The Peculiar Revolution

The Peculiar Revolution

Rethinking the Peruvian Experiment under Military Rule

EDITED BY CARLOS AGUIRRE AND PAULO DRINOT

University of Texas Press ◄► *Austin*

Requests for permission to reproduce material from this work should be sent to:
Permissions
University of Texas Press
P.O. Box 7819
Austin, TX 78713–7819
utpress.utexas.edu/rp-form

⊗ The paper used in this book meets the minimum requirements of
ANSI/NISO Z39.48–1992 (R1997) (Permanence of Paper).

Library of Congress Cataloging Data

Names: Aguirre, Carlos, 1958– editor. | Drinot, Paulo, editor.
Title: The peculiar revolution : rethinking the Peruvian experiment under
    military rule / edited by Carlos Aguirre and Paulo Drinot.
Description: First edition. | Austin : University of Texas Press, 2017. |
    Includes bibliographical references and index.
Identifiers: LCCN 2016040288| ISBN 978-1-4773-1211-7 (cloth : alk. paper) |
    ISBN 978-1-4773-1212-4 (pbk. : alk. paper) | ISBN 978-1-4773-1213-1
    (library e-book) | ISBN 978-1-4773-1214-8 (nonlibrary e-book)
Subjects: LCSH: Peru—Politics and government—1968–1980. | Peru—
    Economic conditions—1968– | Peru—Economic policy. | Peru—Social
    conditions—1968– | Peru—Armed Forces—Political activity. | Military
    government—Peru—History—20th century.
Classification: LCC F3448.2 . P413 2017 | DDC 985.06/33—dc23
LC record available at https://lccn.loc.gov/2016040288

doi:10.7560/312117

Contents

Acknowledgments

This volume began to take shape at a conference held at the Institute of the Americas at University College London in September 2013. The editors would like to acknowledge the support of several institutions, including LSE Ideas, the Society for Latin American Studies, the Peruvian embassy in London, and particularly the Institute of the Americas at UCL. In addition, we are grateful to several individuals who made the conference possible: Maxine Molyneux, former director of the Institute of the Americas; Oscar Martinez Gonzalez, events coordinator at Institute of the Americas; and Ambassador Julio Muñoz Deacon and his staff at the Peruvian embassy in London. Special thanks go to Gonzalo Romero Sommer for his assistance in the run up to and during the conference and to Elizabeth Dore, Rory Miller, Natalia Sobrevilla, and Fiona Wilson, among others, for their contributions from the floor at the conference. The editors are particularly grateful to Kerry Webb and the entire University of Texas Press team for taking on this project and for their sterling work, which has produced a very handsome book. We are deeply grateful to Peter F. Klarén and Cynthia McClintock for their careful reading of the manuscript and their sharp comments and suggestions. Our final and biggest thanks go to the contributors for participating in this project and making the process both pleasant and smooth.

The Peculiar Revolution

Introduction

CARLOS AGUIRRE AND PAULO DRINOT

On the morning of October 3, 1968, the world woke to news about the horrible massacre that had occurred the night before at the Tlatelolco square in Mexico City, where an uncertain number of students (more than three hundred, according to some reports) had been killed by state forces. For Peruvians, the news from Tlatelolco was overshadowed by a much closer but probably no less dramatic event: that same morning they learned that President Fernando Belaúnde Terry, with less than one year left to complete his term (1963–1969), had been deposed by a military coup. Reactions varied, but a common feeling was one of déjà vu: yet another interruption of the constitutional order by military officers defending the status quo and ready to rule through harsh repression. Recent right-wing military interventions in Brazil (1964) and Argentina (1966) were in the minds of many observers in Peru and elsewhere as they tried to make sense of what was behind the latest coup d'état.

For most of the twentieth century, military and authoritarian governments closely allied with traditional social and economic elites had ruled Peru. Since the 1920s, radical projects of transformation, including those advanced by the Communist and American Popular Revolutionary Alliance (APRA) Parties, had attempted to open up avenues for social change, sometimes resorting to violence, but the forces defending the status quo had prevailed. By the 1950s, emerging political and social groups were pushing for modernization and the consolidation of representative democracy. Acción Popular, a center-right political party, won the election in 1963 and brought the architect Fernando Belaúnde Terry to the presidency. Belaúnde Terry had to confront not only fierce opposition from a coalition formed by the now more conservative APRA and the right-wing Unión Nacional Odriísta (UNO) but also the emergence in various parts of the country of guerrilla movements, whose members were inspired by and trained in revolutionary Cuba. Accusations of corruption and a controversy surrounding the negotiation of oil contracts with foreign firms that fueled nationalistic sentiments weakened the legitimacy of Belaúnde's administration. By 1968, Peruvian democracy was in peril, so though not many observers had anticipated another military intervention, when the October 3 coup took place, it did not come as a complete surprise either.

To the shock of many, if not most, however, the new junta led by General Juan Velasco Alvarado quickly dispelled the notion that it would establish another reactionary, right-wing, anti-Communist military project, like those that had ruled Peru in the past and were established in Brazil in 1964 and in the Southern Cone in the following decade. The message Velasco Alvarado broadcast to Peruvians was clear, though it took a while for them to digest it: he was leading a nationalist project aimed at radically transforming Peruvian society, eliminating social injustice, breaking the cycle of foreign domination, redistributing land and wealth, and placing the destiny of Peruvians into their own hands. Political parties, the military thought, had failed to represent the interests of the majority of Peruvians, so it was up to them to carry out the structural transformations needed to put the country on the path toward true sovereignty, independence, and social justice.

It did not take long for the military government to demonstrate that they really meant what they had announced: six days later, on October 9, 1968, they decreed the nationalization of the oil industry, until then controlled mostly by US firms. This was followed by a series of measures affecting virtually every aspect of Peruvian society, from education to labor rights, including, quite prominently, an ambitious land reform project launched on June 24, 1969. The state began to play a central role in economic affairs, the nationalization of foreign-owned companies multiplied, a new focus on promoting and protecting indigenous cultures and peoples was announced, a strong nationalistic rhetoric pervaded official discourse, and a vast apparatus of state propaganda (through print, radio and TV media, posters, songs, festivals, and so forth) accompanied the ambitious "Peruvian experiment," as it came to be known.

The Revolutionary Government of the Armed Forces (RGAF) radically transformed Peruvian society. This is probably the only thing most scholars and analysts of the period would agree on. The RGAF was not without its limitations, contradictions, or setbacks, however, and it had to confront multiple opponents, including so-called traditional political parties (APRA, Acción Popular, and others), sectors of the armed forces that did not agree with the path taken, and to a certain extent the United States and its attempts to prevent the Peruvian process from developing into another Cuba. The accusation of being a "Communist" regime, in fact, was not uncommon. The military government was also opposed by the ultraradical left, in particular Maoist groups with influence in peasant, labor, and student organizations, for whom Velasco Alvarado was leading a Fascist project. But there were also some Peruvian political, labor, intellectual, and economic circles that welcomed the military project and collaborated with it. The pro-Soviet Communist Party of Peru, the Christian Democrat Party, ex-members of the defunct Social Progressive movement, former *guerrilleros*, progressive sectors of the Catholic Church, union leaders, and ex-militants of APRA and other political parties in one way or another applauded the military's agenda and participated in (or otherwise supported) its implementation.

Internally, the Velasco Alvarado regime also faced a number of challenges. The junta he presided over represented the three armed forces—army, air force, and navy—but they were not always in tune with one another. As was to be expected, officers disagreed about the nature, speed, and depth of the social reforms, which led to the formation of various interest groups within the administration and to successive changes in personnel that reflected internal power struggles. As George Philip explains in his chapter in this volume, nationalist generals loyal to Velasco were in the minority, which made the success of the entire project dependent on Velasco's own personal leadership and his ability to keep all the other groups together. Conservative sectors of the armed forces opposed radical measures such as land reform but also the gradual incorporation of leftist and Communist intellectuals and cadres into the administration.

To build popular and institutional support, in 1971 the government created SINAMOS (an acronym for Sistema Nacional de Apoyo a la Movilización Social, or National System of Support for Social Mobilization), an entity that would become the political arm of the military revolution in the absence of a true political party. SINAMOS was in charge of publicizing the government's agenda and measures, carrying out indoctrination campaigns, and mobilizing—using state financial and logistic resources—popular sectors in support of the changes being implemented. SINAMOS's top-down and co-optation tactics led to clashes with autonomous grassroots and popular organizations as well as with APRA and various leftist political parties. It also produced intense friction within the state apparatus. The nickname given to the core group of intellectuals that controlled SINAMOS—*la aplanadora*, or the steamroller—is revealing of popular perceptions about its role in the political process.

In February 1973, Velasco's health problems (an aneurism led to the amputation of his right leg) began to limit his ability to lead such an ambitious project of reforms and to navigate the complicated political situation. In July 1974, the government announced the expropriation of privately owned mass media and their transfer to "social organizations," a measure allegedly aimed at "democratizing" or "socializing" access to information and guaranteeing freedom of expression for all. For the more conservative sectors of the government, this seemed like a move toward a more radical and authoritarian type of regime. They feared that a "Cubanization" of the process was under way. In February 1975, during a police strike, Lima witnessed a couple of days of massive street violence that reflected popular discontent with the government. The SINAMOS headquarters and other government and military buildings, as well as private shops, were the target of popular fury. The government was forced to use extreme measures to repress looting and sacking. Velasco's fate was probably sealed in the wake of the February riots and the ensuing repression.

On August 29, 1975, Velasco Alvarado was removed and replaced by General Francisco Morales Bermúdez, the prime minister and minister of war, through an institutional or palace coup. Velasco's health problems as well as growing "Communist infiltration" were mentioned as key reasons for this change. Although Morales Bermúdez announced that he would continue and even deepen the "structural reforms" initiated in October 1968, the truth is that the "second phase" of the Peruvian revolution quickly began to roll back, dismantle, or at least stall most of those reforms; adopted a clear anti-Communist agenda; and started a gradual process of transfer of power back to civilians. In May 1980, Fernando Belaúnde Terry, the president that had been ousted by the military in 1968, was elected for a second term.

Almost fifty years have passed since the beginning of the Peruvian experiment. During this interval, Peruvian society has gone through significant changes and has been the scenario of dramatic ordeals, including the "internal war" between the Maoist insurgent group known as Shining Path (Sendero Luminoso in Spanish) and the forces of the state that caused almost seventy thousand deaths and enormous human and material destruction. The meaning and legacy of the 1968–1975 experiment, not surprisingly, is still the subject of intense discussions: some blame the military for destroying democracy, hurting economic development, imposing inefficient state controls, and fostering authoritarian methods to address social issues; others recognize the limitations of the military nationalist project but agree that a serious effort was made to implement the social reforms that Peru needed to overcome oppressive forms of exploitation and the marginalization of large sectors of Peruvian society, thus contributing to its democratization. These debates, to be sure, were quite lively during the years of the military government and were successively taken up by scholars in the 1970s and 1980s. Although they never quite subsided, there was a lapse in new scholarly research for twenty years or so. In recent years, a new wave of interest in Peru's military nationalism has begun to produce innovative approaches to our understanding of that period. This volume attempts to bring together some of the most original and creative scholarship on this fascinating period of Peruvian history, and it tries to do so by incorporating themes, regions, and analytical angles that had hitherto not been explored.

The contributions to this volume build on an extensive literature that goes back to the late 1960s and early 1970s. The Peruvian experiment attracted a great deal of attention among scholars, especially political scientists, who were trying to decipher the nature and goals of the military government and identify its social, political, ideological, and institutional foundations. Was it really a revolutionary process? What were the sources and limits of its nationalistic agenda? What was the role of the "masses" in the process? Analysts were generally cautious, if not openly critical.[1] One of the first attempts to explain the military regime led by Velasco Alvarado was that of the Peruvian intellectual Hugo Neira, who would eventually become a collaborator of the military government.[2] For Neira, the October 1968 coup was unjustified and incomprehensible, and he attributed it to the army's anti-APRA sentiments (APRA was expected to win the 1969 election) and to its desire to stop the process of democratization and mobilization that, according to him, had already started in Peru. He denied that the military had any "revolutionary" goals but pointed out that in societies where the ruling elites proved to be incapable of addressing the challenges of social mobilization and leftist organization, the army plays a transitional role, which, he predicted, would be followed by "true and great social reforms."[3]

Another early and critical assessment of military nationalism was that of the Peruvian sociologist Aníbal Quijano. He dismissed attempts to label the Peruvian regime as "populist," "Nasserist," or "Bismarck-ist," and proposed instead an analysis centered on the economic dimensions of the project: Who was benefiting from the reforms? Whose interests was the regime protecting? Locating the Peruvian experiment within shifting international scenarios, Quijano proposed that it was the result of changes in the nature of imperialist domination ("from the agro-extractive to the urban-industrial" sector) and of the erosion of "traditional agents of legitimation" such as the Catholic Church or universities. The military project, guided by notions of "limited nationalism" and "class reconciliation," thus sought to strengthen the role of foreign capital in the more "modern" sectors of the economy and thereby pave the road for a new model of imperial domination, which he dubbed "neo-imperialism."[4] Among international observers, the British Marxist historian Eric Hobsbawm shared some of these critical views about the Peruvian process: If revolutions, he wrote, were defined by the transformations they effect on a given society, the Peruvian experiment was clearly one of them; but if they were to be understood as processes of mass mobilization, then it was not. The masses, observed Hobsbawm, were completely "outside" the changes taking place in their country, and peasants were for the most part a passive element in this process. This was, for Hobsbawm, a "peculiar revolution."[5]

Although scholars began to pay attention to the Peruvian experiment as soon as it was launched, it would take a few years to produce dissertations and monographs, given the time needed to conduct research and complete publication cycles. One of the first contributions was the dissertation, completed in 1973, by the political scientist David Scott Palmer.[6] The focus of his analysis was the extent and nature of political participation in the process. For Palmer, the Peruvian army had initiated a process of reforms in order to guarantee internal security, threatened by guerrillas and other revolutionary efforts, but it was also trying to change "the basic model of politics," building a corporate model that contained a central contradiction: although it emphasized popular "participation," it also needed to guarantee a centralized control of the process. Palmer concluded that Peru's "revolution from above" should be conceived as a preventive effort, what he called "conservative reform."

Two collections of essays, published in 1975 and 1976 respectively, summarized international scholarship on Peru's military regime at a time when it was already being dismantled. Abraham Lowenthal brought together a team of political scientists and economists to analyze the "Peruvian experiment."[7] The overall tone of the contributions can be summarized in the title of Lowenthal's chapter: it was an "ambiguous revolution," that is, anti-Communist in essence but applauded by Fidel Castro and other leftist leaders and parties, both in Peru and elsewhere; authoritarian but not fiercely repressive; allegedly anticapitalist and yet praised by many Peruvian and foreign investors. Like Palmer and Hobsbawm, Lowenthal highlighted the lack of popular support for the regime (he considered it "the toughest challenge" the military faced), despite efforts by SINAMOS, the office in charge of fostering popular mobilization behind military reforms. Failure to ensure "full participation" in the decision-making process was another important setback for the military regime. Overall, Lowenthal identifies an effort toward the redistribution of resources and a "segmentary incorporation" of the population into the process that allowed the military, in his interpretation, to control its pace and boundaries. Once again, the emphasis was on the "limited" or "controlled" nature of the changes being implemented, but Lowenthal also addressed (he was writing in 1974) the potential risks of "expanded participation." The second volume, coordinated by David Chaplin and published in 1976, gathered original and reprinted contributions by Peruvian and foreign scholars.[8] Many of them addressed the various social and political developments that would help explain the rise of military nationalism: guerrillas, peasant mobilization, squatters' movements, and others. In his introduction, the editor, David Chaplin, reiterated the use of the "corporatist" label to characterize the military regime and its goal of guaranteeing popular mobilization behind it. Summarizing points made in several of the contributions, Chaplin insisted on the limitations and contradictions of a model that proclaimed to foster popular participation yet tended to concentrate power and decision making in the hands of the military.[9]

Once Velasco Alvarado was removed from power and the second phase of the process, under Morales Bermúdez, was in full swing, scholarly analyses began to revisit previous interpretations and to advance explanations about the demise of military nationalism. Two books published in 1978 are representative of these views. George Philip attempted to take stock of the "rise and fall" of military nationalism.[10] He reviewed some of the military's key reforms (such as the nationalization of the oil industry and the land reform); the composition of the military government (a pioneering effort in this regard); and the forces of opposition, both internal and external, that the military had to confront. Philip contrasted the "successes" of the military (the destruction of the landed oligarchy, for instance, or the creation of a powerful state economic sector) with the obstacles it had to confront, the central one being its very nature as a military government, which imposed various limits to the possibility of implementing the political changes it had set out to achieve, especially popular participation. In fact, according to Philip, "the problem of political participation is the Achilles heel of radical military regimes" such as the Peruvian one.[11]

The other book published in the aftermath of the Velasco Alvarado ousting was of a completely different nature: it was the transcription of a lengthy debate among Peruvian leftist intellectuals and political leaders such as Ricardo Letts, Carlos Malpica, Francisco Moncloa, and others.[12] As the volume's title suggests, all of them agreed to dub the Velasco Alvarado government a "bourgeois-reformist" regime, akin to, say, Mexico's Institutional Revolutionary Party (Partido Revolucionario Institucional; PRI) or Argentina's Peronism. This characterization implied that it was an attempt (for the most part unsuccessful) to address the deep social problems of Peruvian society without destroying the existing (bourgeois) state and without creating a new structure of power, that is, "popular democracy." For the left, as is clear in the interventions transcribed in this book, military nationalism presented a real and serious challenge, and while some sectors opted to offer their "critical support," others never harbored illusions about the military representing the "real" aspirations of the masses of workers and peasants and chose instead to oppose (and compete with) the government's attempt to control the popular movement.[13]

In the early 1980s, after the second phase of the military government had ended, scholars and analysts went back to revisit the Peruvian experiment. Three collective volumes published in 1983, two in English and one in Spanish, captured the tone of the debates fifteen years after the start of the military regime. Cynthia McClintock and Abraham Lowenthal's volume, *The Peruvian Experiment Reconsidered*, offered a series of essays on the limitations and failures of the Velasco Alvarado–era reforms, especially in the realms of economic growth, redistribution, social justice, reduction of foreign dependence, and popular participation.[14] Somehow departing from the overall tone of the volume, however, Lowenthal argued in his concluding chapter that the military government had actually succeeded in its true original goal: "If one defines the Peruvian experiment as the core program of nationalist affirmation, economic modernization, anti-oligarchical reform, and systematic state-building supported institutionally by the armed forces in 1968, the agenda was implemented to an impressive degree." For Lowenthal, Peru was able to catch up with other populist regimes in the region in closing the gap between "socio-economic realities and its political institutions and public policies."[15]

The other English-language publication, David Booth and Bernardo Sorj's *Military Reformism and Social Classes*, advanced a critique of what its editors saw as a literature shaped by "the preconceptions, preoccupations and passing fashions—as well as the solid scholarly virtues—of mainstream North American political science" and more specifically by an overestimated "institutional" element to the 1968 coup and by the wrongheaded focus on corporatism and the culturalist theory of politics it reflected. Instead, these authors sought to engage more explicitly with the literature on the RGAF produced in Peru by "an initially small but now rather substantial circle of Peruvian social scientists formed under the influence of the new Marxist and radical dependency ideas of the 1960s and early 1970s."[16] Though in some ways disparate in approach, the contributions to this volume, on a range of issues including agrarian reform, public enterprises, and press reform, placed greater emphasis than other English-language publications on class struggle as a key factor shaping the process and outcome of the Velasco regime.

The third publication from this period was a three-volume compendium of essays on "Velasco's Peru" written, for the most part, by former collaborators of the military government.[17] Coordinated by Carlos Franco, it offered both the historical context necessary to understand the emergence of military nationalism (some essays went back to the early twentieth century) and a series of lengthy analyses/testimonies by key participants in the military government (Carlos Franco, Francisco Guerra García, Héctor Béjar, and others). One of the most valuable features of these volumes is precisely the fact that these contributors were writing in their dual role as protagonists and analysts. With the usual nuances and discrepancies, the overall conceptual framework behind these contributions is that the Peruvian experiment constituted an "interrupted revolution," which obviously means that they did consider the military process a "revolutionary" one. In his introduction, Carlos Franco distanced himself from interpretations that dubbed the regime "corporatist" or "Fascist" and those that uncritically embraced the "participatory" nature of the process, but also from Lowenthal's characterization of it as an "ambiguous" process. Franco and his collaborators aspired to offer an alternative interpretation, one that located the Peruvian experiment within the study of the "historical conditions that prevented a popular, bottom-up revolution in Peru,"[18] one that could have carried on the reforms that the military regime ended up implementing. In other words, there were specific conditions that made it *possible* for a process of reforms to be initiated. On the other hand, an explanation of the specific conditions that allowed the military to embrace that "mission" was also part of the preoccupation of these analysts. The supposed "inevitability" of the "military revolution" or its characterization as a "preventive" type of revolution were interpretations that, according to Franco, had been proved wrong. The emphasis, thus, was on those structural conditions that shaped the military's mentality and consciousness and that moved them to act in the way they did. For Franco and the core group of collaborators in this multivolume publication, the ultimate meaning (and justification) of the 1968–1975 military nationalist regime had to be found, first, in the effective destruction of the oligarchic order and, second, in "the beginning of the construction of a national society and state."[19] The interruption of the process in 1975 left this project unfinished.

In contrast to the 1970s and early 1980s, since the mid-1980s the scholarly output on the RGAF has been limited. This relative lack of interest was likely a product of the important changes that Peru experienced in the 1980s and 1990s. The emergence of the Shining Path insurgency in 1980, the development of the internal armed conflict through the rest of that decade and the early 1990s, and the election of Alberto Fujimori and the authoritarian neoliberal "revolution" that he implemented after 1990 shifted scholarly attention to new questions.[20] But the fall in scholarly output also corresponded with a passing of the baton between academic disciplines. The political scientists and sociologists who had led the way in the study of the RGAF, and who in several cases had been drawn to the study of the regime by its apparently sui generis character, shifted their attention to other topics. In the 1990s, anthropologists picked up some of the slack; this is particularly true of anthropologists who were working in rural areas and whose ethnographic studies could not ignore the effect of the Velasco-era agrarian reform on the peasant communities they were studying. In other words, scholars have continued to explore the Velasco regime but do so increasingly indirectly. Historians, however, with a few notable exceptions, had paid relatively little attention to the RGAF until now. One important exception is in the field of diplomatic history, with the work of Richard Walter and Hal Brands adding new perspectives, based on extensive and exemplary research in diplomatic archives in Peru and the United States and, in the case of Walter, on the international relations of the Velasco regime, particularly with the United States.[21] Another is the work of Anna Cant, a contributor to this volume, on the visual culture of the RGAF and its mobilization strategies.[22]

Two general studies of the Velasco regime merit particular attention. Dirk Kruijt's *Revolution by Decree: Peru, 1968–1975* (1994) draws on extensive interviews with key actors in the armed forces.[23] Though it does not provide a major reinterpretation of the Velasco regime, Kruijt's study does contribute to our understanding of the RGAF and its main protagonists through its judicious use of interview material. In particular, the book offers unique insight into the backgrounds and personal motivations of the regime's key actors, including Velasco himself. In Kruijt's fine study, the Velasco regime acquires a much more human dimension and its policies appear to be expressions of a more complex range of factors than in previous studies. Unlike Kruijt, Juan Martín Sánchez does not draw on much original material in his 2002 *La revolución peruana*.[24] Instead, this book, based on the author's doctoral dissertation, is an attempt to provide a new interpretation of the Velasco regime in dialogue with political science theory and in particular with theoretical perspectives on revolutions. Drawing on a careful analysis of several key documents produced by the regime and an assessment of other interpretative frameworks such as populism or corporatism, Sánchez provides a helpful overview of the secondary literature and an intriguing argument about the utility of viewing the regime through the analytical lens of "revolution."

If earlier studies of the Velasco regime had examined the range of reforms it implemented, it is arguably the 1969 agrarian reform that has received the bulk of attention in the last few decades. These studies have continued an earlier interest in exploring the effect of the agrarian reform, a trend that had been set out clearly with the publication in 1976 of José Matos Mar's edited volume *Hacienda, comunidad y campesinado en el Perú* and reassessed in Matos Mar and José Mejía's *Reforma agraria: Logros y contradicciones, 1969–1979*, published in 1984, and continued and developed in the work of authors such as José María Caballero, Cynthia McClintock, Elena Alvarez, and others.[25] In part due to shifts in research paradigms but also no doubt because of the growing awareness of the differentiated effects of the agrarian reform across the country, the studies became more focused on the regional and the local and reliant on grounded or ethnographic research. Linda Seligmann's study of Huanoquite in Cuzco, Carmen Diana Deere's on Cajamarca, and Karin

Apel's on Piura are good examples of this trend.[26] Perhaps inevitably, more recent studies of the 1969 agrarian reform, such as Seligmann's, have sought to explore the ways in which the reform shaped the rise of the Shining Path in the south-central Andean highlands. In this sense, such studies overlap with historical scholarship on the Shining Path that homes in on the ways in which the initiatives of the RGAF, most particularly the agrarian reform and SINAMOS, contributed to creating conditions for the Shining Path to emerge where and when it did.[27]

Published in 2009, Enrique Mayer's *Ugly Stories of the Peruvian Agrarian Reform* is the most important recent contribution to the study of the Velasco period. Building on his own direct experience of the agrarian reform, Mayer's work marks a departure in the literature on the RGAF. It draws on numerous interviews with a whole range of actors directly involved in, or impacted by, the agrarian reform, from those who designed it to those who implemented it, as well as a socially diverse group of characters, including landowners, peasants, intellectuals, academics, and agricultural experts. Unlike other studies of the agrarian reform published in the last couple of decades, Mayer's work attempts a more comprehensive analysis, taking in a number of different experiences from the northern coast, to the central highlands, and to the altiplano in the south. In contrast to some of the earlier work on the agrarian reform, Mayer is interested in recovering the experience and meaning of the agrarian reform for those whose lives were changed by it. Among other things, this approach enables Mayer to show the extent to which the outcome of the agrarian reform differed from the objectives set by its designers and implementers. In the hands of those who benefited from it, the reform took on a life of its own.[28] As in previously mentioned studies, Mayer, too, is concerned with the relation between the agrarian reform and the rise of the Shining Path, though his conclusions are rather cautious.

The chapters in this volume draw on, yet at the same time depart from, the scholarship summarized above. As we have seen, much of it, particularly the contributions made in the 1970s and 1980s, focused on political and economic processes, on issues such as state-military relations and popular mobilization, on determining the character or nature of the RGAF (corporatist, nationalist, populist, revolutionary, and so on), and on assessing the success or failure of particular reforms. By contrast, the chapters in this volume pay greater attention to social and cultural processes, and in particular to the cultural politics of the regime. In so doing, the volume brings into view aspects of the regime virtually unexplored in earlier studies, such as the regime's uses of the past or the collective memory of Velasco and the RGAF. It also sheds new light on previously studied issues such as the regime's education reform, its policies toward the indigenous peasantry, and the military's self-fashioning and culture. Finally, the volume also shifts the focus from the national to the subnational in order to examine in greater detail the ways in which the RGAF's reforms and initiatives were experienced and inflected at the local and regional level in different parts of Peru. In so doing, the volume offers a richer and more complex interpretation of the Velasco regime.

In the first section, the contributions explore aspects of the cultural politics developed by the RGAF and those that it engendered but did not necessarily control. In the first chapter, Carlos Aguirre examines the RGAF's patronage of the sesquicentennial celebrations of Peruvian independence in 1971, and in particular of a project to publish over one hundred volumes of original sources on Peru's independence process. He shows that the apparently contradictory alliance between the military and the conservative historians named to head the special commission charged with overseeing the publication of that collection served the broader purpose of the RGAF to cast its project as one of completing a nationalist emancipatory process and of freeing Peru from external economic dependence and political domination. The sesquicentennial commemoration was seen as an opportunity to legitimize the RGAF by emphasizing the "incompleteness" of the "first" independence process and the need to fully realize the promises of national liberation.

In the next chapter, Charles Walker focuses on the role played by the eighteenth-century rebel leader Túpac Amaru II in the RGAF's cultural politics, and in particular in the context of the sesquicentennial celebrations studied by Aguirre. Walker shows that the regime's championing of Túpac Amaru II was an attempt to create a national symbol that could serve to unify the Peruvian nation around a common project of national liberation that placed Peruvians at the very center of that process. In this reading, it was Túpac Amaru II, rather than the foreign "liberators" like the Argentine José Francisco de San Martín or the Venezuelan Simón Bolívar, who had initiated Peru's independence process, one that the Velasco regime was trying to complete.

In his chapter, Adrián Lerner offers a narrative history of Velasco's funeral. Velasco died in 1977, two years after General Morales Bermúdez had deposed him in a palace coup. However, as Lerner argues, his death and in particular his funeral illustrate many of the characteristics of the regime that he led. Through a detailed reconstruction of the funeral informed by a theoretical engagement with the literature on rituals, Lerner suggests that the massive outpouring of popular sentiment and mobilization during the funeral represented a challenge to the course that the military regime had taken since the ousting of Velasco in 1975. But the sympathy for Velasco manifested in the funeral was not to have a lasting impact, which further reveals the limits of the politics of mobilization that the RGAF promoted.

Paulo Drinot examines the contested collective memories of the RGAF. Drawing on several hundred comments attached to videos about the Velasco period uploaded on YouTube, Drinot examines views expressive of collective memories of the agrarian reform, Velasco's death, Velasco's policies with regard to economic dependency and US power in Latin America, Peru's relations with Chile, and the links between the Velasco "revolution" and the Shining Path insurgency. The Velasco regime and the memories mobilized by and reconstructed through it, Drinot concludes, offer Peruvians a means through which to negotiate, if not necessarily resolve, a number of issues that shape the ways Peruvians feel and think about themselves and their place in the world.

In the second section, the focus turns to the examination of particular policies of the RGAF and its key institutions. Patricia Oliart revisits the education reform implemented by the RGAF. Oliart pays particular attention to the diverse transnational influences that shaped the reform, including Paulo Freire's seminal ideas; to its agents, many of whom, like Augusto Salazar Bondy, were important cultural figures in Peru; and to the radical initiatives that characterized it, which resonated with the regime's critical assessment of the character of Peruvian society and its attempts to transform it. At the same time, Oliart examines the obstacles that the reform encountered. Opposition came from conservative sectors but, more importantly, from teachers aligned with the left-wing teachers' union, Sindicato Único de Trabajadores en la Educación del Perú (SUTEP; Unified Syndicate of Workers in Education of Peru), which viewed the reform as an expression of a bourgeois authoritarian regime.

Jaymie Patricia Heilman similarly considers how land reform impacted a key organized sector of the population: the peasantry. The reform, Heilman shows, produced an intense ideological debate within the Peruvian Peasant Confederation (Confederación Campesina del Perú; CCP) leading to its split into three competing organizations. The establishment of an alternative national peasant confederation by the regime, the National Agrarian Confederation (Confederación Nacional Agraria; CNA), further deepened the division of the organized peasant movement in Peru. As Heilman shows, the impact of the agrarian reform was not limited to the shifts in land tenure explored in numerous studies but also had a profound and long-lasting effect on peasant organization and politics.

Lourdes Hurtado examines what was undoubtedly the central protagonist of the RGAF: the military, and the army in particular. In seeking to understand how Velasco became so central to the project of the armed forces, Hurtado pays special attention to the military culture that developed in Peru in the twentieth century, shaped by gendered (and to a lesser extent racialized) notions about the role of the military in protecting the Peruvian population. Notions of a masculinized army and a feminized nation formed the background against which Velasco emerged as a father or brother figure whose mission was to act as the agent of Peru's emancipation. Because of this close association between Velasco and the fate of the revolution, Hurtado argues, his illness also came to symbolize the weakness and eventual defeat of the process he spearheaded.

In a study that also focuses on the military, George Philip further explores the decline of Velasco's administration. Philip sets out to explain the speed with which the Velasco government collapsed. He acknowledges the role played by economic factors in that collapse (rising debt and an economic slump) and the costs associated with the arms buildup that followed the 1973 Chilean coup. But equally important, Philip suggests, was the type of regime that Velasco established, characterized by personalism but precariously dependent on a coalition of forces. For this reason, Philip concludes, once Velasco's health started to weaken, his hold on power also weakened inevitably and irreparably.

In the third and final section, our contributors explore the local and regional dimensions of the RGAF and its policies. Anna Cant draws on extensive research in provincial archives and interviews she conducted to examine the work of SINAMOS in the context of the implementation of the agrarian reform in three different regions of Peru: Piura, Cuzco, and Tacna. In contrast to the still dominant notion that the reforms of the RGAF were top-down and uniformly applied across the nation, Cant shows that at the local level there was significant engagement between the promoters of the military revolution and those it targeted. Drawing on a keen understanding of local history and problems, SINAMOS developed different communication strategies and narratives to address the particular circumstances of each region. This resulted in significant variation in how the revolution was represented and understood across different regions of the country. At the same time, Cant points to the problems that SINAMOS encountered in each region, which were partly the result of opposition from various local and regional actors and partly the consequence of issues internal to SINAMOS. As Cant shows, the reforms implemented by the RGAF were inflected in different ways in different parts of Peru, an issue that is further explored in the next four chapters.

Mark Carey's study of the giant Chavimochic irrigation project on Peru's northern coast offers new perspectives on the short- and long-term effects of key reforms of the RGAF, in particular the agrarian reform and the 1969 General Water Law. Though Chavimochic was initiated during Alan García's administration (1985–1990) and is still being completed, Carey shows that several developments during the Velasco regime proved critical to its subsequent history. In particular, Carey shows how the impact of the agrarian reform on landownership (the elimination of haciendas), the establishment of the General Water Law and technocratic management of water resources, the mobilization of support for the measure from recently established cooperatives, and the politics of drought management all contributed to creating the conditions that would enable the initiation of the project in the 1980s.

Focused on the town of Chimbote, Nathan Clarke's chapter illustrates the tensions produced by the RGAF's attempt to co-opt the Peruvian labor movement. As the most important fishing port in the world by the 1970s and the heart of Peru's massive fishing industry and emerging steel industry, Chimbote witnessed acute conflict between different labor groups and the emergence of a *clasista* movement, whose leadership sought to align itself with the military regime. In a context of ecological crisis, as fishing stocks fell sharply as a consequence of an El Niño event, and in the midst of the nationalization of the fishing industry, the attempt by the RGAF to curtail labor autonomy in Chimbote resulted in opposition and repression, culminating in the violent Chimbotazo (labor union strike) of May 1973. Clarke suggests that this event marked a point of inflection in the history of the RGAF from which it never fully recovered.

Mark Rice shifts our attention to Cuzco and to an aspect of the RGAF that remains understudied: its tourism policy. Through a detailed examination of Plan COPESCO, the regime's tourism development strategy,

Rice explores the tensions that the implementation of this policy generated in Cuzco, where regional support for tourism promotion, including the building of modern hotel infrastructure in Cuzco and Machu Picchu, faced opposition from the National Institute of Culture, a struggle that pitted regional developmental objectives against Lima-based cultural institutions. The promise of tourism-led regional development also soured when hopes for high-end tourism were confronted with the reality of the growing presence of "hippie" tourists in Cuzco and its environs. Rice concludes by underscoring the limits of the RGAF's tourism policy, which, he argues, failed in its stated objective of providing employment to Cuzco's indigenous population.

Finally, Stefano Varese offers a personal reflection on the impact of the reforms that targeted Amazonian indigenous peoples, reforms that he was involved in and helped design. Varese shows that the small group of anthropologists and other social scientists charged with developing the RGAF's policies toward the Amazonian populations were working in a largely adverse context in which knowledge about the target groups was limited. Much of the initial work involved collating historical and ethnographic sources to map populations. Varese discusses the "revolutionary inventiveness" that went into creating categories such as the "Comunidad Nativa" while at the same time attempting to challenge understandings of Amazonia informed by conceptual frameworks derived from the cases of communities and populations from the Andean highlands. Varese concludes that these initiatives were successful not only in titling indigenous land in the Amazon but also in contributing to the development of ethnopolitical civil institutions that continue to play an important role in preserving the sovereignty of Native communities.

The originality and diversity of the studies included in this volume allow an opportunity to rethink military nationalism in Peru: its policies and institutions, its successes and failures, and its lasting legacies. Building on, but also departing from, the emphases on state institutions, economic processes, and political dynamics, these studies represent some of the most innovative scholarship being produced on this crucial period in Peruvian and Latin American history. New topics, actors, and regions are given attention in these essays, including, quite notably, the cultural dimensions of the revolutionary project and its legacies, the impact of structural reforms at the local level, the dynamics produced by the interaction between state policies and ordinary citizens and labor and peasant organizations, and the careful consideration given to hitherto underexplored areas of the country such as Piura, Chimbote, or Amazonia.

Moving beyond debates about the "characterization" of the military regime (corporatist, Fascist, Nasserist, and the like) and the emphasis on its top-down and authoritarian nature, this volume represents a fresh and diverse intervention in the comparative study of both military power and projects of social transformation in Latin America. The debates around the degree to which the Peruvian military revolution actually succeeded in implementing its policies are illuminated with new evidence and arguments. In the same vein, various chapters in this volume highlight the skepticism and sometimes open hostility with which different social agents reacted to those reforms. What is beyond question, however, is that—as several chapters in this volume highlight—the package of reforms put forward by Velasco Alvarado and his collaborators was quite ambitious: they did attempt to radically transform all realms of Peruvian society, including land-tenure patterns, forms of political participation, the role of the state in the management of natural resources and the economy, and the relationship with foreign capital.

At the same time, it is also true that many of the reforms promoted by the military did not fulfill all their promises and failed to deliver the alleged benefits to the population. Multiple factors contributed to this: excessive bureaucratization, lack of understanding and knowledge about the social realities on the ground, opposition by various social actors, and the contradictions inherent in the very definition of the government's goals. Although several reforms were clearly "leftist" (by the usual definition of what the "left" should promote) and, at least in theory, sought to promote the participation of the population, not all of them shared the same character. As some of the chapters show, there were cases in which the participatory and even the "nationalist" nature of the reforms were, at the very least, questionable. The gap between the ambition and the reality of the reforms is very clearly in evidence in the vivid if conflicted memories of the RGAF that resonate in Peruvian political affairs today.

We are confident that this set of contributions will renew scholarly interest in the Peruvian experiment. This was, we ought to remember, quite an extraordinary and unique initiative: in a context dominated by Latin American right-wing dictatorial regimes and the fight against Communism, the Peruvian armed forces actually embarked on a process aimed at achieving national liberation and promoting social justice that drew on a sobering and unusually candid assessment of the deep historical and structural causes of social inequality and underdevelopment in the country and promoted popular mobilization as the means to achieve social and economic emancipation. That by itself should generate a great deal of interest among scholars and students. The originality of the topics and approaches represented in this volume will shed new light and spark new debates on this fascinating episode of contemporary Latin American history.

Notes

1. We are not including in this review of the literature the numerous articles, pamphlets, and books produced by the military government itself or its collaborators. For an early attempt to defend it, see Carlos Delgado, *El proceso revolucionario peruano: Testimonio de lucha* (Mexico City: Siglo Veintiuno, 1972). Unless otherwise noted, all translations in this introduction are our own.

2. Hugo Neira, *El golpe de estado: Peru, 1968* (Madrid: Editorial Zero Zyx, 1969).

3. Ibid., 61.

4. Aníbal Quijano, *Nationalism and Capitalism in Peru: A Study in Neo-imperialism*, trans. Helen R. Jane (New York: Monthly Review Press, 1971), passim. See also the articles by Quijano and Julio Cotler in *Sociedad y Política*, nos. 1 and 2 (1972). Julio Cotler's classic study *Clases, estado y nación en el Perú*, first published in 1978, offered a historical genealogy of the Velasco revolution.

5. Eric J. Hobsbawm, "Peru: The Peculiar 'Revolution,'" *New York Review of Books*, December 16, 1971.

6. David Scott Palmer, "'Revolution from Above': Military Government and Popular Participation in Peru, 1968–1972" (PhD diss., Cornell University, 1973). See also Palmer's *Peru: The Authoritarian Tradition* (New York: Praeger, 1980).

7. Abraham L. Lowenthal, *The Peruvian Experiment: Continuity and Change Under Military Rule* (Princeton, NJ: Princeton University Press, 1975).

8. David Chaplin, ed., *Peruvian Nationalism: A Corporatist Revolution* (New Brunswick, NJ: Transaction Publishers, 1976).

9. For a fuller discussion of the nature of "corporatism" as applied in the Peruvian case, see Alfred C. Stepan, *The State and Society: Peru in Comparative Perspective* (Princeton, NJ: Princeton University Press, 1979).

10. George D. E. Philip, *The Rise and Fall of the Peruvian Military Radicals, 1968–1976* (London: Athlone, 1978).

11. Ibid., 167.

12. Mirko Lauer, moderator, *El reformismo burgués (1968–1976)* (Lima: Mosca Azul, 1978).

13. For a similar assessment, see "Peru: Bourgeois Revolution and Class Struggle," special issue, *Latin American Perspectives* 4, no. 3 (1977).

14. Cynthia McClintock and Abraham F. Lowenthal, eds., *The Peruvian Experiment Reconsidered* (Princeton, NJ: Princeton University Press, 1983).

15. Ibid., 419.

16. David Booth and Bernardo Sorj, eds., *Military Reformism and Social Classes: The Peruvian Experience, 1968–1980* (New York: St. Martin's Press, 1983), 4.

17. Carlos Franco, ed., *El Perú de Velasco: De la cancelación del Estado oligárquico a la fundación del Estado Nacional*, 3 vols. (Lima: Centro de Estudios para el Desarrollo y la Participación, 1983). Although the date that appears on the copyright page is 1983, the books were printed in 1986. The research was conducted between 1980 and 1984.

18. Ibid., 1:6.

19. Ibid., 1:24.

20. For a discussion of these shifts in scholarly focus, see Paulo Drinot, "Introduction," in *Peru in Theory*, ed. Paulo Drinot (New York: Palgrave, 2014), 1–18.

21. Richard J. Walter, *Peru and the United States, 1960–1975: How Their Ambassadors Managed Foreign Relations in a Turbulent Era* (University Park: Pennsylvania State University Press, 2010); Hal Brands, "The United States and the Peruvian Challenge, 1968–1975," *Diplomacy and Statecraft* 21, no. 3 (2010): 471–490.

22. Anna Cant, "Land for Those Who Work It: A Visual Analysis of Agrarian Reform Posters in Velasco's Peru," *Journal of Latin American Studies* 44, no. 1 (2012): 1–37.

23. Dirk Kruijt, *Revolution by Decree: Peru, 1968–1975* (Amsterdam: Thela, 1994). Earlier versions of this book were published in Dutch and Spanish.

24. Juan Martín Sánchez, *La revolución peruana: Ideología y práctica política de un gobierno militar, 1968–1975* (Seville: CSIC, Universidad de Sevilla, Diputación de Sevilla, 2002).

25. José Matos Mar, ed., *Hacienda, comunidad y campesinado en el Perú* (Lima: IEP, 1976); José Matos Mar and José M. Mejía, *Reforma agraria: Logros y contradicciones, 1969–1979* (Lima: IEP, 1983); José María Caballero, *Agricultura, reforma agraria y pobreza campesina* (Lima: IEP, 1980); Cynthia McClintock, *Peasant Cooperatives and Agrarian Change in Peru* (Princeton, NJ: Princeton University Press, 1981); Elena Alvarez, *Política económica y agricultura en el Perú, 1969–1979* (Lima: IEP, 1983).

26. To be sure, both Deere and Apel consider the agrarian reform in the context of much longer historical studies of the communities. See Linda J. Seligmann, *Between Reform and Revolution: Political Struggles in the Peruvian Andes, 1969–1991* (Stanford, CA: Stanford University Press, 1995); Carmen Diana Deere, *Household and Class Relations: Peasants and Landlords in Northern Peru* (Berkeley: University of California Press, 1990); Karin Apel, *De la hacienda a la comunidad: La sierra de Piura, 1934–1990* (Lima: IEP/CNRS/IFEA, 1996).

27. See, for example, Florencia Mallon, "Chronicle of a Path Foretold? Velasco's Revolution, Vanguardia Revolucionaria, and 'Shining Omens' in the Indigenous Communities of Andahuaylas," in *Shining and Other Paths: War and Society in Peru, 1980–1995*, ed. Steve J. Stern (Durham, NC: Duke University

Press, 1998), 84–117; Jaymie Patricia Heilman, *Before the Shining Path: Politics in Rural Ayacucho, 1895–1980* (Stanford, CA: Stanford University Press, 2010), ch. 6.

28. Enrique Mayer, *Ugly Stories of the Peruvian Agrarian Reform* (Durham, NC: Duke University Press, 2009). The focus on memory is also present in Gonzalo Portocarrero's "Memorias del Velasquismo," in Maritza Hamann et al., *Batallas por la memoria: Antagonismos de la promesa peruana* (Lima: Red para el Desarrollo de las Ciencias Sociales en el Perú, 2003), 229–255.

PART I

SYMBOLS, ICONS, AND CONTESTED MEMORIES: CULTURAL APPROACHES TO THE PERUVIAN REVOLUTION

CHAPTER 1

The Second Liberation? Military Nationalism and the Sesquicentennial Commemoration of Peruvian Independence, 1821–1971

CARLOS AGUIRRE

Only six days after the military coup that ousted President Fernando Belaúnde Terry, the junta led by General Juan Velasco Alvarado nationalized the oil industry, a highly symbolic decision that confirmed the direction the new regime wanted to take. The dispute around the assets of the International Petroleum Company had, in fact, been one of the hottest political issues during the Belaúnde administration, and it had sparked the renewal of nationalistic fervor among certain sectors of the public opinion, including the conservative and highly influential daily *El Comercio*. In his speech announcing the measure, General Velasco Alvarado spoke loudly and clearly: "The Revolutionary Government, raising the flag of *the new emancipation*, now and forever, puts on the lips of every Peruvian the vibrant expression of our national anthem: 'We are free, let's be so forever!'"[1]

The rhetorical mantra of the "new" or "second" emancipation would be pervasive in the official discourse of the Velasco Alvarado regime: again and again Peruvians were told that the revolutionary government was realizing the country's "second independence," the first being the one proclaimed on July 28, 1821, and secured on December 9, 1824, after the Battle of Ayacucho against the forces loyal to Spain. The implication was, of course, that the "first" independence had not been completed, that it had not fulfilled the expectations and needs of the majority of Peruvians, and that to achieve a real and definitive national liberation a series of radical measures were needed. The military regime was justified, to a large extent, on the premise that the only solution to the compounded problems of dependency, underdevelopment, and social injustice was to complete the process of national liberation. The proximity of the 1971 sesquicentennial commemoration of the "first" independence offered the military government the opportunity to both showcase its accomplishments and claim political and historical legitimacy by establishing a direct and explicit connection with the events that culminated in the proclamation of independence 150 years earlier. This chapter explores the cultural and political dimensions of the 1971 commemoration as well as the instrumental use of the past by the military regime.

On September 16, 1969, the government created a National Commission for the Sesquicentennial of Peruvian Independence (hereafter CNSIP, acronym for Comisión Nacional del Sesquicentenario de la Independencia del Perú) and shortly afterward named General Juan Mendoza Rodríguez its president and appointed seventeen other members, including some prominent (and, for the most part, politically conservative) historians who represented a series of institutions such as the University Council, the National Academy of History, the Riva Agüero Institute, the National Library, the San Martín Institute, and others.[2] The historian Carlos Contreras called them "a group of notables."[3] Seen in retrospect, this was indeed a stunning decision: a government that claimed to be revolutionary formed a commission dominated by conservative historians whose work represented what would then be considered "traditional" in Peruvian historiography, including Aurelio Miró Quesada, José Agustín de la Puente Candamo, Félix Denegri Luna, and Armando Nieto Vélez.[4] A number of advisers were also appointed, including scholars such as Jorge Basadre, Luis Valcárcel, and Emilio Romero, who offered in their individual works a different, more critical view of Peruvian history, but whose role in the shaping of the commemoration does not appear to have been relevant.

Five committees were formed within CNSIP. They were in charge of, respectively, documents, publications, public events and monuments, finances, and economic promotion (i.e., fund-raising). The overall plan consisted of a series of initiatives that were, for the most part, of a historical, civic, and symbolic nature but that were also, not surprisingly, imbued with strong political resonances. The single most important and expensive initiative was the compilation and publication of the Colección Documental de la Independencia del Perú (hereafter CDIP), a collection of documents and sources related to the process that led to Peruvian independence in 1821. Originally planned to include 106 volumes, of which only 86 were published, the CDIP series was to include manuscript and printed sources available in Peruvian and foreign archives and libraries that could help demonstrate the efforts and "active participation" by both Peruvians and others from "brother countries" toward "American emancipation."[5] The publication of those documents would "correct the limited and incomplete vision about Peruvian independence," as General Mendoza stated during the ceremony to mark the release of the first set of volumes. Those documents, insisted General Mendoza, will show that "we were not the last ones in the struggle for independence nor were we absent in other latitudes. Quite the opposite: we were the first in the rebellion and in the ideology" promoting independence.[6]

In addition to this massive documentary project, CNSIP included in its plan of activities a number of ceremonies, parades, and rituals, and the erection of monuments that are typical of these commemorations. CNSIP promoted the creation of 18 monuments, 25 busts, 135 memorial plaques, 13 paintings, and 4 bronze friezes, many of them to be placed in the same localities where important events had taken place during the wars of independence.[7] Two fifteen-minute documentaries, *The Peruvian Independence* and *Ayacucho, the Last Battle*, as well as a series of three-minute short, "objective" videos about the many events organized by CNSIP, were also produced under the commission's sponsorship, screened in theaters around the country, and shown by television stations.[8] A series of contests, such as competitions for monographs, anthems, essays, statues, and more, were also organized in an effort to promote the participation of the population. The level and quality of participation, however, were not particularly high. An international contest for historians and writers, for example, titled "The Túpac Amaru Insurrection and Its Projections in the American Independence," received only five works, none of which was considered worthy of the prize, so the contest was declared void. A similar one, this time only for Peruvian authors and titled "The Ideologists of Peruvian Emancipation," also received five submissions. That contest produced two winners, María Luisa Rivara de Tuesta and José Ignacio López Soria, whose books were later published by CNSIP. Various contests for university and high school students were offered as well.[9] A competition announced in March 1970 to choose a "Marcha del Sesquicentenario" ("Anthem of the Sesquicentennial") was also declared null, since none of the ten submissions was considered appropriate; a second try, just a few months later, resulted in the selection of a march composed by Jaime Díaz Orihuela, which was then recorded and issued in a 45 rpm record.[10] A competition of "popular music" related to Peruvian independence in genres such as *vals*, *huayno*, and *marinera* failed twice to produce a winner.[11]

During the second half of July 1971 and most of the month of Au-

Figure 1.1. General Juan Velasco Alvarado delivering the central speech on the sesquicentennial commemoration of Peru's independence, July 28, 1971.

gust, in virtually every city and town around the country, special ceremonies, military parades, inaugurations of monuments, and civic activities were held, although only forty of them were organized by CNSIP: twenty-one were defined as "cultural," thirteen as "civic," and only six as "social." "This was not a program of festivities," proudly reported General Mendoza.[12] On July 28, 1971, the central day of the commemoration, President Velasco Alvarado gave the keynote speech from the governmental palace, which was broadcast live on television and radio and later issued in a 33⅓ rpm double vinyl record. Most of the president's address was devoted to highlighting the reforms being implemented by the government: changes in labor legislation, land reform, the creation of SINAMOS, and others. In closing, he stated that although these transformations may seem "less dramatic and glorious" than the independence of 1821, the battles they were fighting to attain the "definite emancipation" of the country were "tenser and more difficult."[13] Curiously, the painting shown behind Velasco Alvarado during his sesquicentennial speech featured Francisco Pizarro, the conqueror of Peru, instead of one of the heroes of independence (fig. 1.1). Shortly afterward, this painting would be removed and replaced with one of Túpac Amaru, the leader of the 1780 anticolonial rebellion, who, as we will see below, was adopted as a symbol of the military revolution. The name of the main room inside the presidential palace would also be changed to Salón Túpac Amaru.

In retrospect, it is clear that the commemoration of the sesquicentennial anniversary of Peruvian independence was much more sober than, say, the 1921 centennial celebrations, held during the frequently extravagant administration of Augusto B. Leguía. Not much grandeur or luxury was on display in 1971, with the possible exception of a few cocktails served after important events. No popular, carnival-style celebrations have been identified either. Solemn ceremonies, academic events, and military parades dominated the official commemoration program. According to *El Comercio*, the two most important initiatives were the publication of the CDIP and the organization of the 5th Congress of American History (Lima, July 30–August 6, 1971).[14] Part of the explanation for the restraint shown in the commemorations had to do with the fact that on May 31, 1970, a powerful earthquake had caused enormous material and human losses in the central Andean region. Up to two hundred thousand people died as a result of both the earthquake and the landslides that followed it. The government was spending a great deal of resources in the reconstruction efforts, and it would have been frivolous and disrespectful to organize festive celebrations in the aftermath of such a tragedy.[15] It is equally important, however, to stress that the government wanted to use the sesquicentennial commemoration as both a pedagogical and a political tool, and it is clear that Velasco Alvarado's advisers wanted to avoid the frivolity and ostentation that usually accompany these types of celebrations. It is worth highlighting that CNSIP was composed mostly of academics, who, not surprisingly, infused the celebrations with a reserved attitude, focused more on the moral, civic, historical, and intellectual aspects of the commemoration than on its festive ingredients.

General Mendoza emerges from the documents related to the commemoration as a careful administrator, a skillful negotiator, and somebody very closely identified with the military government's political agenda. The historian De la Puente Candamo praised him for performing his duties "with intelligence, firmness, and style (*señorío*), and with indefatigable devotion for Peru."[16] The overall idea behind the commission's plan, Mendoza wrote, was to implement a program shaped by "austerity, dignity, and promotion," by which he meant civic education.[17] Furthermore, "unlike the centennial celebrations of 1921 and 1924, in which everything had to do with social activities and the prominent figures of the liberators" (namely, José de San Martín and Simón Bolívar), "we had to remember and perpetuate the memories of *all the patriots who fought for freedom and independence*."[18] These two features—a restrained attitude and a desire to pay tribute to "all the patriots," not just the leaders of emancipation—represented a solid common ground between the government's agenda and the commissioners' approach to the commemoration.

Besides this commonality of purpose, it is important to identify the central elements in the interpretations about Peruvian independence that were put forward by both the government and the commission. Can we identify a common "official" interpretation of that historical event coming from both the revolutionary government and CNSIP? What were the views on Peruvian independence coming from the various individuals and branches of the government? Although it is to be expected that there were nuances and multiple views among members of the government, the leading voice was that of General Velasco Alvarado, who was a central protagonist in many of the key events of the commemoration. Independence, he suggested, was a "heroic feat that made us free" and it was the *"partial culmination* of an old process of liberation deeply rooted in our people's feelings."[19] That "first independence," however, was a "great but *unfinished* historical achievement," since the living conditions did not change for the majority of the Peruvian population:

> The authentic Peruvian people, to a great extent the carriers of the impulse that made possible the elimination of the colonial status, were not the true beneficiaries of the independence victory. They continued to be exploited and to live miserable lives, and their poverty was the ultimate foundation for the immense fortune of those who, in reality, were the heirs of the wealth and power that, before, were in large part in foreign hands.[20]

The Peruvian people, he added, were "the silent, forgotten, and anonymous victors of a historical battle fought in their name."[21] He considered independence, in short, a "truncated" process, an "unfulfilled promise."[22] It is worth highlighting that Velasco Alvarado's statements included a sometimes explicit criticism of the elites that led the independence movements and ruled the country afterward. The "incomplete" nature of independence and the state of prostration in which the lower classes were maintained were attributed to the elites' selfishness and lack of patriotism. This specific argument would not necessarily be shared or endorsed by CNSIP and its members, whose main focus was to highlight the unity of purpose and the accomplishments of the independence leaders, not their shortcomings.

On July 28, 1969, during his first Independence Day speech, General Velasco Alvarado claimed that on October 3, 1968, a "nationalist revolution" had started, one that would bring to the country its "second independence."[23] History would later recognize, he predicted, that an entire nation and its armed forces "embarked on the path toward their final liberation, established the basis of a genuine development, broke the power of a selfish and colonial oligarchy, recovered its authentic sovereignty vis-à-vis foreign pressures, and started the great task of realizing social justice in Peru."[24] Peru's second independence, he added, "must be an integral realization that encompasses all the areas of our reality."[25] The best possible tribute to the sesquicentennial commemoration was indeed to have started "the struggle for Peru's *definite emancipation* and for the *definite liberation* of its peoples from all forms of domination."[26] The emphasis, thus, was not so much on the achievements but on the shortcomings of the "first" independence.

But Velasco Alvarado and his advisers were very much aware that highlighting the "truncated" nature of the first independence was not enough, given the centrality of the events of 1821 for the formation of a nationalistic interpretation of Peruvian history. Velasco's speeches were first and foremost *political statements* and, as such, they were clearly trying to help legitimize the military nationalistic project. Thus, in addition to pointing to the shortcomings of the 1821 independence, he also claimed an essential continuity between that foundational moment and the changes taking place since October 3, 1968. The first independence was offered, indeed, as a precedent for the military revolution of 1968, thus establishing a genealogy that could further the claim that the military reforms were needed to "complete" the work started 150 years before. During a speech he gave at the Benemérita Sociedad Fundadores de la Independencia, for example, General Velasco Alvarado stated that "the revolution emerged as a logical consequence of the legacy of the heroes of independence (*próceres*), a legacy that did not die but continued to live in the people's soul. The revolution seeks, in fact, *to fulfill the dream of the promoters of our independence.*"[27] In other words, the "dream" existed in 1821, but (for reasons Velasco Alvarado did not elaborate upon) it was not fulfilled. He left no doubt, however, about the connection he saw between the two processes: "Peru is, once again, the scenario of another emancipatory heroic deed. . . . The battle is under way and we will fight until we build a free, dignified, and sovereign fatherland. *We have a sacred commitment to those who preceded us in this struggle.*"[28] The Peruvian revolution, he stated on another occasion, "is the historical continuation of our first libertarian effort."[29] He suggested that the heroes of 1821 made Peru a free country but did not achieve "the ideal of justice," which is what his government was trying to accomplish.[30]

As has been the case with other revolutionary and populist regimes in Latin America (postrevolutionary Mexico, Peronism in Argentina, socialist Cuba, Venezuela's Bolivarian revolution, and others), Velasco Alvarado clearly sought to locate the project he was leading within a historical trajectory that not only made the revolution possible but also necessary: without the radical reforms being implemented by the Revolutionary Government of the Armed Forces (RGAF), the independence being commemorated would have remained incomplete, truncated, unfinished; in other words, it would make no sense at all to celebrate it, since it had not actually fulfilled its promises. At the same time, without the sacrifice and example of the heroes of the first independence, the "second liberation" could not be accomplished. A drawing included in a book aimed at offering a justification of the military coup offered a graphic representation of the kind of connection established by the military regime between the "first" and the "second" independence (fig. 1.2).

Were CNSIP's interpretations of the process of independence aligned with the views put forward by General Velasco Alvarado? General Mendoza offered a useful summary of the interpretive framework that guided the commission's efforts: "The conception [of the documentary collection] responds to an integral view aimed at assessing the situation of the country in the late eighteenth century and at demonstrating not only the diverse manifestations of the Peruvian efforts toward emancipation in various latitudes but also its origins, chronology, thought, and actions—from rebellions and ideology to the patriotic participation of the people and the militancy in the liberation campaigns—within the process of American emancipation."[31] He asserted that the work of historians and researchers confirmed that "we kept the leadership of the rebellion, the ideology, and the blood that was shed" and that "since the late eighteenth century a consciousness about self-determination was in the making."[32] Popular demands for "justice and freedom" arose in various parts of the country. In an article that General Mendoza wrote for a special supplement published on July 28, 1971, he reiterated these points and added others: he wanted to dispel the notion that everything was reduced to "the arrival on Peruvian coasts of the Liberating Expedition," thus trying to counter interpretations about an independence "given to" Peruvians instead of earned by them.[33] Furthermore, "Peruvian independence was neither an isolated episode nor an event that came out of a generous improvisation. It was the result of an enraged (*enardecido*) and protracted effort in defense of the fatherland and its emancipation, which was heightened half a century earlier, marked by rebellions and pronouncements, and illuminated by redeeming ideas that constitute the always fertile seed of freedom."[34]

Figure 1.2. "July 28, 1821. We are free. Let's be so forever. October 3, 1968."
Comando Conjunto de la Fuerza Armada, *3 de octubre de 1968: ¿Por qué?* (Lima,
1968).

With slight variations in tone, this approach built and expanded on the contributions made by different members of CNSIP in their previous work and also in the introductions written to CDIP volumes as well as in statements and articles produced for the commemoration of 1971.[35] Some of them emphasized the "unity" of the efforts toward independence; some, the participation of various sectors of the population (peasants, Indians, blacks, mestizos, Creoles); others, the continuity between the efforts by the "precursors" and those of the actual "liberators"; and still others, the existence, beyond minimal doubt, of a Peruvian national identity that preceded the existence of the Peruvian nation-state.

Generally speaking, the commission's approach to the first independence highlighted the contributions and efforts of the population, not the shortcomings of the postindependence period, as General Velasco Alvarado did. The so-called popular sectors (*sectores populares*), including Indians, peasants, slaves, free blacks, and the urban poor, were seen as part of a larger and cohesive collective that achieved independence on behalf of all Peruvians. For these historians, "popular participation" took the form of informal bands of rebels (known as guerrillas and *montoneras*), the enrollment of lower-class people in the liberation army, the logistic support they offered to patriotic soldiers, and the general enthusiasm they demonstrated toward the cause of independence. Peruvian people behaved heroically, and this could be explained, in turn, by their love for the fatherland. CNSIP and the historians associated with it did not seek to problematize the reasons for that participation, the complexity of the social realities that affected the lower classes, or their multiple and often contradictory attitudes toward the process of independence. In her introduction to the various volumes of documents titled *La acción patriótica del pueblo en la emancipación* (The patriotic action of the people in the emancipation process), published as part of the CDIP, the historian Ella Dunbar Temple summarized this perspective:

> About that period [independence], whose historical and social significance is so remarkable, as vigorous as the [Spanish] conquest, and with the same character of an epic and transitional moment, classic historians present, in contrast, an almost dehumanized profile, one in which only eponymous leaders and defining military episodes prevail. The decisive contribution of the Peruvian population and even the behavior of their patrician figures are silenced; and although their profiles are still largely blurry or unheard of, it is necessary, because of a historical and nationalistic imperative, to offer them a just appreciation in order to vindicate them.[36]

The participation of "the Peruvian people" can be identified, according to Temple, in the actions of "the humble peoples in all towns of Peru," and even if she at some point refers to internal struggles within guerrillas and *montoneras*, she quickly explained them by the fact that they were "men who were not accustomed to military life" but who were "attached to it only because of their love for freedom and independence." There were, she added, "mistakes and deviations," but, as a whole, "they did not depart from *the common denominator.*" The Peruvian peoples, she wrote, quoting a patriotic leader, were not opportunistic actors who "were only awaiting the moment to participate in the struggle."[37]

The overall interpretation offered by CNSIP was one of national unity and widespread and protracted participation of all Peruvians in the independence process. In a lecture on the latter topic, for instance, the historian De la Puente Candamo reiterated the idea that "the proclamation of independence represented the outcome of Peruvians' personal and free attitude; it was a slow process, a free effort of the Peruvian man."[38] An article in *El Comercio* signed by HBG—an author whose identity I have not been able to discover—offered a nice summary of this vision: "Men of lineage and common men, clergymen and freethinkers, wealthy men and poor men, civilian and military: *all of them came together* then, not to choose [for the first time] but to insist on the path toward a Free Fatherland, which was already envisioned centuries earlier by the first representatives of the [Peruvian] national sentiment (*nacionalidad*)."[39] This unitary nationalistic vision that transpires so clearly in the works of CNSIP (but less so in Velasco Alvarado's vision) would be frontally attacked in 1972 by, among others, Heraclio Bonilla and Karen Spalding in their classic essay "La independencia en el Perú: Las palabras y los hechos" (Independence in Peru: The words and the facts), which opened a debate that would continue for years.[40]

As is evident from the previous discussion, there were differences in the visions of independence articulated by General Velasco Alvarado on the one hand, and CNSIP and its members on the other, but the convergences were much more meaningful. The apparent "paradox" of a revolutionary government relying on conservative historians for the production and dissemination of knowledge about Peruvian independence acquires new meaning if we look at those points of convergence. The historian Carlos Contreras suggests that the "relative surprise" of the "rather moderate and conservative character" of the official sesquicentennial commemoration may be explained by the fact that "the Peruvian army was born with the Wars of Independence" and, thus, there was an institutional, that is, military, "historiographical conservatism" on that topic.[41] Without necessarily discarding this thesis, I would like to suggest other elements that may help us explain the apparent paradox. First, both the military government and conservative historians shared a defense of the "sacred institutions" of the fatherland, including the military, particularly in the context of the Cold War and vis-à-vis the serious threats presented by insurrectional movements in various countries in Latin America. The Peruvian experiment initiated in October 1968, despite its revolutionary rhetoric and its radical reforms, could also be interpreted as a project to defend the fatherland against Communism, that is, as a preventive revolution.[42]

Second, the discourse of national unity before and during the first independence, put forward by conservative historians, was not incompatible with the notion of an "incomplete" or "truncated" process, as highlighted by Velasco Alvarado and the military leaders. In fact, this unifying nationalistic discourse worked better for the military than the alternative (radical or Marxist) interpretation that Bonilla and Spalding and others would eventually offer. The latter—which entailed a clearly antinationalist view—would in fact have undermined both the nationalistic thesis of independence and the claims for national unity that the military regime was promoting to legitimize its rule: "The people and the armed forces, united, will prevail" was one of the regime's most widely used slogans. The Peruvian people needed to remain united to fulfill the promise of the second liberation; this was the underlying message that the military wanted to send. Following the example of 1821 would strengthen the chances of fulfilling the promise of a true and definite liberation. A strong attachment to nationalism and "national unity" as central components in the definition of Peruvian identity, past and present, offered a common ground to both the historians' and the army's interpretations of independence. At the inauguration of the monument to the heroes of independence, General Mendoza presented a very explicit call for unity behind the banners of the military government: "Today, when the Armed Forces are guiding the destiny of the nation with success, dignity, and patriotism, we all have the great opportunity to overcome mistakes and omissions, excesses and privileges, that belong to the past. Today is the great opportunity to consolidate aspirations and hopes, to bring together efforts, and to overcome all types of divisions, differences, and distances."[43]

Third, the thesis about "popular participation" in the wars of independence, which was central to the unifying view of the process defended by conservative historians and articulated in several volumes of the CDIP, also served the rhetoric and political goals of the military government very well: if the Peruvian people were able to accomplish independence from Spain in 1821, they would also achieve, with their participation and under the leadership of the military, the second and final liberation. This thesis resonated with a political project that claimed to be building a society of justice and solidarity with full participation of the population and that would eventually be codified in the notion of "social democracy with full participation."[44]

Finally, there was one more element that facilitated, albeit also complicated, this marriage of convenience between the military government and the conservative historians around the commemoration of the sesquicentennial anniversary: the role attributed to Túpac Amaru as a precursor of both the 1821 independence (for the historians) and of the second liberation project (for the Velasco Alvarado government). To be sure, conservative historians had not hitherto fully embraced Túpac Amaru as one of their heroes; very few studies had actually focused on the rebellion, despite its centrality as the largest anticolonial rebellion in Spanish America. But a growing interest in the study of popular revolts and the desire to present independence as a protracted process with its pantheon of precursors and popular heroes made room for the incorporation of Túpac Amaru into the traditional nationalist narrative. Still, it is apparent that the commissioners did not feel completely at ease with the prominence that Túpac Amaru enjoyed as a political symbol for the military government. As Charles Walker discusses in his chapter in this volume, the military brought to the forefront the image of Túpac Amaru both as a historical reference and as a visible symbol, even an icon, for their revolution. Túpac Amaru was the most frequently used historical figure during the Velasco Alvarado regime: he was presented as a fighter for social justice, an enemy of colonialism, a precursor of land reform, and much more. His image, especially in the iconic version by Jesús Ruiz Durand, was used as a logo for many official publications, campaigns, governmental agencies, and even coins and bills.[45] The apocryphal slogan that was emblematic of the 1969 land reform— "Peasant, the landlord will no longer eat from your poverty"—was attributed to Túpac Amaru. A silk-screen poster presented Túpac Amaru as the precursor not to independence but to the Velasco Alvarado–era reforms (fig. 1.3).

CNSIP, on the other hand, gave Túpac Amaru a relatively prominent place but not as central as the military government would probably have liked to see. The CDIP, for instance, opens not with the Túpac

Figure 1.3. "Tupac Amaru promised it. Velasco accomplished it." International Institute of Social History, Amsterdam.

Amaru rebellion but with Creole "ideologists," and the number of pages devoted to each theme reveals where CNSIP's main focus was: while fifteen volumes were devoted to the ideologists, only four covered the Túpac Amaru rebellion. The Monument of the Precursors, proba-bly the most important such monument built in the context of the ses-quicentennial commemoration, inaugurated on July 27, 1971, included Túpac Amaru but alongside three other Creole figures: Juan Pablo Vis-cardo y Guzmán, Toribio Rodríguez de Mendoza, and Francisco de Vidal.[46] A Túpac Amaru monument was planned for the Plaza de Armas in Cuzco, but in the end it was not installed—though, it must be said, it was not the commission's fault.[47] On the other hand, on July 31, 1971, a Túpac Amaru monument was inaugurated in the district of Magdalena, in Lima, with the attendance of Marcos and Leoncia Condorcahua, direct descendants of the hero, who had come from Sicuani to participate in the ceremony. The national anthem was performed in Quechua, and poems were read by Alejandro Romualdo, Magda Portal, and Alberto Chevarría. The San Marcos University Choir interpreted the "Himno a Túpac Amaru," written by the Cuzco poet Luis Nieto.[48] It is evident that different actors were giving different emphases to the place of Túpac Amaru within the process of independence; while he had become the main symbol of the revolutionary government and was made the central figure of the first independence, his place within the overall vision of CNSIP was less prominent.

We can see this in the way the sesquicentennial supplements issued by the conservative daily *El Comercio* and the official newspaper *El Peruano* differed on the images they chose for their covers. The former (a bastion of Peruvian conservatism owned by the Miró Quesada family, one of whose members, Aurelio Miró Quesada, as mentioned above, was a member of CNSIP) had a collage of images of independence heroes with General José de San Martín at the forefront. Although Túpac Amaru's image is very prominent (and bigger), it occupies the second plane (fig 1.4). Furthermore, the main editorial that *El Comercio* published on July 28, 1971, highlighted the symbolic date of 1821 but not the rebellion of 1780, and referred to "the glorious events of 1821 that started with the arrival of the Liberation Army and culminated with the Proclamation of Independence." The only independence hero mentioned in this editorial is José de San Martín, the Argentine general that proclaimed Peruvian independence in 1821.[49] *El Comercio* did not completely ignore Túpac Amaru, however (a much smaller note on the same page called him "the eponymous caudillo, the precursor to independence"), but he clearly occupied a secondary place in the more conservative reconstruction of the independence process.[50]

El Peruano, on the other hand, the official newspaper, titled its supplement "150 Years." Collaborators included both senior and younger historians—Carlos Daniel Valcárcel, Juan José Vega, Heraclio Bonilla, Raúl Rivera Serna, Augusto Tamayo Vargas, Pablo Macera, and others, many of them well known for their leftist political views. The note that announced this special publication stated that "inscribed within

Figure 1.4. Cover of special supplement for the sesquicentennial anniversary of Peruvian independence. *El Comercio*, July 28, 1971.

the *historical continuity* that we wanted to give to the document [that is, the supplement], it also includes the role and the historic work (*obra histórica*) of the Revolutionary Government of the Armed Forces during the short time that it is leading the process that our fatherland is going through."[51] Thus, the supplement's content was not meant to be just about what happened 150 years earlier but also to connect it to the ongoing process of reforms initiated by the military government. The titles for both sections were more than explicit: "First Independence" and "Second Independence," respectively, with the first one featuring just one image: Túpac Amaru (fig. 1.5). For the government, he was *the* hero of that first independence, not José de San Martín. The "Second Independence" section had a peasant holding a Peruvian flag on its cover.

The historical and political relevance of Túpac Amaru was also highlighted in the *El Peruano* supplement by historians such as Carlos Daniel Valcárcel, who suggested that "his uprising left a message to present-day Peru," and Juan José Vega, who considered him "the most important Peruvian character in universal history" and "the first of the great men in our history that tried to give a sense of selfhood (*personería*) to a country that was almost completely alienated."[52] It is clear that for historians and other commentators close to the military government, Túpac Amaru was the most relevant character in the independence process, and his legacy continued to inform efforts toward social justice and liberation.

Ultimately, we must credit politics, not historiography, for the growing visibility of Túpac Amaru in public discourse in the 1970s. Emilio

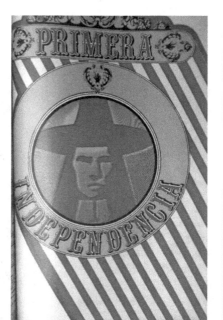

Figure 1.5. Covers of the two sections of the special supplement published by the official newspaper *El Peruano* to commemorate the sesquicentennial anniversary of Peruvian Independence, July 28, 1971.

Romero perceptively noted that "the historian who in future decades will try to reconstruct present-day Peruvian social life will identify as its most exceptional (*insólito*) feature the *rediscovery* or *exhumation* of the figure of Túpac Amaru."[53] This rediscovery took place mostly in the realm of political discourse and symbolism. Although there were important precedents (Carlos Daniel Valcárcel and others), it will take a few more years before historians catch up, thanks especially to the efforts by Alberto Flores Galindo and Scarlett O'Phelan and, more recently, Charles Walker.[54]

Thus, there was no single and homogenous "official" version of independence. The views articulated by General Velasco Alvarado on the one hand and by CNSIP on the other had both coincidences and discrepancies, resulting from, among other things, the fact that the former reflected an unambiguous political agenda that sought to justify, first, the military coup or revolution and, second, the various reforms it was implementing. This required an emphasis on the "shortcomings" of the first independence. For CNSIP, the emphasis was placed on reinforcing the nationalist and unitary interpretation of independence, which in turn required highlighting and praising the positive aspects of the process, including the widespread participation of the population. As mentioned above, however, these differences did not overshadow the multiple coincidences between the two versions, which fundamentally had to do with the affirmation of an essential Peruvian "national identity" that, in their view, explained the process that led to independence in 1821, in one case, and the struggles for the second liberation after 1968.

Conclusion

What was the ultimate impact of the sesquicentennial commemorations? Newspaper headlines tend to suggest that there was an explosion of nationalistic euphoria, and there is evidence of popular participation in public events such as parades, civic processions, artistic shows, or the inauguration of monuments.[55] The event that seems to have gathered the largest crowd was the July 29 military parade (according to *El Comercio*, attended by 250,000), but that was not particularly unusual for the annual display of military force that takes place on that date. Scattered reports from the interior suggest an important degree of participation but not a situation of euphoria. Foreign tourists who happened to be in Peru apparently mingled with local populations at these events.[56]

Although this is always difficult to accurately assess, after reviewing the evidence, I am inclined to suggest that the commemoration did not prompt a wave of nationalistic enthusiasm comparable with, for instance, the one that Peruvians experienced just a year earlier after some successes of the national soccer team.[57]

But probably that is not something to be surprised (or disappointed) by. After all, CNSIP's efforts were not aimed at mobilizing the masses but at generating reflection. The mostly academic tone of many of the official celebrations was not bound to provoke massive popular enthusiasm. Pablo Macera's sarcastic description of them as generating "environmental pollution" and Heraclio Bonilla's harsh depiction of them as reflective of "nationalist intoxication" appear to be related to the intellectual and political resonances of the commemoration, not a widespread sentiment of nationalistic fever.[58] For historians and intellectuals, the commemoration left some long-lasting legacies. The documentary efforts reflected in the eighty-six-volume collection that *El Comercio* called "a true bibliographical monument" and General Velasco Alvarado, "an invaluable treasure on the history of our independence";[59] the many other books published by CNSIP; and the organization of the Fifth Congress of American History constitute, by far, the most important outcomes of the 1971 official commemoration. And although not part of the official program, the other by-product of the sesquicentennial moment was the vigorous and at times acerbic debate that followed the publication of Bonilla's edited volume, which was taken as a threat to the apparent nationalist consensus and was accused of presenting the views of "foreign" scholars (such as Eric Hobsbawm, Pierre Vilar, or Pierre Chaunu) who allegedly did not quite understand Peru's history.[60]

The official commemoration of the sesquicentennial aimed, not surprisingly, at consolidating the emancipatory project of the Revolutionary Government of the Armed Forces. The political uses of the celebration were clear and explicit, not only on the part of the government but even in the case of other institutions such as the Catholic Church, the Municipal Council of Lima, and various civic organizations. The Peruvian Episcopal Assembly, for instance, issued a statement on the occasion of the sesquicentennial celebration that is worth quoting at length because it highlights the way in which the celebration was discursively blended with a clear support of the "revolutionary" process:

> The Catholic Church, by participating in the joy and hope that are generated by this commemoration, wants to bring to light the evangelical

message of *liberation* in order to interpret *the deep meaning of freedom.* . . . The proclamation of independence represented, in the short run, a political change. But in its core, it contains the deep *aspiration for general liberation* . . . that seeks to attain with positive actions a conscious and personal freedom, without external obstacles, and which should mean *the effective freedom of each and every Peruvian.* . . . [T]his sesquicentennial celebration must not be just a lyric remembrance of past glories, but a stimulus to respond to the demands of freedom and justice that Peru is making today with particular urgency and within a process of change, which has to be humanistic and integral.[61]

Lima's cardinal Juan Landázuri, reputedly one of the most progressive members of the Catholic hierarchy, also issued a statement that strongly echoed liberation theology's tenets: "The common good demands from every person of goodwill a serious commitment to the liberation of men; the Church understands it as an integral liberation: liberation from misery and ignorance [and] from all forms of oppression—not only economic and material—that subject people to unacceptable forms of servitude and that are neither humane nor Christian."[62]

On the other hand, at the special session of the Lima municipal council presided over by General Velasco Alvarado that kicked off the sesquicentennial celebrations on July 15, 1971, and ostensibly imitating the 1821 declaration of independence, the council approved its own declaration that special guests and ordinary citizens later adhered to. The declaration expressed its unequivocal support for the "full materialization of the goals of the Peruvian revolution":

The members of the Lima provincial council, gathered in a solemn session to commemorate the sesquicentennial anniversary of the declaration of National Independence, affirm in this historical moment that the general will of the Peruvian people is to attain the country's economic and social emancipation, to break all forms of foreign and local dependency, and to transform traditional structures to create . . . a new society with dignity, freedom, and sovereignty, and capable of achieving the social well-being of all Peruvians of today and tomorrow.[63]

A second statement, a "Declaration of Lima's Citizens" (Declaración de los Vecinos de Lima), pledged that they "will defend with their life, property, and rights the platform (*postulados*) of the Peruvian Revolution."[64] *El Peruano* highlighted the political significance of these declarations and of the overall commemorative program: "Peru lives today through a new revolution, one that even if peaceful is no less gallant and patriotic [than the 1821 one]. This is a new process that reaffirms the independence of our nation and extends it into other realms for the definite realization of its own destiny. This is the glorious atmosphere (*el marco glorioso*) for the sesquicentennial commemoration."[65] It would be difficult to find a more explicit and succinct statement about the whole meaning behind the official commemorations of the sesquicentennial anniversary of Peruvian independence: the transformations effected by the military government were presented as a continuation of the truncated 1821 independence efforts and the fulfillment of a complete and definite national emancipation, one that would bring social justice and dignity for all Peruvians. The commemoration and remembrance of past events, as is always the case, acquired their ultimate meaning in the intervention they had in political battles of the present. Peru's alleged second liberation represented the overall framework within which the sesquicentennial commemoration was conceived and executed.

Notes

1. Juan Velasco Alvarado, *Velasco, la voz de la revolución* (Lima: Oficina Nacional de Difusión del SINAMOS, 1972), 1:3; emphasis added. This and all other translations in this chapter are by the author.

2. Comisión Nacional del Sesquicentenario de la Independencia del Perú, *Memoria presentada por el General de División EP (r) Juan Mendoza Rodríguez, Presidente de la Comisión Nacional del Sesquicentenario de la Independencia del Perú, 1969–1974* (Lima: Editorial Jurídica, 1974), 11; hereafter cited as CNSIP, *Memoria*.

3. Carlos Contreras, "La independencia del Perú: Balance de la historiografía contemporánea," in *Debates sobre las independencias iberoamericanas*, ed. Manuel Chust and José Antonio Serrano (Madrid and Frankfurt: Iberoamericana/Vervuert, 2007), 100.

4. Miró Quesada was a member of the family that owned the conservative newspaper *El Comercio* that would eventually be expropriated, along with other media, by the military government in July 1974. De la Puente Candamo and Armando Nieto Vélez were affiliated with the conservative Riva-Agüero Institute. For an overview of Peruvian historiography in the twentieth century, including the work of these historians, see Alberto Flores Galindo, "La imagen y el espejo: La historiografía peruana 1910–1986," *Márgenes* 2, no. 4 (December 1988): 55–83.

5. CNSIP, *Memoria*, 17.

6. "Ceremonia de entrega de la Colección Documental por la Comisión Nacional del Sesquicentenario al Señor Presidente de la República. Discurso del

Señor General de División EP Juan Mendoza Rodríguez," in *Discursos pronunciados en actuaciones cívicas conmemorativas* (Lima: Publicaciones de la Comisión Nacional del Sesquicentenario de la Independencia del Perú, 1972), 225.

7. CNSIP, *Memoria*, 186.

8. Ibid., 141–144.

9. Ibid., 79–83.

10. Ibid., 125.

11. Ibid., 126.

12. Ibid., 94. *El Peruano*, the official state newspaper, had a daily section called "News of the Sesquicentennial Celebration" that offered information about the many events taking place in different locations.

13. Velasco Alvarado, *Velasco, la voz de la revolución*, 1:143.

14. This international congress included more than 350 participants from Peru and many foreign countries. The five-volume collection of proceedings, published in 1974, included 120 papers.

15. An editorial article in *El Peruano* explicitly stated that the austerity of the commemoration had to do with the May 31, 1970, earthquake. See "Sesquicentenario," *El Peruano*, July 17, 1971.

16. José Agustín de la Puente Candamo, *La independencia* (Lima: BRASA, 1993), 523.

17. CNSIP, *Memoria*, 94.

18. Ibid., 23; emphasis added.

19. Velasco Alvarado, *Velasco, la voz de la revolución*, 2:107; emphasis added.

20. Ibid.; emphasis added.

21. Ibid.

22. Ibid., 2:142, 147.

23. Ibid., 1:59.

24. Ibid.

25. Ibid.

26. Ibid., 2:141; emphasis added.

27. *El Peruano*, July 30, 1971; emphasis added.

28. Ibid.; emphasis added.

29. Velasco Alvarado, *Velasco, la voz de la revolución*, 2:108.

30. Ibid.

31. CNSIP, *Memoria*, 35.

32. Ibid., 36.

33. This issue would be the subject of intense historiographical debates in the 1970s and 1980s. See, in particular, Heraclio Bonilla, ed., *La Independencia en el Perú* (Lima: Instituto de Estudios Peruanos, 1972); Jorge Basadre, *El azar en la historia y sus límites* (Lima: P.L. Villanueva, 1973); and Scarlett O'Phelan, "El mito de la 'independencia concedida': Los programas políticos del siglo XVIII y del temprano XIX en el Perú y alto Perú (1730–1814)," *Histórica* 9, no. 2 (1985): 155–191.

34. *El Comercio*, July 28, 1971.

35. Numerous speeches delivered by members of CNSIP in various civic activities are compiled in the volume *Discursos pronunciados en actuaciones cívicas conmemorativas* (Lima: Publicaciones de la Comisión Nacional del Sesquicentenario de la Independencia del Perú, 1972).

36. Ella Dunbar Temple, ed., *La acción patriótica del pueblo en la emancipación: Guerrillas y montoneras* (Lima: CDIP, 1971), 5: iii.

37. Dunbar Temple, *La acción patriótica del pueblo*, 5: xxviii; emphasis added.

38. "Sobre el papel del pueblo en la Independencia, habló el Dr. de la Puente Candamo," *El Comercio*, July 13, 1971.

39. HBG, "Reafirmación de la Independencia," *El Comercio*, July 18, 1971.

40. Heraclio Bonilla and Karen Spalding, "La independencia en el Perú: Las palabras y los hechos," in Bonilla, *La independencia en el Perú*, 15–64.

41. Contreras, "La independencia del Perú, 100.

42. See, for instance, Dirk Kruijt, "Exercises in State Terrorism: The Counter-Insurgency Campaigns in Guatemala and Peru," in *Societies of Fear: The Legacy of Civil War, Violence and Terror in Latin America*, ed. Kees Koonings and Dirk Kruijt (New York: Zed Books, 1999), 35.

43. "Monumento a Precursores y Próceres de la Independencia se inauguró ayer," *El Comercio*, July 28, 1971.

44. See, for instance, *Bases ideológicas de la revolución peruana. Objetivo: Democracia social de participación plena* (Lima: Gobierno Revolucionario de la Fuerza Armada, 1975).

45. On this, see Leopoldo Lituma Agüero, *El verdadero rostro de Túpac Amaru (Perú, 1969–1975)* (Lima: Facultad de Letras y Ciencias Humanas, Universidad Nacional Mayor de San Marcos, Pakarina Ediciones, 2011).

46. CNSIP, *Memoria*, 97–98.

47. The location in Cuzco was approved by a 27–5 vote. Three different competitions were needed to choose the winning project for the monument, presented by Álvaro Núñez Rebaza, but although he was awarded the prize, it was not built because "it did not produce a good impression in Cuzco." A fourth contest was announced in February 1972, and the winning project was one by Joaquín Ugarte y Ugarte. But when everything was ready to place the monument in the main plaza of Cuzco, the plan was stalled because of "discrepant opinions" about the location. The monument was kept inside an army premise in Lima until the issues were resolved. See CNSIP, *Memoria*, 100–104.

48. *El Peruano*, July 31, 1971.

49. "Sesquicentenario de la Declaración de la Independencia," *El Comercio*, July 28, 1971.

50. "Inauguración del monumento a los próceres peruanos," *El Comercio*, July 28, 1971.

51. "El Peruano editará Suplemento Especial por Sesquicentenario," *El Peruano*, July 13, 1971.

52. Carlos Daniel Valcárcel, "Túpac Amaru, revolucionario," and Juan José Vega, "José Gabriel Túpac Amaru," *El Peruano*, July 28, 1971.

53. Emilio Romero, "Resurrección y gloria de Túpac Amaru," *El Comercio*, July 28, 1971; emphasis added.

54. Alberto Flores Galindo, ed. *Tupac Amaru II: Sociedad colonial y sublevaciones populares* (Lima: Retablo de Papel, 1976); Scarlett O'Phelan, *Rebellions and Revolts in Eighteenth Century Peru and Upper Peru* (Köln: Bohlau, 1985); Charles Walker, *The Tupac Amaru Rebellion* (Cambridge, MA: Harvard University Press, 2014).

55. Newspapers used headlines such as "Crece animación en el país por el

Sesquicentenario," "Reina júbilo en el país por Sesquicentenario," or "Gran júbilo en el país en vísperas del Sesquicentenario."

56. "Gran afluencia de turistas en Cuzco por el 28," *El Comercio*, July 30, 1971.

57. Carlos Aguirre, "Perú campeón: Fiebre futbolística y nacionalismo en 1970," in *Lima siglo XX: Cultura, socialización y cambio*, ed. Carlos Aguirre and Aldo Panfichi (Lima: Pontificia Universidad Católica del Perú, 2013), 383–416.

58. Pablo Macera, review of Bonilla, ed., "La independencia en el Perú," in *Textual*, no. 4 (June 1972): 78–79; Heraclio Bonilla, *Metáfora y realidad de la Independencia en el Perú* (Lima: Instituto de Estudios Peruanos, 2001), 11. Macera sarcastically pointed out that although initiatives such as the CDIP deserved recognition, the celebration of the sesquicentennial anniversary had cost more than what was spent obtaining independence.

59. "El Sesquicentenario de la independencia nacional," *El Comercio*, July 28, 1971; "Discurso del Señor General de División EP Juan Velasco Alvarado, Presidente de la República," July 26, 1971, in *Discursos pronunciados*, 227.

60. See Heraclio Bonilla's response to the critics of his edited volume in "Historia y verdad," *Sociedad y Política*, 1 (June 1972): 51–52. For an excellent review of the historiography on Peruvian independence, see Contreras, "La independencia del Perú."

61. "Mensaje evangélico del Episcopado Peruano en ocasión de celebrarse el 28 de julio los ciento cincuenta años de la Independencia Nacional," *El Peruano*, July 24, 1971; emphases added.

62. "El Cardenal Landázuri pronunció oración gratulatoria por Sesquicentenario Patrio," *El Peruano*, July 30, 1971.

63. "Presidente Velasco presidió ayer la Sesión Solemne del Concejo de Lima," *El Peruano*, July 16, 1971.

64. Ibid.

65. "Sesquicentenario," *El Peruano*, July 17, 1971.

CHAPTER 2

The General and His Rebel: Juan Velasco Alvarado and the Reinvention of Túpac Amaru II

CHARLES F. WALKER

After having been a relegated and uncomfortable figure for official historiography, Túpac Amaru is now undeniably at the forefront. His image appears repeatedly in newspapers, magazines, posters, paintings, movies, etc. He has been converted into an apparently familiar character.
ALBERTO FLORES GALINDO[1]

[The Velasco government] is propagating the glories of the Inca past, of Indian rebels like Túpac Amaru, and of Indian virtues with great enthusiasm, and actually planning schooling in the Quechua language.
ERIC HOBSBAWM[2]

I have long viewed the Velasco Alvarado period as a curious terra incognita of Peruvian history. Not only is it inexcusably understudied (until very recently, at least), but, more interestingly, it divides people in curious and often surprising ways. When I talk to Peruvians about the Incas or about former president Alberto Fujimori, I can usually guess where they will stand. In terms of the Incas, everyone *likes* them, in a range from respect to veneration, although some will quietly or "incorrectly" admit a certain disdain. *Fujimorismo* marks contemporary Peruvian politics like no other issue or figure, and even with the odd and at times dispiriting alliances of late, most opinions are predictable. With Velasco, however, I am often surprised when people tell me that although it was not perfect, the regime did more for Peru than any other government, past and present, or, on the other extreme, when individuals blame 1968–1975 for all of Peru's woes. Some very conservative people have stunned me by acknowledging their respect for Velasco. On the other hand, others express venomous dislike. I have heard taxi drivers blame him for the Lima traffic, and conservatives find him guilty for all of Peru's misfortunes. While those targeted by the Velasco regime—the *oligarchy*, to use the lazy term of the period, or at least all those who lost land—detest him, others say that they supported an agrarian reform, but not his, or that he was only a step better than the fascist thugs of the Southern Cone. Velasco radically altered Peru, for better or for worse, and historians and Peruvians still have not come to terms with his period and him.

The Velasco government used the image of the eighteenth-century anticolonial rebel José Gabriel Condorcanqui, or Túpac Amaru II, widely.[3] The redesigned iconic face and invented quotation ("Campesino, el patrón no comerá más de tu pobreza"; "Peasant, the lord will no longer eat from your poverty") adorned posters, banners, and publications, while statues, plaques, and renamed streets commemorated the rebel leader. The regime named a plan, a hall, avenues, towns, new shantytowns, an information center, and much more after him. The use of Túpac Amaru as the historical face of the regime represents an interesting moment in Latin American hero cults. It also constituted an important recasting of the Peruvian wars of independence at the time of the 1971 sesquicentennial.

This chapter analyzes why the Velasco government selected Túpac Amaru and how the government and its supporters reinvented him. I examine the nature of publications on Túpac Amaru leading up to the 1968 coup, how historians and others envisioned him, and why he attracted increasing international attention. I then explore Velasco's use of Túpac Amaru, particularly in the commemoration of the 150th anniversary of Peru's independence in 1971.[4] He and the Velasco regime turned out to be a very good fit. The recasting of Túpac Amaru as the initiator of Peru's truncated struggle for independence—a battle that Velasco vowed to finish—sparked debates about the wars of independence that continue today.

Túpac Amaru was everywhere during the Velasco period. In the words of Enrique Mayer, "Everything revolutionary and nationalistic during the Velasco regime had the name Túpac Amaru. New statues, plazas, and streets were dedicated to him in every city. The Ministry of Agriculture and its agrarian reform posters had Túpac Amaru on them. Expropriated haciendas with aristocratic Spanish names were renamed after him, and even the state-run food distribution system had a stylized stencil symbol of Túpac Amaru with a black-brimmed, tall top hat

Figure 2.1. Túpac Amaru depicted on the fifty-sol bill in 1969, drawn by Germán Suárez Vértiz. Author's collection.

and a stern face."⁵ This ubiquitous latter image, created by Jesús Ruiz Durand, morphed into younger, darker, and even pop-infused versions. A dour Túpac Amaru with a bowler hat and flowing hair adorned the fifty-sol note from 1969 and that of one hundred soles in 1976 as well as the ten-sol coin from 1974 (fig. 2.1).⁶ Workers placed plaques honoring this "precursor and martyr of the independence of the Americas" in Tungasuca, Surimana, Tinta, and Iberia (Madre de Dios) and others commemorating the uprising in Sangarará, Cuzco, Puno, and Lampa.⁷

In a 1973 speech in Cuzco, General Leonidas Rodríguez Figueroa, a close collaborator with Velasco and director of the all-important Sistema Nacional de Apoyo a la Movilización Social, or SINAMOS (National System of Support for Social Mobilization), explained the centrality of Túpac Amaru for the regime, deeming him "the heroic link between our ancestors and ourselves! He is the heroic link between the ancient struggle against Spanish domination and today's struggle against imperialism. . . . That's why Túpac Amaru defines the personality of our fatherland; that's why Túpac Amaru roots the national revolution [Velasco's] in our history; that's why Túpac Amaru is the historical inspiration for the independent and nationalist quest of the Peruvian revolution."[8] In late September 1971, Velasco traveled to southern Peru. He began his September 27 speech in Cuzco with these words: "To reach Cuzco, land of Túpac Amaru, is to reach the heart of our history."[9] One account noted how people choked up when Velasco got on his knees to lift up an elderly campesina, an encounter "with the humble, those from below, as the president himself would state, precisely in the belly of the ancient Inca Empire, in the base of the Túpac Amaru liberation movement, whose flags this revolution has raised."[10]

The military revolutionary government picked its symbol well. José Gabriel Condorcanqui, or Túpac Amaru II, led a massive anticolonial uprising, the largest in Spanish American colonial history. Spreading from its base just south of Cuzco to Lake Titicaca and into Charcas or what became Bolivia, the 1780–1783 conflagration (it continued for two years after the May 1781 execution of Túpac Amaru; his wife, Micaela Bastidas; and their inner circle) nearly toppled Spanish control of South America. The brutal execution of Túpac Amaru and his wife— Micaela had her tongue slashed and was then strangled with a garrote, while Túpac Amaru was quartered by four horses and then hanged— converted them into martyrs. The rebellion encouraged other dissidents throughout South America and beyond; its death toll reached one hundred thousand.[11] He was a great fit for a leftist regime seeking images and icons. Túpac Amaru was a provincial (non-Lima, nonreformist) revolutionary with Inca roots (the name Túpac Amaru refers to his shared lineage with one of the Inca martyrs of the Spanish Conquest) who had challenged the Spanish yet, after centuries, had not taken his place in the pantheon of national heroes in Peru. Túpac Amaru had not, however, been forgotten, either in popular memory or by historians.

In the able hands of Jesús Ruiz Durand, Augusto Díaz Mori, Milner Cajahuaringa, Germán Suárez Vértiz, and other artists, he became a ruggedly handsome *andino* who resonated with a large part of Peru, particularly the campesinos whom Velasco sought to aid (and receive the support of) through his agrarian reform. In stressing visuals, particularly the lovely posters produced by SINAMOS and other institutions, the regime smartly recognized the limitations of the print media in Peru, where many citizens were illiterate (40% according to the 1961 census, overwhelmingly rural people) and had no access to newspapers or television.[12] Yet the impact went beyond campesinos and rural people who might see themselves as the descendants of Túpac Amaru and Micaela Bastidas. The image of a dark-skinned, ponytailed male resonated with the leading political and aesthetic inclinations of the period, the late 1960s and early 1970s: Third Worldism. In their simplicity and resonance, the representations of Túpac Amaru paralleled the iconic image of Ernesto Che Guevara.[13]

Timing was important. Military ideologues saw their revolutionary government as a struggle to overcome the failures of nearly 150 years of postindependence governments and to win the battle begun by Túpac Amaru. The sesquicentennial weighed heavily on them. They posited that Túpac Amaru had initiated the struggle for emancipation from Spain and that many of the goals and promises of the long war of independence (more than forty years if Túpac Amaru is seen as the initiator) remained unfulfilled. The Velasco government, however, did not invent Túpac Amaru out of thin air from the historical penchant of an erudite *ministro* or some musty colonial documents from Seville or Cuzco. Túpac Amaru was already a much-debated, highly vaunted figure in Peru and beyond. The chapter turns now to this point, the primary material from which historians and others converted him into a revolutionary icon.

In 1964, Antonio Cisneros published the pithy poem "Túpac Amaru Relegated":

There are liberators
with long sideburns
who saw the dead and wounded brought back
after the battles. Soon their names
became history, and the sideburns
growing into their old uniforms
proclaimed them founders of the nation.

Others with less luck have taken up
two pages of text
with four horses and their death.[14]

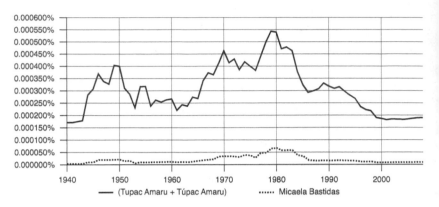

Chart 2.1. Frequency of use of terms "Túpac," "Túpac Amaru," and "Micaela Bastidas" in Spanish-language books, 1940–2014. Google Books Ngram Viewer.

The poem captures how historians and official celebrations had written dark-skinned rebel leaders out of the story, favoring the better-known heroes and martyrs of European descent. Yet the text also reflects, curiously, the growing interest in Túpac Amaru in Peru and beyond in the 1950s and 1960s. Cisneros did not have to name Túpac Amaru. Readers knew who he was with the mere mention of four horses, a reference to his brutal execution on May 18, 1781. Túpac Amaru's name and image circulated widely in Peru before 1968. However, he needed to be *revindicated*, to use a favored verb of the era.

The number of books published on the Túpac Amaru Rebellion grew steadily from the 1940s to the 1980s. Chart 2.1 indicates the frequency with which the terms "Túpac," "Túpac Amaru," and "Micaela Bastidas" appeared in books published in Spanish between 1940 and 2014.[15] The increase leading up to and during the Velasco government stands out.

Who were these authors that provided the prime material for the political reinterpretation and aesthetic remaking of Túpac Amaru in the late 1960s and 1970s? Beginning in the 1940s with his *Rebeliones indígenas* and *La rebelión de Túpac Amaru*, Carlos Daniel Valcárcel (1911–2007) published numerous accounts of the uprising. A professor at San Marcos University in Lima, he depicted the battle as an epic struggle between indigenous fighters and Spanish royalists, extolling Túpac Amaru and Micaela Bastidas. He paid little attention to intermediate groups or women and left almost no room for neutrality or doubt—men were either rebels or royalists. Valcárcel cast Túpac Amaru as an overlooked hero and, in nationalist terms, chided Peruvians for turning their back on the Andean rebels. His books circulated widely beyond Peru. The Fondo de Cultura Económica in Mexico published *La rebelión de Túpac Amaru* in 1947 and in its Colección Popular in 1965 and *Rebeliones indígenas* in 1982. Numerous versions were released in Peru, including *La rebelión de Túpac Amaru* in the ubiquitous Biblioteca Peruana series (published by PEISA and sponsored by the Velasco government) in 1973.[16]

Other authors wrote important books on Túpac Amaru. Jorge Cornejo Bouroncle (1898–1995), who worked as an administrator and professor at the Universidad San Antonio Abad del Cuzco from 1936 to 1964, published *Túpac Amaru, la revolución precursora de la emancipación continental* in 1949. Its title stresses both the role of Túpac Amaru as a *precursor*, an important term in the revival of the uprising under Velasco, and the rebellion's hemispheric importance. Cornejo Bouroncle presented some of the key documents about the uprising and provided a useful chronology and narrative. The analysis, however, lags.[17] In contrast, Boleslao Lewin wrote a number of exceptionally analytic and deeply researched studies from the 1940s into the 1970s. This Polish-Argentine historian, a World War II Jewish refugee, makes implicit comparisons between the uprising and the Holocaust. Incorporating European historical sensibilities and a massive amount of archival material, Lewin wrote, for me, the most sophisticated studies of the uprising. He published more than a dozen books in Spanish, with translations in German and Japanese.[18]

Other authors should be mentioned as well. Juan José Vega (1932–2003), for example, in his 1969 monograph, *José Gabriel Túpac Amaru*, provided a more militant tone. Indicative of the *"clasista"* trend of the era, section one is titled "José Gabriel Túpac Amaru and the Social Classes of His Time." Vega published numerous well-researched (although with questionable referencing style) monographs on Túpac Amaru and was a much-cited authority during the Velasco period.[19]

One striking element about these books and, in general, Peruvian historical works from the mid-twentieth century, is how little they dialogued. They made minimal references to one another, yet built off the same sources. Francisco Loayza's wonderful series of documents, Los Pequeños Grandes Libros de Historia Americana, which featured six titles on some facet of the rebellion, proved essential to historians such as Valcárcel, Lewin, and many others.[20] These historians also depended on nineteenth-century document collections such as those published by Pedro de Angelis or Manuel de Odriozola.[21] Most of these writers cited the others minimally (if at all), and did not contextualize their work or highlight their findings and their critiques in relation to others.[22] Book reviews were not common or particularly important, and each author set his own course. In fact, Lewin denounced Valcárcel in 1979 for not recognizing his work even when he used both Lewin's arguments and his documents. Lewin also lambasted Valcárcel for publishing documents copied, transcribed, and published by Francisco Loayza without proper citation.[23] This polemic was much more the exception than the rule. These historians differed in backgrounds (Valcárcel was from Lima, Cornejo Bouroncle was from Arequipa with decades in Cuzco, and Lewin was Polish-Argentine—important distinctions), and Vega was much more forthright about his leftist views. But, besides the one exception, Lewin's tirade, the disagreements need to be read between the lines or in citation *absences* more than in open arguments.

Despite this lack of dialogue and the differences in focus and quality, this body of work (and other historians could be cited) presents a coherent vision of the rebellion. It casts Túpac Amaru and, to a lesser extent, Micaela Bastidas as overlooked heroes who initiated the decades-long struggle against the Spanish. As Cornejo Bouroncle's title suggests, the rebels were precursors who had a hemispheric impact. These historians present Indians as victims who had not been, in more than a century since independence, vindicated or integrated into the national body. Thus, Túpac Amaru's mission had not been fulfilled. Not surprisingly, these works from the 1940s into the 1960s presented categories such as *indios* as ironclad and did not probe the complexities and contradictions of racial terms and national identity. They did, however, present a comprehensible vision of Túpac Amaru as a neglected hero whose frustrated project to overthrow colonialism and incorporate indigenous people into the Peruvian nation remained not only relevant but also urgent.

These studies did share many features: They focused on Túpac Amaru himself, not moving the analysis much either geographically or chronologically. They wrote little about Micaela Bastidas and those who led the second phase of the uprising (Diego Cristóbal Túpac Amaru, Mariano Túpac Amaru, and Andrés Mendigure). When they addressed the Kataristas, the series of uprisings taking place simultaneously with those of Túpac Amaru but in Charcas, or what became Bolivia, they tended to present them as Túpac Amaru's followers or, to put it crudely, inferiors. (Boleslao Lewin would be the exception on this front.) Serious comparative work would not begin until the research of Scarlett O'Phelan Godoy in the 1970s. O'Phelan Godoy and others benefited greatly from the indexed documents published in the Colección Documental de la Independencia del Perú (1971–1976, 86 volumes, originally slated to be 106) and later the seven-volume Colección Documental del Bicentenario de la Rebelión de Túpac Amaru (1980–1982).[24] These studies, which provided the bibliographic foundation for Velasco's invocation of Túpac Amaru, took a nationalist stance and drew clearly demarcated battle lines between the malevolent Spanish and the heroic rebels. Cornejo Bouroncle, Vega, and Valcárcel paid scant attention to Creoles or indigenous people who supported the royalists or to the role of the Catholic Church in defeating the rebels (Lewin was superior on these topics).[25] In general, they cast Túpac Amaru in hagiographic terms, lauding him for his courage, foresight, and martyrdom. Some authors made tactical quibbles—wondering why he waited to attack the city of Cuzco or whether he underestimated the royalist offensive in early 1781—but nevertheless presented him as Peru's long-lost hero. (In doing so, they neglected Micaela Bastidas's centrality as a strategist.) These studies provided ample material for ideologues to turn Túpac Amaru into a precursor or *padre de la patria*.

Both Valcárcel and Vega published widely on Túpac Amaru in outlets that glorified the work of the Velasco government and echoed its identification with Túpac Amaru. For example, on November 6, 1970, the magazine *Oiga* commemorated the 190th anniversary of the outbreak of the rebellion (November 4, 1780) with an article by Valcárcel entitled "Túpac Amaru y los criollos de Lima." A caption just below the title and alongside an awkward sketch of Túpac Amaru stated, "Rescued from the four or five paragraphs in which he was hidden in official texts, the undefeated figure of Túpac Amaru, through the people's and the armed forces' revolutionary government, has taken his true place in the daily life of Peru's contemporary struggles." The article discussed Túpac Amaru's stay in Lima in 1777 and 1778, building on well-known documents from the Archivo de Indias in Spain. After blaming the rebellion's demise on divisions among caciques (also called *kurakas*), the local ethnic authorities who provided important support and opposition to the uprisings, the article ends with: "The history of Túpac Amaru is that of the process of a hero shifting from royalist to separatist, from rebel to anticolonial revolutionary." After Velasco's coup in 1968, Valcárcel increasingly referred to Túpac Amaru as a revolutionary.[26] Vega published a short piece on Túpac Amaru in a November 1968 issue of *Oiga*. He deems the Cuzco rebel, "the most important Peruvian in world history," and deplores how the National Academy of History and the "fallacious, reactionary history taught in text books" had marginalized the uprising and its leader.[27]

Historians were not the only intellectuals discovering and extolling Túpac Amaru from the 1940s into the 1960s. Enrique Mayer underlines the role of *indigenismo* (a movement that stressed the role of indigenous people in the nation-state) in the Velasco intelligentsia and in the revival of interest in Túpac Amaru. He examines the emergence of *cine campesino*, or peasant cinema, in the 1960s and 1970s.[28] The anthropologist and writer José María Arguedas turned his curiosity to the rebellion. In 1962, he published *Tupac Amaru kamaq taytanchisman (Haylli-Taki)/A nuestro padre creador Tupac Amaru (Himno-Canción)*. In a letter to John Murra, Arguedas explained, "I wrote the poem 'Tupac Amaru' in the sad days when they were killing Indians," referring to the repression of peasant mobilization in the early 1960s.[29] Arguedas formed part of a wonderful poetic tradition on Túpac Amaru, from Alejandro Romualdo (*Canto coral que es la libertad*) to Pablo Neruda (*Canto general*) and beyond. Novelists have had less success.[30]

Of course, print and film were not the only media in which intellectuals and artists reworked the image of Túpac Amaru. In the November 15, 1968, edition of *Oiga*, a letter writer ("un lector amigo") questioned the weekly magazine's contention that in the November 4 holiday celebrating the 188th anniversary of the Túpac Amaru uprising, "very few knew that it was in honor of Túpac Amaru." The writer pointed out that "now that the first revolutionary of the Americas has been rescued from official silence, it's important to remember that in Lima, Buenos Aires, and other cities, *peñas*, or social clubs composed of writers and artists, have been honoring Túpac Amaru for years. The Lima *peña* includes Magda Portal, Esteben Pavletich, José Varallanos, Raúl Valencia, Víctor Villanueva, Carlos Daniel Valcárcel, and others." The writer described how members of the Lima *peña* had met on November 4 at the "Piselli restaurant" (in the district of Pueblo Libre) and then taken flowers to the "cheap bust of the hero, lost amid an everyday small plaza in the San Miguel district."[31]

Music and recordings were also important formats to honor Túpac Amaru and highlight his association with Velasco. For example, in 1969, Smith Discos and Ediciones Viva Voz released a 45 rpm record with Alejandro Romualdo's evocative poem "Canto coral a Túpac Amaru/Tupaqamarauman Ukhuti Takina Taki" in Spanish and Quechua.[32] The same year, a number of acclaimed musicians released the LP *Canciones de la nueva patria*, with songs supporting Velasco. SINAMOS itself produced pro-Velasco records.[33] In 1970, the Municipal Theater held a light-and-sound-show performance of renowned composer Edgar Valcárcel's work based on Romualdo's poem. Edgar Valcárcel had written this piece in 1965, and in 1975 he created a composition honoring Pedro Vilca Apaza, a leading rebel of the Túpac Amaru era, based near Puno.[34]

The 1960s witnessed a growing interest in the Andes, in peasants as victims and even political agents, and in Túpac Amaru. In Peru, the peasant insurgencies in the 1950s and early 1960s in La Convención, Cuzco, ultimately led by Hugo Blanco, and the guerrilla movements of the Ejército de Liberación Nacional (ELN; National Liberation Army) and the Movimiento de Izquierda Revolucionaria (MIR; Revolutionary Left Movement) in the 1960s forced Lima to look toward the sierra. In fact, the MIR named their column in the central Andes, led by Guillermo Lobatón and Máximo Velando (both killed in 1965), after Túpac Amaru. While the Peruvian roots of this attention (some would say temporary) to the Andes need to be examined, ranging from the guerrillas to Arguedas, it can also be understood as part of worldwide interest in the Third World. The Vietnam War shocked the world and kept its attention, as did Africa's liberation wars. The seriousness of this new or renewed interest in the Third World ranged from the rethinking of revolutions (taking into account cases from Cuba to Angola) to what Tom Wolfe deemed in 1970 "radical chic."[35] The anticolonial struggles in Vietnam, Africa, and elsewhere and the rise of the New Left prompted a search for fresh revolutionary heroes. Che was not alone. The intriguing question is, how did a military regime such as that of Velasco appropriate and develop such an image? Military officers in Peru and beyond are generally quite distant from the groups that promoted these new progressive heroes: the left, historically attuned intellectuals, and the followers of the radical chic. Velasco was an exception.

Breaking Intellectual Barriers

Authors have long sought to pinpoint why and how the officers who took power in October 1968 became interested in Peru's deep socioeconomic problems. Most stress their experience and background and mention the campaigns against the peasants led by Hugo Blanco in La Convención, and two years later, against the MIR and ELN guerrillas. Forced out of the barracks and into the countryside in order to repress these insurgencies, the ascending officers in the early and mid-1960s saw the poverty and injustice evident in the Peruvian countryside. Some felt sympathy for the guerrillas' motivations; most if not all knew that conditions had to change in order to prevent more rural unrest.[36] Héctor Béjar mentions the officers' disgust with the infighting and banality of elite politics as well as the experience fighting the guerrillas as "some of the many paths that led them to question representative democracy, which in reality only represented the politicians of Peru's old right."[37]

Scholars also point to the social background of the officers themselves—many, most notably Velasco, were from the provinces and few were from the upper classes. In terms of training, in the 1960s the Centro de Altos Estudios Militares (CAEM) increasingly addressed national problems and social and political analysis.[38] For example, Dirk Kruijt notes that officers read articles by Hildebrando Castro Pozo on Inca collectivism and other *indigenista* literature. The work of Virgilio Roel Pineda as an instructor at CAEM and a much-read author must also be taken into account. In dozens of books and articles, Roel Pineda underlined lower-class participation in Peruvian history, particularly in the wars of independence, and preached statist approaches to development and the reduction of inequality.[39]

The wars of independence weighed heavily in the discussions and rhetoric of the military officers. It's indicative that the regime spent so much time and resources on the eighty-six-volume Colección Documental de la Independencia del Perú (CDIP), the most ambitious document collection ever undertaken in Peru. The collection, discussed in this volume by Carlos Aguirre, indicates the centrality history has (or had) in political discussions in Peru as well as the hubris around Peru's 150th anniversary of independence, celebrated on July 28, 1971.

In September 1969, General Juan Mendoza Rodríguez was put in charge of the national commission to celebrate the 150th anniversary, with the creation of the CDIP being one of its major duties. General Mendoza Rodriguez (1902–1995) had a distinguished career with a variety of administrations, having served twice, 1948–1952 and 1955–1956, as minister of education. Not one of the younger firebrands surrounding Velasco but instead a seasoned career military officer with extensive public service, Mendoza Rodríguez recruited a heterogeneous group of historians and scholars, with more than a dozen public and private institutions represented, to supervise the CDIP. It received the support of numerous conservative historians, such as José de la Puente Candamo and Félix Denegri Luna.[40] In the July 1971 ceremony celebrating the completion of the Colección Documental, General Mendoza acknowledged the work of twelve historians: Ella Dunbar Temple (who quit the commission in 1970, replaced as director of the Comité de Documentos by De la Puente); Felipe de la Barra; Félix Denegri Luna; Guillermo Durand Flórez; Capitán Julio J. Elías M.; Guillermo Lohmann Villena; Aurelio Miró Quesada Sosa; RP Armando Nieto Vélez, S.J.; Estuardo Núñez Hague; Gustavo Pons Muzzo; José de la Puente Candamo; and Alberto Tauro del Pino.[41] This is an impressive group but not one that you would necessarily associate with a left-wing military government. Many friends of these scholars presumably despised Velasco (some having lost land to the agrarian reform) and criticized the collaboration.[42] Clearly, many people participated who were not avid supporters of Velasco, an unusual sign of nonpartisanship by both the state and the participants.

The eighty-six volumes in the CDIP present a broad, nationalist view of Peruvian independence. Thematically, it features ideologues, institutions (the navy, for example), and the events from 1815 to 1824, the "coastal phase" of the long war (or wars). As Carlos Aguirre and Carlos Contreras have noted, it was surprisingly conservative in light of Velasco's radical rhetoric and expropriations. Yet it also included four volumes on Túpac Amaru, ten on lesser-known conspiracies and uprisings, six on guerrillas and *montoneras*, and several on theater and literature. Its organization, with twenty-four subtopics ranging from institutional history to the guerrilla wars, could seemingly satisfy all members of the diverse Comisión Nacional del Sesquicentenario de la Independencia del Perú, or CNSIP (National Commission for the Sesquicentennial of Peruvian Independence). Perhaps more surprising than the collection's moderate, nationalist tone is its quality and the very fact that the eighty-six books saw the light. By the time most of them were released, in the early to mid-1970s, Velasco himself was flailing, the Peruvian economy declining. The CDIP, of course, is not perfect, with some volumes overlooking important documents or inadequately citing the sources, but nonetheless constitutes a priceless contribution that permitted a resurgence of scholarship on the wars of independence and on specific topics ranging from the Cortes de Cádiz to Lima theater. Decades after the CDIP was published, the historian José de la Puente Candamo deemed it "the most important publishing event of the [twentieth] century . . . a contribution of unlimited significance."[43]

The CDIP buttressed the Velasco position that Túpac Amaru had begun the war of independence and that Velasco would achieve many of his unfinished goals. As one beautiful Jesús Ruiz Durand poster declared, "190 Years Later, Túpac Amaru Is Winning the War" (fig. 2.2). Articles referred to Túpac Amaru as "undefeated," while Velasco himself, in a September 1970 speech, declared that "our work in Peru today represents the continuity of a mass but truncated historical effort that we must complete."[44] In a September 1971 speech in Cuzco, Velasco referred to the region's "shining history" and its many struggles, conflating the Incas, Túpac Amaru, and the peasant struggles of the 1950s and 1960s.[45]

This discourse placed Túpac Amaru as the first American revolutionary, the precursor or pioneer. Positioning the Velasco regime as the fulfillment of Túpac Amaru's frustrated but yet-to-be-defeated revolution makes sense on many fronts. It tightened the links he sought with campesinos, Cuzco, and the Incas. The association made marketing sense, although I don't believe that Velasco's advisers were ever so crass as to present it solely in that way. It also unified more than divided, echoing the nationalist historiography surveyed above. Everyone, with the exception of the vilified oligarchy and landowners, could support Túpac Amaru. He became an official national symbol. The fact that Peru lacked independence war heroes must have bothered the nationalist military officers. In reunions with their colleagues from Argentina and Venezuela, for example, they no doubt heard endless stories about those countries' liberators José de San Martín and Simón Bolívar. I assume that some expressed Peru's need for a hero from the epoch; others must have contested that it had one, Túpac Amaru.[46]

An additional quote by the conservative historian José de la Puente Candamo, part of a speech given at the Fifth Congreso Internacional de Historia de América (1971), demonstrates how Túpac Amaru served as a symbol for the right and the left.

> Túpac Amaru rises in arms against authority precisely because he used up all the legal avenues to demand justice in the multiple arenas available in the eighteenth-century viceroyalty. Túpac Amaru, in his behavior and in his texts, addresses all Peruvians, the Peruvian people, those born in this country, in a broad reflection. The caudillo of the Cuzco revolution embodies the search for justice in social life and a vision of another side, just and integrated, of the human context in Peru.[47]

De la Puente presents Túpac Amaru as a serene leader of all Peruvians (those born there), who sought justice (social rather than economic) through violence only after exhausting all other venues. This was a very different perspective from that expressed by other historians in the early 1970s such as Juan José Vega or members of the international left

Figure 2.2. Jesús Ruiz Durand, 1969. The author thanks Ruiz Durand for providing this and other images.

(for example, the Tupamaros in Uruguay or the Black Panther reading groups in the United States) who adopted Túpac Amaru as a symbol or model. They envisioned Túpac Amaru as a revolutionary who sought to overthrow the Spanish and destroy colonial injustices based on class and race. Velasco ideologues stressed that the long wars of independence had managed to break the tyranny of Spain but had not truly freed its people. This task was left for Velasco.[48]

In various speeches and texts, Velasco himself insisted on the centrality of Peruvians in the wars of independence, challenging the idea that only the arrival of San Martín and Bolívar had led to liberation. In one speech, Velasco stressed, "Throughout these noble emancipatory struggles, it was above all else our ancestors, Peruvians, who were actors and protagonists, and with their sacrifice they earned the fatherland the first emancipation."[49] That all Peruvians, poor and rich, from Lima to the high Andes, participated was the essence of his message about the wars of independence. The CDIP allowed multiple perspectives on the independence period, providing rich sources on a variety of topics. At its core, however, stood the argument that Peruvians fought for their independence, in a struggle begun by Túpac Amaru and ultimately to be completed by the revolutionary military regime.[50]

In decrying how scholars and the general public had overlooked Túpac Amaru and, in general, Peruvian contributions to the wars of independence, Velasquistas did not criticize historians. Instead, they argued that *the lack of published sources* had impeded a true understanding of the long war (singular) of independence, 1780–1821/1968, thus justifying the expense of the CDIP. In the 1971 ceremony celebrating the release of the first tome of the CDIP, General Juan Mendoza Rodríguez lamented the paucity of published primary sources. He was precise, noting Manuel de Odriozola's two collections and citing several others. He explained the motivation behind the CDIP:

> We have not prepared this work as a bibliographical display to show-case the proven capacity and dynamism of our historians. We have organically put together these primary sources with the patriotic objective of integration, to present an eloquent testimony of Peruvian efforts for emancipation; and above all to show, chronologically, the thought and actions of our precursors and heroes who had a true Americanist orientation, as they understood the struggle for emancipation in its continental dimension, surging from the inherent force of the human person and quest for self-determination, which characterize societies conscious and

proud of their ancestral values, that understand their responsibility and see themselves as owners of their own destinies.[51]

Velasco himself also explained the shameful loss of primary sources: "Some fell into the hands of peddlers of patriotic goods and [were] sold overseas; another part was lost during the War of the Pacific (1879–1883); another burned in the libraries themselves to erase tradition; and what was left was forgotten."[52] The CDIP sought to right these injustices, placing Peruvians at the forefront and providing the primary material for further study. Not only did Velasco assume a nationalist position, but he also blamed archive gaps rather than historians for not having written the true story of Peru's independence.

Velasco and his collaborators succeeded in turning Túpac Amaru into a symbol of national unity, of justice and liberation deferred.[53] As Aguirre shows in his chapter, Velasco, similar to Fidel Castro and the War of 1898, stressed the frustrations of the unfulfilled emancipation, and presented himself as Peru's historical emancipator. For example, he declared in October 1969, "In one year, we have done much more for Peru and for its people than all of the previous governments. . . . With the recovery of our oil, we have also recovered our dignity as a nation."[54] A wide panorama of people could accept the interpretation of Túpac Amaru as national hero and precursor, from the almost Christian-Democratic tone of De la Puente Candamo to the more radical use of Túpac Amaru in the agrarian reform propaganda war and in spheres overseen by SINAMOS and others.[55] Obviously, people understood Túpac Amaru in radically different ways. For Quechua speakers, he led an uprising whose embers continued to smolder, whose message of fighting injustice and looking to the Incas continued to resonate. For more conservative people, Túpac Amaru took his place alongside the more renowned heroes of European descent, the "Liberators of long sideburns" in the rich metaphor of Antonio Cisneros's poem cited above. Though historians would soon begin to argue about the two central Velasquista premises (that Túpac Amaru had begun the revolution and that Peruvians had united to fight the Spanish), historians and Peruvians of very different viewpoints agreed on Túpac Amaru's importance and his deserved place as a national hero.

In 1971, the Uruguayan writer Eduardo Galeano, a leading figure of the literary left, wrote, "Nearly two centuries had to pass after Túpac Amaru's death before the nationalist general Juan Velasco would take up Túpac's resounding, never forgotten words: 'Campesino, your poverty shall no longer feed the master.'"[56] On very few historical issues, it seems safe to assume, do Galeano and historians such as De la Puente Candamo concur. Túpac Amaru was one of them.

Rare Success

The construction of Túpac Amaru as a national hero, a precursor, was one of the rare symbolic victories of the regime. In political terms, they faced hostile and powerful enemies and did not have mass backing. The right controlled the press until the expropriations of 1971 and 1974, and the regime had to work diligently to gain support and legitimacy. The fragmented left was largely unsympathetic, unwilling to support a military regime. Growing economic problems took the wind out of the sails of the regime's more populist reforms.[57] My impression is that, like most military regimes, they had a tin ear. Besides the Túpac Amaru pop symbolism, they came across like other military regimes: misogynist and conservative on social issues. They had little patience with the winds blowing from the north—from feminism to marijuana—and their speeches and language seem stereotypically military (although with a strong dose from the left) and, well, turgid or square. These issues did not matter much in the countryside, but I believe they played a role in why, to their great frustration, so much of the urban middle class turned its back on them. Despite their sympathy toward the nationalist and left-leaning nature of Velasquismo, urban youth did not by and large support the regime. This is, again, an impression, but it seems that the conversion of Túpac Amaru into a national hero, a pioneer whose project would be fulfilled by the Gobierno Revolucionario de las Fuerzas Armadas, was one of the lone discursive victories of the regime.[58]

Why this success? As argued in this chapter, Túpac Amaru was already a well-known and respected historical symbol, lovingly crafted by historians and other intellectuals before 1968 into a hero. No single author, school, or government "invented" him, in that his fame had changed but never disappeared since his execution in 1781.[59] Moreover, Velasco's use of Túpac Amaru was not just rhetoric, hyperbole, and nationalist hubris—Túpac Amaru and his movement deserved and deserve a greater place in national memory. In other words, the *materia prima* was excellent for the construction of a nationalist icon. On the other hand, the regime and its ideologues and artists crafted a sympathetic figure whose uprising could be understood as a first coming of the agrarian reform and other radical changes that the Velasco government envisioned. They not only connected Túpac Amaru and Velasco but also built on international trends that sought Third World heroes, preferably dark-skinned, defiant, and muscular, as José Gabriel Condorcanqui, or Túpac Amaru, had always been depicted. Túpac Amaru did seem to epitomize the best of the Velasco regime.

Notes

1. Alberto Flores Galindo, *Tupac Amaru II-1780: Sociedad colonial y sublevaciones populares* (Lima: Retablo de Papel, 1976), 7. This and all other translations in this chapter are by the author.
2. Eric Hobsbawm, "Peruvian 'Indians,'" *New York Review of Books,* June 15, 1972.
3. I have used the more common spelling Túpac rather than Tupac throughout the text.
4. See Carlos Aguirre's chapter in this volume.
5. Enrique Mayer, *Ugly Stories of the Peruvian Agrarian Reform* (Durham, NC: Duke University Press, 2009), 43.
6. See the excellent Leopoldo Lituma Agüero, *El verdadero rostro de Túpac Amaru (Perú, 1969–1975)* (Lima: Facultad de Letras y Ciencias Humanas, Universidad Nacional Mayor de San Marcos, Pakarina Ediciones, 2011), especially chapter two. Germán Suárez Vértiz designed the fifty-sol bill, which was reproduced, with modifications, in 1976. Also valuable is Alfonso Castrillón Vizcarra, *La generación del 68: Entre la agonía y la fiesta de la modernidad* (Lima: ICPNA, 2003).
7. *Discursos pronunciados en actuaciones cívicas conmemorativas, 1. Etapa Sanmartiniana* (Lima: Comisión Nacional del Sesquicentenario de la Independencia del Perú, 1972), 613–615 and 604–606.
8. Malgorzata Nalewajko, "La imagen de la revolución peruana en las declaraciones oficiales del gobierno militar," *Estudios Latinoamericanos* 7 (1980): 83–102, quote on 86. Leonidas Rodríguez was subsequently one of the founders of the Partido Socialista Revolucionario. Enrique Bernales, "Partido Socialista Revolucionario (Perú)," *Nueva Sociedad* 91 (1987): 78–79. For a reenactment of his November 1973 speech commemorating the revolution's fifth anniversary, with many references to Túpac Amaru, see http://vinilosperuanos.blogspot .com/2013/06/sinamos-disco-de-propaganda-del-inkari.html. See also *Oiga,* no. 550, November 9, 1973. For further information on SINAMOS, see Anna Cant's chapter in this collection.
9. Juan Velasco Alvarado, *Velasco: La voz de la revolución. Discursos del Presidente de la República General de División Juan Velasco Alvarado, 1970–1972* (Lima: Oficina Nacional de Difusión del SINAMOS, 1972), 2:173.
10. *Oiga,* no. 443, October 1, 1971, 9.
11. Sergio Serulnikov, *Revolution in the Andes: The Age of Túpac Amaru* (Durham, NC: Duke University Press, 2013); Charles Walker, *The Tupac Amaru Rebellion* (Cambridge, MA: Harvard University Press, 2014).
12. Anna Cant, "'Land for Those Who Work It': A Visual Analysis of

Agrarian Reform Posters in Velasco's Peru," *Journal of Latin American Studies* 44, no. 1 (2012): 1–37; Lituma Agüero, *El verdadero rostro*. I found the illiteracy rate at http://proyectos.inei.gob.pe/web/biblioineipub/bancopub/Est /Lib0024/2.htm.

13. Michael J. Casey, *Che's Afterlife: The Legacy of an Image* (New York: Vintage, 2009); Jon Lee Anderson, *Che Guevara: A Revolutionary Life* (New York: Grove, 2010). For an excellent survey of new approaches on the 1960s in Latin America, see "Special Issue: Latin America in the Global Sixties," *The Americas* 70, no. 3 (January 2014). A postcard with images and slogans of Túpac and Che circulated in Lima in 1969. *Oiga*, 344, October 3, 1969.

14. Antonio Cisneros, *Postales para Lima* (Lima: Ediciones Colihue, 2001), 35; my translation.

15. Source: Google Books Ngram Viewer, http://books.google.com/ngrams.

16. It's surprising how little is written about Valcárcel and other mid-twentieth-century historians. Valcárcel published many books on Túpac Amaru, often with minor changes among them. His titles include *La rebelión de Túpac Amaru* (Mexico City: Fondo de Cultura Económica, 1947); *Túpac Amaru* (Lima: Universidad Nacional Mayor de San Marcos, 1977); and *Rebeliones indígenas* (Lima: PTCM, 1946). He also published several document collections, such as *Túpac Amaru* (Lima: Moncloa-Campodónico Editores Asociados, 1970). Of course, the authors reviewed here were not the first to treat Túpac Amaru. For the early twentieth century, see Emilio del Solar, *Insurrección de Túpac Amaru, sus antecedentes y efectos* (Lima: La Opinión Nacional, 1926). For an incisive analysis of the treatment of Túpac Amaru by earlier authors, see Gonzalo Portocarrero and Patricia Oliart, *El Perú desde la escuela* (Lima: Instituto de Apoyo Agrario, 1989), 65–102.

17. Jorge Cornejo Bouroncle, *Túpac Amaru, la revolución precursora de la emancipación continental* (Cuzco: Universidad Nacional de San Antonio Abad del Cuzco, 1949). The Universidad Nacional de San Antonio Abad del Cuzco recently published a new edition. For information about Cornejo Bouroncle, I have drawn from José Augusto Tamayo Herrera's prologue to this new edition (Cuzco: Universidad Nacional de San Antonio Abad del Cuzco, Facultad de Ciencias Sociales, 2013), xxiii–xxv.

18. Boleslao Lewin, *La rebelión de Túpac Amaru*, 3rd ed. (Buenos Aires: SELA, 1967).

19. Juan José Vega, *José Gabriel Túpac Amaru* (Lima: Editorial Universo, 1969); *Túpac Amaru y sus compañeros*, 2 vols. (Cuzco: Municipalidad del Qosqo, 1995). It is interesting that in 1970, Moncloa-Campodónico released the Valcárcel book cited above and labeled it *Túpac Amaru el revolucionario* on the cover, but on the title page and elsewhere reduced it to *Túpac Amaru*. This is the only time Valcárcel used the term "revolution" in one of his titles. I found it listed with and without *el revolucionario* in WorldCat.

20. These include Francisco A. Loayza, *Genealogía de Túpac Amaru* (Lima: Librería e Imprenta D. Miranda, 1946); Francisco A. Loayza, ed., *La verdad desnuda, o Las dos faces de un obispo: Escrita en 1780 por un imparcial religioso* (Lima: Los Pequeños Grandes Libros de Historia Americana, 1943); Francisco A. Loayza, *Mártires y heroínas: Documentos inéditos del año de 1780 a 1782* (Lima:

Librería e Imprenta D. Miranda, 1945); Raphael José Sahuaraura Titu Atauchi (Francisco Loayza, ed.), *Estado del Perú: Códice escrito en 1780 y que contiene datos importantes sobre la revolución de José Gabriel Túpac Amaru por Raphael José Sahuaraura Titu Atauchi* (Lima: Librería e Imprenta D. Miranda, 1944); Francisco A. Loayza, *Preliminares del incendio: Documentos del año de 1776 a 1780, en su mayoría inéditos, anteriores y sobre la Revolución Libertadora que engendró y dio vida José Gabriel Túpac Amaru, en 1780* (Lima: Librería e Imprenta D. Miranda, 1947); Juan Bautista Túpac Amaru, *Cuarenta años de cautiverio: Memorias del inka Juan Bautista Túpac Amaru*, ed. Francisco A. Loayza (Lima: Librería e Imprenta D. Miranda, 1945).

21. Pedro de Angelis, *Documentos para la historia de la sublevación de José Gabriel de Túpac Amaru, cacique de la provincia de Tinta en el Perú* (Buenos Aires: Imprenta del Estado, 1836); Manuel de Odriozola, *Documentos históricos del Perú en las épocas del coloniaje después de la conquista y de la independencia hasta la presente*, vol. 1 (Lima: Tipografía de Aurelio Alfaro, 1863).

22. As noted, scholars have written very little about these historians and their generations. It is not only a problem of Peru—Lewin deserves more attention in Argentina.

23. Boleslao Lewin, *Túpac Amaru en la independencia de América* (Buenos Aires: Plus Ultra, 1979), 9–12. I have not found a response from Valcárcel. In 1975, Valcárcel received first prize in an Organization of American States–sponsored competition for the best book on Peru's sesquicentennial, and Lewin received an honorable mention. Valcárcel published this study in 1977, providing a two-page bibliographic introduction. Carlos Daniel Valcárcel, *Túpac Amaru* (Lima: Universidad Nacional Mayor de San Marcos, 1977).

24. Scarlett O'Phelan Godoy, *Un siglo de rebeliones anticoloniales: Perú y Bolivia 1700–1783* (Cuzco: Centro de Estudios Bartolomé de Las Casas, 1988). The Colección Documental de la Independencia del Perú (CDIP) originally was to have 106 volumes but ended up with 86 (divided into *tomos* and each of these subdivided into *volúmenes*). CDIP (Lima: Comisión Nacional del Sesquicentenario de la Independencia del Perú, 1971–1976). See *tomo* 2, *La rebelión de Túpac Amaru*, 4 vols. (1971–1972). The Colección Documental del Bicentenario de la Revolución Emancipadora de Túpac Amaru (CDBRETA) published five document collections (I, II, III-I, IV-II, V-III), one anthology, and one collection of articles from a conference (Lima: Comisión Nacional del Bicentenario de la Rebelión Emancipadora de Túpac Amaru, 1981–1982).

25. Lewin, in contrast, was very critical of Bishop Moscoso y Peralta, whom he (correctly in my mind) presented as a major factor in the rebellion's defeat. Vega did pay more attention to this in his *Túpac Amaru y sus compañeros*.

26. *Oiga*, no. 398, November 6, 1970, 11–12. This issue includes a picture of the recently elected Salvador Allende in the article "Chile also Takes the Túpac Amaru Path."

27. *Oiga*, no. 298, November 8, 1968, 17–18.

28. Mayer, *Dirty Stories*, 41–74. Saturnino Huillca, *Habla un campesino peruano* (Lima: PEISA, 1974).

29. José María Arguedas, *Tupac Amaru kamaq taytanchisman (Haylli-Taki)/A nuestro padre creador Tupac Amaru (Himno-Canción)* (Lima: Ediciones Salqan-

tayt, 1962). Letter in John Murra and Mercedes López-Baralt, *Las cartas de Arguedas* (Lima: Pontificia Universidad Católica, 1998), 84. See also Gordon Brotherston, *The Emergence of the Latin American Novel* (Cambridge: Cambridge University Press, 1977), chap. 7, "Tupac Amaru Dismembered: José María Arguedas."

30. César Angeles Caballero, *Túpac Amaru y Micaela Bastidas en la poesía nacional* (Lima: Comisión Nacional del Bicentenario de la Rebelión Emancipadora de Túpac Amaru, 1980).

31. *Oiga*, no. 299, November 15, 1968. The *Oiga* issue from the week before had complained about the lack of attention to the November 4 anniversary of the uprising, even though it had been declared a "civic workday," or a holiday without the day off. *Oiga*, no. 298, November 8, 1968. This became an almost annual complaint in *Oiga*. It complained about the "incredible silence" on November 4, 1969. *Oiga*, no. 349, November 7, 1969; see also *Oiga*, no. 500, November 10, 1972. I thank Angel Ragas for finding this.

32. Ediciones Viva Voz/Smith Records, 1969, 45 rpm.

33. See the excellent blog on Peruvian records at http://vinilosperuanos .blogspot.com/2013/06/sinamos-disco-de-propaganda-del-inkari.html.

34. Winston Orrillo, "'Canto coral' Arte de Vanguardia, Arte Revolucionario," *Oiga*, no. 398, November 6, 1970. For another record released by SINAMOS, see http://vinilosperuanos.blogspot.com/2013/06/sinamos-disco -de-propaganda-del-inkari.html. On Edgar Valcárcel: http://www.filarmonia .org/page/Edgar-Valcarcel.aspx. I thank Raúl Romero for his help with this.

35. Tom Wolfe, "Radical Chic: That Party at Lenny's," *New York Magazine*, June 8, 1970.

36. Luigi R. Einaudi, *Peruvian Military Relations with the United States*, RAND paper P-4389 (Santa Monica, CA: Rand Corporation, 1970); Víctor Villanueva, *¿Nueva mentalidad militar en el Perú?* (Lima: Editorial Juan Mejía Baca, 1969); Juan Martín Sánchez, *La revolución peruana: Ideología y práctica política de un gobierno militar 1968–1975* (Seville: CSIC, Universidad de Sevilla, Diputación de Sevilla, 2002), 152–153.

37. Héctor Béjar, "Velasco," 5, undated electronic publication, available at http://www.hectorbejar.com/docs/libros/velasco.pdf (no longer available online).

38. Víctor Villanueva, *El CAEM y la revolución de la Fuerza Armada* (Lima: Instituto de Estudios Peruanos/Campodónico Ediciones, 1972), especially chapter 3. He marks 1961 as the "gran cambio" (great change) as the oligarchy fought the curriculum changes in the CAEM and the growing presence of the military outside the barracks. Dirk Kruijt believes that Villanueva exaggerates the impact of the CAEM. Dirk Kruijt, *Revolution by Decree, Peru 1968–1975* (Amsterdam: Thela Publishers, 1994), 37–42.

39. Virgilio Roel Pineda, *Los libertadores* (Lima: Editorial Gráfica Labor, 1971).

40. Carlos Contreras, "La independencia del Perú: Balance de la historiografía contemporánea," in *Debates sobre las independencias iberoamericanas*, ed. Manuel Chust and José Antonio Serrano (Madrid: AHILA-Iberoamericana-Vervuert, 2007), 99–117, especially 99–108. Universities per se were not represented, and the commission was also very Lima-centric.

41. The list is from *Discursos pronunciados*, 223. Dunbar Temple's resignation is mentioned in Juan Mendoza Rodríguez, *Memoria* (Lima: Colección Documental de la Independencia Peruana, 1974), 17. See Contreras, "La independencia del Perú," 101–104, for a list of the sixty-one *"responsables"* for the different tomes. Many individuals were involved with more than one tome.

42. *Discursos pronunciados*, 223.

43. José de la Puente Candamo, "La historiografía peruana sobre la independencia en el siglo XX," in *La independencia del Perú: De los Borbones a Bolívar*, ed. Scarlett O'Phelan Godoy (Lima: Pontificia Universidad Católica, IRA, 2001), 11–12.

44. Velasco Alvarado, *Velasco, la voz de la revolución*, 1:264.

45. Ibid., 2:170.

46. Heraclio Bonilla and Karen Spalding delivered an influential critique of the era's nationalist views on independence. See Heraclio Bonilla, ed., *La independencia en el Perú* (Lima: Instituto de Estudios Peruanos, 1972), especially Bonilla, "Clases populares y Estado en el contexto de la crisis colonial," 13–69, and Bonilla and Spalding, "La independencia en el Perú: Las palabras y los hechos," 70–113. See also Contreras, "La independencia," for an overview of the literature.

47. *Discursos pronunciados*, 310. This book exemplifies the military's obsession with ceremonies and speeches.

48. Régis Debray uses Túpac Amaru as an example of armed spontaneity in his 1967 *Revolution in the Revolution? Armed Struggle and Political Struggle in Latin America*, translated from French and Spanish by Bobbye Ortiz (New York: Grove Press, 1967), 29. It is a one-paragraph reference that incorrectly claims that "reconquest was achieved without difficulty."

49. "Discurso del Señor General de División EP Juan Velasco Alvarado, Presidente de la República," in *Discursos pronunciados*, 227.

50. The articles in Bonilla, *La independencia en el Perú*, were an immediate, critical response to this interpretation. See also Scarlett O'Phelan Godoy, "El mito de la 'independencia concedida,'" *Histórica* 9, no. 2 (1985): 155–191.

51. *Discursos pronunciados*, 224–225. The reference is to Odriozola, *Documentos históricos*.

52. "Discurso del Señor General de División EP Juan Velasco Alvarado, Presidente de la República," *Discursos pronunciados*, 227.

53. This is an assertion, but one I would argue for at length.

54. Speech from October 8, 1969, Piura, in Velasco Alvarado, *Velasco: La voz de la revolución*, 1:115–116.

55. I cite, again, Lituma Agüero, *El verdadero rostro*; Cant, "Land for Those Who Work It." The literature on Cuba, Fidel, and 1898 is massive. A good starting point is Louis A. Pérez Jr., *The War of 1898: The United States and Cuba in History and Historiography* (Chapel Hill: University of North Carolina Press, 1998).

56. Eduardo Galeano, *Open Veins of Latin America: Five Centuries of the Pillage of a Continent* (London: Latin American Bureau, 1997), 45.

57. For an overview of the regime and its limitations, see Cynthia McClintock and Abraham F. Lowenthal, eds. *The Peruvian Experiment Reconsidered* (Princeton, NJ: Princeton University Press, 1983).

58. In 1994, Carlos Iván Degregori described Peru's "indigenista" alliance between the Velasco-led state, intellectuals, and peasant leaders as "ephemeral" but "intense." Among a list of measures and cultural phenomena, he includes the "rescue of the figure of Túpac Amaru." Carlos Iván Degregori, "El estudio del otro," in *Peru 1964–1994: Economía, sociedad y política*, ed. Julio Cotler (Lima: IEP, 1995), 303–332, quotes from 313.

59. The long history of the image of Túpac Amaru is waiting to be written.

CHAPTER 3

Who Drove the Revolution's Hearse?
The Funeral of Juan Velasco Alvarado

ADRIÁN LERNER

When General Guillermo Arbulú and his wife entered General Juan Velasco Alvarado's room at Lima's military hospital on the evening of December 23, 1977, Velasco was lying in his bed, breathing with difficulty, heavily and slowly, his forehead covered in sweat. He had been awake for only a few hours and would not remain conscious for long. He and his family had been receiving people who wanted to bid him a final farewell, but time was now running out. Once an all-powerful man, he had been so fragile in the final years. Still, he had a role to play. Arbulú was by then commander in chief, minister of war, and prime minister of General Francisco Morales Bermúdez's so-called Second Phase of the Revolution. His presence represented that of the government of the Second Phase and was therefore largely a matter of protocol.

It must have been an awkward scene. Like many of the generals in power during the Second Phase, Arbulú owed his importance to a certain extent to Velasco, but he had also been an accomplice to Velasco's overthrow by Morales Bermúdez. At the same time, once Velasco's health started to worsen, Arbulú had helped with his travel expenses and the medical bills. It took Velasco a few seconds, but after greeting them, he sat up in his bed. He looked into Arbulú's eyes and suddenly asked him, as if attempting to show that he could still be in charge: "What the fuck are you doing with the Revolution?"[1]

In the following days, the events that surrounded Velasco's memorial services showed that he was far from alone in questioning the changes brought about by the Second Phase. Furthermore, the sheer scale and the nature of popular participation in his funeral revealed important changes in the fabric of Peruvian society and politics. Only minutes after Velasco's death was announced, and in the days that followed, thousands of citizens from different parts of Lima and from all across Peru gathered to pray for the dead general's soul, to talk to his dead body, and to sing together. Others, either as anonymous individuals or as members of unions or associations, often in more explicitly political fashion, issued statements that declared Velasco the only president who had ever really done anything for the Peruvian people and openly ridiculed the leaders of the Second Phase. In these and other ways, just as Velasco had done with Arbulú, a mobilized public challenged the protocol that the military government of the Second Phase had imposed. In so doing, they asserted their right to make of his death what they wished.

The funeral took place in the context of the profoundly liminal juncture of the Second Phase of the Revolution, a period generally characterized by revolutionary recoil in the face of intramilitary conflict, economic crisis, and massive social unrest. The agitated years between the Morales Bermúdez coup and the return of the military to the barracks in 1980 are perhaps *the* paradigmatic transition in the political history of modern Peru: from revolution to counterrevolution, from "the Peruvian Experiment" to an authoritarian liberalization, and later from military rule to democracy. It is not easy to think of a more convoluted moment. It is as part of this process that I understand Velasco's funeral.[2]

Funerals, of course, rank among the most quintessential of liminal events themselves. They are rituals, often in the form of collective performances, during which social structures become evident and can thus be reinforced or challenged: alternative texts and unexpected actors can radically alter the script and the meanings of the performance. Anthropologists and ethnographically oriented historians have often stressed these rituals as stabilizing forces within given societies, and when they have explored their disruptive potential, they usually have done so by focusing on their symbols and representations at the theatrical level. Consequently, even when "the possibility that something could go wrong" in a ritual is recognized as having a subversive potential, such potential tends to be seen as merely adding "urgency and unpredictability to the drama."[3] Therefore, rituals like funerals are usually seen as capable of subverting the sociopolitical order in indirect ways.

As performed rituals, state-sanctioned and state-orchestrated funerals of notable individuals such as statesmen or national heroes provide potential grounds for challenges to official protocols in which interpretations of the lives and deaths of these men and women are often inscribed. Struggles over rituals can thus be about the meanings of those lives and deaths.[4] But since these official rituals often are events during which political power is explicitly deployed, and thus rendered vulnerable *in a very material sense*, these challenges are not necessarily limited to the realm of the symbolic. Because they are liminal moments that often constitute sites of encounters between official and popular practices, rituals like conspicuous and politically charged funerals are shaped by the meaningful contexts in which they take place, but they can also directly shape them.[5]

This chapter approaches the death and the funeral of Juan Velasco during and after Christmas of 1977 as one such liminal moment. The death of a revolutionary authoritarian leader like Velasco, even if by then he had been politically defeated and relatively isolated by foes and by sickness, was still capable of shaking the political arena. I argue that the events that surrounded Velasco's death and funeral were related to, part of, and consequential for several important and interconnected issues in the politics of the Second Phase, the revolutionary process as a whole, and even larger processes like the emergence of populism and the overwhelming of the state by civil society. These include the conflicts between popular mobilization and governmental control and between participation and representation, the political relevance of the figure of Velasco, the cycle of radical massive mobilization that had started in 1971 and the counterrevolutionary politics that followed it, and, finally, the political plausibility of the revolution as understood by the coalition that had supported the more radical aspects of the government: in other words, of some form of Velasquismo without Velasco.

Velasco's funeral revealed a combination of massive popular mobilization around a charismatic leader turned into a myth, redistributive politics, and nationalistic rhetoric. Though his regime was far from a procedural democracy, Velasco's funeral was the site of an antielitist, popular politics at a pre-electoral juncture: at least during that specific context, it included most of the characteristic elements of Latin America's populism.[6] At the same time, the problems associated with governmental attempts to control popular mobilization in a context of economic crisis and massive urban growth highlighted by the funeral illuminate an understudied but telling episode of the classic trope of *desborde popular* (popular overflow). The overwhelming of the state apparatus during the funeral was related to the emergence of new urban classes that the state could not incorporate. These groups brought new forms of political mobilization, which in turn had played a central role during the Revolutionary Government of the Armed Forces (RGAF).[7] Both issues are related to new forms of mass, direct popular participation in politics.

The funeral constitutes an overlooked chapter in the history of the Peruvian democratic transition of the late 1970s. The struggles to bury

Velasco's body illustrate an essential particularity of the period: the fact that it was a double transition, first from one progressive military dictatorship to a more repressive one, and then to democracy. During these consecutive shifts, discourses of rupture and of continuity were similarly problematic. Political participation through social mobilization was key to the Peruvian Revolution's ideals and practices, but its radicalization also played a major role in its collapse. The need to tighten governmental control over radical social movements then became, again, a focal point of the Second Phase, and its failure to tighten that control was a key factor in its demise. Massive mobilization was even put in the service of attempts to reestablish the revolution or to help some of its remaining leaders reclaim power.

Velasco's death represented a political opportunity for an array of actors, but it also exposed the limitations of their political praxis. It led to one of the last successful episodes of a revolutionary politics with populist traits, based on the power of social mobilization. Emanating from a particularly agitated juncture, it channeled discontent directed against the regime of the Second Phase. Meanwhile, it also highlighted some of the key contradictions of Velasco's regime. The subversion of the official ritual revealed an uneasy legacy in which incentives to mobilization coexisted with attempts to control it and with dependence on an ailing (and then dead) leader with the hopes of a revolutionary project capable of transcending him. Ultimately, the funeral revealed the dawn of a new political regime, as social mobilization was becoming an electoral platform. If Velasco's death was one of the occurrences during which it seemed as if the ideal of a progressive transfer of power to the organized masses could be achieved through democratic means, the long term proved to be a reality check. The funeral itself ended inconspicuously, with the ritual order restored by the military through the use of force.

Customs, representational conventions, individual decisions, feelings, and contingency played a major role in the events of December 1977. In order to render at least part of the cultural and political texture of those days, I have chosen to present a narrative account of the funeral preceded by a contextualization.

Death in Context; or, The Revolution's Illness: Velasco, Popular Mobilization, and the Second Phase

Since this is the story of a death, it seems only logical to begin with disease. After months of rumors about his health, in March 1973, an aneurysm almost took General Juan Velasco Alvarado's life. In May of the same year, Velasco lost a leg in a subsequent medical complication. It was as bad a time as any for Velasco to fall seriously sick: it coincided with the beginning of the end of the honeymoon between the revolutionary government and the increasingly mobilized peoples in whose names it was ruling, the first signs of a global economic crisis, and growing opposition within the military's own right-wing sectors.[8] Amid rumors of other generals seeking to replace Velasco, over the course of the following days the government's mobilization apparatus organized demonstrations of support for the president.[9] Velasco remained in power, but as his physical condition worsened, the regime began to be perceived as increasingly frail. Velasco was key to its stability.[10]

Until 1974, the balance of power had clearly been in favor of the radicals within the military. During the first two years of the decade, the RGAF had created platforms for popular mobilization intended to integrate social movements into its structural reforms, but also to co-opt and control them.[11] The National System of Support for Social Mobilization (Sistema Nacional de Apoyo a la Movilización Social; SINAMOS), created in 1971, and the recognition of a record-shattering number of unions and indigenous communities were the centerpieces of the efforts to channel mobilization.[12]

The Peruvian Revolution soon proved unable to cope with the demands created by the degree of popular mobilization it had incentivized.[13] Even "success stories" like the Confederación Nacional Agraria (CNA; National Agrarian Confederation) were tainted by this phenomenon.[14] The government's largely ineffective reaction consisted in the age-old strategy of creating parallel unions. This coincided with the displacement of the original radical generals that had supported the coup, which damaged the cohesiveness of the regime.[15]

The economic crisis that accompanied this process did not do the regime any favors. Between 1973 and 1975, the frequency and intensity of strikes reached unprecedented levels.[16] This, along with the navy's disaffection toward the radical generals, created a sense of political crisis. The regime answered with desperate measures, such as the expropriation of newspapers of national circulation in 1974, which galvanized accusations of totalitarianism and worsened internal divisions.[17] The strike of the Guardia Civil (an important police force) and subsequent urban riots and repression on February 5, 1975, compromised any remaining sense of an alliance between the military government and the lower classes.[18] To top it all off, weeks later, on February 28, Velasco suffered a stroke that once again raised doubts about his ability to rule.[19]

This was the background of the Francisco Morales Bermúdez coup of August 28, 1975.[20] None of Velasco's allies took to the streets to oppose his ousting. The unions of peasants, industrial workers, and shantytown dwellers; the members of the Communist Party; his ministers; and even his classmates in the army who still held key military positions—all remained silent. In the following months, Velasco was forced to stay secluded in a de facto house arrest.[21] Despite his rhetoric and some early signs emphasizing revolutionary continuity, Morales Bermúdez curtailed crucial revolutionary measures, and the new government quickly resorted to widespread repression. After a series of large strikes, on July 1, 1976, a yearlong state of exception was declared, during which militants, opposition journalists, and radical generals were arrested and deported. The Second Phase was betraying the ideals of the revolution, and therefore losing whatever legitimacy it had inherited.[22]

The impulse given to mobilization during the Velasco years had created momentum, and popular organizations decidedly opposed the regime. Since 1976, the new government had begun approaching political parties, and in early 1977 it announced a four-year transition to democracy that included elections for a constituent assembly. The general strike of July 19, 1977, the most important demonstration since the struggles for the eight-hour day in 1919, was conceived in this scenario.[23] Particularly intense in urban settings, the strike revealed the strength, unity, and unruliness of the popular movements.[24] Barely weeks after the strike, Morales Bermúdez announced early elections for the constituent assembly and lifted the state of exception. Amid a general opening of the political arena, new parties were created, including the Velasquista Partido Socialista Revolucionario (PSR; Socialist Revolutionary Party). This mix of mass popular mobilization, repression, and political opening was the context in which the death and the funeral of Juan Velasco took place in late 1977.[25]

The Revolution's Death: Velasco's Funeral and Popular Mobilization against the Second Phase

In November 1977, General Velasco traveled to Houston, where he successfully underwent surgery for a second aneurysm. Soon after he returned to Lima, however, he began to suffer from an inflammation of the pancreas. Allegedly because of his taste for traditional heavy food (*comida criolla*), the problem rapidly developed into severe pancreatitis, followed by internal hemorrhages. After less than a month, he was diagnosed with septicemia. By the evening of December 23, after two additional surgeries and amid constant rumors of his death, his physicians at the Military Hospital declared that there was nothing they could do.[26] The political agenda was extremely agitated, but when Velasco's health began to deteriorate, he became the center of public attention again.

After Arbulú and his wife left, only family members were allowed to remain for the night. General Velasco finally fell asleep around four, and died at ten past eight on the morning of December 24, 1977.[27] A section of the hospital had been reserved for the family, but a few journalists managed to sneak into the lobby. One of them, who was in the right place at the right time, heard Velasco's sister-in-law make a call from a pay phone: "Juanito has passed." From then on, the news of Velasco's death spread throughout the world. It was too late for the newspapers to break the news, but it was all over the radio. Within minutes, hundreds of citizens gathered and waited for hours until the hospital's chapel opened and they were allowed to join the first part of the wake.

Many important people visited the chapel that day, but it was the large crowd and the presence of the proverbial man on the street that captured the attention of journalists. One such individual, for example, identified as Jacinto Criollo, an eighty-eight-year-old poor man from Lima, was described as carrying a three-foot-long wooden cross, and as having been loudly praying to it for the soul of "General Juanito." At some point, a mysterious woman walked toward him and kissed one of the edges on the top of the cross. She then disappeared into the middle of the crowd. Jacinto, who was bowing low, never even noticed her presence. No other word was written about any of them, but the way in which the scene was portrayed depicted the popular manifestations of fervor toward Velasco that instantly followed his death.[28]

When the doors of the hospital chapel opened at four o'clock in the afternoon, there was already a large gathering outside. The Peruvian flag was flown at half-mast, and the crowd began to sing the national anthem—for the first of many times during that weekend.[29] People waited in a long line to enter the chapel. Once inside, they saw the coffin, crossed themselves, and gave their condolences to the family. Many of them carried flowers. The chapel remained open to visitors until midnight. Early on the following morning, the remains of Juan Velasco were picked up in a black, army-owned car, to be taken to El Sagrario, the side chapel next to the cathedral in Lima's main square, the Plaza de Armas. Along the route, thousands greeted the car, which was escorted by official motorcycles and some twenty vehicles carrying Velasco's relatives and government officials.[30]

In late 1977, many of the newspapers that had been expropriated and given to representatives of civil society as "social property" remained loyal to Velasco and to the principles of the First Phase of the Revolution, although at the same time they tended to avoid direct confrontation with the new administration of Morales Bermúdez. Others openly embraced the new status quo, but there was still room for more critical positions. Several new daily publications and magazines had been created since 1975. Plurality and freedom, nevertheless, had to be understood as limited. The government, through censorship and the threat of jail or deportation, still held leverage over the press.[31]

The morning of December 25, all the newspaper front pages were about Velasco. During his tenure, he had decided that Santa Claus was an imperialist figure and tried to establish instead the much more Peruvian Niño Manuelito, an Andean depiction of Christ as a child, as the central icon of Christmas celebrations. In 1977, Santa Claus was back, but Christmas was going to be all about Velasco. Some readers even sent letters to their favorite publications complaining about the excessive attention granted to Velasco in the media during the holidays. He had stolen Christmas again. The contingent circumstance of Velasco's death and funeral happening close to a major holiday also created both conflicts and an opportunity: an array of organizations demanded the extension of the holiday for a couple of extra days as a sign of mourning. That would allow a much more impressive turnout and permit the attention of the whole country to be focused on the funeral. In a context in which nationwide media were generally precarious, massive direct presence was an important element in political events.[32]

There was something contradictory about the contents of the papers during those days. On December 25 and 26, they all reproduced with excruciating detail the official protocol dictated by the military government: the hours the coffin could be visited, who would be allowed to do so, how it would be transported to the cathedral for the religious ceremony, which streets it would be taken through, who was supposed to sit in each part of the cathedral, who would speak and when, and so forth. There was no room for direct popular involvement in the government's program, and the coffin would be guarded at all times by military or police officers or under their strict supervision. Moreover, the Ministry of the Interior, in charge of internal security, published a statement declaring that it had acquired knowledge about "the intentions of subversive elements" that would attempt to use the occasion to disrupt public order and the established protocol. Security measures would therefore be redoubled, and any attempt to alter public order would be "severely punished"—quite a threat coming from a repressive military dictatorship.[33]

This was a response to Velasco's paradoxical resurgence in popularity during his final months. Since his time in house arrest, rumors of a Velasquista coalition that championed the continuity of the revolution gained strength. First gravely ill and isolated, and then dead, the figure of Velasco still loomed large. Even from the heights of power he had not been capable of gathering enough political strength to resist the coup that ousted him, but Velasco was still feared of being capable of bringing together a potentially formidable leftist opposition to the Second Phase. Likewise, to the image of Velasco as a leader and hero that had been propagated by the revolution, now that of him as a martyr was added, the latter bringing one of the recurrent tropes about the prominent and politically contested dead in the history of Latin America. Velasco himself may have seen the situation in similar terms. A close collaborator who visited him during his house arrest at the end of 1976 later wrote about the general's disappointment: "Can you please explain to me," Velasco reportedly asked him, "how they can keep talking about the Revolution . . . when I was the Revolution?"[34]

At the same time that they were bombarding the public with strict rules and government threats, the newspapers were enthusiastically reproducing and commenting on calls for mass popular participation in the funeral. They all circulated a statement issued by a dozen left-wing organizations, most of which had already been quite vocal about their dislike of the Second Phase of the Revolution.[35] It was yet another show of unity. Many of the organizations that had previously worked together to challenge the Morales Bermúdez regime in the massive national strike of July 1977 were doing the same by offering an alternative protocol to the one that the government was so emphatically imposing.

In the statement, they declared that the "revolutionary people" had a duty to participate in the funeral of Velasco, the only president in the history of the republic who had ever done anything for them. Despite all the problems that his own government had faced in relation to popular mobilization, but also because at least in part it had encouraged it, his image was useful specifically for mobilizing people in the streets. In an explicit challenge to the government's program, the statement in the newspapers declared that the popular organizations had decided that the coffin was to be carried to the cemetery on the shoulders of "the people." It was also up to them to choose two representatives from their own ranks to deliver a speech during the funeral. In this way, they expressed what was one of the overarching conflicts of the Peruvian Revolution, one that would become particularly evident, at a micro level, during Velasco's funeral: the difference between representation and participation.[36] The government had designated representatives of popular movements and political organizations to make speeches and carry the coffin, but the organizations demanded to make that decision for themselves and to participate in the act in much more direct ways. They summoned their membership to the main square at eight in the morning.[37]

When the gray coffin and the cortege arrived at the side chapel on the extremely hot morning of December 26, the turnout at the Plaza de Armas consisted of a few thousand people. More impressive than the crowd seems to have been the police cordon that separated it from the side chapel. When the casket was taken from the hearse to be carried inside, however, hundreds of enthusiasts who wanted to get close to Velasco's dead body briefly broke the cordon, only to be easily contained by the police. In view of the situation, family and friends hurriedly carried the coffin themselves, leaving behind the group of Afro-Peruvians dressed in tuxedos, who, as tradition demanded, had been hired for that duty.[38] As soon as the casket was brought in, covered with the Peruvian flag and with Velasco's kepi and sword on top, the bells of the cathedral started tolling. Many in the crowd started crying. The national anthem was spontaneously sung for the second time since Velasco's death. This time new chants were added: "Velasco Revolution!" "Velasco, with you until the end!" "Long live the Revolution!" "Velasco, you will never die!" "Goodbye, Chino!"[39]

Inside, three candlesticks flanked the coffin on each side, and a silver crucifix was set in front. Officers of the Peruvian Legion Guard, created by General José de San Martín in 1821, stood to the left and right of Velasco. Flower arrangements and funeral wreaths had been brought to the church by the hundreds, and it did not take long before they filled the atrium and beyond. A brief Mass was performed; then the chapel was opened. This time, the lines were four or five blocks long and lasted all day. People of all social strata paraded in, but the majority were blue-collar workers, peasants, children, and poor housewives from the shantytowns and from towns far away from Lima. It was a mix of people: some were there as members of organizations, but many had decided to come on their own. Most of them crossed themselves as soon as they entered and saw the coffin, within which lay the general, dressed in his ornate uniform: a white jacket with braids made of gold and beige trousers. Some rapidly went by, others stared at the embalmed body. Some even talked to it before they approached Velasco's widow, Consuelo González, and the rest of the family. One woman in particular hugged the coffin for several minutes while she prayed, before loudly breaking into tears, making everyone else around her cry in the process. The side chapel remained open until eight o'clock in the morning of December 27.[40]

Many people were still waiting to pay their respects when the police arrived to close the side chapel and disperse the crowd toward the main square. In the hour that elapsed between the closing of the Sagrario and the transportation of the coffin to the cathedral next door, the plaza filled up. The second Mass in the cathedral started at ten in the morning. By then, the crowd in the square had grown to proportions rarely seen. Demonstrators brought banners with the names of their organizations, but also with messages such as "We will follow your example, General of the poor"; "The path has been made, comrade; socialism will triumph"; "Velasco has not died; he will live forever in the heart of the people." The crowd sang political songs and popular music: "In the sky, the stars; on Earth, injustice; and in our hearts, the Peruvian Revolution." They could not hear what was going on inside the cathedral, but those inside, despite the archbishop of Lima's Mass and the music of the National Symphonic Orchestra, heard them loud and clear.[41]

Sections of the crowd unsuccessfully attempted to break the cordon a few times. At one point, however, a woman identified by the media as Julia Rosa Cabanillas, a thirty-year-old who had come all the way from the northern department of Cajamarca, interrupted the Mass. She had spent the night inside the side chapel, and then somehow had managed to break into the cathedral. Suddenly, she started singing as loud as she could: "Peruvian Inca, your name is Juan Velasco. Today your people claim you and cry. Rise, rise, can't you see your people waiting for you? Juan Velasco Alvarado, dauntless, Peruvian pride, good and brave hero. Rise, rise, can't you see your people waiting for you?"[42]

In the main square, it was even hotter than the previous day. When the Mass was over at eleven o'clock, the invitees started to leave the cathedral. The crowd booed and insulted the members of the government

as they paraded, starting with the revolutionary junta, of which Arbulú was part. Morales Bermúdez had not shown up, honoring a specific
request from the Velasco family, but he was not forgotten: "¡Morales
to the coffin, Velasco to the palace!" "Velasco to history; Morales, go
fuck yourself!" This was another particularly interesting moment. The
events that surrounded the funeral were partly about ascribing meaning
to the revolution and, more specifically, to the end of the revolution. At
stake was a dispute about who could be part of, and even administrate,
the ritual that consecrated the death of the revolution. Perhaps it was
also about who was responsible for its death. The fact that Morales Bermúdez, the president of the republic in a time of military dictatorship,
had not been allowed to attend but still was publicly insulted—in what
was no doubt, as newspapers later denounced, the political decision of a
few organizations but also a popular reaction—was no small detail. Publicly insulting the head of state of a repressive military dictatorship in a
solemn ceremony is never an apolitical or a trivial act. It certainly reinforced the image of Velasco as a martyr.

Then, when the coffin appeared, the crowd roared, and the noise was
as loud as the old Plaza de Armas had ever heard. The bells tolled again.
The national anthem was sung yet another time. The crowd tried once
more to break the police cordon, but they were successfully contained,
just as before, although this time the use of force, in the form of police
batons, was required. Helicopters intimidatingly flew over the square.
The multitude kept singing: "On the shoulders of the people!" "Velasco
is from the people and he belongs to the people!"[43] The police and military officers in charge would have none of it. There was a protocol and it
would be followed. The coffin had to be carried on mourners' shoulders
to San Francisco Square, some three blocks from the Plaza de Armas,
but the names of those honored with the task had already been clearly
established. First, it would be army officers and then friends and representatives of grassroots organizations—a total of thirty people, six at a
time. Once at San Francisco, the coffin would be put inside the hearse,
and a new cortege would leave for El Ángel Cemetery, located some five
kilometers away. The burial of Velasco's body would start at noon, and
only those invited would be allowed to take part.

The walk to San Francisco proved longer and tougher than expected.
The crowd by then was at least one hundred thousand strong, and they
were not going to be easily contained. The narrow streets of the old colonial city did not make things go any faster. At a street corner, after
only one block, part of the crowd kept pushing the policemen in an at-

tempt to get to the coffin; in the meantime, the rest took to another street and ran toward San Francisco. When the coffin arrived there, the hearse was already waiting with the back door open. The members of the junta and other officials were also waiting in their cars. A group of about a hundred people tried to intercept the coffin, but the mounted police managed to disperse them. Velasco remained inside the hearse; the protocol had not been broken.

Except that there were far too many people by then. The hearse was surrounded, and in seconds the police wall disappeared, as if consumed by the crowd. The multitude swooped against the hearse, which still managed to move, albeit extremely slowly. It was a tremendously tense moment. Most of the members of the junta left their cars to seek refuge in one of the official buildings in the area. Arbulú stayed in his car. Some people knelt in front the hearse. Others tried to put nails in the tires. They all did what they could to stop the hearse. The car's engine was now overheating, and it was forced to slow down even more. Suddenly, during the struggle and confusion, someone stole the keys from the driver through the window. After minutes of confusion, at ten past noon, a military officer, very likely Arbulú himself, agreed with Velasco's family to allow the crowd to carry the coffin to the cemetery on their shoulders.[44]

It was five kilometers between downtown and El Ángel Cemetery, mostly along the wide Abancay Avenue. The procession, reportedly about 250,000 strong at that point, moved extremely slowly. People stole flowers from the gardens of the houses they passed and from the parks they crossed and put them on the coffin. Petals and confetti were thrown from the upper stories of the buildings that surrounded Abancay Avenue. Thousands leaned out of their windows or stood on the sidewalks and cheered. In the procession, people took short, orderly turns carrying Velasco's coffin in groups of six, seven, or eight, depending on their size and strength. They also talked to him: "Here I am, Chino, like I had promised you"; "Here I am, my General: I am a worker and I am fulfilling my duty to you and to the revolution"; "We will miss you, but we will follow your example and will never surrender the fight"; "Only God knows how much we will miss you, because you were very good, and poor just like us."[45]

It took five hours to get to Avenida Los Incas, where the cemetery is located. A police squad had followed the crowd all along, and a much larger one, this time armed with antiriot gear and vehicles, awaited. In an extremely aggressive operation, they quickly beat down thousands of people and made it clear that the crowd was not going to be able to enter the cemetery. In just a few minutes, the police regained control of the coffin and managed to bring it inside the cemetery. The crowd went back to singing: "Velasco belongs to the people, not to the gorillas!" "The people in uniforms are also exploited!"[46]

Of the 250,000, only about 100 managed to enter the cemetery. Even one of the designated speakers, the union leader Guzmán Rivera Castañeda, was left out. Consuelo and the rest of the family had gotten there before noon and had been waiting in a military lodging nearby. A few people managed to climb the trees and the walls to watch the burial and listen to the speeches by Luis Bambarén (the progressive "bishop of the shantytowns" who had collaborated with Velasco), a representative of the family, and members of the armed forces. Others looked through the old metallic grilles of the cemetery walls, but most of them just stayed outside. They kept singing for Velasco and protesting against the government, looking victorious. The crowd included peasants, industrial workers, shantytown dwellers, and members of the Communist Party. Even Velasco's former ministers and his classmates in the army were there.

At fifteen past four, a trumpet announced the beginning of a minute of silence, which meant that the coffin was being buried. There, in tomb number 7475 of Garden L, called San Baltazar, Velasco was being interred, the object for which they had been struggling all day. Silence around the cemetery was interrupted only by twenty-one cannon shots. This time, those outside had heard the noise from inside.[47] That day, having the last word had required controlling the ritual, taking over the streets, attempting to drive the revolution's hearse, and burying Velasco. Many people had managed to make their voices heard, but Velasco and the revolution were ultimately buried, after an antiriot operation carried out by the military.

Epilogue

The funeral was an extremely important moment for Velasquismo, or at least for the political sectors that presented themselves as heirs of Velasco's political bequest. Devoid of political power at the highest spheres since the coup of August 1975, but now without Velasco himself alive, they saw in the dictator's burial an opportunity to assert themselves as a political force. They managed to do so at least as far as popular mobilization went—and popular mobilization was not a minor factor at the time. Even as the Second Phase of the military regime kept attempting to limit their power, many of these organizations made yet another powerful demonstration of strength with a new national general strike on May 22–23, 1978. That strike was even larger and more intense than the one in July 1977. From this perspective, the history of Velasco's funeral underlines both the potential of ritual as a locus for contentious politics and the importance that massive popular mobilization had acquired in Peru at the dusk of the Velasco era.

Looking forward, on the other hand, the funeral was part of an especially anticipated preelectoral juncture. In that context, those who had stakes in claiming Velasco's legacy at that time—men like Social Christian political leader Héctor Cornejo Chávez, peasant organizer Avelino Mar, or General Aníbal Meza Cuadra, who were particularly active during the funeral—saw in the occasion an opportunity to affirm their association with Velasco and the potential that his image, indeed his body, had for massive popular mobilization, as they paid tribute to his life and death. Whether that would pay off for an enduring political project remained to be seen. The success of Avelino Mar and, more importantly, the election of six representatives of the pro-Velasco Partido Socialista Revolucionario (PSR; Socialist Revolutionary Party) to the constituent assembly in 1978 were sources of optimism regarding the future of Velasquismo.[48]

In the long term, however, as part of the general patterns of division, electoral collapse, and violence that trapped the Peruvian left, the funeral had little impact. The parallel rise of electoral politics and a bloody armed struggle diminished the importance of massive mobilizations. Combative demonstrations that exalted the image of a left-leaning general in a country torn by an internal armed conflict that pitted a faction of the Maoist left against the military must have hardly seemed like an attractive alternative. In the political logic of December 1977, massive popular mobilization had proved to be an extremely powerful political tool, but it was one that would not fare well in Peru during the 1980s. Fernando Belaúnde Terry, the very man against whom Velasco had organized his coup in 1968, was back in power, while the extreme left considered Velasco a Fascist. In June 1980, the Shining Path dynamited his tomb in El Ángel.[49]

In other words, Velasco's funeral can be seen as an expression of resistance to Morales Bermúdez and his Second Phase dictatorship, but resistance does not necessarily lead to the creation of a new sustainable political alternative, let alone a new order. The subversion of rituals has the potential to unsettle power relations, but not to determine the larger arc of politics.[50] In Peru, by the end of 1977 and beyond, that larger arc revolved around the return of electoral politics; an extremely bloody insurgent-counterinsurgent war; and a deep economic, social, and political crisis during the 1980s. The following decade, in turn, witnessed yet another authoritarian regime, this time the neoliberal, corrupt, and no less violent government of Alberto Fujimori (1990–2000). Social movements suffered heavily during all those years, under the combined weight of the violence of the Shining Path and the Peruvian armed forces and neoliberal legislation. The left, moreover, despite its encouraging electoral forays throughout the 1980s, finally fell into disarray, prey to both its own divisions and an extremely difficult context in which all "traditional" political parties foundered.

This is not to say that Velasco's body, as such, has remained an important issue in Peruvian politics beyond 1980. In fact, while the Revolutionary Government of the Armed Forces is still one of the most contentious topics in public debates about recent Peruvian history, discussions about Juan Velasco himself are often reduced to extreme polarizations.[51] It is as if his historical figure has not been capable of withstanding the pulling and tugging of memory politics. Lest that symbolic dismemberment keep obscuring an important part of Peruvian political history, his funeral should be understood as a defining episode in the histories of the transition to democracy and of the politics of social mobilization in Peru.

Notes

I want to thank María Claudia Huerta at the Pontificia Universidad Católica del Perú for exceptional research assistance. Professor John Demos and several of my fellow students in the Spring 2013 "Narrative (and Other) Histories" Seminar at Yale University made comments to the earliest versions of this paper. The participants of the "Rethinking Military Nationalism" Conference at University College London, in October 2013, as well as Gil Joseph, Enrique Mayer, Adolfo Polo y La Borda, and Cynthia McClintock read and commented on later drafts, and Eduardo Dargent and Ángel Ragas made bibliographic suggestions. Finally, I would like to thank the editors of this volume for the invitation to participate in this project and for their insightful suggestions.

1. Augusto Zimmermann Zavala, *Los últimos días del general Velasco. ¿Quién recoge la bandera?* (Lima: Self-published, 1978), 150. Zimmerman, a journalist, was one of Velasco's closest collaborators and his press secretary. Unless otherwise noted, all translations in this chapter are my own.

2. The classic studies of the Morales Bermúdez regime as a transition are Nicolás Lynch, *La transición conservadora: Movimiento social y democracia en el Perú, 1975–1978* (Lima: El Zorro de Abajo Editores, 1992), and Julio Cotler, "Military Interventions and 'Transfer of Power to Civilians' in Peru," in *Transitions from Authoritarian Rule: Latin America*, ed. Guillermo O'Donnell, Philippe C. Schmitter, and Laurence Whitehead (Baltimore, MD: Johns Hopkins University Press, 1986), 148–172. See also Abraham Lowenthal, ed., *The Peruvian Experiment: Continuity and Change Under Military Rule* (Princeton, NJ: Princeton University Press, 1975), and Juan Martín Sánchez, *La revolución peruana: Ideología y práctica política de un gobierno militar, 1968–1975* (Seville: CSIC, Universidad de Sevilla, Diputación de Sevilla, 2002).

3. Nicholas B. Dirks, "Ritual and Resistance: Subversion as a Social Fact," in *Culture/Power/History: A Reader in Contemporary Social Theory*, ed. Nicholas B. Dirks, Geoff Eley, and Sherry B. Ortner (Princeton, NJ: Princeton University Press, 1993), 498. See also Victor Turner, *The Ritual Process: Structure and Anti-Structure* (New York: Aldine de Gruyer, 1969).

4. Lyman L. Johnson, "Why Dead Bodies Talk: An Introduction," in *Death, Dismemberment, and Memory: Body Politics in Latin America*, ed. Lyman L. Johnson (Albuquerque: University of New Mexico Press, 2004), 11, 16.

5. Eric Van Young, "Conclusion: The State as Vampire—Hegemonic Projects, Public Ritual, and Popular Culture in Mexico, 1600–1990," in *Rituals of Rule, Rituals of Resistance: Public Celebrations and Popular Culture in Mexico*, ed. William H. Beezley, Cheryl English Martin, and William H. French (Wilmington, DE: Scholarly Resources, 1994), 349. See also William Roseberry, quoted in Gilbert M. Joseph and Daniel Nugent, "Popular Culture and State Formation in Revolutionary Mexico," in *Everyday Forms of State Formation: Revolution and the Negotiation of Rule in Modern Mexico*, ed. Gilbert M. Joseph and Daniel Nugent (Durham, NC: Duke University Press, 1994), 17.

6. See Alan Knight, "Democratic and Revolutionary Traditions in Latin America," *Bulletin of Latin American Research* 20, no. 2 (2001): 147–186. See also Alan Knight, "Populism and Neo-Populism in Latin America, Especially Mexico," *Journal of Latin American Studies* 30, no. 2 (1998): 223–248; Alberto Vergara, *Ni amnésicos ni irracionales: Las elecciones peruanas de 2006 en perspectiva histórica* (Lima: Solar, 2007), 74; Steve Stein, "The Paths to Populism in Peru," in *Populism in Latin America*, ed. Michael L. Conniff, 2nd ed. (Tuscaloosa: University of Alabama Press, 2012), 110–131; and John Crabtree, "Populisms Old and New: The Peruvian Case," *Bulletin of Latin American Research* 19, no. 2, (2000): 163–176. Interestingly, some contemporaries described Velasco's regime as "military populism": see Julio Cotler, "Political Crisis and Military Populism in Peru," *Studies in Comparative International Development* 6, no. 5 (1970): 95–113.

7. José Matos Mar, *Desborde popular y crisis del Estado: Veinte años después* (Lima: Fondo Editorial del Congreso del Perú, 2004). See also Julio Calderón Cockburn, *La ciudad ilegal: Lima en el siglo XX* (Lima: Universidad Nacional Mayor de San Marcos, 2005), and Carlos Iván Degregori, Cecilia Blondet, and Nicolás Lynch, *Conquistadores de un nuevo mundo: De invasores a ciudadanos en San Martín de Porres* (Lima: Instituto de Estudios Peruanos, 1986). The history of urban "invasions" shows that efforts to integrate these new groups anteceded

the revolutionary government, and thus questions the *desborde* thesis. Nevertheless, the Velasco regime both radicalized attempts at integration and sowed the seeds for subsequent difficulties in achieving it. Cf. David Collier, *Squatters and Oligarchs: Authoritarian Rule and Policy Change in Peru* (Baltimore: Johns Hopkins University Press, 1976), and Matteo Stiglich, "Estado, pobladores y la creación de Villa El Salvador" (unpublished manuscript).

8. From the left, the teachers' union (SUTEP) and the mining federation led the opposition, increasingly taking their grievances to the streets.

9. Henry Pease, *El ocaso del poder oligárquico: Lucha política en la escena oficial, 1968–1975* (Lima: DESCO, 1977), 106.

10. Martín Sánchez, *La revolución peruana*, 186; Pease, *El ocaso del poder oligárquico*, 175.

11. The crucial and most ambitious of which were the agrarian reform and the creation of the industrial community.

12. See Denis Sulmont, *El movimiento obrero peruano (1890–1980): Reseña histórica* (Lima: Tarea, 1980), 101–103; Evelyne Huber Stephens, *The Politics of Workers' Participation: The Peruvian Approach in Comparative Perspective* (New York: Academic Press, 1980), 151; Cynthia McClintock, *Peasant Cooperatives and Political Change in Peru* (Princeton, NJ: Princeton University Press, 1981), 263–264.

13. Martín Sánchez, *La revolución peruana*, 94–95. Governmental co-optation worked among associations of dwellers of the *pueblos jóvenes* (shantytowns), which were growing in the areas surrounding Lima, and, to a lesser degree, among the agrarian federations united in the CNA. See Alfred Stepan, *The State and Society: Peru in Comparative Perspective* (Princeton, NJ: Princeton University Press, 1978), 174; Luis Pásara, "When the Military Dreams," in *The Peruvian Experiment Reconsidered*, ed. Cynthia McClintock and Abraham Lowenthal (Princeton, NJ: Princeton University Press, 1983), 311. On Velasco and shantytowns, see Collier, *Squatters and Oligarchs*, and Stiglich, "Estado, pobladores y la creación de Villa El Salvador."

14. The CNA was an ambitious federation of peasant unions and a symbol of the government's new politics. See Jaymie Patricia Heilman's chapter in this volume and Susan Stokes, *Cultures in Conflict: Social Movements and the State in Peru* (Berkeley: University of California Press, 1995), 44; Nigel Haworth, "Conflict or Incorporation: The Peruvian Working Class, 1968–79," in *Military Reformism and Social Classes: The Peruvian Experience, 1968–80*, ed. David Booth and Bernardo Sorj (London: Macmillan, 1983), 94.

15. Among several accounts of this process, see Héctor Béjar, *La revolución en la trampa* (Lima: Ediciones Socialismo y Participación, 1976), chapter 5. See also Guillermo Thorndike's fictionalized account, *No, mi general* (Lima: Mosca Azul, 1976).

16. Huber Stephens, *The Politics of Workers' Participation*, 210–212; Martín Sánchez, *La revolución peruana*, 92.

17. This announcement came after another radical revolutionary measure, the creation of the "social ownership" (*propiedad social*) sector, in April 1974, and the expropriation of media in July of the same year. In theory, "productive groups" would actually own newspapers and other media. Both were announced as part of a retrospective government plan of sorts, El Plan Inca. See

David Booth, "The Reform of the Press: Myths and Realities," in David Booth and Bernardo Sorj, *Military Reformism and Social Classes*, 141–184; Pease, *El ocaso del poder oligárquico*, 122; Juan Martín Sánchez, *Perú 28 de julio: Discurso y acción política el día de Fiestas Patrias, 1969–1999* (Sevilla: CSIC/Instituto Mora, 2002), 114–131.

18. Estimates of the casualties of this episode range between the official 86 deaths and 155 wounded to several thousands.

19. Velasco's last months in power were characterized by an increase in repression, as shown by the deportation of more than twenty-seven journalists in early August and by the closure of the leftist newspaper *Marka*. Lynch, *La transición conservadora*, 101; Martín Sánchez, *La revolución peruana*, 97; Huber Stephens, *The Politics of Workers' Participation*, 228.

20. Until then, Morales Bermúdez had been a crucial general in the revolution. Besides a brilliant military career, during which he was employed in several important governmental positions, he had been minister of finance and commerce during Fernando Belaúnde Terry's first administration (1963–1968) and had held that same position and those of minister of economy, minister of war, and prime minister during the Velasco regime. See Federico Prieto Celi, *Regreso a la democracia: Entrevista biográfica al general Francisco Morales Bermúdez Cerruti, presidente del Perú (1975–1980)* (Lima: Realidades, 1996), 152, 161. On conflicts among the generals, see George D. E. Philip, *The Rise and Fall of the Peruvian Military Radicals, 1968–1976* (London: Athlone Press, 1978).

21. Dirk Kruijt, *Revolution by Decree: Peru 1968–1975*, 2nd ed. (West Lafayette, IN: Purdue University Press, 2003 [1994]), chapters 6 and 7; Alfonso Baella Tuesta, *El miserable* (Lima: Self-published, 1978), 437, 440; Henry A. Dietz, *Poverty and Problem-Solving under Military Rule: The Urban Poor in Lima, Peru* (Austin: University of Texas Press, 1980); Henry Dietz, *Urban Poverty, Political Participation, and the State: Lima, 1970–1990* (Pittsburgh: University of Pittsburgh Press, 1998), 121. The Peruvian Communist Party had by then exploded into dozens of factions, but for practical purposes, I will here refer to the "pro-Moscow" Partido Comunista Peruano-Unidad (PCP-U), the largest faction, as "the Communist Party."

22. Huber Stephens, *The Politics of Workers' Participation*, 230–233; Pease, *El ocaso del poder oligárquico*, 187; Lynch, *La transición conservadora*, 118–119.

23. The strike was organized by a Consejo Unitario de Organizaciones Sindicales (CUOS; Unifying Council of Union Organizations) and a Comando Unitario de Lucha, which included the participation of the Confederación General de Trabajadores del Perú (CGTP); the Aprista Confederación Nacional del Trabajo (CNT; National Confederation of Labor); Lima unions affiliated with the Confederación de Trabajadores de la Revolución Peruana (CTRP; Confederation of Workers of the Peruvian Revolution), the CNA, and the Confederación Campesina del Perú (CCP; Peruvian Peasant Confederation); squatters and shantytown dwellers; and independent unions.

24. The demands of the strike, however, were not fulfilled for the most part, and union leaders were fired from their jobs in subsequent months with the help of the regime's promulgation of new antiunion legislation. The immediate cost, moreover, was eighteen dead protesters and several hundred wounded.

25. These two paragraphs are based on Manuel Valladares Quijano, "Movi-

mientos sociales y dictadura militar: La experiencia política del Paro Nacional del 19 de julio de 1977," *Investigaciones Sociales* 11, no. 18 (2007): 243–276, and Manuel Valladares Quijano, *El Paro Nacional del 19 de julio: Movimientos sociales en la época del "Gobierno Revolucionario de las Fuerzas Armadas"* (Lima: Universidad Nacional Mayor de San Marcos/Grupo Pakarina, 2013). See also Daniel Masterson, *Militarism and Politics in Latin America: Peru from Sánchez Cerro to Sendero Luminoso* (Westport: Greenwood, 1991), 262–263; Lynch, *La transición conservadora*, 127–128; Pease, *El ocaso del poder oligárquico*, 251–252; Sulmont, *El movimiento obrero peruano*, 122–113; Stokes, *Cultures in Conflict*, 45–46; Huber Stephens, *The Politics of Workers' Participation*, 229.

26. All the major newspapers in Lima closely followed Velasco's illness between late November and late December 1977.

27. "Una infección incontrolable venció su gran fortaleza," *La Crónica*, December 25, 1977, 2.

28. "Hombre del pueblo oró con una cruz a cuestas," *Correo*, December 25, 1977, 4; "Rezan por Velasco," *Ojo*, December 25, 1977, 4.

29. The singing of the national anthem was a customary ritual in Peruvian popular mobilizations of the time; the Velasco government's nationalist rhetoric likely had incentivized it.

30. "Ayer un pueblo consternado y dolido anticipó su adiós al ex presidente Velasco Alvarado," *El Comercio*, December 26, 1977, 1.

31. Juan Gargurevich, *Historia de la prensa peruana (1594–1990)* (Lima: La Voz, 1991), 215–228; Alfonso Baella Tuesta, *Prensa Libre* (Lima: El Tiempo, 1979), 5–12.

32. On Velasco's anti–Santa Claus campaign, see Enrique Mayer, *Ugly Stories of the Peruvian Agrarian Reform* (Durham, NC: Duke University Press, 2009), 6; Jorge Castro de los Ríos, "Velasco: Sic Transit Gloria Mundi," *Gente, La Revista del Perú*, January 16, 1978, 46; on readers' complaints about excessive coverage of Velasco's death, see "Sepelio de Velasco," *Caretas*, January 12, 1978, 2.

33. "Comunicado del Ministerio del Interior sobre el sepelio" and "Comunicado Oficial No. 19-ORRPPMI," both published in all newspapers on December 25 and 26, 1977.

34. Quoted in Carlos Franco, "Los significados de la experiencia velasquista: Forma política y contenido social," in *El Perú de Velasco*, ed. Carlos Franco (Lima: CEDEP, 1983), 2:415. On the martyr idea, see Lyman L. Johnson, "Preface" to *Death, Dismemberment, and Memory*, xvi.

35. Those organizations included more than twenty Communist and socialist factions, the CNA, the Aprista CNT, the CTRP-Lima, and many other organizations.

36. Lynch, *La transición conservadora*, 41.

37. This statement was also published in all newspapers on December 25 and 26, 1977.

38. Upscale funerals in Peru customarily feature black carriers. That an official ceremony such as this one followed the tradition reflects the degree to which certain forms of labor were racialized, an issue that has been studied, among others, in Paulo Drinot, *The Allure of Labor: Workers, Race, and the Mak-*

ing of the Peruvian State (Durham, NC: Duke University Press, 2011). See also Tanya Golash-Boza, *Yo Soy Negro: Blackness in Peru* (Gainesville: University Press of Florida, 2011).

39. "Multitudinario homenaje popular se tributó ayer a Juan Velasco," *El Comercio*, December 26, 1977, 4. Velasco was nicknamed "El Chino," or "the Chinese man."

40. "El dolor era de todos en la capilla ardiente," *Correo*, December 26, 1977, 3; "Millares de personas desfilaron ante restos del General Velasco," *La Crónica*, December 26, 1977, 3.

41. "La multitud entonó canciones populares," *Ojo*, December 27, 1977, 3; "Consuelo mostró dolida serenidad en el sepelio," *Correo*, December 27, 1977, 8.

42. "Inca peruano, te llamas Juan Velasco," *Correo*, December 27, 1977, 14.

43. "El camino está hecho," *Correo*, December 27, 1977, 8.

44. The best account of the scene is "Cronología del entierro y sepelio del General Velasco," *Marka*, December 29, 1977, 12.

45. "En el traslado de los restos de J. Velasco, multitud recorrió más de 5 kilómetros en 5 horas 20 minutos," *El Comercio*, December 27, 1977, 7; "No solo lo cargaban . . . ¡hablaban con él!," *Correo*, December 27, 1977, 9.

46. "Cronología del entierro y sepelio del General Velasco," *Marka*, December 29, 1977, 13.

47. "Emocionada multitud acompañó el cortejo," *Expreso*, December 29, 1977, 4b; "El ataúd fue llevado a pie a lo largo de 50 cuadras," *La Prensa*, December 27, 1977, 1.

48. The left, in general, had a durable imprint in the Constitution of 1978, which was then replaced by the Fujimori regime in 1993. PSR later participated in the general elections of 1980 and 1985, as part of the most important leftist electoral coalition in Peruvian history, Izquierda Unida, and presented candidates in the municipal elections of 1980, 1983, and 1986. It also took part, with little success, in elections in 1989 and 1990. Some of its founders and most important militants were former high-profile Velasquista generals like Leonidas Rodríguez Figueroa and Jorge Fernández Maldonado. After years in oblivion, it reemerged as an extremely small member of the coalition that supported Ollanta Humala in the 2011 presidential election. See Constante Traverso Flores, *La izquierda en el Perú: Entre el dogma y el sectarismo. Una historia que no ha concluido* (Lima: Proesa, 2013), 146.

49. On the attack to Velasco's tomb, see Nelson Manrique, "Pensamiento, acción y base política del movimiento Sendero Luminoso: La guerra y las primeras respuestas de los comuneros (1964–1983)," in *Historizar el pasado vivo en América Latina*, ed. Anne Pérotin-Dumon (2007), http://www.historizarel pasadovivo.cl/downloads/manrique.pdf.

50. Dirks, "Ritual and Resistance," 501; James C. Scott, *Domination and the Arts of Resistance: Hidden Transcripts* (New Haven, CT: Yale University Press, 1990).

51. See Paulo Drinot's chapter in this volume.

CHAPTER 4

Remembering Velasco: Contested Memories of the Revolutionary Government of the Armed Forces

PAULO DRINOT

As the election of Ollanta Humala in 2011 confirmed, and as the recent 2016 elections demonstrated once more, memories of the Revolutionary Government of the Armed Forces (RGAF) are regularly mobilized in Peru.[1] However, the collective memories of the Velasco regime have not received much scholarly attention. In 2003, Gonzalo Portocarrero published a short paper that drew on interviews and on an analysis of how different intellectuals framed the military regime. According to Portocarrero, dominant evaluations of the Velasco regime are shaped by class: "For the dominant classes, Velasquismo should never have existed. It is an anomaly that must be forgotten as quickly as possible. But the subaltern classes consider the Velasco government to be one of the best in recent history."[2] His interviews with informants both old and young, rich and poor, confirm that the period is remembered, and therefore actualized, in different and contested ways. More recently, Enrique Mayer has explored the Velasco period through the memories of a range of people, from landowners to union leaders to peasants who participated in or were affected by the agrarian reform of 1969.[3] While both studies offer important insight into how the Velasco regime is remembered and, to some extent, operationalized politically and culturally in contemporary Peru, it is clear that much remains to be done to uncover the contested memories of the period.

I approach the collective memories of the Velasco regime through an analysis of circa fifteen hundred comments attached to three video uploads on YouTube. As is well known, YouTube, part of the Google Corporation, is an online video-sharing platform that allows anyone with an account to upload videos and share them with as many people as are interested in watching them. But the YouTube platform also allows visitors or users to post comments on the videos. As I showed in a previous study on collective memories of the War of the Pacific (1879–1883), an analysis of such comments provides useful insight into what Elizabeth Jelin has called "the labour(s) of memory."[4] YouTube video uploads, like many other digital artifacts, can function as online *lieux de mémoire*, or (web)sites of memory, not unlike the more traditional "sites of memory" studied by Pierre Nora, the French historian who introduced the concept, referring to places such as monuments, memorials, or what are increasingly known as trauma sites: locations associated with traumatic past events, such as, most famously in the case of Latin America, the Escuela Superior de Mecánica de la Armada (ESMA, now the Space for Memory and for the Promotion and Defense of Human Rights) in Buenos Aires or Villa Grimaldi in Santiago de Chile.[5] However, because these online comments are interactive, recording responses to the video recently viewed by the poster or to other comments, they operate as vehicles of memory (Jelin) or technologies of memory (Sturken) that help us explore the memory practices of specific, if largely faceless, individuals that are in turn expressive of collective memory practices.[6] The comments of these individuals illustrate in interesting ways how collective memory, ostensibly a framework for remembering (and forgetting) and making sense of the past, is mobilized or operationalized in order to make sense of the present.[7]

The comments attached to the videos, and the memories they reflect and mobilize, therefore, point to the current valence of the Velasco period. After briefly introducing each video, I focus on some of the key issues that posters or users of YouTube comment on. First, I explore the contested memories of the agrarian reform and suggest that these memories converge on the idea that the failure of the reform was a consequence not of Velasco's own failings but of the unpreparedness of those who were given responsibility for making the reform successful: the indigenous peasantry. I suggest that this interpretation of the failure of the reform is expressive of racialized assumptions about indigeneity in Peru. I then turn to a number of other issues, including the death of Velasco, Velasco's policies with regard to economic dependency and US power in Latin America, Peru's relations with Chile, and the links between the Velasco "revolution" and the Shining Path insurgency. I suggest that the ways in which these events or processes are remembered (and forgotten) are expressive of the role that is assigned by Peruvians to Velasco himself and, to a lesser extent, to the Revolutionary Government of the Armed Forces in making sense of Peru's past, present, and future. The Velasco regime and the memories mobilized by and re-constructed through it offer Peruvians a means through which to work through, if not necessarily resolve, a number of issues that shape how Peruvians feel and think about themselves and their place in the world.

The Videos

The three videos in question were uploaded at different times, by different YouTube users, or, more precisely, produsers.[8] They did so with different goals in mind. The video titled "Juan Velasco Alvarado . . . Speech . . . Agrarian Reform" was uploaded on September 22, 2009, by a produser with the tag "ciberchango."[9] It includes an audio recording of Velasco's speech announcing the agrarian reform. The speech is presented alongside a slide show of still images, which include a photograph of the book that contained the law, an image of Velasco giving a speech with a large painting of Túpac Amaru breaking his chains in the background, a photograph of Velasco in a motorcade, and a photograph of Velasco in a football stadium. This speech, delivered by Velasco on June 24, 1969, is of course one of the most famous and era-defining speeches in Peruvian history. It ends with the sentence or aphorism that has come to define not only the agrarian reform but the whole Velasco government: "We can now say to the man who works the land [*hombre de la tierra*], using the immortal and liberating words of Túpac Amaru: 'Peasant, the landlord will no longer eat from your poverty!'"[10] The video, which lasts ten minutes, has been watched 94,756 times at the time of writing and has elicited 465 comments. When uploading the video, ciberchango added not only a title but also a short description, set in uppercase letters, that leaves little doubt as to the sentiments motivating the creation and dissemination of the video: "THE GENERAL OF THE POOR OF PERU . . . YOU LIVE FOREVER IN OUR MIND AND HEART . . . LONG LIVE PERU DAMN IT . . ."

The video titled "Coup of Juan Velasco Alvarado" was uploaded on May 2, 2011, by a produser with the tag "NoalSocialismo2011."[11] At the time of writing, it had been viewed 149,303 times and had elicited 811 comments. The political position of this produser is made clear both by the tag used and by the icon chosen: a hammer and sickle inside a road sign indicating "no" (a red circle with a diagonal red line) and by the added description: "For all young people who do not know about the worst period in Peru's history we present Ollanta Humala's hero, this is the model he draws on for inspiration, open your eyes, socialism leads to nothing good, only to the debacle." As this suggests, the 2011 Peruvian national elections provided the context for the upload of this video by whoever stood behind the tag NoalSocialismo2011. Following the first round of voting on April 10, Ollanta Humala, who ran on a left-of-center ticket (later largely abandoned), was pitted against Keiko Fujimori, the daughter of former president Alberto Fujimori, who is serving a long jail term for human rights abuses and corruption. Humala defeated Keiko Fujimori in the second round elections on June 5 and was sworn in as president on July 28. The video should perhaps be thought of as part of a broader campaign that sought to associate Humala not only with Velasco, with whom Humala had a clear affinity, but also with Venezuela's Hugo Chávez and, more generally, with authoritarianism and, particularly, statist development policies.

Indeed, in contrast to the first video, which appears to be an amateur production put together by the produser, this video is simply an upload of a professional video prepared by an online news outlet called Willax TV. This is an online news channel, which, by its own admission, is committed to a neoliberal agenda.[12] The video, introduced by a reporter, is clearly hostile to the Velasco regime. Lasting thirteen minutes, it includes archive footage of October 3, 1968, the day of the coup, with images of tanks patrolling the streets of Lima; of the speech Velasco gave the day of the expropriation of the International Petroleum Company's Talara refinery; of Fernando Belaúnde Terry, the president deposed by the coup; of the expropriation of newspapers and television channels; and of the February 1975 police revolt that was put down by the regime. It also uses a number of still images of the period, including some of the images used in the previously described video. This footage and the images are interspersed with or overlaid by the reporter's commentary, which focuses on the nationalization of private firms, such as Cerro de Pasco, a US mining company, or the numerous fishing companies involved in the fishmeal sector, and on the creation of state entities. The reporter argues that in favoring social justice over "business efficiency," these measures were implemented "without consideration of the economic sustainability of the project." The reporter ends the piece by recounting the end of the regime and the transition to democracy in 1980 and adds: "But the reforms and nationalizations that brought about the economy's backwardness could only be repealed many years later; now we have recovered lost time and arrived at where we are today: one of the countries with the highest growth rates in the world."

The third video, "Juan Velasco Alvarado—Presidente del Perú de 1968 a 1975," was uploaded by a produser with the tag "ARCHIVO TV PIURA" on August 29, 2009.[13] It had been viewed 91,056 times and had elicited 201 comments by the time of this writing. It contains some of the same footage used in the previously described video (video 2). The video includes a voiceover that presents a negative view of the Velasco regime and the 1968 coup. After describing Velasco's arrival at the presidential palace in a helicopter, the voiceover states: "The country did not know that behind the flags of nationalism hid a dictactorship that would change Peru, that would undermine individual freedoms, and would take us down the mistaken path of statism that has done so much harm to Peru." However, the produser who uploaded the video included a long description that ends with the following: "Note: What's important about the video are the images and not what the narrator says, which may appear truthful to some but not to the majority of Peruvians." The description offers a short biography of Velasco, who, we are told, was born in Piura in 1909 "to a working-class family," and an overview of the regime. The short biography describes Velasco's rapid ascent in the military ranks, which is attributed to his "dedication and effort" after he joined the army in 1929 with the rank of private. The assessment of the regime offered attempts to strike a balance: "The social and economic reforms brought about an unprecedented level of change in the country, the working classes obtained the recognition that they had always been denied, but agricultural production virtually disappeared, which produced mass migration from the countryside to the city. These changes continue to affect the country until today."

Not everyone who views these videos leaves a comment. In total, and assuming that each visitor views the video only once (which may not be a fair assumption), some 350,000 people had viewed these three videos. But there are only approximately 1,500 comments and many users leave more than one comment. Nevertheless, the universe of comments is sufficiently large to offer useful insight into the collective memories of the Velasco regime.

Overwhelmingly, the comments are by Peruvian visitors to the YouTube videos under consideration. Only very occasionally do users, or posters, identify themselves as being of a different nationality. In fact, it is very difficult to know very much about these posters. Their tags may tell us something about how they wish to be identified, and very occasionally a poster will reveal some personal information, typically whether they are young or old or male or female. Many posters are highly critical of Velasco and the military regime. One leitmotif in the comments—also expressed in one of the videos, as we have seen—is the idea that the dictatorship reversed Peru's development by thirty or fifty years. Luis Marca's comment that "this revolution cost us thirty years of backwardness (*retraso*) and poverty because neither the peasants nor the state were in a position to generate wealth. Instead they only produced politicking" (video 1) is typical of such comments.[14] However, the majority of comments are positive: most visitors to the YouTube pages remember Velasco fondly, and the policies of the regime are judged to have often been necessary and well intentioned if not always successful. In many cases, the lack of success of the reforms implemented by the regime, as I discuss below, is blamed not on the regime, and certainly not on Velasco, but rather on other factors. As bobzone85 notes, in allusion to claims that Velasco put the country back decades: "When Velazco took over, Peru had a 200-year lag (*estaba retrasado 200 anhos* [*sic*])" (video 1).[15]

The memories mobilized by the videos seem to confirm that remembering is "a dynamic process that is the result of the practices of individuals and groups."[16] Although they evoke the past, memories are produced or reconstructed in relation to contemporary processes.[17] They reflect what has been variously called "social" or "cultural" memory, a memory that is not necessarily acquired through direct experience of an event or process. In a few cases, we learn that users' memories of Velasco are a product of generational transfer: they are what Marianne Hirsch has called "postmemories."[18] Dianaxrk, for example, says: "well, I wasn't alive during his government, but my parents were, and they say that despite the fact that many people were opposed to him, he made Peru a better place" (video 3). MsWilkis similarly states: "it's incredible to hear the voice of Juan Velazco Alvarado . . . this is a historic moment for me . . . I only know about him because of my parents . . ." (video 3). Luzsteffy's postmemories of Velasco were transmitted by someone who knew Velasco personally: "my father, his bodyguard Pedro Guerrero, always spoke well of him" (video 3). Nelson huanca ramirez recalls the emotion that listening to Velasco's agrarian reform speech produced in his father: "thanks to this law the lives of millions of people who lived on the edge of slavery changed and for this reason, thank you Mr Velasco, my father cried when he heard this speech" (video 1). In a comment that addresses a point made by a number of users regarding a potential war with Chile that Velasco had been allegedly preparing for, Carlos Martinez recalls: "I remember when my father would tell me about how the tanks paraded in front of his house in Ica, the war was set to start, but [Francisco] Morales [Bermúdez] stopped it. History would have been different otherwise" (video 3). In other cases, the comments indicate that awareness of the Velasco regime came about through a process that Alison Landsberg has referred to as "prosthetic memory," that is, a form of memory that is acquired through participation in mass culture.[19] Hecast90, for example, states: "Velasco, you will not be forgotten by the young people who have rediscovered your deeds" (video 1).

The Agrarian Reform

The agrarian reform is one of the key issues that comment posters debate in relation to the videos. Many posters view it as an unmitigated disaster that impacted negatively on agricultural productivity and economic growth and did nothing to address poverty in the countryside. As xarlo1000 states in response to Velasco's agrarian reform speech:

> Yes, of course, a very nice speech, bullshit! The only thing they achieved was to fuck up productivity in the country. After 40 years since the [agrarian] reform—which, by the way, has been declared unconstitutional—we know what results it has produced: more poor peasants and the worst thing of all is that now they sell the land and get into fights with each other over land. . . . So don't tell me about the "nice speech" . . . this imbecile screwed up Peru . . . read up a bit and stop messing around! (video 1)

This is a view repeated by several posters, including Albenvenutti: "Velasco, how the hell did you undertake a badly planned agrarian reform and you brought much hunger and poverty on the country, a poverty that even today we have to contend with; damn cripple, I hope you are burning in hell!!!" (video 1). As this suggests, several posters express the idea that the reform was badly planned, which ultimately meant that the outcome was the opposite of what was intended and that the peasantry ended up worse off than they started. As fer13cho02 suggests:

> the agrarian reform was really badly planned, it wasn't the right time to redeem the peasants, not like that, it should have been thought through better. Today, the poor peasant, although he enjoys freedom to think and make his own decisions, this freedom is of no use to him because

he is still poor and poorer than he was before the reform, because at least he had something to eat under the *gamonal* [the hacienda landlord] (I know of cases in the sierra) but now he does not know how to produce or how to eat. (video 1)

For many posters, the agrarian reform was doomed by the fact that it handed over land to people who did not know what to do with it. Mirko GF, for example, argues that

Velasco did nothing other than to damage the economy of Peru, even of the peasants, what's the point of giving land to people who have no way of sowing it! Sugar and cotton exports fell immediately. I am a planter (*agricultor*) and I know people who lived through those times and they told me that the solution was worse than the problem. The intelligent thing would be to establish and enforce rights, extra hours, profit shares, insurance, health benefits. To give land to those who cannot sow it! Stupidity! (video 1)[20]

Andrés Ara, similarly, frames the agrarian reform in terms of a transfer of wealth from the entrepreneurial to the lazy: "Thanks to him, many people who, with great effort, had haciendas, land . . . etc., lost them. He is not the general of the poor of Peru, he is the general of the lazy, because the poor are provided with opportunities to make a living and the lazy are given everything for free" (video 1). Ruido Blanco makes a similar argument that the agrarian reform favored the undeserving: "The Agrarian Reform represents for my country the forward march of ignorance, when many people were able to obtain a patch of land that they had never worked, they took it like 'free inheritance' from the government, that's why there was great poverty and some cholos [*sic*] who now have big houses, it's normal, rather than work they devoted themselves to grab those plots of land for their personal benefit. Velasco, I hope you are in hell" (video 1).

Several posters experienced this process directly as it impacted their families. Christian Gamero states:

I'm glad this bastard is dead!! They took my grandmother's hacienda because of this idiot who believes in giving the same to everyone and in nationalization (*estatitzar*) [*sic*] instead of giving opportunities so that everyone can achieve their goals by virtue of their effort and hard work. [It was a mistake] to give land to so many ignorant Indians who don't even know how to manage an hacienda (*administrar*). God save us from these damned emotionally repressed people (*malditos reprimidos*)! (video 1)

Similarly, mochiwakawaka, whose grandparents were affected by the land reform, suggests that it was a total failure, the worst thing that could have happened to Peru. The only thing that the agrarian reform achieved was to make peasants even poorer and to turn them into alcoholics: "you give land and money to ignorant people what do they do they take . . . that's what my grandparents and relatives who were affected because of this soldier (*militar*) saw . . . thanks so much for having taken apart agriculture in Peru and made the economy stagnate for thirty or more years . . . the day of the peasant . . . for me it's the day of the assassin and the thief" (video 1).

Yet not all whose families were affected or who were on the losing side of the agrarian reform have negative memories. ChoaKing,s joaquin, who claims to be the son of landowners, applauds the reforms that Velasco initiated and the attempt to regain Arica from Chile and, more generally, what he sees as the radical change that Velasco was trying to bring about. He or she concludes: "[you get] a president like this one every hundred years" (video 1). Nenkofer Montenegro, moreover, attacks those he or she sees as "alienated snobs (*pituquitos alienados*)" who will never forgive Velasco for having taken the land of their grandparents. These elites, he or she contends, are a minority. For the majority, "which was always excluded from the colonialist banquet," the Velasco regime represented a new dawn, even though the project was incomplete: "It is up to the sons of Peru to continue the path that you showed us toward a society of justice and equality" (video 1).

However, the agrarian reform is remembered not only for its impact on rural Peru, agricultural productivity, or the well-being of the peasantry; it is also remembered for its broader impact on Peruvian society. In particular, a number of posters view the agrarian reform in terms of its supposed consequences for the social and racial makeup of Lima, arguing that it contributed to the wave of migration from the highlands to the capital, which, in turn, radically transformed what was until then a largely criollo, or white, city. For example, Nicolas velasquez sanchez suggests that Velasco was responsible for the fact that many peasants who benefited from the agrarian reform lost their lands because they did not know how to manage them, "and that as a consequence [they] migrated to the capital, causing overpopulation. I'm not saying they were

wrong to migrate, but perhaps if General Velasco had made better decisions, there would not be so many poor people in Lima, most of whom
are migrants" (video 3). This same argument is made in overtly racist
ways in some cases. Jan adam, for example, states: "he was a fucking Indian, a cholo, because of him the cholos fucked up Lima, the city was
made 100% by Europeans and now it's a disaster full of combis [public
transport vans], filthy markets, Indians begging in the streets and other
shit. . . . Peru can thank the fucking cholo grunt (*milico*) Vlasco [*sic*] Alvarado, funded by the soviet KGB via fucking Fidel . . . Down with the
cholos and Indians who will never progress" (video 3). Domart11 makes
a very similar point: "hahaha imbeciles, Velazco so you know once and
for all stole your parents' land with that agrarian reform bullshit, as a
consequence of that your forefathers (*antepasados*) migrated to Lima, that
is to say, they invaded Lima to work as servants and that is why we need
to put up with this invasion of darkies (*cobrizos*) that we see now in Lima
with all their delinquency, thefts, gangs, and corruption" (video 1).

For many more, however, the agrarian reform amounted to an emancipation of Peru's peasant and indigenous population. The term "*esclavitud*" (slavery) is used frequently by those who make this point. Alberto
Rodriguez, for example, says that the peasants "were the serfs of the
great hacendados, little more than slaves, Velasco freed them" (video 3).
Although many agree that the agrarian reform was not a resounding
success, it was first and foremost a process that gave many Peruvians
their freedom or, put differently, made them citizens. Jhonatan erick
Godoy states: "it is true that the agrarian reform failed but it was [a] social accomplishment (*logro social*), the peasants were no longer slaves"
(video 1). Similarly, Lalo Quillo argues: "Despite the fact that the agrarian reform was not the success that had been planned and today the little gamonales and the privileged take advantage and blame the Chino
Velasco for all the ills that Peru faces, it was the ideological liberation
of the most oppressed" (video 1). Several posters point to the ways in
which enslavement was replaced by dignity. Engineerlhas, for example,
states: "the most important thing is that Peruvians who lived in the Andes, enslaved and in infrahuman conditions, were given dignity; nobody
remembers or cares about them. Peruvians are not only those who live
in Lima, or do the rest not matter? Remember that the Day of the Indian became the Day of the Peasant, which is an adequate name. The
national was made valuable." Indeed, the agrarian reform not only freed
and dignified the peasantry; it also made them aware of their rights as
citizens. Shilicaso argues: "Thanks to Velasco, the humble peasant woke

up, or at least he began to know certain rights; many were no longer humiliated" (video 1).

As these comments indicate, memories of the Velasco regime are highly focused on Velasco as an individual. Velasco, rather than the regime or the intellectual architects of the regime, is identified as the source or originator of important reforms, such as the agrarian reform, or other initiatives, such as Peru's military rearmament with a view to attack Chile in order to recover Arica and Tarapacá, the two provinces lost to Peru's southern neighbor during the War of the Pacific, a question I return to below. Numerous posters state that unlike most Peruvian presidents before and since, Velasco was a great leader. WGUARDIAPERU says that he was "THE ONLY WORLD-CLASS PRESIDENT THAT PERU HAS EVER HAD" (video 1). He is compared favorably to only a handful of other Peruvian leaders. The most common comparison is to Ramón Castilla, who, many Peruvians believe, was responsible for the emancipation of Peru's slaves in the mid-nineteenth century, and Andrés Avelino Cáceres, one of the heroes of the War of the Pacific. As Roger Evans states: "If you study Peru's history, you realize that it was always governed by criminals and traitors: Piérola, Leguía, Benavides, Prado, Belaúnde, Morales Bermúdez, Alan García, Fujimori, Toledo, etc. There have only been three patriot leaders who have governed Peru with patriotism, without seeking to enrich themselves and introducing laws that favored the poor: Marshall Ramón Castilla, Marshall Andrés Avelino Caceres [sic] and GENERAL JUAN VELASCO ALVARADO" (video 1). Occasionally he is also compared to Túpac Amaru.[21] By contrast, posters often accuse Francisco Morales Bermúdez, who deposed Velasco in 1975, of having been a traitor. As ilbeckio states: "Velasco was Peru's best president. Morales Bermudes [sic] messed it all up . . . he sold out" (video 2).

Almost invariably the idea that Velasco was a great leader is conveyed through two statements that invoke heteronormativity and hypermasculinity. Velasco, posters claim, had "*huevos*" (balls) and wore "*pantalones*" (trousers), that is to say, he was brave. David Loayza, for example, says that Velasco was "the only president who had the BALLS to take on capitalism" (video 2). For unmsm008, Velasco "was the only president who had the courage (*ha tenido pantalones*) to take on the Americans (gringos)" (video 2). Coral técnicas unidas says: "he was a man who wore trousers, remember that he was the only one who said stop to the Chileans" (video 2). William mendoza puma suggests that "since Velasco died, there has not been another general with balls" (video 2). Jaslyr espinoza, meanwhile, compares Velasco to Humala: "this man wore trousers damn it, not like Ollanta [Humala] who shits in his pants (*que le tienblan* [*sic*] *los huevos*)" (video 2). Occasionally, a poster berates Velasco in similar terms for not having followed through with some measures: "he didn't have enough balls to recover Arica and Tarapacá," says astonveraz (video 2). This highly gendered language, with its reference to both the male genitals and trousers, an item of clothing associated with masculinity, is of course expressive of the ways in which leadership is associated in Peru and elsewhere with male and, indeed, hypermasculine characteristics. It also suggests, perhaps less directly, a perception of Velasco as a father figure who could engender a new generation of Peruvians. By contrast, it is interesting to note that General Francisco Morales Bermúdez, in addition to being branded a traitor, is called by several posters a "maricón" and a "puto" (a homosexual).[22] He is in this way presented as a man of, at best, dubious masculinity.

Through these comments about his leadership and hypermasculine qualities, Velasco is presented as a sort of Übermensch. This characteristic is retained in discussions that assess the failure of the reforms that Velasco championed, where posters often shift the blame from Velasco, who as an Übermensch could not have been responsible for failure, to those who were supposed to oversee or implement the reforms. In fact, posters on both sides of the spectrum make this point repeatedly. [W]ilber peche, for example, suggests that "THE IDEA THAT PERUVIANS SHOULD BECOME OWNERS OF THEIR OWN WEALTH WAS GOOD, BUT HE FAILED TO TRAIN PEOPLE IN LEADERSHIP AND PROFESSIONALS WITH THE SKILLS TO MANAGE EVERYTHING THAT WAS EXPROPRIATED; THAT'S WHAT WAS MISSING" (video 3). By contrast, creepkun shifts the blame from the lack of professionals to those who received the land: "because of this guy, many people went from being employees to becoming owners but they did not know what to do with the land, they went bankrupt and became very poor" (video 3). This view is echoed by carlitoshyd, who clearly views the broader process initiated by the military regime positively, but concedes that there were errors in the way that the reform was implemented, and that a key error was that those who were given responsibility for running the new agricultural cooperatives were not sufficiently "prepared": "For the young who do not know about this historic moment. In 1968 people would not talk of boss (*jefe*) but of lord (*patron*) [*sic*], yes my lord, etc. Velasco gave them dignity and brought democracy to the country. The error was that the people were

not prepared (trained) to take responsibility in the cooperatives, etc."
(video 2). Others, however, blame a whole range of factors. Rubiazul1,
for example, includes the role of elites who scuppered the reform process in his broader assessment: "It is such a shame that this great man
was no[t] able to continue his project, I think the people were not sufficiently prepared [and] that's why the agrarian reform failed [, because
of] the absence of technical knowledge, lack of machinery, lack of roads,
the extreme poverty of the peasantry, the rich and racist elites [—all
these contributed to] the failure of that government" (video 3).

The lack of "preparedness" of those who were given control over collective agricultural units is sometimes presented in connection to the
argument that, as a direct consequence of the agrarian reform, Peru
lost its place as one of the leading agricultural exporters, particularly
of commodities like sugar. RafoAQP, for example, states: "the great
problem that this law had, and which made the transformation fail, is
that it did not train (*no capacitó*) these people, who all of sudden had a
plot of land, that's why we went from being the first-place producers of
sugarcane to second and third place and now we are not even among
the top ten" (video 2). Similarly, Pablo Eduardo Coha Luna writes: "At
that time they also expropriated the sugar plantations that were admired throughout Latin America and we went from being [one of the]
top sugar producers to importing sugar. The peasants who were on the
edge of slavery moved to the edge of poverty, those who[se properties]
were expropriated have still not received compensation for their land.
The peasants were not educated to become more productive. If you do
not educate people[,] no reform can be successful" (video 1).

While in some cases the blame is placed on the military regime for
not adequately preparing or educating the peasants, in others, the peasantry itself is blamed in ways that are overtly racist. Gitano261, for example, challenges a statement by another poster that Velasco gave the
indigenous dignity: "what dignity[,] you moron? In the agrarian reform
Velasco gave them machinery and seeds, land, etc., and what did the Indians do? They sat on their arses and let the machinery and seeds go to
waste. They never worked out how to start a tractor. They went back to
their mountains, to their coca, and continued to breed more children
and more poverty. They didn't give a shit about the [agrarian] reform"
(video 2).

These memories of the agrarian reform, elicited by the videos, clearly
point to the contested ways in which the reform is remembered. But
both those who see the agrarian reform as an entirely negative process

and those who choose to emphasize its positive aspects mobilize broader assumptions about the nature of Peruvian society and economic development. The recurring idea that whether well intentioned and planned or not, the agrarian reform was doomed by the decision to hand over land to those who were "unprepared" to manage it and make it productive expresses much more deeply held beliefs about the sources of progress and backwardness in Peru. Indeed, beneath the explicitly racist commentary that often inflects debates or comments on the agrarian reform is a more generally shared racialized assumption, sometimes expressed in explicitly racist terms, that the reform failed because the peasants who received the land, in their state at the time, could not possibly have made that land productive. This is an assumption that is in turn shaped by the ways in which the indigenous population in Peru has historically been perceived as incommensurable with labor, that is to say, with productive activity, as I have suggested elsewhere.[23] The unarticulated assumption that guides comments on the agrarian reform, therefore, is that Indians qua Indians could not have been the agents of a successful agrarian reform. The implication is that the reform should have been carried out by those who were already "prepared," and who were therefore not indigenous peasants, or by peasants who, once properly prepared, would no longer be, properly speaking, indigenous.

Death, Dependency, Chile, and Sendero Luminoso

Beyond the agrarian reform, the posters debate several other questions that are equally expressive of broader historical and contemporary issues. One recurrent theme is the idea that Velasco did not die of complications following the aneurism he suffered in 1973 but rather that he was assassinated. As josecarlpluto states, with sarcasm: "Aneurism? I didn't know lead was called aneurism" (video 2). Typically, posters argue that the United States, and sometimes more specifically the CIA, often in collaboration with the Chilean government, was responsible for Velasco's death. [I]van perez egoavil, for example, states: "aneurism . . . it was the Yankee sons of bitches under the cover of the CIA, the CIA killed Velasco and on top of that they sent him to the United States to kill him, damned liars . . . they shot him full of bullets filled with cyanide and sent him to die in the USA; bastards . . . people are easily fooled . . . the damned Yankees control the press" (video 2). [D]arwin huaylla macedo meanwhile frames the assassination of Velasco more squarely in the context of his attempts to recover land that had been lost to Chile during the War of the Pacific and to the US reaction to this project: "Peru was going to defeat Chile in a war to recover what they had stolen from us, like Arica and Tarapacá, but Velasco was betrayed by [Morales] Bermudez [*sic*] and then nothing happened and the American CIA killed him with a poisoned bullet to his right foot, giving him gangrene, and then he died; that's why the Yankees don't like revolutionaries who no longer pay royalties and then repress the poorer countries" (video 1). Finally, in one case, a poster links the death of Velasco to the more recent death of Hugo Chávez. According to Angel edition Walfa (I retain the original syntax): "Juan Velasco Alvarado because of the USA in a CIA intervention he was killed because he represented a threat helped by Chile too, as happened with Hugo Chavez, the USA always tries to subject [Latin] American countries for their own ends. The gringos killed Hugo Chavez with the Chentrails project, and [they killed] Juan Velasco Alvarado" (video 3). This comparison to a supposed assassination of Chávez clearly serves to frame the Velasco regime, and his reforms, in a more recent example of supposed anti-imperialism.

The idea that Velasco did not die from ill health but was assassinated is consistent with the idea that he was an Übermensch, as discussed above. A man with his "*huevos*" and who wore "*pantalones*" the way he did could not have been defeated by a simple disease. He had to have been killed. Moreover, he had to have been killed by an overwhelming force. That this force was the United States is logical not only because the United States was the most overwhelming force around but also because, as many posters stress, Velasco challenged and indeed undermined US imperialism. Elizabeth dj, for example, uses those very terms: "that coup and the takeover of the IPC [International Petroleum Company], was a coup against the empire, it was a transcendental act, we showed South America that we were not afraid of the government of the United States, of all their CIA agents, and you need balls to do that" (video 3). MIVAN AHMED makes a similar point: "HAAA HE KICKED THEM IN THOSE USA IMPERIALISTS IN THE ARSE IN LA BREA Y PARIÑAS THEY STOLE ALL OUR OIL IN ADDITION TO MINING COMPANIES AND OTHER AMERICAN COMPANIES . . . LONG LIVE VELASCO DAMN IT" (video 2). Jesus villanev aran, meanwhile, in addition to applauding the measures that were taken to address inequality in the countryside, stresses the regime's able management of the Cold War context to further Peru's interests: "I think this government had positive aspects such as the search for social equality[,] which was absent in the countryside at that time. The countryside was characterized by extreme social exclusion and by landlords who exploited [the peasantry. I]t was a nationalist government which stood up to US imperialism and sought to take advantage of the Cold War to further national objectives" (video 2).

These and many other comments (including references to Velasco's dealings with the Soviets), and the ubiquity of references to "soberanía" (sovereignty), suggest that for many posters, Velasco represents a moment or process when, as happened with peasants after the agrarian reform, Peru as a nation-state gained a degree of freedom.[24] This notion of freedom, or independence, is expressed in several comments that focus on the extent to which Velasco's economic reforms sought to reduce the external "dependence" of the Peruvian economy, particularly the economy's reliance on primary exports. This involved directly challenging the power of both foreign capital and the local elites allied to it, which controlled most of the Peruvian economy. Carlos P, for example, states: "It is not socialism that we must applaud Velasco for. It is rather that he tried to stop Peru being dependent on foreign capital" (video 2). Several posters agree that foreign capital and the local elites with which it was allied siphoned all the benefits from economic activity, leaving nothing for Peruvians. [P]eterocco1980, for example, writes: "Those foreign capitalists and national oligarchs did not pay a single miserable cent in taxes, that's why what Velasco did was so necessary[,] otherwise we Peruvian[s] would not have evolved as human beings" (video 1). Similarly, Perth2705 argues:

> Before most of the land belonged to foreign capitalists and national oligarchs, they argued that we were a world-leading agricultural nation but people never saw any benefit. Today many Peruvians own land and they have been able to send their children to school. Belaúnde was a great man but a poor president and he showed that in his two last governments . . . in the last we suffered very high inflation. Some say we would be better off [without the reforms initiated by Velasco] . . . I doubt it. (video 1)

At the same time that he challenged the power of foreign capital and of the national oligarchy, many posters contend, Velasco pushed through reforms that directly reduced Peru's dependent relation to First World economies by favoring the development of the internal market. [J]alagar, for example, recalls favorably the attempts made during the

Velasco regime to shift the Peruvian economy away from its dependence on primary exports and to develop a national industry: "I have to admit that in order to make a revolution Velasco had to have balls because he changed completely Peruvians' mentality and above all [he gave them] dignity. . . . Do you remember? With Velasco we had car assembly plants . . . Moraveco. . . . And now Peru has become a mere exporter of raw materials, oil, gas, and other minerals that have very low prices. . . . Peru could do with another revolution" (video 3). One poster, camino angosto evangelio, sees these reforms as having brought Peru back from the brink of collapse and, perhaps surprisingly, compares them favorably with the reforms of the Fujimori regime: "he strengthened the mining sector, oil, fishing, the foreigners would take things and not pay[;] before Velasco the people in the countryside were exploited by the landlords. Peru before Velasco was in ruins and he fixed it. In 1990 Fujimori arrives and also fixed Peru. The first time in 1970 it was Velasco, the second time Alberto Fujimori . . . thanks to both these men Peru changed" (video 2). The comparison with Fujimori may seem odd when we consider the diametrically opposed policies associated with each leader. However, it is less surprising when we remember that many see Fujimori, like Velasco, as a great leader with *huevos* and *pantalones*.

It is in comments that refer to Peru's relations with Chile that Velasco's role as a leader and as an Übermensch almost single-handedly capable of increasing Peru's standing in the world is expressed most clearly and vehemently. According to many posters, under Velasco, other countries in Latin America, and particularly Chile, began to respect Peru. As elprimero34 states: "Juan Velasco gave dignity back to Peru and to Peruvians, everyone respected us in South America, and Chile feared Velasco, but today they mock us and they do as they like with our country" (video 3). Several posters suggest that the rearmament the Velasco regime orchestrated was crucial to this new state of affairs. For example, LimaPorno argues—while also making reference to the current dispute over the two countries' maritime border at the International Court at The Hague—that "if it had not been for Velasco who strengthened our armed forces[,] Chile would have invaded us a second time . . . forget about The Hague" (video 2). The purchase of Soviet weapons is clearly remembered by several posters who are able to list the type of military hardware obtained by the Peruvian military at the time. As coc6969ful states: "VELASCO WAS GOING TO GET ARICA AND TARAPACA BACK AND NOT ONLY THAT HE WAS GOING

TO WIPE CHILE FROM THE MAP, WE HAD 55 STATE OF THE ART SU-22 FIGHTER-BOMBERS BOUGHT ESPECIALLY FOR THAT PURPOSE, WE HAD 500 T-55 TANKS BOUGHT FROM RUSSIA, WE HAD STATE OF THE ART SURFACE TO AIR MISSILES SUCH AS SHILKA AND ALSO SA-3 PECHORA, AND THAT'S THE SAME HARDWARE THAT WE SEE TO-DAY 35 YEARS LATER" (video 3). As the last sentence suggests, for this and for other posters, the military purchases that were made during the Velasco period become all the more relevant by the fact that since that time Peru has not updated its tanks or other weapons.

For many posters, the real reason Velasco was removed from power was that he planned to attack Chile and regain the provinces lost to Chile in the War of the Pacific: Arica and Tarapacá. This planned war, posters contend, did not sit well with the United States and, as a consequence, Velasco was the victim of a conspiracy against him. [W]endel delgado herrera states: "everything was ready to blow the Chileans to bits and get back Arica but a coup by [Morales] Bermudez [sic] and the USA screwed it all up" (video 3). Similarly, damian lucifer writes: "THAT'S WHAT I'M TALKING ABOUT!!!!! WE WOULD TAKE BACK WHAT IS OURS AT ANY COST. ARICA AND TARA-PACA WILL BE PERUVIAN ONCE MORE!!!!!! OUR GENERAL VELASCO HAD IT ALL PLANNED OUT BUT HE WAS SUR-ROUNDED BY TRAITORS WHO FINISHED HIM OFF, BUT HIS IDEALS ARE ALIVE IN PATRIOTS WHO WILL MAKE THEM A REALITY SOONER OR LATER.... LONG LIVE PERU DAMN IT!!!!!" (video 3).

Some posters claim direct experience of the aborted military campaign, such as ivanx1972, who was living in Tacna in 1974 and 1975 and studied at the local university. He recalls having been called to the front along with his friends: "it was time to take back Arica, Iquique and we even thought we would take what had once belonged to Bolivia, but [Morales] Bermudez [sic] betrayed us" (video 2). For posters such as fransdh, Velasco's decision to attack Chile was a product of his own personal experience of Chilean abuse in Peru: "as a child he saw how foreign companies took our resources without paying for them and exploited the Peruvian workers . . . when he kicked them out of the country he cried, he was emotional. He hated the Chileans who walked around Lima raping women and girls" (video 3). As this suggests, memories of the Velasco regime elicit further memories of Peru's conflicted relations with its southern neighbor that date back at least to the experience of military defeat in the War of the Pacific. These memories are shaped by a sense of national inferiority and a desire for revenge (*revanchisme*). This positive remembrance of Velasco homes in, not surprisingly, on his promise of national redress.

A final important issue that mobilizes memories of the Velasco government is the relation between the reforms implemented during the military regime and the rise of the Maoist insurgent group known as Sendero Luminoso (Shining Path).[25] Here, opinions again are divided. Several posters argue that the regime's reforms, and more specifically the agrarian reform, weakened the impact of the Shining Path insurgency. Wachy67, for example, suggests that thanks to the agrarian reform, the peasantry who gained ownership of the land felt they had something to lose from backing Shining Path. As a consequence, a potential war was averted: "Thanks to the incomplete agrarian reform, Sendero Luminoso did not have the support of the peasantry, who were poor but owned their land and [felt that they] had something to lose with the insurgency. If Sendero Luminoso had been confronted with landlords and exploited peasants, our country would have divided and experienced a civil war" (video 1). Others make a similar point. Clickeclick, for example, states: "with or without the agrarian reform the country was going to ruin, but what Velasco achieved was to reduce human casualties because [without the agrarian reform] the internal war would have been far bloodier" (video 1). For XM95K, similarly, the agrarian reform weakened the appeal of revolutionary groups: "if Velasco had not pushed that through then MIR, ELN, FIR, PCP and SL [all references to armed insurgent groups] would have started a revolution along with peasants and workers and Peru would have become communist. If you want to blame someone, blame the United States[,] which sent Velasco, Pinochet, and Videla to Latin America to stop the guerrillas. The reform was positive because otherwise we would still live in a feudal state in the twenty-first century" (video 2). Others, such as walberto chanca buque, suggest that if Velasco had not implemented the agrarian reform, it would have been implemented by more radical groups, including Sendero Luminoso, with far worse consequences: "What would [have] happened if the savages of Sendero Luminoso had implemented the agrarian reform? It is likely that many landlords of that time would have been hanged and murdered with their entire families or handed over to the revengeful peasants or suffered worse things yet. Thank GOD that the revolutionary government of Velasco implemented [the reform]. It was done legally and peacefully" (video 1).

By contrast, other posters argue that the Velasco period was the breeding ground for the rise of Sendero Luminoso. HELL77 makes this point categorically: "this coup d'etat was the historical process that propitiated terrorism in Peru" (video 2). So does campanita: "VELASCO YOU RAT, ROT IN HELL/YOU MADE PERU POORER AND YOU CREATED TERRORISM" (video 1). Posters suggest different links between Velasco and Sendero Luminoso. For Rolondrilo, the link is socialism, which was a common language and project to both movements: "the Velasco dictatorship was the inspiration for Sendero and the MRTA [Movimiento Revolucionario Túpac Amaru; Túpac Amaru Revolutionary Movement] . . . take power by a coup and claim that it is socialism" (video 2). Avantixsiempre offers a similar argument, but focuses more on the effects of socialist measures that created the conditions for the rise of Shining Path:

> things have to be assessed with regard to their outcomes, and what benefit did this country obtain from the socialist dictator? Only more inequality, misery, backwardness; the poor from the Andes migrated en masse to Lima because the agrarian reform was a complete failure because it followed the leftwing recipe of "justice making" by taking from those who have the most to give to the poor, all of this created the perfect context in which the most savage extremist groups like Sendero could grow and emerge. (video 2)

This is also the argument put forward by Lobito30000, although he or she focuses more squarely on the excessive spending practices of the regime:

> what a stupid general. Although it was [a] social achievement, the agrarian reform did not have the expected result, there was no transfer plan. The peasants lacked [the] capacity to undertake production and the agrarian sector stagnated. Velasco was escalating the arms race. He spent all the money on tanks and planes and in the end he decided against an attack [on] Chile. This excessive expenditure generated the external debt, the crisis of the 1980s, and the worst thing is that it opened the door to terrorism. (video 1)

These divergent interpretations of the links between the Velasco regime and the rise of Shining Path reflect, though they do not neatly map onto, the different ways in which the internal armed conflict is itself remembered. As I have suggested elsewhere, two narratives of the conflict dominate public discussion.[26] The first is a narrative associated with a "memory of salvation," put forward by Fujimori and his supporters, which frames the rise of Shining Path primarily and sometimes exclusively in terms of the decisions made by an extreme and violent insurgent movement, decisions consistent with an equally violent and extreme ideology that is anathema to Peruvian society. The second narrative, associated with the human rights community in Peru and more specifically with the final report of the Truth and Reconciliation Commission (2003), frames the rise of Shining Path in a sociohistorical analysis that emphasizes the ways in which entrenched and intersecting inequalities, especially in the highlands where Velasco's agrarian reform was implemented, were reflected in and reproduced by the internal armed conflict (while recognizing the responsibility of armed actors— Shining Path first and foremost—for the violence). Although some posters reproduce the idea that violence was intrinsic to left-wing ideologies shared by Velasco and Shining Path, the extent to which the agrarian reform weakened or sharpened those inequalities, and therefore increased or decreased the likelihood of violence, is ultimately the main question that different posters return to in order to assess the link between the Velasco regime and the internal armed conflict. In this way, memories of the Velasco regime and memories of the internal armed conflict are mobilized to explain the other process.

Conclusions

The past is the past. But how we make sense of the past and what meaning it has for us is always subject to contestation and change. Individuals and groups remember and forget the past selectively. They mobilize specific memories for particular purposes. The video *producers* are memory entrepreneurs: they seek to mobilize, through their YouTube videos, particular memories of the Velasco regime. Their interventions are intended to shape both how the past is remembered and how the present is interpreted. They also seek to shape expectations of the future.[27] But the posters of comments on the videos are also memory entrepreneurs. Through their interventions in the debates that the videos enable and promote, they, too, attempt to influence how the past is remembered and how the present and future are envisioned. The negative memories of the Velasco regime serve to mobilize first and foremost a critique of statism and, by extension, of the left. They are a critique of the critique of neoliberalism. Velasco is a lesson to be learned, an experiment never to be repeated. Velasco, these mobilized memories suggest, is an example in the past of a future in which the current model of development in Peru is altered. In some ways, these negative memories of Velasco are a particularly Peruvian version of the injunction that came to characterize postdictatorship processes in the Southern Cone: "Nunca más" (Never again). In Peru, however, "nunca más" refers not to dictatorship or human rights abuses but to state-led development.

The more positive memories of the Velasco regime point to what many see as the key issues that Peruvians face today. Several posters express nostalgia for a period when (military) order reigned. Like Luis754301, many remember the military regime as a time when political corruption did not exist: "HOW WE MISS THOSE SOLDIERS, WHO FREED US FROM THE ABUSES OF CORRUPT POLITICIANS, THE MILITARY TODAY ARE A BUNCH OF SCARED MEDIOCRE COWARDS AND TRAITORS WHO SERVE THE POLITICIANS" (video 2). Others, like Leo horacio, remember the military regime as a time when military service instilled proper values in the young: "we no longer have military service and as a consequence we have thieves, drug addicts, prostitution in the streets, sons who kill their fathers or rape their mothers, now killing is common among gangs" (video 2). But, more generally, as we have seen, the positive memories of the Velasco period are associated with terms like "dignity," "sovereignty" (economic and political), "independence," "*huevos*," and "*pantalones*." These terms arguably express collective aspirations not only for order but also for social justice, greater social equity, a sense of community, and the hope that Peru can gain a more elevated position in the world (not least vis-à-vis Chile). Although he did not succeed, many believe that this is what Velasco strove for. This is why, almost half a century after the coup of 1968, many Peruvians remember Velasco fondly.

Notes

1. During the 2006 and 2011 elections, both those who supported Humala and those who opposed him raised the specter of Velasco (and of course Hugo Chávez, particularly in 2006) to either attack or praise the electoral candidate who would later become president. In 2011, for example, right-wing news-

papers like *El Comercio* noted that Humala's government plan, "La gran transformación," praised the reforms introduced by the RGAF. See "Humala no ha cambiado: Su plan de gobierno es estatista y autoritario," *El Comercio*, March 25, 2011. Supporters of Humala, by contrast, viewed the association of the two leaders in a more positive light, with some campaign posters (probably not officially sanctioned by Humala, who in 2011, in contrast to 2006, sought to present a much more moderate image) portraying Humala and Velasco together. See http://www.netjoven.pe/actualidad/61844/Ollanta-Humala-y-Velasco-juntos -en-propaganda-de-Gana-Peru-en-Huaura.html. In the 2016 elections, the specter of Velasco reappeared in the debates that shaped the electoral process, particularly in the context of the rise of a left-wing movement, the Frente Amplio, and also as a consequence of candidacy of Velasco's son, Javier Velasco González, which did not prosper. See http://larepublica.pe/politica/715781 -elecciones-2016-hijo-de-velasco-quiere-ser-presidente-y-propone-drasticas -politicas. Unless otherwise noted, all translations in this chapter are my own.

2. Gonzalo Portocarrero, "Memorias del Velasquismo," in *Batallas por la memoria: Antagonismos de la promesa peruana*, ed. María Esther Hamann, Santiago López Maguiña, Gonzalo Portocarrero Maisch, and Victor Vich (Lima: Red para el Desarrollo de las Ciencias Sociales en el Perú, 2003), 229.

3. Enrique Mayer, *Ugly Stories of the Peruvian Agrarian Reform* (Durham, NC: Duke University Press, 2009).

4. Paulo Drinot, "Website of Memory: The War of the Pacific (1879–1884) in the Global Age of YouTube," *Memory Studies* 4, no. 4 (2011): 370–385; Elizabeth Jelin, *Los trabajos de la memoria* (Buenos Aires: Siglo XXI, 2002).

5. See, among others, Pierre Nora, "Between Memory and History: Les Lieux de Mémoire," *Representations* 26 (Spring 1989): 7–24; Elizabeth Jelin and Victoria Langland, eds., *Monumentos, memoriales y marcas territoriales* (Buenos Aires: Siglo XXI, 2003).

6. As Jelin suggests, "One does not remember on one's own, but rather with the help of the memories of others and with shared cultural codes, even when memories are personal and unique." Jelin, *Los trabajos de la memoria*, 20. On "vehicles of memory," see Jelin, *Los trabajos de la memoria*, 37. On "technologies of memory," see Marita Sturken, "Memory, Consumerism and Media: Reflections on the Emergence of the Field," *Memory Studies* 1, no. 1 (2008): 74.

7. Again, as Jelin notes, "The past that is remembered and forgotten is activated in the present and with a view to future expectations." Jelin, *Los trabajos de la memoria*, 18.

8. On the concepts of "produser" and "produsage," see Axel Bruns, *Blogs, Wikipedia, Second Life, and Beyond* (Oxford: Peter Lang, 2008).

9. https://www.youtube.com/watch?v=6oyAC2kDx70. This is the first part of five of the whole speech. It is identified in the text as (video 1). The others are also available on YouTube.

10. See http://www.marxists.org/espanol/tematica/agro/peru/velasco1969 .htm.

11. https://www.youtube.com/watch?v=Rz2uTq3SkWs. Identified in the text as (video 2).

12. See http://willax.tv/acerca-de-nosotros [URL no longer active].

13. http://www.youtube.com/watch?v=QJrmcaKaUVY. Identified in the text as (video 3).

14. I have identified the video to which each comment is attached by adding (video 1), (video 2), or (video 3) after each quotation.

15. I have kept the original spelling of all the tags or nicknames used by comment posters, including capitalization or lack thereof and some obvious spelling errors of well-known words or names such as "Velazco" for "Velasco."

16. Sturken, "Memory, Consumerism and Media," 74.

17. Jan Assmann and John Czaplicka, "Collective Memory and Cultural Identity," *New German Critique* 65 (1995): 125–133.

18. Marianne Hirsch, *Family Frames: Photography, Narrative and Postmemory* (Cambridge, MA: Harvard University Press, 1997).

19. Alison Landsberg, *Prosthetic Memory: The Transformation of American Remembrance in the Age of Mass Culture* (New York: Columbia University Press, 2004).

20. Interestingly, this same poster concedes that not all of Velasco's policies were wrong: "But we have to admit that he did a lot on the social front. He put those landlords and despot planters in their place. That was fair, it seems to me. On the other hand, Peru was respected militarily speaking; neither Chile nor any other country dared to mock us. I remember phrases like 'we will spend new year's eve in Santiago' but as I say below on the economic front it was criminal!!!" (video 1).

21. According to shilicaso: "J.Velasco will always be remembered just like Tupac Amaru, he was a soldier who never looked the other way in exchange for a wad of money, he was a *provinciano* [from one of the provinces, i.e., not from Lima] with big balls" (video 3).

22. Cerefore, for example, accuses Morales Bermúdez of being not only a *"maricón"* (fag) but also a Chilean bootlicker (*chupamedias chileno*) (video 3). For 99026478, Morales Bermúdez was responsible for halting a positive transformation in a whole range of social and cultural practices that Velasco had initiated: "That's how it was damn it!!! We sang the national anthem; we studied the history of Peru during the whole school year; we had books on the history of Peru; children were fed at school; the peasants obtained their rights! Damn it! A moment of glory for Peru, a moment when Peru could have changed if it had not been for the *puto* Morales Bermúdez" (video 3).

23. See Paulo Drinot, *The Allure of Labor: Workers, Race, and the Making of the Peruvian State* (Durham, NC: Duke University Press, 2011).

24. It is worth noting that this assessment is broadly consistent with recent research on Peru's foreign relations during this period. See Richard J. Walter, *Peru and the United States, 1960–1975: How Their Ambassadors Managed Foreign Relations in a Turbulent Era* (University Park: Penn State University Press, 2010).

25. This is an issue that has received some scholarly discussion. See, among others, the concluding sections of Mayer, *Ugly Stories of the Peruvian Agrarian Reform*; Linda J. Seligmann, *Between Reform and Revolution: Political Struggles in the Peruvian Andes, 1969–1991* (Stanford: Stanford University Press, 1995); and

Florencia E. Mallon, "Chronicle of a Path Foretold? Velasco's Revolution, Vanguardia Revolucionaria, and 'Shining Omens' in the Indigenous Communities of Andahuaylas," in *Shining and Other Paths: War and Society in Peru, 1980–1995,* ed. Steve Stern (Durham, NC: Duke University Press, 1998), 84–117.

26. See Paulo Drinot, "For Whom the Eye Cries: Memory, Monumentality, and the Ontologies of Violence in Peru," *Journal of Latin American Cultural Studies* 18, no. 1 (2009): 15–32.

27. On "memory entrepreneurs," see Jelin, *Los trabajos de la memoria,* passim.

PART II

TEACHERS, PEASANTS, GENERALS: MILITARY NATIONALISM AND ITS AGENTS

CHAPTER 5

Politicizing Education: The 1972 Reform in Peru

PATRICIA OLIART

Summing up, the end goal of education is the free and thoroughly developed individual, capable of acting creatively in a truly independent and prosperous nation, harmoniously integrated to the international community, free of marginalization and oppression. Therefore, the new education policy should be liberating, and at the same time, inward looking, able to raise profound awareness and commitment to confront and transform our society.[1]

In 1969, the Revolutionary Government of the Armed Forces (RGAF) appointed more than one hundred specialists to form the Comisión de la Reforma de la Educación (CRE; Education Reform Commission). The briefing they received from the Comité de Asesoramiento de la Presidencia (COAP; Presidential Advisory Board) was to work on a reform project that would modernize the education system in Peru, in tune with the social and economic changes pursued by the military regime.[2] The CRE included philosophers, social scientists, psychologists, writers, and pedagogues. A few specialists who had participated in a process of important changes in the education system led by General Mendoza during the Manuel Odría regime (1948–1956) were also part of it.[3] The result of this unprecedented effort was the publication of the *Reforma de la educación peruana: Informe general* (hereafter *Informe general*),[4] a best-seller at street kiosks at the time, also known colloquially as the *Blue Book* (*Libro azul*). The analysis and recommendations provided by this report closely informed Education Reform Law 19326, finally promulgated in March 1972.

Even though the CRE was dissolved shortly before the publication of the *Informe general*, many of its members joined the Ministry of Education and other relevant institutions to promote the implementation of the law.[5] Unlike the unscholarly and improvised nature of other reforms, the education reform project was the result of an exceptional collaboration between the military and a highly interdisciplinary group of experts, who were aware of and participants in the academic and political critique of pedagogy and the school system taking place in Europe, the United States, and Latin America.[6] In many ways, the *Informe general* and the text of Education Reform Law 19326 were innovative and radical by the standards of the time. In fact, some of their guiding ideas are still considered relevant for examining education projects in Peru and elsewhere. In José Rivero's words, the final formulation of the reform law is "even now, regarded by experts and international education agencies as one of the attempts at a most original and creative educational transformation in developing countries."[7]

This regard for the pioneering nature of the project may explain why, unlike the fate of most public figures linked to the Velasco regime, and in spite of the reform's failure, members of the CRE did not lose prestige or legitimacy in the education community in Peru after the fall of the RGAF. They remained important voices for public opinion for decades and played a crucial role in the formulation of a consensus-based educational project in 2006.

However, the short-lived education reform showed modest results,[8] and academic analyses of the Velasco regime only rarely include this reform. One exception is Abraham Lowenthal's compilation,[9] in which Robert S. Drysdale and Robert G. Myers's lucid contribution, written while the reform was under way, sharply identified both the flaws and the main tensions the reform was facing, and predicted it would be politically and technically unsustainable.[10] Later studies have focused on specific aspects of the education reform in different fields; for example, the very active use that the RGAF made of the school system and state-run cultural institutions for the dissemination of an anti-imperialist version of nationalism.[11] The pioneering role of the RGAF in the official recognition of Quechua as a national language and the establishment of bilingual education policies in the context of the education reform have been used as classic examples when studying the relationship between the state and indigenous peoples in twentieth-century Peru.[12] The social tensions sparked by the implementation of the reform[13] and the particularly difficult relationship with the teachers union have also received attention when studying this period.[14]

This chapter considers the legacy of the education reform project in contemporary Peru. After presenting the main political objectives of the reform and the way they were translated for their implementation in the school system and the wider society until 1975, the following pages show how, in spite of its controversial application and the aggressive process of dismantling it that came after the Velasco regime, conspicuous members of the reform commission and their ideas have maintained prestige, legitimacy, and currency among the Peruvian intellectual community interested in education even to the present day. As Luis Pásara and José Matos Mar pointed out at the time, the RGAF irreversibly politicized the debate about education in Peru.[15] My research suggests that the education reform's influence played an unsung role in the way the World Bank–led education reform was "neutralized" or shaped by the education community in Peru in the 1990s. In spite of the shortcomings and controversial implementation of the education reform of 1972, revisiting its legacy is timely in the current context of intense global debates in the fields of education and development, pedagogy, and the politics of education. The failure of the World Bank Education Reform implemented in Latin America in the 1990s[16] has brought back debates that were prominent in the 1972 Peruvian education reform. Issues such as the role of formal education in forging citizenship or the role of the school curriculum in the dissemination of knowledge that is relevant for the future of a sovereign nation are part of important debates in Brazil, Argentina, Uruguay, Bolivia, Ecuador, and Venezuela.[17] As we shall see in the following pages, even the Peruvian teachers union, which was firmly opposed to the Velasco Alvarado regime and the reform at the time, has reconsidered its evaluation of the education reform project of 1972 and formulated a different appreciation of the project in recent public statements.

The Education System under Scrutiny

The elaboration of the RGAF education reform project occurred at a time when a second wave of deep criticism of school systems and pedagogy was taking place in Europe and the United States.[18] Concurrently in Latin America and in several African countries that had recently gained independence, discussions about the political nature of state-run education projects were intense and very productive, linking them to national liberation political agendas.[19] The issues considered in those formulations ranged from the role of the education system in the creation of a sovereign national identity to the relationship between labor and academic knowledge and to equal access to education for all groups of society as a secure path to full citizenship. All of these ideas were included in the 1972 Education Law 19326 in Peru.

The first wave of criticism aimed at the school as an institution started in Europe and the United States in the 1930s, when it became evident that the democratic promise of public, compulsory schooling was not being accomplished, as it was failing the working classes and becoming yet another tool for capitalist social reproduction.[20] Those were the years when alternative pedagogies better suited for the working classes marshaled some education reform movements in the United States and Europe and enjoyed support and legitimacy mainly through the development of John Dewey's ideas (interestingly, they were brought back in the late 1960s and 1970s).[21] The global growth of the school system after the Second World War led to the professionalization of the teaching career; education and pedagogy developed as higher-education subjects, as did the sociology of education, and developmental psychology. This allowed for the development of postgraduate studies in education in the 1960s, particularly in Europe and the United States, where criticism of pedagogy and the school system's social role was intense.[22]

Emerging critical interpretations of education and schooling in the 1960s stated that because of capitalism, democracy had retracted its commitment to social justice.[23] On both sides of the Atlantic, influential analyses made evident the role of schools in supporting capitalism and in guaranteeing the reproduction of social inequalities.[24] Pierre Bourdieu denounced the idea that schools could simply be considered an effective space for advancing the democratization of society. When higher levels of schooling become widely accessible, the large-scale qualifications it provides lose their value. This leads the economically and culturally powerful groups to increase their investment in their children's education in order to protect the expected significant gap in the market opportunities for their children.[25] Thus is unveiled the contradictory nature of the school system: along with creating opportunities for social mobility, it is also used by the middle classes and emerging groups as an important mechanism for social differentiation.[26]

A few years before those publications came out, Giorgio Alberti and Julio Cotler led a series of studies in Peru on the impact of education in rural areas in the 1960s.[27] Their nuanced interpretation of the relationship between education and social change went beyond denouncing the role of education in reproducing the oligarchic regime. Theirs was the first study, among many others to follow, showing how the growth of the education system, evident in the 1960s in Peru, had been the result of a massive and very proactive demand for this service from the most remote rural communities to urban marginal populations, and how it was an important element to consider in the analysis of the fracture of the oligarchic regime.[28]

In fact, the social and political crisis of the oligarchic regime had been accompanied by a vigorous growth of the education system, whose advocates pushed for a consistent increase of almost 10 percent of the national budget for education from 1955 to 1965.[29] The electoral campaign of 1956 reflected how important the growth of the education system was, when most contending political forces promised the creation of teacher colleges for their provinces.[30] In 1958, President Manuel Pardo passed Law 12997, which encouraged communities to build their own schools. It stated that once the school had been built, they could ask the Ministry of Education to provide both teachers and official acreditation. President Fernando Belaúnde Terry (1963–1968) continued support for this law by donating first the drawings for a simple school design, and once it was built, a bronze plaque with the inscription "Made by the People."[31]

The 1970 *Informe general* acknowledged the recent growth of the education system but characterized it as inefficient and a failure to the hopes invested in it by the communities who had fostered the creation of schools, teacher training colleges, and regional state-funded universities. In their analysis, the authors of the report concluded that facts such as the inability of the system to keep rural students in primary school for more than three years had led the school system to "produce more illiterate people than [it] received."[32] For the education reformers, the Peruvian education system had failed the country because it was not guided by national interests. It was not simply a problem of inefficient allocation and use of resources or poor results. It was a matter of political orientation: "[F]oreign social models have been applied systematically, disseminating authority and subordination patterns to the benefit of the dominant groups or hegemonic powers of the world."[33]

Education for Social Change

Juan Martín Sánchez has studied the discursive practices of Velasquismo and pointed out that the presentation of each of the reforms began with a critical assessment of the previous situation in the area of intervention, against which the relevant reform was presented as the result of an independent and sovereign choice that would follow the necessary steps to break with the colonial past that had not been overcome after independence from Spain.[34] Thus, the RGAF justified their reforms beginning with the denunciation of the ravages of capitalism in the country, and the failure of developmental strategies promoting modernity and progress. Such strategies were considered irrelevant for the unavoidable task of transforming the dominant structures of society and achieving liberation from imperialism. In stark contrast with *developmentalism* at the time, which envisioned the overcoming of poverty through the gradual modernization of societies, the RGAF associated development with liberation from a foreign design for the future of the country.[35] Following this conceptual and discursive demarcation that sought to break with the past, each reform arose as the right formulation for the transformations the RGAF wanted to achieve.

The *Informe general* followed the same pattern, but it was not written by the RGAF. The president of the CRE was Emilio Barrantes, a former schoolteacher and APRA militant who had been involved with important changes in the education system during the government of José Luis Bustamante y Rivero (1945–1948). In turn, Barrantes named the philosopher, journalist, and university professor Augusto Salazar Bondy vice-chair of the reform team. Barrantes's writings clearly demonstrate a keen interest in connecting the reform project with the history of the school system in Peru within the context of the growth of schooling in the world. He wanted to combine the reformist innovative spirit with previous valuable contributions and experiences that had been abandoned by the state. Barrantes was very keen on promoting the dynamic integration of the latest schools of thought in education and pedagogy in the world into the reform project.[36] The educational psychologist Carmen Lora took part in the group of specialists, formulating a pioneering program for preschool education. She had just arrived from Belgium after finishing a master's degree in developmental psychology and was swiftly absorbed by the vibrant atmosphere and stimulating challenges posed to the working group led by Carlos Castillo Ríos. One main task was to bring awareness about the integral nature of school education for all levels, preschool through high school, not just for young children: "We innovated the approach to education in many important ways that are still relevant: the need to understand education linked to child development; the awareness of Piaget's contributions to psychology and pedagogy; the need to develop a view of state-funded attention to children that integrated nutrition, health, justice, and education. You could feel that in all areas of work there was an awareness about what was going on internationally and that, intellectually, aims were very high."[37]

The production of the *Informe general* was a collaborative endeavor. Each area of education (i.e., preschool, primary school, secondary school, adult education) had groups of specialists analyzing relevant issues and then sending their conclusions to the CRE, where the main writers were Augusto Salazar Bondy, Carlos Delgado, Walter Peñaloza, and Leopoldo Chiappo.[38] The predominant imprint of Augusto Salazar Bondy is clear, however, from the front pages of the text of the *Informe general*. He became a public advocate of the reform and used his academic writing and his newspaper columns in *Expreso*, a daily that had been expropriated by the military regime, as a platform from which to stress the sense of urgency for the reform. He presented the education system as a major factor in the structures of domination and in the underdevelopment of the country, and, conversely, as an important space for the necessary transformations to take place.

The *Informe general* describes the Peruvian education system as elitist, alienating, dependent, and inefficient. In tune with the critique of the role of education systems under capitalism, it denounces the fallacy of the ideological neutrality of schooling. Furthermore, the report stresses that the education system needed to assume a specific ideological orientation in order to effectively contribute to an independent national development. Therefore, education policy and the actions of the revolutionary regime had to be linked to the major changes taking place in society. When General Velasco referred to the ongoing work of the CRE, he said: "Only an effective, profound, and permanent transformation of Peruvian education will ensure the success and continuity of the other structural reforms of the revolution. Hence, this education reform, perhaps the more complex but also the most important of all, constitutes an essential need for the development of Peru, the central objective of our revolution."[39] His words closely resonate with those of Salazar Bondy, writing about domination in Peru: "No effective social transformation will take place, nor will we be able to establish a new national social order capable of overcoming the chronic evils of underdevelopment, if we do not deeply transform the education system, in parallel with the other social and economic reforms. These seek to cancel the bonds of internal and external domination and eliminate the dichotomy concentration-marginalization that affects the distribution of power and property in Peru."[40]

The *Informe general* proclaimed that what the country needed was an education that encouraged personal and national independence, "the spirit of a conscious but unwavering struggle against injustice and oppression, the zeal to affirm and enhance the truly positive achievements of the Peruvian nation."[41] Education, then, acquired a meaning that went beyond schooling. The cultural alienation resulting from imperialist domination needed changing, and the envisioned way to establish the values of the new society was to take control of the education system and other official channels for the dissemination of ideas to foster cultural and political transformation. Thus, education reform and control over the media became crucial means to transform Peruvian society. People and institutions involved in the process would all become vehicles for providing opportunities to raise awareness and educate, to bring "a message" aimed at developing greater knowledge, to liberate people from cultural domination, and to become allies of the transformations taking place.

The substantial cultural intervention of the revolution in society included the creation of the National Tele-education Institute (Instituto Nacional de Tele-educación; INTE) to provide support services to the education reform through the production of films, radio shows, and television programs. Following the expropriation of the press, the newspaper *Expreso* made education one of its main areas of focus. On television, Channel 7 and a few radio stations in the country took an active part in a campaign that sought to involve the whole population in education reform. The RGAF created the National Culture Institute (Instituto Nacional de Cultura; INC), a state agency in charge of protecting the national cultural heritage and of sponsoring cultural institutions and activities in the country. The similarities between these guidelines and the relevant sections of the General Resolution of the Cultural Congress held in Havana in 1968 are striking.[42] It states that given that "foreign oppressors use every resource in their power to substitute local cultural values," a revolution in power should take control of the mass media and put them at the service of the revolution. "Mass media must inform, educate, guide and unify the entire people. They must help the great masses to understand the world that surrounds them and to create a revolutionary culture."[43]

In a manner similar to the cultural policies implemented in Cuba and the Eastern European Socialist Bloc during the Cold War, the RGAF sponsored the creation of state-funded schools and companies for the arts (music, theater, and dance), giving the artists involved in these initiatives the opportunity to work for the state and contribute to the creation and development of a greater appreciation of national culture within and outside the country. Some important measures included the creation of the National Folklore Company, directed by Victoria Santa Cruz, and of the National Popular Theatre, directed by Alonso Alegría, and the inclusion of the Popular Song Workshop led by Celso Garrido Lecca at the National School of Music, to name a few.

To guarantee an audience for these new companies, Lima saw the creation of modern open-air stages and the refurbishment of various cultural venues. In the rest of the country, an interesting boost to the local tourism industry took place, with the development of state-run "Tourist Hotels" and a national campaign under the slogan "Discover Peru First," as Mark Rice discusses elsewhere in this volume. In this context of affirmation and support for Peruvian culture, many artistic events in the country found a historic opportunity to win legitimacy and recognition not only in the capital but also in other regions. Annual events, such as Inkarrí, promoted the economic and cultural integration of the different regions through agricultural fairs and folk performances linked to peasants' organizations.[44]

All of these platforms were used to carry out the *tarea concientizadora* (consciousness-raising task) necessary to fulfill the revolutionary transformations with the support of the population. The agenda for the *concientización* was clearly laid out in the *Informe general*. It included explanations of the historical and social problems of underdeveloped countries, the requirements and benefits of structural changes pursued by the RGAF's development model, the core values of the Peruvian nation, the role of Peru in the Third World, and the image and meaning of the new human society that should emerge from the revolutionary changes. It also included reminders about the importance of community participation in the development effort and the benefits of practices to preserve health, such as improvements in nutrition levels and housing in order to increase productivity at work.[45]

In their quest to raise social awareness and educate the population on the revolutionary values, reformers attributed a very important role to the classroom. The reform required not just an understanding of the historical, social, and political flaws of the school system to promote democratic access to citizenship; it was also important to revolutionize pedagogy in the classroom and get students involved in the process. The rationale for fostering high levels of personal and community involvement in the implementation of the reforms was inspired in ideas about liberation stemming from Paulo Freire's book *Pedagogy of the Oppressed*.[46] According to Freire, liberation is a collective endeavor and is the result of a process of education in which reflection and action must be combined to achieve independence "from the inside" of individuals, from the consciousness of their situation in the world.[47] "*Concientización*," the Freireian word translated by bell hooks as social awareness and commitment,[48] had to be addressed not only through the inclusion of new subjects in the curriculum, but also by the dissemination of a critical agenda using all the outlets over which the state had control. Unlike other experiences where political goals were linked to education reforms but lacked a strategy to transform pedagogy and the curriculum,[49] the education reform project in Peru had innovative ideas in both areas.

Changing the Shape and Content of Education

At the time of the educational reform, and occurring alongside political criticism of the education system, ideas and experiences suggesting the new role that schools could play in educating a generation of citizens striving to change the world emerged in Europe and the United States.[50] In that context, the development of critical pedagogy attributed great importance to the role teachers could play in any change to be implemented in education because of their absolute control of the classroom. It was important to reflect on how to change power relations in the classroom so that a productive experience of freedom, respect, and personal and collective responsibility could be created.[51] Following this quest, in the 1970s and early 1980s, innovative formulations inspired different educational experiments in Europe and some communities in the United States, which developed under severe scrutiny and criticism and yielded very mixed results. Those were the decades for the creation of alternative education schools.[52]

An important project of Salazar Bondy's was to bridge the separation between schoolwork and enjoyment that capitalism entails. He criticized the traditional education culture for not teaching young people to enjoy what they do in the classroom. Thus, and considering that as humans we express our creative essence in labor, education should not be reduced to the passive reception of teaching, but offer opportunities for creativity and discovery through personal and group work. Following these criteria, students were put in groups; subjects were rearranged, emphasizing similarities and connections between them; the role of research according to students' interests was promoted; and the curriculum was discussed and reshaped, taking into account its relevance to the reality of the students. The justification for those changes was that any knowledge taught without the voluntary participation of students represented a form of alienated labor that curtailed the harmonic development of the individual.

Another concern for Salazar Bondy was the separation between general and technical education, which reinforced social class divisions and unequal access to universal knowledge. At the same time, it denied students in either type of schooling the chance to develop their potential in the skills not considered in their area of education. Thus, both types of education were integrated, and a vocational higher education pathway was created—the Higher Education Professional Schools (Escuelas Superiores de Educación Profesional; ESEP)—for those students not interested in pursuing university studies. These schools featured six to eight semesters of training after basic education and provided professional degrees in unconventional careers.

Among the curricular changes, and mirroring what was going on in Europe and the United States at the time, the reformers' criticism of the lack of integrated knowledge in the curriculum resulted in the combining of history, geography, and what was formerly known as civic education into a single subject named *ciencias histórico-sociales* (sociohistorical sciences). This subject became a major focus of the work with in-service teachers, as it was intended to contribute to the formation of a new type of student. It had to serve the purpose of providing or enabling an understanding of Peruvian society and history that "unmasked social conflict, the violence, suffering, and struggles of the Peruvian peoples, to instill the spirit of rebelliousness against all forms of discrimination and prejudice."[53]

The representation of Peruvians in school textbooks for primary and secondary education changed. Images of workers, peasants, and people of various regions of Peru were included to represent the family in primary school textbooks, while the oligarchy appeared as "the cultural other," a social group alien to the interests of the country and the majority.[54] The predominant visual and narrative representation of the Spanish Conquest and colonization was one of a violent and predatory process.[55] Finally, a clear sense of place, of belonging to a local or regional history and the country, made teachers the main articulators and instigators of the *amor a lo nuestro* (love for what is ours).[56]

In pursuit of the objectives of eliminating all types of discrimination in the school system and fostering respect for the rights and opportunities of all the disenfranchised or discriminated against, Education Reform Law 19326 granted women access to all kinds of training and leadership posts within the education system. Helen Orvig, a Norwegian feminist activist and Salazar Bondy's wife, drafted Article 11 of the law upon his request. Apart from denouncing the situation of marginalization of women, which was drastically cut in the final version, it also contained provisions for the creation of an inter-sector commission formed by the Ministries of Education, Labor, Health, and Transport, together with SINAMOS, with the mandate of protecting women's rights and fostering their participation in the revolutionary process across the country.[57]

Tensions and Confrontations around the Reform

The aspiration that Salazar Bondy made explicit in his writings was that *peruanidad* (Peruvianness) should be a forward-looking, integrative synthesis of all cultures. He openly disagreed with those who defended one culture above others as being "more" representative of Peru. For Salazar Bondy, Peruvian society should be modern and Western but with its own identity resulting from the combination of all components of the nation. To him, no Peruvian citizen should be excluded because of his or her ethnicity, cultural background, or socioeconomic status. Stepping aside from the dominant discourse in the West during the Cold War, which linked political freedom to the existence of democratically elected regimes, the Peruvian education reformers linked personal freedom to liberation from oppression and from lack of representation: "The new man, the new society, the new culture, may not emerge in Peru until the legions missing from the guiding decisions of Peruvian life are incorporated as a free and creative force in the nation-building process."[58]

The education reform was fraught with the ambiguities of a modernizing project and advanced objectives that now would be considered Eurocentric. On the one hand, the Education Reform Law acknowledged the multilingual situation in Peru, noting that schools "should use the vernacular language when necessary," with teachers being able to use the students' mother tongue in both directions. It also stated that at least 30 percent of the school curriculum should be dedicated to promoting the appreciation of different cultures and languages of the country.[59] On the other hand, some of the statements in the *Informe general* lack a sense of understanding and respect toward the particularities of indigenous cultures. The use of indigenous languages in schools was merely a tool for improving literacy rates following a United Nations recommendation from 1953, which considered them necessary only in the first two years of school. At the same time, getting rid of the "magical and naive visions" of the indigenous Peruvians appears to be instrumental in making Peru a modern, cosmopolitan nation.[60]

One of the major achievements of the reform was the reduction of illiteracy from 27 to 2 percent.[61] It also increased the recruitment of children of school age in all three regions. The state presence in rural areas was, for the first time, the result of a coordinated effort between several ministries, and rural schools were at the center of the experiment.[62] In order to grant access to education to every child of school age, the reform attempted to implement a flexible school calendar at intermediate and local levels to suit particular characteristics, namely the rainy seasons and the agricultural calendar. The Graduate Civil Service (Servicio Civil de Graduandos; SECIGRA) became a mandatory part of university education to ensure that new graduates would reach remote areas of the country but also to enthuse a greater commitment to the development of the nation among young professionals of different disciplines by reaching communities that otherwise would not have access to their services.

The reform not only focused on repairing injustice in education at the lower echelons of society; it also opened up a battlefront with the urban middle classes. To comply with the aim of liberating the school of its role as "an instrument of cultural imposition," Law 19326 imposed some regulations for private schools that created great controversy. The reform targeted a group of bilingual schools originally created to cater to an international body of students who spoke English, French, or German as their primary language, but which were in great demand among the local middle and upper classes. Teachers were hired abroad, the curriculum was in line with the education curriculum of the sponsoring countries, the headmaster was often not Peruvian, and certain subjects were taught entirely in the relevant language. The reform banned the use of English in nursery schools. Foreign languages were to be taught only after first grade and as a separate subject. Schools run by foreign bodies were required to have a Peruvian headmaster.

The documentation needed to obtain official approval to open a new private school required the promoters of the school to declare their commitment to join the struggle against social discrimination. Private schools were required to grant scholarships to 10 percent of the student body and to establish a system of tuition payment to suit a range of family incomes. Finally, a nationwide common school uniform was introduced:[63] "The implementation of the single uniform model for use by all Peruvian children also serves to express through external appearance the determined will of the government to give equal treatment to all Peruvians according to the demands of people's dignity and the desire to promote rapprochement and understanding of all learners."[64]

Parents associations of private schools in Lima, Arequipa, and Trujillo found some of these measures too radical and unacceptable.[65] The reform also became a controversial issue for the Religious Schools Sports Association (Asociación Deportiva de Colegios Religiosos; ADECORE). Some religious orders, such as the Jesuits and the Dominicans, supported the reform and its egalitarian aims with great enthusiasm, as it coincided with the expanding influence of liberation theology among them. Others were very concerned about the impact of such measures on the families they catered to.[66] Another area of discursive opposition and practical resistance to the reform among urban and rural middle classes was the demand for participation. The slogan used by the regime to foster the reform was "Education, Everybody's Duty" ("Educación, tarea de todos"). To reach all schools and the education communities (comprising students, parents, teachers, and local authorities), the Ministry of Education created the Núcleos Educativos Comunales (NEC; Communal Education Clusters), the basic entities in charge of guaranteeing that the local education authorities fostered the reform as part of the revolutionary process, procuring the individual commitment of teachers, students, and parents to the transformations taking place. Each school had an educational council with 40 percent representation for the teaching community, 30 percent for the parents organization, and 30 percent for members of the community. Each NEC had to organize many activities in order to increase the participation of families in the educational process. This nuclear structure created by the education reform was well received in some rural areas, as it was helpful in facilitating access to other ministries,[67] but the NEC encountered great resistance in the cities.

The NEC demanded meetings and organized various activities and development projects, but this type of commitment was completely foreign to the urban middle-class culture regarding the role of the school, and having to participate in meetings and other activities was experienced as an imposition. Middle-class parents in both Lima and the provinces complained that the education system had become part of the regime's propaganda apparatus and the school environment was being politicized. They proposed that indoctrination should be resisted.[68] The reform also generated tensions between parents and schools when teachers embraced the call to encourage the involvement of young people in addressing the problems of society, as was the case in some Catholic private schools, where students were taught about the importance of committing to social change.[69]

Another unwelcome decision among the provincial middle classes was the closure of one hundred teacher-training schools. The poor quality of their performance was blamed for the stark decline in the teachers' academic level. To start an organized intervention that the regime could afford, they decided to strengthen and invest in the thirty best teachers colleges.[70] General Ramón Miranda Ampuero explained:

> We did this out of a deep sense of responsibility. Clearly it would not be well accepted by communities in the provinces, the aspiration being that each would have its own teaching school; it was a sign of status, and it allowed young people to achieve higher education without having to migrate. But that in itself was a problem. [Teachers colleges] were the only alternative for achieving higher education, attracting people to the profession for reasons that had nothing to do with the teaching profession. [It is a fact that] lack of vocation threatens the quality of education.[71]

The Role of Teachers

According to George Psacharopolous, several educational reform projects, particularly in independent African countries, failed in the 1970s and 1980s. This was because even with well-defined political targets, adequate technical resources, and a clear financial strategy, sustaining the proposed changes requires widespread consensus and support in the larger society.[72] The state-funded education system is a fairly complex ground where various stakeholders are constantly negotiating their interests.[73] Beyond a clear formulation, attempting a reform requires close political management of the dynamic tension between a centralizing and controlling state and the decentralized complexity of regional and local social conflicts, where fragments of different educational projects are negotiated and frequently linked to regional power struggles.[74] In reality, a fundamental part of the reform takes place in the classroom; teachers' engagement with the reform guidelines is only part of what is necessary. The adoption and implementation of those directives depend on each teacher's conscious option to develop a radical practice in the classroom. Besides, the very process of transferring a radical pedagogy entails many risks, such as the simplification of ideas and criticism of past forms of teaching without a clear grasp of what needs to be changed and why.[75]

Gaining teachers' support for the 1972 reform project was of utmost importance in Peru. As recalled by General Miranda Ampuero, minister of education during the RGAF:

> An idea that became very clear in the *Informe general* is that it was crucial to change the devalued image of the teaching profession. The teachers' role in the success of the reform was clearly understood. We knew that without teachers, the reform would not happen, so we looked for ways of integrating them into the process. The problem was that it was a revolutionary process, it was a dictatorship, and as such, much of the population did not agree with the process. And for better or for worse, the teachers' union was highly politicized, it was not a pluralist union; they were opposed to the revolutionary process. . . . This was a major problem, because for us it was very clear that teachers had to take a leading role as active agents in the transformation of the education system.[76]

In fact, the largest teachers union, the Sindicato Único de Trabajadores en la Educación del Perú (SUTEP; Unified Syndicate of Workers in Education of Peru), sustained an open and outright rejection of the reform from the start. SUTEP was founded in Cuzco, in 1972, as a result of the unification of teachers of different levels in a single union. It was born in open confrontation with the RGAF and with an agenda that went beyond a salary dispute. On the one hand, the defense of Law 15215, or Ley del Estatuto y Escalafón del Magisterio Peruano (Law of Peruvian Teachers' Statute and Pay Scale), was perceived as the defense of the teaching profession. The suspension of this law was one of the issues that deeply soured the relationship between the RGAF and SUTEP from the start. This law passed in 1966, during the Belaúnde Terry regime. It guaranteed gradual increases in teachers' salaries. The RGAF considered this law to be technically unsustainable and in conflict with their stabilization plans for the economy after the crisis of 1967.[77] On the other hand, the union resisted the RGAF because it was a dictatorship favoring the bourgeoisie. Until the teachers strike of 1971, the pro-Moscow faction of the Communist Party led by Jorge Del Prado (which published the *Unidad* newspaper) had some control over the teachers union. However, because this political party supported the RGAF reforms, they were displaced by a new group of provincial young leaders, very radicalized and largely associated with the Maoist-oriented Communist Party (which published the *Patria Roja* newspaper), linked to important regional movements from Arequipa, Cuzco, and Puno.[78]

The teachers union's agenda included the defense of law 15215; the struggle against corruption among national, regional, and local authorities of the Ministry of Education; and the autonomy of trade unions in the face of RGAF attempts to control workers organizations. The historian Iván Hinojosa and the sociologist Nicolás Lynch have described how proselytism techniques in political parties on the left in the 1970s did not respect the united front character of labor organizations. Instead, gaining control of a particular union meant that the party line would be imposed on the union organization, forcing identification of the union organization with the party.[79] Consequently, SUTEP was identified for several years with the political line of the Communist Party of Peru—*Patria Roja*, which explicitly sought to transcend the nature of union organizations, as can be seen in this quote attributed to Julio Pedro Armacanqui Flores, the founder of SUTEP:

> From the constitution of SUTEP, a qualitative change has occurred in the teachers organization: We no longer protest for our working conditions alone. We have to understand our struggles as linked to the struggles of other workers in the country. We need to convey to our affiliates that our mission is not only to impart knowledge in the classroom, but that we also have the responsibility of educating a new generation, emphasizing the values of solidarity, equity, justice, to lay the foundation of a great movement to form new leaders capable of leading larger movements in our country.[80]

The *Patria Roja* leadership infused SUTEP with a militant character and offered frontal opposition to the military regime. According to César Barrera Bazán (the former national leader of SUTEP and a militant of *Patria Roja*):

A central feature of the labor movement in those years was its politicization. It was very, very strong. The Velasco regime did not understand that the movement needed autonomy. That was a profound error that led to deep resentment toward the regime in the union movement. Authoritarianism and repression completely contaminated the possibilities of understanding and engaging the conscious participation of teachers in the education reform project, which had many positive aspects, as we have come to acknowledge recently.[81]

The union considered the reform to be paternalistic because a group of experts had assumed the task of formulating it without including teachers organizations in the process. César Barrera Bazán, who was a young union leader at the time, remembers: "We felt that the commission of specialists had taken ownership of the reform, telling us 'the truth' as if it was error free, and no real discussion about the project was allowed."[82]

Outside of the union militancy and rhetoric, the reform represented a professionally challenging situation for the teachers experiencing the process. The acknowledgment of the vital social role played by teachers in the school system was followed by the design of a "retraining program" that started before the law was made public. First a cohort of four hundred teachers was enrolled for three months, in the hope that they would infuse enthusiasm for the reform among their colleagues. Later, once the reform law was published, training sessions involved two or three days in a secluded venue outside of Lima, where teachers received a copy of the *Informe general* for discussion. As part of their training, they met members of the CRE, many of whom were also acknowledged intellectuals and public figures associated with education, and some of them were the authors of new textbooks. According to the educator and Jesuit priest Ricardo Morales, also a member of the CRE: "In those years we conducted a radical review of traditional forms of education, and teachers engaged with that criticism. They had a chance to sit and quietly reflect on the connections between education—as a collective endeavor—and politics."[83]

From personal experience (as a school student in those years, as the daughter and niece of teachers, and years later, as a researcher), I realized that for some teachers who went through the experience, the reform was a major milestone, not only for questioning and disseminating a new pedagogy, but also for bringing intellectual and academic relevance to their work.[84]

The regime's official discourse was to present teachers as agents of social change, and the classroom as a space where ideas about the social and economic transformation of the country should be discussed. Many teachers were pleased to be able to say they were getting an education that was "Marxist-inspired," as they were encouraged to develop a critical revision of traditional historical narratives, to focus on the role of social conflict as a generator of change, and to emphasize the key role of grassroots movements in social and political transformations and historical events, instead of the traditional enhancement of individual heroes.[85]

Yet, along with their interest in some aspects of the reform, many of those same teachers were also loyal members of SUTEP, opposing the repression toward the union and rejecting the regime's attempts to compete with SUTEP through a newly created organization, the Union of Educators of the Peruvian Revolution (Sindicato de Educadores de la Revolución Peruana; SERP), affiliated with SINAMOS. Thus they participated in the strikes and other union-led industrial actions. The repression unleashed by the military regime against labor organizations was severe. In 1973, after a nationwide strike by teachers under the direction of SUTEP, more than five hundred teachers were imprisoned. The regime also resorted to raids on local union branches, transferring teachers in leading positions to other regions, as well as dismissals, imprisonment, and deportation.

Augusto Salazar Bondy and many of the intellectuals supporting the reforms were extremely worried about the growing abyss between the regime and teachers in the country. In several of his columns in *Expreso*, Salazar Bondy tried to separate teachers from the "*ultra izquierda*" that opposed the regime, calling on teachers to assume their role as advocates of social change to create a society "without exploiters, anticapitalist, and anti-imperialist," and suggesting that supporting the "revolutionary process" was the only way to achieve these goals. He invoked the "constant creativity of teachers and students, without whose support the revolutionary process would be hampered."[86]

As some analysts have identified, an important element in the political scenario in those years was the oversimplified version of Marxism that was embraced dogmatically by the emerging radical left.[87] Maoist groups rejected the RGAF's reforms because of their class character (if the armed forces were part of the bourgeois system, its political program could not pick up the interests of the revolutionary classes). Yet this explanation is not sufficient to understand the fierce loyalty and commitment of the teachers' and the students' movements, both under Maoist leadership in those years. According to several authors, Maoist radicalism deeply connected with the demands and feelings of an aspiring middle class, predominantly provincial, who found in the union and radical political militancy the resources to push for the recognition and legitimacy of their aspirations to be recognized, overcoming the reluctance of a closed, racist, and conservative society.[88] Alan Angell found early SUTEP documents ardently arguing that the hierarchy and importance of the teaching profession should be established and respected by the government.[89] An expression of this aspiration was the teachers' rejection of the reform, as Norman Gall reported after witnessing how teachers in rural and marginal urban areas opposed the reform because they saw their authority threatened by the level of participation that the reform demanded from the local communities, making them important actors in the education community.[90]

SUTEP called on teachers to reject the reform training sessions until they realized that they could be converted into an opportunity for ideological discussion and dissemination of the union demands. However, over the years, SUTEP leaders have critically reconsidered their stance against the education reform. In the words of César Barrera Bazán: "With the benefit of hindsight, we have become self-critical because we should have been more thoughtful in considering the importance of the education reform project. There were very good people working there, with important and novel approaches, particularly on issues such as the role of education in developing and asserting our national identity, or the need to critically study history and society."[91]

Looking Back

A systematic campaign to dismantle the RGAF reforms started during the Morales Bermúdez regime in 1975 and continued through the Belaúnde Terry regime of the early 1980s. But one element of the education reform had a lasting legacy: the commission that formulated it. Their understanding of the education system, their attention to innovative ideas, and the expertise they contributed in the formulation of the project were crucial for the development of an active group of organizations and experts that did not disappear with the Velasco regime.[92] They have played a key role in the development of a consensual vision for the development of education in the country that materialized in the National Plan for Education signed in 2006, which aims to ensure universal access to quality education, to strengthen democracy, and to allow the participation of the community in the education system.[93] There are clear coincidences between the main goals of this plan and important issues that were raised during the education reform of the 1970s. The plan envisions an education system that recognizes, celebrates, and works with cultural diversity in the classroom; ensures teacher training that has national and local relevance; and is committed to treating teachers with dignity. It clearly formulates the need to provide higher education that responds to the needs of the country, and considers to be of crucial importance setting in place mechanisms to guarantee the participation of the wider community in the education system. The challenge of transforming these orientations into specific policies is still difficult to meet, but they certainly resonate with Emilio Barrantes's words about his hopes for the future, that time would allow the country to bring back the "most important ideas" of the 1972 reform project "for the sake of the country's education and its protagonists."[94]

Notes

1. Ministerio de Educación, *Reforma de la educación peruana: Informe general* (Lima: Ministerio de Educación, 1970); hereafter *Informe general*. All translations from Spanish are mine unless otherwise indicated.

2. Robert S. Drysdale and Robert G. Myers, "Continuity and Change: Peruvian Education," in *The Peruvian Experiment: Continuity and Change Under Military Rule*, ed. Abraham F. Lowenthal (Princeton, NJ: Princeton University Press, 1975), 254–301.

3. Emilio Barrantes, *Historia de la educación en el Perú* (Lima: Mosca Azul, 1989).

4. Ministerio de Educación, *Informe general*.

5. Drysdale and Myers, "Continuity and Change"; José Rivero, *Educación, docencia y clase política en el Perú* (Lima: Tarea, 2007).

6. Michael W. Apple, *Education and Power* (New York: Routledge, 1982); Roy Lowe, *The Death of Progressive Education: How Teachers Lost Control of the Classroom* (New York: Routledge, 2007).

7. Rivero, *Educación, docencia y clase política*, 364.

8. Teresa Tovar, *Aportes de las políticas del Estado al desarrollo magisterial* (Lima: Foro Educativo, 2004).

9. Abraham F. Lowenthal, ed., *The Peruvian Experiment: Continuity and Change Under Military Rule* (Princeton, NJ: Princeton University Press, 1975).

10. Drysdale and Myers, "Continuity and Change."

11. José Itzigsohn and Matthias vom Hau, "Unfinished Imagined Communities: States, Social Movements, and Nationalism in Latin America," *The-*

ory and Society 35, no. 2 (2006): 193–212; Matthias vom Hau, "Unpacking the School: Textbooks, Teachers, and the Construction of Nationhood in Mexico, Argentina, and Peru," *Latin American Research Review* 44, no. 3 (2009): 127–154.

12. Tracy Lynne Devine, "Indigenous Identity and Identification in Peru: *Indigenismo*, Education, and Contradictions in State Discourses," *Journal of Latin American Cultural Studies* 8, no. 1 (1999): 63–74; Maria Elena García, *Making Indigenous Citizens: Identities, Education, and Multicultural Development in Peru* (Stanford, CA: Stanford University Press, 2005); Nancy H. Hornberger, *Bilingual Education and Language Maintenance: A Southern Peruvian Quechua Case* (Dordrecht: Foris, 1988).

13. Norman Gall, *La reforma educativa peruana* (Lima: Mosca Azul, 1974).

14. Alan Angell, "Classroom Maoists: The Politics of Peruvian School-teachers under Military Government," *Bulletin of Latin American Research* 1, no. 2 (1982): 1–20; Eduardo Ballón, Luis Peirano, and César Pezo, *El magisterio y sus luchas* (Lima: Desco, 1984).

15. José Matos Mar, "Presentación," in *Aspectos sociales de la educación rural en el Perú*, ed. Giorgio Alberti and Julio Cotler (Lima: Instituto de Estudios Peruanos, 1972); Luis Pásara, "When the Military Dreams," in *The Peruvian Experiment Reconsidered*, ed. Cynthia McClintock and Abraham F. Lowenthal (Princeton, NJ: Princeton University Press, 1983).

16. Stephen J. Ball, Gustavo E. Fischman, and Silvina Gvirtz, *Crisis and Hope: The Educational Hopscotch of Latin America* (London: Routledge Falmer, 2003).

17. Jorge M. Gorostiaga and César G. Tello, "Globalización y reforma educativa en América Latina: Un análisis inter-textual," *Revista Brasileira de Educação* 16, no. 47 (2011): 363–388; Confederaciones de Trabajadores de la Educación de la República Argentina, Brasil, Chile y Uruguay, *Las reformas educativas en los países del Cono Sur: Un balance crítico* (Buenos Aires: CLACSO, 2005).

18. Michael W. Apple, "Facing the Complexity of Power: For a Parallelist Position in Critical Educational Studies," in *Bowles and Gintis Revisited: Correspondence and Contradiction in Educational Theory*, ed. Mike Cole (New York: Falmer, 1988); Lowe, *Death of Progressive Education.*

19. George Psacharopoulos, "Why Educational Reforms Fail: A Comparative Analysis," *International Review of Education* 35, no. 2 (1989): 179–195.

20. Apple, *Education and Power.*

21. Arthur Zilversmit, *Changing Schools: Progressive Education Theory and Practice, 1930–1960* (Chicago: University of Chicago Press, 1993).

22. Lowe, *Death of Progressive Education.*

23. Henry A. Giroux, *Theory and Resistance in Education: Towards a Pedagogy for the Opposition* (Westport, CT: Bergin and Garvey, 2001).

24. Samuel Bowles and Herbert Gintis, *Schooling in Capitalist America: Educational Reform and the Contradictions of Economic Life*, vol. 57 (New York: Basic Books, 1976); Pierre Bourdieu and Jean-Claude Passeron, *La reproduction: Éléments pour une théorie du système d'enseignement* (Paris: Editions de Minuit, 1970).

25. Pierre Bourdieu, *Distinction: A Social Critique of the Judgment of Taste* (Cambridge, MA: Harvard University Press, 1984), 130–137.

26. Bradley A. Levinson, Douglas E. Foley, and Dorothy C. Holland, eds.,

The Cultural Production of the Educated Person: Critical Ethnographies of Schooling and Local Practice (Albany: State University of New York Press, 1996).

27. Giorgio Alberti and Julio Cotler, *Aspectos sociales de la educación rural en el Perú* (Lima: Instituto de Estudios Peruanos, 1972).

28. Patricia Ames, *Mejorando la escuela rural: Tres décadas de experiencias educativas en el Perú* (Lima: Instituto de Estudios Peruanos, 1999); Carlos Iván Degregori, "Del mito de Inkarrí al mito del progreso: Poblaciones andinas, cultura e identidad nacional," *Socialismo y Participación* no. 36 (1986): 49–56; Juan Ansión, *La escuela en la comunidad campesina* (Lima: FAO, Ministerio de Agricultura, 1989).

29. Gonzalo Portocarrero and Patricia Oliart, *El Perú desde la escuela* (Lima: Instituto de Apoyo Agrario, 1989).

30. Teresa Tovar, *Reforma de la educación: Balance y perspectivas* (Lima: Desco, 1985).

31. Patricia Oliart, *Políticas educativas y la cultura del sistema escolar en el Perú* (Lima: Instituto de Estudios Peruanos–TAREA, 2011).

32. Ministerio de Educación, *Informe general*, 16.

33. Ibid., 19.

34. Juan Martín Sánchez, *La revolución peruana, 1968–1975: Ideología y práctica de un gobierno militar* (Seville: CSIC, Universidad de Sevilla, Diputación de Sevilla, 2002).

35. On developmentalism, see Arturo Escobar, *Encountering Development: The Making and Unmaking of the Third World* (Princeton, NJ: Princeton University Press, 1995).

36. Barrantes, *Historia de la educación en el Perú*.

37. Interview with Carmen Lora, October 14, 2014.

38. Ibid., 103.

39. Fragment of the message to the nation by General Velasco on July 28, 1970. *El Peruano*, July 29, 1970.

40. Augusto Salazar Bondy, *La cultura de la dominación* (Lima: Instituto de Estudios Peruanos, 1972), 29.

41. Ministerio de Educación, *Informe general*, 19.

42. A full version of the agreement is available at https://elsudamericano.wordpress.com/2013/06/16/resolucion-general-del-congreso-cultural-de-la-habana-1968/.

43. Fragment of the agreement translated in https://nacla.org/article/cultural-congress-havana.

44. This enthusiasm for the national culture also had a controversial side to it: the censorship of cultural expressions considered "alienating," such as rock and roll. Bands from the United States and the United Kingdom were almost banned from radio and television in order to stop "cultural penetration," even in a context in which many rock bands and musicians were critical of the economic and cultural systems of their countries. This was also detrimental to national rock musicians, who were going through a good moment of creativity and growth. Pedro Cornejo, *Alta tensión: Los cortocircuitos del rock peruano* (Lima: Emedece Ediciones, 2002); Carlos Torres Rotondo, *Demoler: Un viaje personal por la primera escena del rock en el Perú, 1957–1975* (Lima: Revuelta Editores, 2009).

45. Ministerio de Educación, *Informe general*, 166–167.

46. I recall at least three of my schoolteachers reading him and recommending the book to us.

47. Paulo Freire, *Pedagogia do oprimido* (Rio de Janeiro: Paz e Terra, 1970), 57.

48. bell hooks, *Teaching to Transgress: Education as the Practice of Freedom* (New York: Routledge, 1992), 15.

49. Psacharopoulos, "Why Educational Reforms Fail"; Jennifer Gore, *The Struggle for Pedagogies* (New York: Routledge, 1992).

50. Apple, "Facing the Complexity of Power."

51. David Hursh, "Social Studies within the Neo-Liberal State: The Commodification of Knowledge and the End of Imagination," *Theory and Research in Social Education* 29, no. 2 (2001): 349–356; Lowe, *Death of Progressive Education.*

52. For an account on alternative schools in Perú, see Martín Benavides, Verónica Villarán, and Santiago Cueto, "Socialización escolar y educación en valores democráticos: El caso de las escuelas alternativas," in *Juventud: Sociedad y cultura*, ed. Aldo Panfichi (Lima: Fondo Editorial, Pontificia Universidad Católica, 1999), 133–170.

53. Augusto Salazar Bondy, "Educación liberadora y trabajo," *Expreso*, February 13, 1972.

54. Vom Hau, "Unpacking the School," 140.

55. Ibid.; Portocarrero and Oliart, *El Perú desde la escuela.*

56. Barrantes, *Historia de la educación en el Perú*, 39.

57. Conversation with Helen Orvig, Lima, July 2015.

58. Augusto Salazar Bondy, "Educación, dependencia y reforma," *Expreso*, May 5, 1970.

59. In my school, for example, folk dance lessons were included as part of physical education classes.

60. Ministerio de Educación, *Informe general*, 101.

61. Tovar, *Reforma de la educación.*

62. Gall, *La reforma educativa.*

63. I vividly remember discussing this rule in class assembly the year before it became mandatory nationwide. One of my classmates bitterly stated that she would feel uncomfortable leaving the house at school time, wearing the same uniform as her maid's children.

64. Ministerio de Educación, *Informe general*, 200.

65. Gall, *La reforma educativa.*

66. Jeffrey Klaiber, "The Battle over Private Education in Peru, 1968–1980," *The Americas* 43, no. 2 (1986): 137–158.

67. This was the case, for example, of the collaboration with the Ministry of Agriculture for the implementation and monitoring of the agrarian reform.

68. Rivero, *Educación, docencia y clase política.*

69. Interview with Ricardo Morales, S.J., about the role of parents associations in Catholic schools in Lima, in Patricia Oliart, *Los maestros como transmisores de imágenes sobre el país: El caso de los maestros de ciencias sociales en la educación secundaria urbana* (Lima: Pontificia Universidad Católica del Perú, 1986).

70. Teresa Tovar, *Aportes de las políticas del Estado al desarrollo magisterial* (Lima: Foro Educativo, 2004), 69.

71. Oliart, *Políticas educativas*, 49.

72. Psacharopoulos, "Why Educational Reforms Fail."

73. Stephen J. Ball, *The Micro-Politics of the School: Towards a Theory of School Organization* (London: Methuen, 1987).

74. Bret Gustafson, *New Languages of the State: Indigenous Resurgence and the Politics of Knowledge in Bolivia* (Durham, NC: Duke University Press, 2009).

75. Gore, *The Struggle for Pedagogies*.

76. Interview with General Ramón Miranda Ampuero, Lima, October 12, 2001.

77. Martín Sánchez, *La revolución peruana*.

78. Ricardo Letts, *La izquierda peruana: Organización y tendencias* (Lima: Mosca Azul, 1981); Angell, "Classroom Maoists"; Ballón, Peirano, and Pezo, *El magisterio y sus luchas*.

79. Iván Hinojosa, "On Poor Relations and the Nouveau Riche: Shining Path and the Radical Peruvian Left," in *Shining and Other Paths: War and Society in Peru, 1980–1995*, ed. Steve J. Stern (Durham, NC: Duke University Press, 1995), 60–83; Nicolás Lynch, *Los jóvenes rojos de San Marcos: El radicalismo universitario de los años setenta* (Lima: Ediciones El Zorro de Abajo, 1990).

80. Raúl Fernando Moscol León, *Los años heroicos del magisterio* (Piura: ABC Espacial, 2011), 68.

81. Interview with César Barrera Bazán, Lima, April 13, 2012.

82. Ibid.

83. Interview with Ricardo Morales, Lima, June 1985.

84. Many of the 120 teachers whose interviews I analyzed for my BA thesis in 1985 had ambiguous memories of the reform. They were from nine cities in the three regions of Peru. Several of the older teachers mentioned the education reform training as the most valuable learning experience they had had. It is quite telling that they particularly valued having experienced decent treatment, the interest shown in them as professionals, and the shared understanding of the importance of teachers in the educational process. Oliart, *Los maestros como transmisores*.

85. Portocarrero and Oliart, *El Perú desde la escuela*.

86. Augusto Salazar Bondy, "Desmitificando la educación peruana," *Expreso*, September 10, 1972.

87. Carlos Iván Degregori, "La revolucion de los manuales: La expansión del marxismo-leninismo en las ciencias sociales y el surgimiento de Sendero Luminoso," *Revista Peruana de Ciencias Sociales* 3 (1990): 102–125.

88. Angell, "Classroom Maoists"; Lynch, *Los jóvenes rojos*; Hinojosa, "On Poor Relations and the Nouveau Riche."

89. Angell, "Classroom Maoists."

90. Gall, *La reforma educativa*.

91. Interview with César Barrera Bazán, Lima, April 13, 2012.

92. Patricia Oliart, *Educar en tiempos de cambio: 1968–1975* (Lima: Derrama Magisterial, 2013).

93. Ministerio de Educación, Consejo Nacional de Educación, *Proyecto Educativo Nacional*, 2006.

94. Barrantes, *Historia de la educación en el Perú*, 104.

CHAPTER 6

Through Fire and Blood: The Peruvian Peasant Confederation and the Velasco Regime

JAYMIE PATRICIA HEILMAN

Seated beneath a large painted portrait of General Juan Velasco Alvarado, a rural activist named Marcelino Bustamante López explained why he quit Peru's largest campesino organization—the Peruvian Peasant Confederation, or CCP (Confederación Campesina del Perú)—in the early 1970s. He recalled that the CCP had "very politicized leaders, and they didn't accept the agrarian reform that General Velasco enacted. They didn't accept it because the CCP's plan, its ideal, for agrarian reform was that land should be acquired through fire and blood."[1] Upon leaving the CCP, Bustamante immediately joined the Velasco government's newly created rural organization, the National Agrarian Confederation (Confederación Nacional Agraria; CNA). This chapter explores how the CCP responded to the Velasco regime's rural reforms. Members of the CCP were sharply divided over how—or whether—to engage the military government's ambitious agrarian reform law, and those divisions exacerbated existing fissures in the organization, breaking the peasant organization into three competing factions. Those factions then had to face a new challenge from the Velasco regime: Decree Law 19400, which called for the dissolution of all existing rural organizations and their replacement with state-sponsored bodies. Although all three factions staunchly opposed the regime's efforts to displace the CCP, their differences proved impossible to surmount and the national peasant movement remained bitterly fractured.

The Velasco agrarian reform has received much careful attention from scholars. A burst of studies appeared in the 1970s and early 1980s, assessing the reform's shape and exploring its social and economic impact on Peru's countryside.[2] More recent studies by Linda Seligmann, Elmer Arce Espinoza, and Enrique Mayer examine how campesinos engaged the reform and how they navigated the major changes—and the major frustrations—initiated by the law.[3] Yet for all these studies of Velasco's rural reforms, much work remains to be done. As the historian Anna Cant has noted, few scholars have investigated the agrarian reform's cultural and ideological sides.[4] This chapter takes up the question of ideology, showing that Velasco's dramatic rural reforms generated a major ideological crisis within the Peruvian Peasant Confederation, triggering a three-way split of the organization. Confederation members fought angrily over how to interpret and engage the agrarian reform, and their differing opinions quickly proved irreconcilable.

The CCP leadership's uncompromising rejection of Velasco's agrarian reform offers a stark counternarrative to the well-established story of Peruvian campesinos' general response to the law: initial excitement followed by increasing disillusionment and disappointment. Precisely because the CCP had made agrarian reform its central demand at its 1962 national congress, the CCP's leaders worried about their organization's relevance after the Velasco regime issued its agrarian reform measure, Decree Law 17716. If the CCP's primary purpose was to fight for agrarian reform, then Velasco's law threatened to make the CCP's mandate obsolete. As Iván Hinojosa has noted, the existence of "a military regime that seemed to preempt the Left" generated serious problems for Peru's leftist political parties.[5] The same was true for the CCP, which also feared for its very institutional survival, as Decree Law 19400 created new, state-sponsored rural organizations to supplant all existing ones. Given the threat Velasco's sweeping reforms posed to the CCP, it is not surprising that the organization's leaders so staunchly rejected the regime and its laws. Yet for all the CCP's vocal opposition to the Velasco regime's reforms, the organization remains surprisingly understudied by scholars.[6]

The CCP's opposition to Velasco's rural reforms also provides a twist on the interplay between reform and revolution. Many scholars have argued that the Revolutionary Government of the Armed Forces (RGAF) launched its ambitious reform program to stave off revolution, introducing socioeconomic and political changes to Peru to drain popular support from those groups advocating Marxist principles and revolutionary solutions to injustice.[7] Many of the CCP's leaders opposed the Velasco reforms for exactly the same reasons, fearing that the regime's extensive rural reforms would douse revolutionary sentiment in the countryside. But not all members of the CCP shared that conviction. Some were eager to benefit from the Velasco reforms and left the CCP in protest.

Others—especially those linked to the political party Vanguardia Revolucionaria (VR)—regarded the military government as bourgeois and insufficiently radical, but felt that outright rejection of the regime's reforms would be counterproductive.[8] The passionate and conflicting attitudes of CCP activists toward Velasco's agrarian reform reveal that the law's radical impact stretched well beyond upheavals in land tenure and dramatic changes inside rural communities.

Founded in 1947, the Peruvian Peasant Confederation was forced into inactivity shortly after General Manuel Odría's 1948 coup. The organization revived in the late 1950s, under the direction and tacit leadership of the Ancash lawyer and Peruvian Communist Party activist Saturnino Paredes. In 1962, the CCP resumed active political work, holding its second national congress and electing a new secretary general, an indigenous peasant activist from Ayacucho named Manuel Llamojha Mitma. The Peruvian Peasant Confederation soon became Peru's largest and most important campesino organization. Paredes served as the CCP's secretary of defense, and the peasant organization allied closely with the political party he led: the Maoist Peruvian Communist Party–Bandera Roja, which was formed upon the 1964 split of the Peruvian Communist Party into pro-China and pro-Soviet parties. Not all members of the CCP, however, were Bandera Roja members. Manuel Llamojha never formally affiliated with any political party, and the CCP's sub-secretary general, Ramón Núñez La Fore, allied with the pro-Soviet PCP–Unidad (although, admittedly, that allegiance got him kicked out of the CCP in 1964).[9] Ricardo Letts Colmenares, in turn, began working with the CCP in 1962 and, three years later, he cofounded the eclectic leftist political party Vanguardia Revolucionaria.[10] Several other members of Vanguardia Revolucionaria joined Letts in the CCP, although few held leadership positions before the confederation's 1973 fracture.

Agrarian reform was the CCP's central demand, but the peasant organization's leadership staunchly denounced Decree Law 17716, which initiated a massive redistribution of land, expropriating highland haciendas and coastal estates and reorganizing the seized lands into large agricultural cooperatives. Peasant participation in the agrarian reform was organized, in part, through the National System of Support for Social Mobilization (Sistema Nacional de Apoyo a la Movilización Social, or SINAMOS), an organization created by the Velasco regime in 1971. Speaking to a national assembly of CCP delegates in 1972, Secretary General Manuel Llamojha decried the "pro-*latifundista* [large landlord], antipopular, pro-Yankee, and repressive essence" of the agrarian reform law.[11] The CCP leadership also called for "a true agrarian reform of antifeudal and anti-imperialist character" and stressed that "the basic principle of authentic agrarian reform is the CONFISCATION OF LAND AND ITS DELIVERY TO THE PEASANTS WHO WORK IT" (emphasis in original).[12] Nearly a decade after the passage of the agrarian reform, CCP activists allied with Saturnino Paredes offered a similar casting of Decree Law 17716, asserting that "the false agrarian reform of the Fascist government is of a landlord character and is nothing but a trick that, in the end, favors the large landowners and the enemies of the working people."[13]

The CCP leadership's opposition to the Velasco agrarian reform centered on four key issues: the reform's motivation, control of the reform, the so-called agrarian debt, and the establishment of cooperatives. The CCP's leaders insisted that the Velasco regime introduced the agrarian reform law because of pressure from the United States and the dictates of the American Alliance for Progress program. In his report to the national assembly of CCP delegates, Llamojha explained that the United States had given instructions to all Latin American countries "so that they make 'reforms' in their respective countries with the aim of calming the masses who fight for land and for their liberation from the clutches of capitalist exploitation."[14]

The CCP's leadership also felt that true agrarian reform had to be driven by the masses, not by the state. As they agreed in 1972, "antifeudal and anti-imperialist agrarian reform can only be accomplished through the combative attitude of the peasants . . . under the direction of the working class and in alliance with it and other exploited sectors."[15] The CCP made the same point the following year, stressing that "a true 'agrarian reform' cannot be directed or oriented by North American imperialism. Instead, it must be carried out by the campesinos themselves, directed by the working class."[16] Rejecting the military regime's reform outright, the CCP's leaders were making an implicit argument about their continuing relevance: only they, as the true leaders of the rural masses, could bring about legitimate agrarian reform.

The CCP's leadership also objected to the structure of the reform. One feature of the law was the requirement that peasant beneficiaries of the agrarian reform pay an "agrarian debt" to help compensate hacendados for their expropriated lands. Llamojha asserted that the agrarian reform "is an instrument that supports and benefits the large hacendados and *latifundistas*, as it pays them great sums of money for lands snatched from the campesinos themselves."[17] The principle of land without payment became a priority for many CCP leaders. As the former CCP secretary of press and propaganda Pelayo Oré remembered it, "The frontal struggle that the CCP carried out was against hacendados, to liquidate the feudal slavery that reigned in the country. Our specific orientation was the struggle of the CCP for the liberation of the peasantry, but through an agrarian reform without any payment whatsoever."[18]

CCP leaders' opposition to Decree Law 17716 also stemmed from their rejection of agrarian cooperatives. As several activists wrote, "In the agrarian or communal cooperatives, the campesino is stripped of all decision-making abilities. It is state functionaries who decide everything. The peasant participates as a simple supplier of labor force."[19] Reflecting on the Velasco agrarian reform decades later, Llamojha explained:

> The campesinos realized what a cooperative was, and that cooperatives weren't in the peasantry's favor. . . . When they formed the cooperative, the hacendados themselves were the managers! With the harvest, the harvest of corn, potatoes, everything, they only gave the peasants one *arroba* [about thirty pounds] per family.
>
> The campesinos turned bitter. They said, "How are we going to live for a full year on just one arroba of corn or wheat? We want our own production from our own land." Saying that, they rejected the cooperatives.[20]

Relatedly, the CCP's leadership opposed the Campesino Community Statute, a 1970 law that created new communal leadership bodies and aimed to cooperativize peasant communities. At the 1970 National Congress, the CCP's leadership resolved that the statute "establishes the requirement to convert communities into cooperatives, without respect for the will of their members, their traditional form, or their particular forms of development." They also warned that by forcing communities to become cooperatives, they would "completely lose their organizational and classist character, as well as their social, familial, and human character."[21]

Crucially, not all sectors of the CCP shared their leadership's hostility toward the agrarian reform. Some individual members like Marcelino Bustamante—the Ancash campesino activist quoted at the start of this chapter—saw the Velasco agrarian reform as an incredible opportunity that peasants needed to seize. As Bustamante phrased it, "One had to take advantage of such an important moment. Facing the inhumane exploitation of our indigenous brothers, one had to accept this [agrarian reform] law. . . . How could you wait? So, that was the polemic, the disagreement we had with our comrades from the CCP."[22]

Many members of Vanguardia Revolucionaria likewise objected to the CCP leadership's attitude toward the agrarian reform. Characterizing the Velasco regime as a "bourgeois reformist military government," VR activists believed that the CCP could—and should—take full advantage of the government's agrarian reform, pushing it as far as possible in campesinos' favor.[23] It wasn't that Vanguardia Revolucionaria fully supported the Velasco regime—in the party activist Andrés Luna Vargas's words, "We said that reforms are reforms and not revolution"— but rather that VR activists thought they could radicalize the reforms through peasant actions like land invasions, an idea they soon put into practice.[24] VR activists also argued that while the government's agrarian reform had many problems, including the agrarian debt and state control of cooperatives, simply boycotting the agrarian reform would prove detrimental to peasants' interests.[25] A 1974 VR document criticized CCP secretary general Manuel Llamojha's attitude toward Decree Law 17716, charging that "the infantile tactic of ignoring the bourgeois agrarian reform has put the brakes on the mass movement" and had allowed "SINAMOS to penetrate the countryside."[26] In effect, Vanguardia Revolucionaria wanted to ensure that it—rather than the Velasco government—directed peasant participation in the process of reshaping Peru's countryside.

These differing perspectives on the agrarian reform surfaced during the CCP's third national congress in October 1970. Reflecting on that event, Llamojha later wrote: "At the Third National Congress of the Peasant Confederation, the existence of two lines within the heart of the confederation was clearly established." The core division, he stated, rested on the "difference in analysis of the Law of Agrarian Reform 17716." Llamojha characterized these differences as being between individuals who "defended the landlord's path" and those who supported "the peasant's path, of those who openly defended the buying and selling of land and those who would confiscate it."[27]

These tensions within the CCP finally exploded in May 1973, during the organization's fourth national congress. Held in Eccash, Ancash, the congress soon became the scene of a major clash between Paredes's supporters and Vanguardia Revolucionaria activists. (CCP secretary general Manuel Llamojha Mitma had already split from Paredes—for reasons I explore in the coming pages—by the time of the Eccash congress, so he did not attend the event.) Paredes and his supporters did not welcome Vanguardia Revolucionaria's participation in the congress. A VR activist named Fernando Eguren told the historian José Luis Rénique, "I think Saturnino held the meeting in such a remote and inhospitable place on purpose," adding that he suspected Paredes "was surprised by our attendance."[28] Paredes loyalists, in turn, subsequently described the participation of "the overwhelming majority of authentic representatives of the peasantry" and contrasted that attendance with the "group of infiltrators, yellows [traitorous conservatives], officialist elements, and Trotskyists."[29]

Conflict erupted almost immediately over issues of participation. Delegates sympathetic to Vanguardia Revolucionaria argued that Paredes and his supporters had arbitrarily extended credentials to too many campesinos from Eccash and its annexes, giving a disproportionately strong voice to Paredes supporters. In addition, Paredes's supporters organized an armed campesino guard and filled it with Paredes loyalists. Peasant delegates sympathetic to Vanguardia Revolucionaria demanded a review of plenary delegates' credentials and the establishment of a campesino guard whose members were elected, rather than imposed by Paredes. Campesinos made these demands because, as Luna Vargas phrased it, the Peruvian Peasant Confederation "is not the property of any political party."[30] Predictably enough, Paredes and his supporters denied the requests. With that rejection, campesino delegates sympathetic to VR withdrew from the congress.[31]

Upon their retreat from Eccash—at least according to pro-Paredes sources—Vanguardia Revolucionaria members and sympathizers approached regional authorities and reported the presence of armed campesino groups at the congress. As one Paredes supporter described it, "Having been unmasked, the cowardly fled, but not without first engaging in denunciation and snitchery, reporting to repressive authorities the existence of 'armed shock groups' in Eccash."[32] Pro-Paredes CCP leader Pelayo Oré remembered that "they retreated from the congress, denouncing us, saying that we had weapons over here and over there."[33]

After VR's withdrawal from Eccash, Paredes and his followers continued with the congress, passing a series of resolutions. They also elected a new secretary general to replace Llamojha, whom they now deemed a traitor. The man elected to the post was Justiniano Minaya Sosa, a mining activist from Eccash who had joined the CCP in 1966. But less than a month after his election at the Eccash congress, Minaya was murdered. Upon leaving a peasant community in Ancash, Minaya was ambushed by a local hacendado and his supporters. The men bound Minaya's hands and feet, beat him with stones and sticks, and then shot him.[34] Paredes and his supporters held Llamojha and Vanguardia Revolucionaria partially responsible for the killing; they claimed that the denunciations about armed campesino groups in Eccash led to increased repression against the leadership of Paredes's CCP, culminating in Minaya's death. In their words, Minaya "was assassinated by the reaction and by imperialism on May 20, 1973, as a result of his revolutionary importance and the incriminating denunciations made by Letts Colmenares, Luna Vargas, [and] Manuel Llamoja [sic]."[35]

The Vanguardia Revolucionaria activists who broke from Paredes at Eccash initially enjoyed the support of the CCP's previous secretary general, Manuel Llamojha. He attended VR's National Campesino Assembly in Mazo, Huaura Province, Department of Lima, during which Vanguardia Revolucionaria established its own CCP.[36] At that August 1973 meeting, Llamojha stood as a candidate in the election for president of the campesino assembly, but he lost the race to the VR activist Andrés Luna Vargas, who was subsequently elected secretary general of VR's CCP. Soon thereafter, Llamojha broke from Vanguardia Revolucionaria's CCP and established his own Peruvian Peasant Confederation. Suddenly, there were three rival CCPs.

The fracture of the CCP generated bitter acrimony between the three factions. Paredes supporters charged that Vanguardia Revolucionaria activists had a "plan to divert the entire national peasantry from their true path. They are the principal implementers of the so-called 'Agrarian Reform' of the regime that they categorize as 'bourgeois reformist,' creating illusions in the peasantry that it is sufficient to 'deepen' the current landlord's path of the 'Agrarian Reform.'"[37] Turning their attention to Manuel Llamojha, Paredes loyalists asserted that Llamojha "has fallen into the dirtiest political and social degeneration, turning into a dummy of Trotskyist and officialist puppets."[38] They asserted that Llamojha headed a "small faction of renegade yellow traitors . . . who hurl a series of stupid calumnies and prejudicial lies."[39] In the casting of Paredes's supporters, Llamojha, Andrés Luna Vargas, and the well-known Trotskyist leader Hugo Blanco were all "enemies of the peasantry and agents of exploiters" who should be "unmasked and condemned by the peasant masses."[40]

Vanguardia Revolucionaria activists responded in kind, denouncing both Paredes and Llamojha and criticizing the "true ultraleftists, who, with radical extremist charlatanism, usurped the direction of the CCP in its previous era, at the same time that they immobilized and disarmed the masses, facilitating in this manner the ideological and organic penetration of the government's bourgeois reformism, leading the CCP to disorganization and its isolation from the peasant masses."[41] Manuel Llamojha, in turn, offered his own critiques of Vanguardia Revolucionaria. Decades later, he commented that "they aided Velasco. They were always on the side of the bourgeoisie, and for that reason, I didn't agree with them. I explained this to the campesinos. Our clear position was to make agrarian reform with our own hands."[42]

Competing opinions about the Velasco regime and its rural reforms drove the CCP's fracture. A former Peruvian Communist Party–Bandera Roja activist and member of the CCP's executive committee stressed that the split at Eccash occurred precisely because of differing attitudes toward the agrarian reform.[43] But contrasting opinions about the agrarian reform and the military government were not the only factors behind the CCP's split. Instead, those disparate visions generated new fissures within the CCP, exacerbating other tensions within the organization. One such preexisting tension was the fact that activists in Vanguardia Revolucionaria felt that Paredes and Llamojha had done a poor job leading the CCP. This sentiment came through in the report produced after VR's Fourth National Campesino Congress at Huaral. Assessing the CCP's work in the year 1962, a year when major agrarian struggles broke out across the country, VR activists accused the CCP of having failed to capture and direct the momentum of Peru's campesinos, as it was "incapable of ensuring advances in the forging of an alliance of the proletariat with the peasantry."[44] Vanguardia Revolucionaria maintained that by the time of the CCP's 1970 Congress, "the participation of the bases was insignificant, the proceedings were bureaucratic," and the CCP did not "play the role of coordinator, organizer, centralizer, nor effective leader."[45] All of these shortcomings, by VR's telling, "drove the peasant organization toward its liquidation."[46]

Unlike VR's split from Paredes and Llamojha, the break between Llamojha and Paredes emerged from a sharp dispute over loyalty and money, a conflict that originated during Llamojha's trip to China in 1965. Llamojha explained: "It's that Paredes cheated us badly. He went to China, to ask for money, saying that he was making revolution, that there were already two liberated pueblos, when there was nothing. He wanted arms from China, for nothing." When Llamojha's Chinese hosts inquired about the progress of Paredes's revolutionary work, Llamojha revealed the truth: "I said, 'There is nothing. It's a lie.' . . . So China sent investigators, delegates from China, to investigate. And so they discovered the truth and they cut this aid to Paredes. So Paredes went over to another country, the socialists . . . in Europe."[47] Llamojha also recalled how Paredes and his supporters immediately turned against him, accusing him of collaboration with the Velasco regime and even trying to kill him.[48]

Llamojha's story is a compelling one, and it sits well with other activists' assertions that Paredes turned to Albania simply because it proved more willing to fund his political efforts.[49] Paredes's supporters, not surprisingly, offer a very different explanation of their leader's political decision. Pelayo Oré explained that Paredes broke with China because "it wasn't the political line that we wanted. We wanted the formation or implementation of the socialist system, but Mao wasn't thinking about this. He was just a nationalist and anti-imperialist. His political position was not correct." That differed, by Oré's telling, from the Albanians. "In Albania, Enver Hoxha had a correct position; as a disciple of Stalin, he had constructed socialism for over forty years . . . with the correct line of Marxism-Leninism."[50]

Paredes's Albanian turn—a switch that most likely happened after the 1973 fracture of the CCP—only further alienated Vanguardia Revolucionaria activists who already thought Paredes was excessively dogmatic.[51] Andrés Luna Vargas remembered that Paredes's ideological stance "turned extreme" when he embraced the Albanian line of Enver Hoxha. "What esotericism," Luna Vargas laughed. "Imagine that! Here? No way!" To Luna Vargas, Paredes's ideological views were completely divorced from the experiences and needs of Peru's campesinos, and that ideological disconnect was "one of the factors that, I believe, ended up completely distancing him, completely, from reality and from the bases."[52] Ricardo Letts Colmenares offered a similar perspective. He commented that "Saturnino separated himself from the Chinese line and went to the Albanian line of Enver Hoxha. What craziness!" Letts also expressed sadness that Paredes had taken such a "dogmatic and sectarian" turn.[53]

The CCP's fracture was also compounded by other political animosities. Members of the Peruvian Communist Party–Shining Path (Sendero Luminoso), whose leader, Abimael Guzmán, had broken with Paredes in 1969, experimented with peasant union activities during the first half of the 1970s by participating in Llamojha's faction of the CCP.[54] Although Llamojha himself never joined the Shining Path, Paredes supporters were quick to denounce the collaboration, commenting that Llamojha "has been picked up by the miniscule opportunist group named 'Shining,' a pseudo-revolutionary faction that carries out the government's strategic instruction to further divide the pueblo and the peasantry and at the same time diminish their struggles."[55] Paredes supporters also charged that "the politics of these 'Shining Ones' is really dubious, stupid, and consciously traitorous to the peasant movement."[56]

The CCP factions loyal to Paredes and Llamojha also decried the presence of Trotskyist activists inside Vanguardia Revolucionaria's CCP. The objection was largely specious: the Trotskyist faction had been forced out of Vanguardia Revolucionaria back in 1971. Yet it is true that the prominent Trotskyist activist Hugo Blanco—leader of Peru's most famous land invasions in the 1960s—decided to ally with Vanguardia Revolucionaria's CCP in the mid-1970s.[57] Blanco explained in 1976 that he had chosen to work with VR's CCP despite the fact that he did not belong to Vanguardia Revolucionaria. He made that choice, Blanco explained, because "it's only as a united group that we can defeat the government."[58] Though Blanco made that statement without intentional irony, the reality was that Blanco's presence in Vanguardia Revolucionaria's CCP only further entrenched the divides between the three CCP factions. Llamojha charged that "Hugo Blanco also wrecked things because he's a Trotskyist, nothing more than a provocateur," and he recalled how Blanco insulted him and tried to prevent him from speaking at a political event in Cuzco.[59] Paredes supporters, in turn, routinely derided VR's CCP for collaborating with Trotskyists.[60]

Following the split at Eccash, the three competing CCPs continued to fight over how to engage the Velasco regime and its agrarian reform. That fight grew particularly intense after a series of land invasions that Vanguardia Revolucionaria activists led in Andahuaylas in 1974, helping an estimated thirty thousand peasants seize almost seventy haciendas.[61] Following the invasions, representatives of VR and the Andahuaylas peasant federation negotiated with the Velasco government and struck an agreement with the regime. By the terms of these controversial accords, the regime acknowledged the legitimacy of Andahuaylas campesinos' claims to the seized lands. Campesinos, in turn, were required to pay the "agrarian debt" to compensate the affected hacendados. Many Peruvian leftists—including several members of Vanguardia Revolucionaria—saw these accords as an unacceptable compromise tantamount to betrayal of the masses and traitorous allegiance to the Velasco regime.[62]

Although the military government soon reversed its course and ar-

rested many Andahuaylas peasant leaders and Vanguardia Revolucionaria activists, Llamojha and Paredes—and their respective CCPs—nonetheless excoriated VR's CCP as collaborators with the Velasco regime.[63]
Llamojha remembered that "Vanguardia organized to seize land, but
with the end of delivering it to SINAMOS."[64] Activists in Paredes's
CCP made similar accusations, charging that Vanguardia Revolucionaria, "in agreement with the government and SINAMOS, brought
about the land seizures in Querecotillo and Andahuaylas, 'deepening'
the agrarian reform by implanting the CAPS, SAIS, Communal Enterprises [all forms of cooperatives]. They committed the peasantry to
payment for the land."[65] Their charges seemed all the stronger, given
that two of the most prominent VR activists who worked in Andahuaylas—Félix Loayza and Lino Quintanilla—had both briefly worked for
SINAMOS.[66]

Vanguardia Revolucionaria activists dismissed these criticisms. In a
1974 document, VR's CCP asserted that Llamojha was "childishly declaring that land seizures by the peasantry favor landlords and the military government."[67] The VR activist Lino Quintanilla, in turn, charged
that Llamojha was "hypocritically lying to the bases, saying that these
seizures that we were carrying out were in favor of the government, the
same way other infantilists who had never set foot in the countryside
slandered us."[68] Andrés Luna Vargas remembered: "Those sectors that
we deemed 'ultras' . . . said that to enter into land seizures was to get involved in the counterrevolutionary process of an agrarian reform that
came from the Pentagon. All of this was a terrain that was very ideological, political, abstract—because that's not what happened in reality."[69]

The dispute over land seizures obscured the principles shared by the
three rival CCPs. All three wanted peasants to have land, all three criticized the agrarian debt, and all three objected to SINAMOS and its efforts to control popular participation.[70] In addition, all three factions argued against state-controlled cooperatives, with VR activists assisting
several peasant invasions of cooperatives.[71] But while they shared many
similar ideas and attitudes, the three CCPs ultimately spent more energy and time fighting each other than confronting the military government and its reforms.[72]

The agrarian reform was not the only challenge the CCP faced. CCP
activists also had to confront the Velasco regime's determined effort to
overhaul peasant organizations inside Peru and further control rural
participation in the agrarian reform. With Decree Law 19400 passed in
May 1972, the RGAF mandated the creation of a new system of peasant

organizations: the establishment of Agrarian Leagues at the provincial level, Agrarian Federations at the departmental level, and the National Agrarian Confederation (CNA) at the national level. Just as importantly, Decree Law 19400 called for the dissolution of all existing rural organizations, effectively outlawing the CCP.[73]

The CNA officially began operations in October 1974.[74] The Velasco regime provided the nascent CNA—and the Agrarian Leagues and Agrarian Federations—with significant material support. The assets of newly dissolved landowners' associations—including the National Agrarian Society, the National Association of Cotton Producers, and the National Society of Cattle Ranchers—all passed into the CNA's hands.[75] The military government further supported its state-sponsored peasant organizations by offering them extensive publicity and ideological support. The Trotskyist peasant activist and former SINAMOS employee Antonio Cartolín recalled that his work with SINAMOS and with Ayacucho's Agrarian Federation involved "going to our communities, the bases of our federation, to give talks, to train, to talk to them [campesinos] with—as they say—our heart in hand."[76] The CNA was able to use government support to issue radio announcements, hold press conferences, and publish bulletins.[77] The government also required the prominent newspaper *El Comercio* to start publishing a supplement entitled *El Campesino* that celebrated the achievements of the Velasco regime in the countryside, including the work of the CNA.[78]

According to *Marka*, a left-wing periodical staunchly allied with VR's CCP, the CNA quickly became the largest peasant organization in Peru, with twenty departmental federations and 679,825 affiliates.[79] There is no doubt that much of the CNA's support came at the expense of the CCP. Many activists shared the views of Marcelino Bustamante, the Ancash campesino activist whose reflections opened this chapter. The Trotskyist activist Antonio Cartolín likewise broke from the CCP to join the CNA. Cartolín had played a major role in Ayacucho peasant organizing during the 1960s, serving as head of the CCP-allied Departmental Federation of Ayacucho Communities and Campesinos. But in the early 1970s, Cartolín accepted the government's invitation to work with SINAMOS, and he led the establishment of the government-sponsored Departmental Agrarian Federation of Ayacucho, the FADA (Federación Agraria Departamental de Ayacucho).[80] A FADA activist named Evaristo Quispe recalled CCP activists' outrage at Cartolín's decision. As he phrased it, "Antonio went to work at SINAMOS, and for that reason, they just about lynched him."[81] Reflecting on the CCP's leaders, Antonio Cartolín stressed that their ideological rigidity and their factionalism proved to be their undoing, stating that "they were little palisades with their dogmatism." He added that they suffered "because of their sectarianism, because they wanted to be the light that gave fire, but which in itself, from day to day, turned to ashes until there was nothing left."[82]

There was also a repressive dimension to the CNA's growth. Although peasant beneficiaries of the agrarian reform were not automatically required to become members of the CNA—or its affiliated Agrarian Leagues or Federations—many likely felt that state-sponsored organizations were the only safe options for rural activism. *Marka* noted that many union leaders had been charged with "the crime of sabotage against the agrarian reform" or simply jailed without explanation.[83] The periodical *Sur* offered a similar assessment, commenting that the CNA's "creation and function, linked to governmental decisions and support, made the CNA an organization in which the affiliation of the bases was practically coercive."[84] These periodicals were not exaggerating. Numerous CCP activists were indeed arrested by the Velasco regime, the CCP's central office was raided in 1973, and the Velasco government ordered the deportation of several CCP activists.[85]

Not surprisingly, all three factions of the CCP denounced Decree Law 19400 and the CNA, mobilizing charges of corporatism and Fascism. Manuel Llamojha Mitma wrote that the law "represented the vertical, corporatist organization of Fascism."[86] VR's Andrés Luna Vargas likewise decried the Velasco government's "intentions to control the peasantry through Law 19400."[87] Another Vanguardia Revolucionaria activist wrote that "the classist sectors of the peasantry and their leaders face repression, persecution, trials, and threats of deportation for fighting for their interests according to their principles, opposing Decree Law 19400 and the action of SINAMOS and other bodies that the government has sent to the countryside to combat the worker-peasant alliance."[88]

CCP activists aligned with Saturnino Paredes offered similar invectives against Decree Law 19400, asserting that "through an express legal mechanism, Decree Law 19400, . . . the military government is trying to destroy the antifeudal, classist organizations of the peasantry, replacing them with others in which exploited and exploiters of reactionary character are grouped together, under the control and orientation of the military regime."[89]

Activists from the CNA and its related Agrarian Federations today remember the antipathy CCP activists felt toward them. Evaristo Quispe, who worked with the Departmental Agrarian Federation of Ayacucho (FADA), recalled that CCP activists labeled FADA members "opportunists" and "rams, sheep of a criminal dictator."[90] The CNA activist Marcelino Bustamante similarly remembered that "the CCP thought it [the CNA] was a Fascist organization, a pro-government organization, managed, manipulable. But it wasn't like that."[91]

The fracturing of the CCP hampered the organization's ability to challenge the CNA; the members of the rival CCPs were too busy fighting one another to effectively fight the CNA. But the CNA could not take full advantage of the CCP's split, for the CNA itself was deeply divided. Some members of the CNA prioritized close collaboration with the military government, while others were prepared to challenge the regime in order to better advance peasants' interests.[92]

The split within the CNA worsened significantly after the August 1975 internal military coup that ousted General Velasco from power. Under the leadership of General Francisco Morales Bermúdez, the "Second Phase" of the Revolutionary Government of the Armed Forces slowed the course of agrarian reform and reversed many of Velasco's reforms. The more radical sectors of the CNA were quick to denounce the regime's actions, but many members of the CNA disagreed with this oppositional approach, believing the peasantry's best hopes lay in continued alliance with the military regime.[93] Following the 1977 election of Avelino Mar Arias as president of the CNA, a victory for the organization's more radical elements, the Morales Bermúdez regime soon began working to undermine the CNA from within, urging provincial and departmental peasant leagues and federations to block their leadership's directives.[94] The CNA's relationship with the military regime continued to deteriorate, and on May 30, 1978, the government issued Decree Law 22199, which disbanded the CNA.[95] Although the government withdrew all financial and material support from the CNA, the peasant association continued to operate.[96] In Avelino Mar's words, "The CNA will exist so long as it has bases, so long as the peasantry recognizes it."[97]

With the legal dissolution of the CNA, the slowing of the agrarian reform process, and the military government's 1977 announcement that Peru would transition back to democracy in 1980, all three CCPs made motions toward reuniting Peru's deeply divided peasant organizations. Members of Paredes's CCP invited those who belonged to the newly outlawed CNA to join their organization.[98] Paredes's CCP also sent Pelayo Oré to the Special National Congress of Unification of the

Peruvian Peasantry in Quillabamba, Cuzco, a meeting organized by the Provincial Federation of Campesinos of La Convención and Lares. At that August 1978 meeting, however, old hostilities quickly resurfaced. The periodical *Sur* reported that Oré "accused Llamojha and Luna Vargas of having broken the unity of the peasantry" with their retreat from Eccash, charging that they were "SINAMOS and imperialis[t] infiltrators."[99]

Manuel Llamojha Mitma likewise attended the Quillabamba meeting. He offered a heartfelt self-criticism regarding his role in the CCP's division and was subsequently elected president of the National Commission of Unification of the Peruvian Peasantry.[100] That election no doubt owed to the fact that Cuzco peasants—who represented eighty-eight of the ninety-eight delegates in attendance—had remained Llamojha's core base of support following the 1973 split of the CCP.[101]

Vanguardia Revolucionaria's CCP also took seriously the possibility of uniting the country's peasant organizations. At the Vanguardia Revolucionaria CCP's Fifth National Congress in August 1978 in Equeco Chacán, Cuzco—following on the heels of the Quillabamba meeting—delegates voted on three unification proposals: unification with the CNA and other "dispersed classist forces," integration of the CNA's ranks into the CCP, or unification of the three rival CCPs. In the end, members of VR's CCP voted for the first option—unification with the CNA—rejecting the possibility of reuniting the three CCP factions.[102]

Yet even unity with the CNA proved elusive. Although both the CNA and Vanguardia Revolucionaria's CCP issued repeated overtures for unification across the remainder of the 1970s and through the early 1980s, the two organizations never merged.[103] The differences between the organizations simply remained too great, and both the CNA and VR's CCP struggled with their own major internal divisions.[104] The other two CCPs, in turn, effectively ceased to exist. Llamojha ended his involvement in the CCP after the Equeco Chacán meeting, and Paredes's CCP halted its activities at the outset of the 1980s.[105]

At the 1978 national congress of Vanguardia Revolucionaria's CCP, a group of peasants stood holding a large sign that read "For Peasant Unification," but unity proved an impossible goal.[106] The Velasco regime's ambitious agrarian reform and its efforts to control peasant participation had sparked an ideological crisis within the CCP, generating enormous tensions and exacerbating existing divisions inside the organization. Those tensions and divisions were ones that Peruvian Peasant Confederation activists ultimately proved unwilling or unable to surmount.

The CCP did not face this ideological crisis alone; its experiences formed part of the larger history of the Peruvian left during the Velasco years. The rise of the Revolutionary Government of the Armed Forces provoked sharp divides inside the Peruvian left, as it did within the CCP. Many leftist activists chose to work with the Velasco regime, excited by the prospect of a government that promised long-overdue social and economic justice. Others took a more cautious approach, hoping they could radicalize the government's reforms. And still others rejected the regime entirely, deeming it corporatist and Fascist. These leftists insisted that revolutionary change could be driven only by the masses, not by the state, and they feared that government reformism might drain popular revolutionary sentiment. Some also worried that the regime might displace their parties and organizations, as the Velasco government pledged to fulfill long-standing leftist demands and as it created new state-directed bodies to mobilize Peruvian workers and other impoverished citizens.[107]

As happened with CCP activists, Peru's leftists faced serious obstacles in their efforts to confront the Velasco regime: many were harassed, others were arrested, and some were even deported by the government. These activists also expended tremendous energy fighting against one another in bitter factional disputes, rather than working together to challenge the regime. But when they saw popular protests and labor strikes explode in early 1975, many of these leftists probably thought Peru was on the cusp of a revolution that would be achieved through fire and blood.[108] What they witnessed instead was Velasco's ouster and the installation of a Second Phase military regime that proved far less progressive and decidedly more repressive than its predecessor.

Notes

I thank Alicia Carrasco Gutiérrez for research assistance and Ricardo Caro Cárdenas for providing access to key documents. The research for this chapter was funded by the Social Sciences and Humanities Research Council of Canada.

1. Interview with Marcelino Bustamante López, Lima, April 10, 2013. Unless otherwise noted, all interviews were conducted by Alicia Carrasco Gutiérrez, utilizing scripted interview questions I had prepared in advance. All translations to English are my own. Some of the material in this chapter appears in

Chapter 5 of *Now Peru Is Mine: The Life and Times of a Campesino Activist*, by Manuel Llamojha Mitma and Jaymie Patricia Heilman (Durham, NC: Duke University Press, 2016).

2. Key works include Mariano Valderrama, *7 años de reforma agraria peruana, 1969–1976* (Lima: Pontificia Universidad Católica del Perú, 1976); José Matos Mar and José Manuel Mejía, *La reforma agraria en el Perú* (Lima: IEP, 1980); José María Caballero, *Agricultura, reforma agraria y pobreza campesina* (Lima: IEP, 1980); Cynthia McClintock, *Peasant Cooperatives and Political Change in Peru* (Princeton, NJ: Princeton University Press, 1981); Abraham F. Lowenthal, ed., *The Peruvian Experiment: Continuity and Change Under Military Rule* (Princeton, NJ: Princeton University Press, 1975).

3. Linda J. Seligmann, *Between Reform and Revolution: Political Struggles in the Peruvian Andes, 1969–1991* (Stanford, CA: Stanford University Press, 1991); Elmer Arce Espinoza, *Perú 1969–1976: Movimientos agrarios y campesinos* (Lima: CEDEP, 2004); Enrique Mayer, *Ugly Stories of the Peruvian Agrarian Reform* (Durham, NC: Duke University Press, 2009).

4. Anna Cant, "'Land for Those Who Work It': A Visual Analysis of Agrarian Reform Posters in Velasco's Peru," *Journal of Latin American Studies* 44, no. 1 (February 2012): 3.

5. Iván Hinojosa, "On Poor Relations and the Nouveau Riche: Shining Path and the Radical Peruvian Left," in *Shining and Other Paths: War and Society in Peru, 1980–1995*, ed. Steve J. Stern (Durham, NC: Duke University Press, 1998), 69.

6. The CNA has received much more attention than the CCP. See Mariano Valderrama, "Movimiento campesino y la reforma agraria en el Perú," *Nueva Sociedad* 35 (March–April 1978): 103–113; Peter S. Cleaves and Martin J. Scurrah, *Agriculture, Bureaucracy and Military Government in Peru* (Ithaca, NY: Cornell University Press, 1980); Susan C. Bourque and David Scott Palmer, "Transforming the Rural Sector: Government Policy and Peasant Response," in Lowenthal, *The Peruvian Experiment*, 179–219; Arce Espinoza, *Perú 1969–1976*, 39–43, 76–79.

7. See Jane S. Jaquette, "Belaúnde and Velasco: On the Limits of Ideological Politics," in Lowenthal, *The Peruvian Experiment*, 408.

8. Ricardo Caro Cárdenas, "Vanguardia Revolucionaria: Una introducción a los orígenes y desarrollo de la Nueva Izquierda peruana, 1965–1972" (Licenciatura Thesis, Sociology, Pontificia Universidad Católica del Perú, 1998).

9. *Bandera Roja* March 20, 1964, 8; Hugo Neira, *Los Andes: Tierra o muerte* (Madrid: Editorial Zyx, 1968), 224.

10. Caro Cárdenas, "Vanguardia Revolucionaria," part 2, 2.

11. "Informe a la Asamblea Nacional de Delegados de la Confederación Campesina del Perú," *Informativo Agrario: Círculo de Estudios Artemio Zavala* 3 (August 1973): N.p.

12. "Resoluciones del III Congreso Nacional Campesino [1970]," *Informativo Agrario: Círculo de Estudios Artemio Zavala* 3 (August 1973): N.p.

13. CCP "Central Auténtica," *Conclusiones y resoluciones del V Congreso Nacional de la Confederación Campesina del Peru "Justiniano Minaya Sosa"* (N.p.: n.p., 1978), 5.

14. "Informe a la Asamblea Nacional de Delegados," n.p.

15. Ibid.

16. Confederación Campesina del Perú, *IV Congreso Nacional: Eccash, Ancash, 1973: Conclusiones y resoluciones* (Peru: Ediciones Voz Campesina, 1978), 10.

17. "Informe a la Asamblea Nacional de Delegados," n.p.

18. Interview with Pelayo Oré, Lima, August 11, 2011.

19. Confederación Campesina del Perú, *IV Congreso Nacional: Eccash, Ancash, 1973*, 16.

20. Defensoría del Pueblo, Centro de Información para la Memoria Colectiva y los Derechos Humanos (CIMCDH), interview with Manuel Llamocca [*sic*] Mitma.

21. "Resoluciones del III Congreso Nacional Campesino," n.p. See also, Confederación Campesina del Perú, *IV Congreso Nacional: Eccash, Ancash, 1973*, 23.

22. Interview with Marcelino Bustamante López, Lima, April 10, 2013.

23. Confederación Campesina del Perú, *IV Congreso Nacional Campesino: Torreblanca, Huaral, 5, 6, 7 de Mayo 1974. Informe Central* (N.p.: n.d.), 16.

24. Author interview with Andrés Luna Vargas, Lima, June 23, 2011.

25. Author interview with Andrés Luna Vargas, Lima, June 23, 2011; Confederación Campesina del Perú, *IV Congreso Nacional Campesino*, 27–30.

26. Confederación Campesina del Perú (CCP), *Manifiesto: Por la Unificación de las Luchas Populares* (November 15, 1974), n.p., in *Documenting the Peruvian Insurrection* (Woodbridge: Primary Source Microfilm, 2005); Lenin used the term "infantilist" to criticize ultraleft extremism. See Hinojosa, "On Poor Relations," 79n9.

27. "La lucha entre dos líneas y la reconstitución de la Confederación Campesina del Perú," *Informativo Agrario: Círculo de Estudios Artemio Zavala* 3 (August 1973): N.p.

28. José Luis Rénique, *La batalla por Puno: Conflicto agrario y nación en los Andes peruanos* (Lima: IEP, 2004), 193. Rénique's discussion of the events in Eccash is one of the few academic treatments of the CCP's fracture.

29. Confederación Campesina del Perú, *IV Congreso Nacional: Eccash, Ancash, 1973: Conclusiones y resoluciones* (Peru: Ediciones Voz Campesina, 1978), 7.

30. Author interview with Andrés Luna Vargas, Lima, June 23, 2011.

31. Confederación Campesina del Perú, *IV Congreso Nacional Campesino: Torreblanca, Huaral*, 10.

32. Carlos Herbozo Martínez, "Justiniano Minaya Sosa y el movimiento campesino en el Perú," *Tierra y Liberación: Revista de Crítica e Investigación Agraria*, no. 1 (September 1978): 64.

33. Interview with Pelayo Oré, Lima, August 11, 2011.

34. Ibid.; Herbozo Martínez, "Justiniano Minaya Sosa," 64.

35. Confederación Campesina del Perú, *IV Congreso Nacional: Eccash, Ancash, 1973*, 4. Herbozo Martínez, in "Justiniano Minaya Sosa," states that the murder occurred on May 28, 1973.

36. Mariano Valderrama, "Movimiento campesino y la reforma agraria en el Perú," *Nueva Sociedad* 35 (March–April 1978): 103–113; author interview with Andrés Luna Vargas, Lima, June 23, 2011.

37. Saturnino Paredes, *El trabajo en el frente campesino*, 2nd ed. (Lima: Ediciones Trabajo y Lucha, 1976), 4. Pages 1–36 of this book form an introduction written by unnamed editors.

38. *Bandera Roja* 11, no. 52 (September 1973): 18.

39. *Tierra y Liberación: Órgano de la Federación Departamental de Comunidades y Campesinos de Ayacucho (FEDCCA)* 1, no. 1 (January 1975): 3.

40. CCP "Central Auténtica," *Conclusiones y resoluciones del V Congreso Nacional de la Confederación Campesina del Perú "Justiniano Minaya Sosa"* (N.p., 1978), 14.

41. Confederación Campesina del Perú, *IV Congreso Nacional Campesino: Torreblanca, Huaral*, 3.

42. CIMCDH, interview with Manuel Llamocca [*sic*] Mitma.

43. Author interview with Armando Castillo (pseudonym), Ayacucho, May 20, 2011.

44. Confederación Campesina del Perú, *IV Congreso Nacional Campesino: Torreblanca, Huaral*, 8.

45. Ibid., 10.

46. Ibid., 10. It is possible that there were also quiet tensions of race and class driving the divides between these activists. The leaders of Vanguardia Revolucionaria were relatively wealthy, urban activists who were not indigenous, while both Paredes and Llamojha were from the indigenous Andean countryside. Such tensions, however, did not surface in an explicit way in either the written record or in oral history interviews.

47. Interview with Manuel Llamojha, Concepción, January 26, 2011.

48. Ibid.

49. Interview with Franco Silva (pseudonym), Ayacucho, February 14, 2012.

50. Interview with Pelayo Oré, Lima, December 24, 2011.

51. Interview with Ricardo Letts, Lima, October 22, 2012. The exact date of Paredes's Albanian turn is difficult to pinpoint. Pelayo Oré remembered only that it happened before Mao's death in 1976. There was no mention of Albania in the documents produced by Paredes supporters immediately after the 1973 Eccash congress, yet their 1978 congress featured a visit from two Albanian representatives and the congress proceedings repeatedly lauded Albania and criticized China. It is thus likely that Paredes changed his political allegiance between 1973 and 1976.

52. Author interview with Andrés Luna Vargas, Lima, June 23, 2011.

53. Interview with Ricardo Letts Colmenares, Lima, October 22, 2012.

54. The PCP-SL abandoned Llamojha's CCP following a national congress in Ayacucho in 1975, deciding that union activity was counterrevolutionary. See Llamojha Mitma and Heilman, *Now Peru Is Mine*, Chapter 5.

55. *Tierra y Liberación: Órgano de FEDCCA* 1, no. 1 (January 1975): 11.

56. Paredes, *El trabajo en el frente campesino*, 25.

57. Caro Cárdenas, "Vanguardia Revolucionaria," part 4, chapter 10.

58. *World Outlook* (January 30, 1976): 19.

59. CIMCDH, interview with Manuel Llamocca [*sic*] Mitma; author interview with Manuel Llamojha, Concepción, May 05, 2013.

60. *Voz Campesina "Auténtica"* 32, no. 30 (February 1979): 7.

61. Florencia Mallon, "Chronicle of a Path Foretold? Velasco's Revolution, Vanguardia Revolucionaria, and 'Shining Omens' in the Indigenous Communities of Andahuaylas," in Stern, *Shining and Other Paths*, 84–117; Rodrigo Sánchez Enríquez, *Toma de tierras y conciencia política campesina: Las lecciones de Andahuaylas* (Lima: IEP, 1981).

62. Mallon, "Chronicle of a Path Foretold?," 108–111.

63. Ibid., 109.

64. CIMCDH, interview with Manuel Llamocca [*sic*] Mitma.

65. *Tierra y Liberación*, no. 1 (September 1978): 81.

66. Mallon, "Chronicle of a Path Foretold?," 95.

67. Confederación Campesina del Perú (CCP), *Manifiesto*, n.p.

68. Lino Quintanilla, *Testimonio de Andahuaylas* (Lima: Círculo de Cultura e Investigación José María Arguedas, 1974), 15.

69. Author interview with Andrés Luna Vargas, Lima, June 23, 2011.

70. Confederación Campesina del Perú, *IV Congreso Nacional Campesino: Torreblanca, Huaral*, 11.

71. Diego García-Sayán, *Tomas de tierras en el Perú* (Lima: DESCO, 1982), 35–36, 123–217; Tanya Korovkin, *Politics of Agricultural Co-Operativism: Peru, 1969–1983* (Vancouver: University of British Columbia Press, 1990), 33; Mayer, *Ugly Stories*, 156–157.

72. The divides and fights that plagued the CCP were far from unusual: similar ideological arguments, splits, and internecine battles were common within both the Peruvian left and the larger Latin American left. See Hinojosa, "On Poor Relations," 64–66; Alan Angell, "The Left in Latin America since c. 1920," in *Cambridge History of Latin America Volume 6: 1930 to the Present, Part 2: Politics and Society*, ed. Leslie Bethell (Cambridge: Cambridge University Press, 1995), 163.

73. http://docs.peru.justia.com/federales/decretos-leyes/19400-may-9-1972 .pdf.

74. "C.N.A.," *Sur* 1, no. 3 (June 1978), 9.

75. "La implicancia de la C.N.A.," *El Campesino: Revista Semanal de El Comercio*, June 24, 1975, 1.

76. Interview with Antonio Cartolín, Lima, April 13, 2013.

77. "La labor de la C.N.A.," *El Campesino: Revista Semanal de El Comercio*, June 24, 1975, 1.

78. *El Comercio* was actually supposed to pass into the CNA's control, but this never occurred. See McClintock, *Peasant Cooperatives*, 268.

79. "¿Quién es quién en el campo?," *Marka*, July 19, 1979, 28.

80. Interview with Antonio Cartolín, Lima, April 13, 2013.

81. Author interview with Evaristo Quispe, Ayacucho, May 25, 2011.

82. Interview with Antonio Cartolín, Lima, April 13, 2013.

83. "Política oficial y movilización campesina," *Marka*, June 24, 1976, 20.

84. "Organizaciones campesinas," *Sur* 3, no. 23 (January 1980): 55.

85. Sánchez, *Toma de tierras*, 124; Andrés Luna Vargas, *Historia de un luchador campesino: Andrés Luna Vargas, Secretario general de la CCP* (Lima: Centro Peruano de Estudios Sociales, 1979), 49; Confederación Campesina del Perú, *IV Congreso Nacional: Eccash, Ancash, 1973*, 17–18; Arce, *Perú 1969–1976*, 123.

86. "La lucha entre dos líneas y la reconstitución de la Confederación Campesina del Perú," *Informativo Agrario: Círculo de Estudios Artemio Zavala* 3 (August 1973): N.p.

87. Andrés Luna Vargas quoted in "CCP: Una línea de masas," *Marka*, June 24, 1976, 22.

88. Confederación Campesina del Perú, *IV Congreso Nacional Campesino: Torreblanca, Huaral*, 21.

89. Confederación Campesina del Perú, *IV Congreso Nacional: Eccash, Ancash, 1973*, 17.

90. Author interview with Evaristo Quispe, Ayacucho, May 25, 2011.

91. Interview with Marcelino Bustamante López, Lima, April 10, 2013.

92. Korovkin, *Politics of Agricultural Co-operativism*, 36; "CNA: Reforma o Revolución," *Marka*, September 27, 1979, 34.

93. "La denuncia de la CNA," *Revolución Proletaria: Órgano del Partido Obrero Marxista Revolucionario* 27 (September 23, 1976): 16.

94. Ibid.; "CNA: El proceso devora a sus hijos," *Marka*, November 17, 1977, 22–23; "Entrevista a la CNA," *Marka*, January 19, 1978, 19.

95. "C.N.A.," *Sur* 1, no. 3 (June 1978): 16.

96. "Congreso nacional de la CNA," *Sur* 2, no. 21 (November 1979): 1.

97. "Mitin unitario multitudinario," *Sur* 1, no. 6 (August 1978): 79.

98. CCP "Central Auténtica," *Conclusiones y resoluciones del V Congreso Nacional*, 16.

99. "Congreso Campesino en Quillabamba," *Sur* 1, no. 7 (October 1978): 3.

100. Ibid.

101. Ibid., 1.

102. "Centralización sindical campesina y popular," *Sur* 1, no. 6 (August 1978): 68.

103. On the continuing efforts for VR-CCP/CNA unity, see "Entrevista a Andrés Luna Vargas," *Sur* 2, no. 19 (September 1979): 11; "Por una central única campesina," *Equis X*, June 24, 1985, 32.

104. "CNA: Reforma o Revolución," *Marka*, September 27, 1979, 34; "Congreso Nacional de la CNA," *Sur* 2, no. 21 (November 1979): 1; "Centralización sindical campesina y popular," *Sur* 1, no. 6 (August 1978): 68.

105. Today, a handful of Paredes loyalists are working to revive their CCP, once again asserting their status as the true and authentic CCP. See "Exitoso VI Congreso Nacional de 1 CCP," http://altopiura.blogspot.ca/2008/10/exitoso-vi-congreso-nacional-de-la-ccp.html.

106. "Centralización sindical campesina y popular," *Sur* 1, no. 6 (August 1978): 69.

107. Hinojosa, "On Poor Relations," 64, 68–70; Julio Cotler, "Democracy and National Integration in Peru," in McClintock and Lowenthal, *The Peruvian Experiment Reconsidered*, 32–35.

108. Hinojosa, "On Poor Relations," 66, 70; Cynthia McClintock, "Velasco, Officers, and Citizens: The Politics of Stealth," in McClintock and Lowenthal, *The Peruvian Experiment Reconsidered*, 300.

CHAPTER 7

Velasco, Nationalist Rhetoric, and Military Culture in Cold War Peru

LOURDES HURTADO

The future of our country depends on the historical responsibility that the armed forces are fulfilling now.
GENERAL JUAN VELASCO ALVARADO, 1971[1]

In twenty-first-century Peru, no military building carries the name of General Juan Velasco. A quick search in the historical section of the army's institutional web page describes 1968 as the year in which certain "circumstances" forced the army to stop depending on US weaponry and to rely on Soviet armament instead. The same official page characterizes the 1970s as the decade when the army opened the Training School for Noncommissioned Officers, and when the Peruvian military sent peacekeeping missions abroad for the first time.[2] The only reference to General Velasco is a marginal entry in the list of generals who were chiefs of staff after the 1960s.[3] The virtual disappearance of Velasco's memory from the army's official narratives starkly contrasts with the centrality that his image played during the First Phase of the Revolutionary Government of the Armed Forces (RGAF; 1968–1975), and with the very present collective, if contested, memories as discussed in Paulo Drinot's chapter elsewhere in this volume.

The army has sent Velasco's memory to the bottom of its collective "memory box," that space which, according to Steve Stern, is a community's foundational component, a "precious box to which people are drawn, to which they add or rearrange pictures and scripts, and about which they quarrel and even scuffle."[4] Throughout the twentieth century, the army filled that box with images of dead heroes that reminded military males of the sacrifices that other men who belonged to this institution made for the fatherland.[5] It also filled the box with discourses about the army's uniqueness, its importance and standing in Peruvian history. During the First Phase of the RGAF, the army's memory box enshrined the image of General Velasco: it acknowledged his role as the revolution's leader and assigned him the role of the older brother of the Peruvian nation. After Velasco was overthrown by a coup in 1975, he became ostracized until his death in 1977, and he disappeared from the army's official record. Nevertheless, Velasco's image remained alive at the margins of the institution: among some younger officers who identified themselves with Velasco's social reforms, among the rank-and-file, the military veterans known as *licenciados*, and radical groups such as *etnocacerista* officers.[6]

This chapter examines military culture in twentieth-century Peru. It discusses how the army articulated a complex and sometimes contradictory rhetoric that addressed its institutional and psychological shortcomings and that used concepts such as "institutional adulthood," "inferiority complex," and "institutional superiority." General Velasco's rhetoric was nurtured by a military culture that highlighted the Peruvian army's manliness, heroism, and leading role in the making of the nation. The general advanced this discourse by glorifying the army's popular origins, redefining this institution's historical responsibility in relation to Peru's contemporary present, and skillfully honoring its gender and patriarchal expectations.

As discussed in the introduction to this volume, the literature on the Peruvian military experiences of 1968–1980 is vast. Most of it discusses the political and economic characteristics of the regime. Some institutional histories such as Daniel Masterson's consider the coup of 1968 as the last step the military took to redefine their political role in Peru.[7] For Juan Martín Sánchez, the regime incorporated a blend of Catholic social thought and aimed to create a sovereign and developed state where military discipline was essential. This project was not related to any foreign ideology, and it had to be implemented in a peaceful and organized way.[8] In this literature we can also situate Cecilia Méndez's work in which she explores the relationship between the peasantry and the military in the nineteenth and twentieth centuries. As the army became more professionalized, its interactions with the peasantry became more vertical and hierarchical. Méndez considers Velasco's period of rule one of several authoritarian regimes that was attentive to the interests of the peasantry.[9]

A strand of the literature on the Peruvian military studies the army's cultural and social characteristics. Víctor Villanueva pays attention to the army's institutional culture and explores the military's constant search for self-legitimation throughout the twentieth century. Army officers developed an inferiority complex as a consequence of the defeat they suffered in the war of 1879 against Chile.[10] Dirk Kruijt focuses on the backgrounds of the officers involved in the 1968 coup. They came from the lower middle class and low classes in the provinces; this made them different from their peers in both the navy and the air force because these institutions attracted men from the upper and middle urban classes. This different social background constituted a factor of autonomy with regard to the oligarchy, one of self-legitimation and identification with the popular classes.[11]

This chapter contributes to the study of the Peruvian army during General Velasco's regime. It builds on Dirk Kruijt's idea of how army officers' social origins became an element of self-legitimation and identification with the people and on Villanueva's discussion about the army's notion of institutional superiority. It illustrates how General Velasco used his own humble origins to legitimize his position as the leader of the revolution. The first section examines the army's military culture before 1968, its notions of manliness and a successful military masculinity. Section two analyzes General Velasco's persona under the light of that military culture and examines the general's views about the army's adulthood and the recovery of national honor. Section three discusses the general's decline.

Transforming the Army into a Manly Institution

Throughout the twentieth century, the Peruvian army was interested in professionalizing its officer corps as well as educating the recruits that year after year filled its barracks.[12] Apart from its focus on education and nation building, the army created a pantheon of heroic figures that provided its officers with a historical narrative that legitimized the army's leading role in Peruvian society.[13]

General Manuel A. Odría, president of Peru between 1948 and 1956, made the most aggressive conscious choices to position the army as one of Peru's most important and privileged institutions. He elevated the status of army officers, increased their economic benefits and salaries, gave free medical insurance to active duty and retired officers, extended these benefits to their families, and established a high-quality retirement fund that was equivalent to thirty salaries at the moment officers retired, in addition to their pension.[14] Odría also allowed officers to import cars without paying taxes and created military bazaars that imported all types of merchandise, including luxury items, tax free. With all these prerogatives, Peruvian army officers enjoyed some of the comforts and benefits of the middle and upper echelons of Peruvian society.

General Odría also introduced reforms in the army's educational system, such as changes in the training of officers. The Organic Law of the Army of 1950 stated that the Chorrillos Military Academy (Escuela Militar de Chorrillos; EMCH) was the only institution in Peru that could train new army officers. In 1950, he opened the Center of Advanced Military Studies (Centro de Altos Estudios Militares; CAEM), the army's think tank that offered postgraduate programs for colonels and generals.[15] In the classrooms of CAEM, the Peruvian War College, and the School of Intelligence, the newer generations of Peruvian senior officers discussed Peru's economic and political problems and the ways to overcome them.[16]

Odría's regime also established the legal and institutional settings that promoted a new pantheon of heroic figures that embodied a manlier and more masculine bearing within the army. A series of decrees published in 1951 stated that Peruvians needed "new symbols and expressions" that reminded them of the moral lessons they had learned from their past. Odría declared Francisco Bolognesi the army's patron (*patrono*) and enshrined other nineteenth-century heroic figures such as Andrés A. Cáceres, Ramón Castilla, Pedro Ruiz Gallo, and José J. Inclán as patrons of the infantry, cavalry, engineering corps, and artillery, respectively. Promoting new military heroes who were mostly connected with the War of the Pacific had deeper implications for the army's ideological makeup.[17]

Víctor Villanueva, one of the few military intellectuals who wrote critically about Peruvian military culture, stated that Peru's defeat by Chile in the War of the Pacific (1879–1883) had shaped the pattern of interactions between the military and civilians in twentieth-century Peru. This war brought about not only the invasion of Peruvian territory by Chilean forces but also the loss of the rich provinces of Arica and Tarapacá. Later, in 1931, Peru would experience another defeat in the war with Colombia. As a consequence of that war, Peru lost the province of Leticia, in the Amazonian rain forest. Villanueva stated that the army's incapacity to defend Peru's physical integrity triggered "an institutional inferiority complex and a psychological trauma."[18] This complex had to be solved by "overcompensation," a process through which army officers crafted and spread an institutional discourse in which they and their military community appeared "heroic," "courageous," and "better" than the rest of Peruvians. As Villanueva says, "One of the mechanisms that the Peruvian army used to heal its psychological traumas and overcome its frustrations . . . was overcompensation. The army made this conscious choice to stand out and increase its own sense of self-worth and annihilate the inferiority complex caused by humiliating military defeats."[19]

The army's desire to overcome its legacies of defeat can be seen in the way that General Odría reworked Bolognesi's public image. Between 1905 and 1953, the centric Bolognesi Square displayed the hero's statue made by the Italian artist Mariano Querol. This image represented the hero holding the Peruvian flag at the very moment when he was dying in the Battle of Arica. In 1954, however, after Odría passed the decrees that officially declared Bolognesi the army's institutional patron, he commissioned the artist Artemio Ocaña to create a new image of the hero that portrayed him with a more manly military bearing.[20] Ocaña's statue was placed in the plaza in 1954. It represented Bolognesi holding the Peruvian flag in his right hand and a pistol in the other, ready to "fire the last round."[21] This new image of the hero conveyed the winning and more assertive attitude that the Peruvian army promoted beginning in the 1950s.

Odría's refashioning of the army's heroic figures was only one of several changes that expressed a new moment in this institution's historical consciousness, and that would be more evident in the 1960s. For example, in the *Historia de la Escuela Militar del Perú*, a book published in 1962 to commemorate the fiftieth anniversary of the Military Academy, the army stated that never again would it expose itself to a situation that might lead to defeat. The war with Chile still influenced the Peruvian military's self-perception. The *Historia de la Escuela Militar* said that it was important to maintain a living memory of the War of the Pacific (1879–1883), of the "tragedy of 1879," and it reminded readers that the Military Academy was located in Chorrillos, a neighborhood in southwest Lima, as "a constant reminder of the old pains and bloody battles" that the army had endured during the war.[22] This was an allusion to the Battles of San Juan and Miraflores (January 1881), near Chorrillos, during which Peruvian soldiers and civilians tried unsuccessfully to defend Lima from the Chilean invasion.

In the 1960s, however, and as a consequence of the reforms that had taken place in the previous decade, Peruvian army officers were convinced that their institution had become stronger and that they were in a much better situation than in the past. As they stated when they referred to the Peruvian Military Academy (Escuela Militar de Chorrillos): "The Military Academy has become a powerful educational center that has allowed us [the officers] to overcome any inferiority complex. We are now assertive about our physical, moral, and mental capacity to make of this country a great nation, as it was in ancient times."[23]

This institutional rhetoric at the turn of the 1960s was further complicated by the spread of Cold War anxieties in Latin America, fueled by class and gender differences and by the threat of Communism. The Peruvian army embraced and glorified a warrior masculinity that focused on the defense of Peru's national security against external and internal enemies that had caused anxiety for the military since at least the 1930s, when the army targeted the Alianza Popular Revolucionaria Americana (APRA), a center-left populist party led by Víctor Raúl Haya de la Torre.

The November 1963 cover of *Actualidad Militar*, the army's official publication, reveals some of the anxieties and assumptions that Peruvian cold warriors had to deal with at that time. On this cover, we see a soldier wearing a uniform, carrying a gun across his chest and standing on Peruvian territory. Next to the soldier there are three men wearing the clothes that stereotypically associate them with Peru's three principal regions: the coast, the highlands, and the rain forest. There is also an urban family, with a man wearing a suit and a woman wearing a dress carrying her baby. All these people are very small and seem overshadowed by the imposing presence of the soldier, who stands boldly in the middle, almost as if he was on a pedestal. On the left of the picture, in the middle of a cloud, we see the Four Horsemen of the Apocalypse menacing Peru and Peruvians. The soldier, however, is stopping them with his right hand. He will not allow them to get close to Peruvian territory. His left hand, held still and next to his body, is making a fist. Under the soldier is the caption "The Army: Sentry of the Nation" (fig. 7.1). This image illustrates the Peruvian army's Cold War discourse in the 1960s: the male Peruvian army would not allow any evil/foreign forces to take control of or penetrate Peruvian territory, the feminized fatherland, as had occurred during the War of the Pacific. The *Actualidad Militar* picture positioned the soldier as the defender of the Peruvian nation and as the highest example of the country's identity and power. In the editorial of the same issue, the military stated that the Horsemen of the Apocalypse—war, famine, death, and pestilence—"affected countries that, despite their vast natural resources, had been unable to reach

Figure 7.1. Cold War Soldier. *Actualidad Militar*, November 30, 1963.

civic maturity" but that in Peru the army sought to counter the country's lack of "civism."[24] In the 1960s, as they stated in the 1962 *Historia de la Escuela Militar*, army officers had already "overcome" their old "inferiority complex" and were "assertive about their physical, moral, and mental capacity" to make of Peru "a great nation."[25] As the image of *Actualidad Militar* conveyed, the Peruvian soldier was able to protect everybody in the nation, not only women and children, but other men, too, because he embodied the ideal of a hegemonic masculinity and was superior to those other men.[26] The analysis of the army's rhetoric during the 1960s, as it appeared in several military publications, suggests that this discourse not only aimed to "compensate" for the army's incapacity to defend Peru's national borders in the nineteenth and early twentieth centuries but also tried to "redeem" its popular and Andean origins in relation to other military branches such as the navy and the air force. After all, the army had an "indigenous face" that the other Peruvian military institutions did not have.[27]

In the 1960s, drawing on the teachings of CAEM and on an international context that fostered revolution, national liberation, and the spread of the Catholic Church's social doctrine, the army blamed the Peruvian oligarchy for maintaining the conditions that favored exploitation of indigenous peoples. From the army's perspective, the barracks erased social and ethnic differences, and all the components of the Peruvian military—officers, noncommissioned officers (NCOs), and enlisted men—were equally important for the army. However, rhetoric was not reality, and the military family indeed reproduced the hierarchies operating in Peruvian society in mid-twentieth-century Peru. The army officer corps usually came from "whiter" middle-class and lower-middle-class sectors, whereas NCOs came from more popular backgrounds, and the army's rank-and-file had indigenous and rural origins.

Despite this internal stratification, however, in relation to the other military branches, the army's officer corps was less "white." The reason for this lay in the army's spatial distribution. Since it was the largest military institution and had a stronger presence throughout Peruvian national territory, the army offered more chances for social mobility to men from popular sectors and regional mestizo elites than the navy or the air force. Also, until 1950, noncommissioned officers in good standing who had served in the army for many years had the chance to obtain a commission after passing a set of qualification exams.[28] And young men who enrolled in military service for at least one year received additional points on their admission exams for the Military Academy.

If we consider that in Peru military service had usually been stigmatized because it was associated with the indigenous and the poor, and if we acknowledge that some army officers actually rose through the ranks after performing military service, we can understand why this military branch was more associated with Peru's popular sectors in the 1960s. An example of this situation was the composition of the Revolutionary Government of the Armed Forces. The majority of the leading generals and colonels who participated in the coup of 1968 came from humble urban origins or from farming families from the countryside. Several of them had fulfilled their compulsory military service before being admitted to the Military Academy to pursue a military career.[29]

The army's "ethnicization," that is to say, the fact that this institution presented a more racially and ethnically diverse composition than the other military branches in Peru in the 1960s, was also represented in Peruvian urban contemporary literature. Mario Vargas Llosa, in *The Time of the Hero* (1966), portrayed how the army-run Leoncio Prado High School evoked opposite meanings for the novel's main characters. Thus, when the friends of upper-class Alberto Fernández, "The Poet," found out that he was going to study at Leoncio Prado, they took pity on him and teased him for attending a "school for *cholos*" (acculturated indigenous people) and risking the loss of his "white" social status. The same school, however, had a different meaning for Porfirio Cava, "The Serrano," a *cholo* student who came from a city in the highlands. Cava regarded his attendance at Leoncio Prado as a preliminary step to being admitted into the Military Academy (Escuela Militar de Chorrillos) to become an artillery commissioned officer, and thereby achieve his goal of social and economic mobility.[30]

This was the army that nurtured General Juan Velasco and the cultural milieu the allowed his rise to power. The army of the late 1960s was an institution concerned about its real capacities to defend Peru from the menaces of the Latin American Cold War. It endorsed renewed ideals about the primacy of a military masculinity over other subordinate ones, and it was aware of the racial and social differences that made it a unique institution.

Velasco and the Army's New Mission

General Velasco Alvarado's initiation into power began with a public demonstration of force and a spectacle on the eve of October 3, 1968.

That night, President Fernando Belaúnde Terry was informed by his presidential guard that a coup was in the making and that the army requested that he peacefully leave the Government Palace. Tanks and armored vehicles from the nearby Armored Division (the División Aerotransportada, located in El Rímac) surrounded Lima's main square; a strong contingent of paratroopers was also stationed around the plaza. President Belaúnde had to abandon the palace in the middle of the night, unharmed but humiliated, incapable of sparking loyalties among the officers closest to him.

Early the next day, General Velasco arrived at the Government Palace in a helicopter, and a new phase in Peruvian contemporary history began. By displaying the male signs of power and military might, Velasco's takeover was similar to other military regimes in Latin America that also endorsed foundational purposes and attempted to bring "order" to their new societies.[31] This display of force, however, was the only coincidence between General Velasco's regime and dictatorships in Argentina or Chile, because the Peruvian military attempted to undertake a social revolution and transform Peru's deeply ingrained social and economic inequalities, whereas the others did not.

During the Cold War, Latin American militaries had to deal with the tension of defending their countries from external menaces and internal enemies that became much more evident with the triumph of the Cuban Revolution in 1959. In the case of Peru and Brazil, local armies envisioned a doctrine that equated security with development.[32] General Velasco and the officers who supported him in the coup took the army's security doctrine to a higher level, and the general stated that to achieve development, the army's mission was to make revolution.

For General Velasco, the army's legitimacy to implement a revolution came from his institution's historical origins. Throughout the twentieth century, the army nurtured the idea that it was the institution that had allowed the independence of Peru in the nineteenth century, and it promoted the concept that the founding fathers of the Peruvian nation were military men. In fact, the army acknowledges the Battle of Ayacucho, which took place on December 9, 1824, as its foundational moment.[33] For Velasco, the army's "glorious" origins and its role as the forger of the Peruvian nation gave it "the historical responsibility" to conduct reforms in Peru.[34]

According to the general, the army was capable of leading a revolution because it had reached a "level of institutional maturity" that entitled it to implement transformations. As a consequence of its institutional adulthood, in the 1960s the army had developed a new "historical consciousness" that led its officers to reflect on the role they played in contemporary Peru.[35] Velasco was aware of the new moment that the Peruvian army was going through. He was the spokesperson of a section within the army that felt that the time had come to make a revolution because "the deep reforms that Peru needed were impossible within the traditional political system."[36] He also acknowledged that although in the nineteenth century the army had contributed to Peru's independence, during the twentieth century the oligarchy had used this institution to defend its own economic and political interests. The general clearly stated that "those who historically were responsible for the deep crisis in which Peru was before the revolution [i.e., the oligarchy] always flattered our armed forces. Deep down, however, they felt for us the same contempt that they felt for the people. And they felt it that way because they knew that we, the men from the Peruvian army, came from the people [*el pueblo*], and they knew that sooner or later we would go back to it."[37]

General Velasco was also very outspoken against US political and economic influence in Peru because it affected the country's sovereignty. He also acknowledged that the United States' economic interests in Peru were a humiliating issue for Peruvian sovereignty. In the 1977 interview that he gave to César Hildebrandt, he stated:

> [After 1968] Peru was no longer a subjugated country [*un país vendido*], a nation that had to kneel down. How were things here before? Here, the American ambassador had to ask for an appointment and [I] kept him six feet distant. I didn't allow them [the Americans] to foul things up. I kicked them away! Here there were fifty or sixty American chiefs, and the Peruvian government had to pay them their salaries, their plane ticket, and even the cat that the family brought with them. And they also provided the CIA with information. We didn't need them, we had grown up enough and we did not need to ask them about everything. Here our army schools were very good. We could even have trained them [the Americans].[38]

"We didn't need them"; "We had grown up enough"—in these remarks, the general conveys the widespread notion that the Peruvian army had become mature enough to pursue larger issues. Under that logic, it was possible for the army to even pursue the social and economic transformations that Peru needed, and the time had come for the army to act autonomously. General Velasco specifically talked about the very advanced level of professionalization that the Peruvian military enjoyed by the 1960s. He also made reference to the fact that Peru was an emasculated country, and he acknowledged the growth of the Peruvian army by the time of the 1968 coup.

From Velasco's perspective, both the army and the people had been oppressed. The people had been subdued by the oligarchy and foreign influences, and the oligarchy had used the army as a political pawn to fight for its own interests. However, the general said, in the second half of the twentieth century, the army had developed a new historical consciousness. Its officers became aware of the wide gap that separated the oligarchy from the army and realized that their mission was not "to reinforce an order of injustice but to eradicate it," and that the army's role was not to "strengthen foreign domination" but to "destroy it."[39] For Velasco, in late-1960s Peru, the army had nothing in common with the oligarchy because "the lines were very well established between [it and] them [the oligarchy]."[40] The two camps were well defined.

The wider the gap that existed between the oligarchy and the armed forces, the closer the army grew to the Peruvian people. This connection and proximity between the army and the poor and the excluded also legitimized the Peruvian Revolution. The RGAF created a term, the "Binomio Pueblo–Fuerza Armada," to address that body made up of the people and the armed forces. They both had been oppressed by the oligarchy, and after reversing their subjugation, together they would be able to implement transformations in Peru. The "Revolution Anthem," a song written in 1969 to commemorate the first anniversary of the revolution, and that was later played at all of Velasco's public presentations, expressed these feelings:

The armed forces are with the people,
and Velasco is leading Peru.
Today they both embody the principles of justice
for the oppressed people of Peru.
Today they both impose their redemptive flag
over [the people's] memories of pain and slavery.[41]

Because of his own social origins, Velasco himself was the embodiment of the Binomio Pueblo–Fuerza Armada. In his speeches, he usually made reference to his humble background in the barrio of Castilla, in the city of Piura, to remind the people that he was one of them. He liked talking to the masses with "sincere and simple words" because he favored a language that "the people understood."[42] And he also had the capacity to connect with Peruvians at a very emotional level. As he said in one of his appearances in Piura in 1970:

> My home was here and my roots are here. I still remember . . . the years of my provincial and happy adolescence. My family were humble people, without any lineages, and one day they saw me depart toward the capital, where I began my military career as a simple private[, . . . and now] I am the child who returns home after so many years, carrying on my shoulders the responsibility of being the representative of the deep revolution that our nation is experiencing.[43]

The image of the young and inexperienced recruit who left his home village and later returned to his community as a grown-up man was a common trope in military publications in the 1960s and 1970s.[44] In the quote above, the general connected his own personal narrative to the experience of thousands of men who, like him, had had to leave their homes to perform military service, and to the families whose children had been enlisted and who waited for them to come home. In another speech in that same visit to Piura in 1970, he told the people in Castilla's main square that they probably thought that since he had returned as the president of Peru, he might "no longer remember the hardships and sacrifices that humble people have to deal with." But the general reassured them and said that he had never forgotten the people and that they were the reason he had decided to undertake the revolution.[45]

Apart from General Velasco's and the army's humble origins, the military's legitimacy to rule Peru was based on its capacity to recover national honor. Velasco had stated that the army's mission was not to "strengthen foreign domination" but to "destroy it."[46] The event that symbolized the recovery of national honor was the occupation of Talara's oil wells, under the control of the US-owned International Petroleum Company (IPC).

The IPC had monopolized oil exploitation in Piura since the 1920s and had developed extremely unequal labor relations with the local workers. Throughout the 1960s, the issue of sovereignty over the wells had been a source of tension among Peruvian politicians. Average Peruvians and even Peruvian military men were prohibited from entering the oil town in Talara unless authorized. The Stars and Stripes rather than the Peruvian flag flew in that area. The scandal surrounding the disappearance of the eleventh and final page of the new contract that the Peruvian state had signed with the IPC, and the obscurity that shadowed these relations, provoked collective distress and anger in the weeks before the October coup of 1968. For Velasco, the IPC's presence in Talara represented Peru's "national shame."[47] As he stated, "[Talara] was a piece of Peruvian soil that was alien to all Peruvians. It was surrounded by barbed wire; [it was] a discriminatory field where we were foreigners!"[48]

The coup was on October 3, and on October 9, the regime militarily occupied the oil wells in La Brea and Pariñas with the soldiers and armored vehicles from the Eighth Light Division. In this endeavor, the army had the support of the Peruvian workers who were on duty that day.[49] Once the army occupied the Talara oil fields, they hoisted the Peruvian flag there as a "vindication of Peru's sovereignty and dignity."[50] The reinstatement of Peruvian control over national soil in Talara was portrayed as an act that healed Peruvian national pride. If, in the past, and despite the heroism of its leading figures, the army had not been able to defend Peru's national sovereignty from the foreign aggressions of Chile and Colombia, in the 1960s, a stronger, manlier, and revolutionary army had been able to do so.

For Velasco and the military, recovering Talara was an act of redress.[51] In the televised speech that he delivered at the very moment when the troops were occupying La Brea and Pariñas, General Velasco said that the IPC's role in Peru had been "a painful wound," "a chapter of ignominy and shame because it represent[ed] an affront to the nation's dignity, honor, and sovereignty."[52] The foreign presence in Talara acquired deeper undertones for the general because he was from Piura, and as a young officer he had been commissioned there. He had seen firsthand the types of interactions that occurred between the IPC and the local population.

The military said that October 9 was to be declared the Day of National Dignity, a holiday that would allow Peruvians to commemorate the revolution's first historical act.[53] With Talara's physical reoccupation, Peru and its army had reclaimed the national honor that they had tried to recover for so long. The stanzas of the "Revolutionary Anthem" reveal the feelings of pride and satisfaction that, from a military perspective, Peruvians should feel after 1968:

With Velasco Peru
has reached a high place, has reached a position
of pride—of pride,
of heroism, and of honor[54]

In the army's perspective, the sense of achievement about the revolution's goals was shared by the majority of the army's officer corps. In an article published in *Actualidad Militar* in 1972, a female high school student wrote an interview with her father, an infantry major who identified himself as a revolutionary officer. She had decided to interview him for a newspaper competition because she thought he was "a reflection of all those Peruvians who wanted things to change." The conversation between father and daughter expressed the importance that issues of social justice had acquired among army officers after 1968. The piece was also a pedagogical narrative about the meanings and the intentions of the revolution in Peru.

DAUGHTER: Dad, I have heard people talk a lot about the revolution. What is the revolution?

OFFICER: The revolution is no more than the moment of transition from a bad and decadent moment to another, better one that will provide a better future to all Peruvians. This transition is fast, and we [the military] have decided to do it.

DAUGHTER: Dad, are you a revolutionary man?

OFFICER: All men who really love their families and, as a consequence, their fatherland are revolutionary. I was born a revolutionary man. I always wanted us Peruvians to live better and to have fewer problems. . . . Daughter, you are still young and you are privileged because you were born in a home that, although modest, can give you the basic comforts of life. Why? Because I, your father, can provide for you. And because I—due to my own effort and the opportunities I had in life—was able to get an education and culture, and I can give you that.[55]

For this military father, to love the fatherland was equated with the love toward one's own family. He had been "born" a revolutionary not because he carried the ideals of revolution in his biological makeup but because he had been exposed to these principles when he was reborn as a "new man"—an officer—through several rites of passage and initiation in the Military Academy. In his commissions throughout the country, he became aware of Peru's inequalities because people did not enjoy the same "opportunities" to "get an education and culture" as he had.

The father continued his pedagogical role by making reference to Peru's economic contradictions and the poverty in which people in the highlands lived because they did not have the same opportunities as other Peruvians.

OFFICER: Do you think, dear, that it is fair that you study peacefully and tomorrow you wake up and have breakfast, that you have rested in a good bed, and that you know that your life and your brothers' are safe?

DAUGHTER: Yes, because it is fair, and you have earned it.

OFFICER: Now then, do you think it is fair that others cannot enjoy these things because they have no opportunities? What would you have done if you had lived in an inhospitable *puna* [Andean plateau], if you were cold and hungry, without any hope? . . . Those poor people [there] barely earn enough to survive.

The conversation finished with a reiteration of the revolution's transformative capacities for Peru.

DAUGHTER: Dad, do you think that the revolution is changing these people's life conditions?

OFFICER: Absolutely! And I am proud of being a participant in it. I am lucky to have been born in this time when we are finally glimpsing true justice.[56]

This exchange between father and daughter can also be read as the Peruvian army's need to instruct Peruvians about the process of transformation that Peru was undergoing in the 1970s. The revolution was happening from above and it had to be explained by the military "fathers" to their uninformed Peruvian "children." They had to justify why being a revolutionary military man was right and necessary in Peru.

Being a revolutionary officer in Peru meant endorsing the army's role as an agent of social justice, a trope that usually appeared in the army's cultural artifacts. Social justice was addressed in the "Revolution Anthem" in 1969 and in the "Army's Anthem" in 1973. The "Army's Anthem" is perhaps the cultural artifact that best summarizes the army's imaginings crafted in the second half of the twentieth century. This song was performed at all official and unofficial army gatherings, and it portrayed the army as the institution that was related to Peru's history through a "fertile and virile tradition." Spanish is a gendered language, and the anthem contained several gendered words that highlighted the army's manly condition in Peru.

The song made several references to the army's military masculinity and its popular nationalism that positioned contemporary officers as heirs of Incas. It also highlighted the centrality of Colonel Francisco

Bolognesi, the paradigm of military heroism and sacrifice. More importantly, the anthem emphasized the army's revolutionary mission and its interest in achieving social justice. The last stanza reads:

> The army receives weapons from the people
> and it is a stronghold of social justice.
> The army proudly protects Peru's borders
> because it is the guardian of national honor.
> I am a soldier and to the troops I belong.
> My duties to the Motherland I will fulfill.
> I will devote my life to her
> and I will fight or die for her.

The historian Carmen McEvoy has suggested that imaginings are mediated through the continuous selection of tradition and social memory. This is a process through which the makers of cultural products work as active builders of national identity, and in which institutions and cultural practices play an important role in shaping the links between present and past.[57] The army's anthem was a cultural product that connected the army's past (forging the nation) with its contemporary present (achieving social justice). It is ironic, however, that the anthem was created in 1973, the same year that General Velasco became ill and started to lose the power that he had at the beginning of his regime.

Velasco's Decline

Velasco suffered from diabetes, and in February 1973, he had an abdominal aneurism. He had to be hospitalized and his leg was amputated. This event diminished him physically and symbolically. The father of the revolution was no longer able to stand by himself, and he would not be able to fight against the antirevolutionary forces that would emerge from within the army. Velasco's serious condition moved Peruvians, and a crowd waited for news outside the military hospital. Some weeks later, in its March issue, *Actualidad Militar* published a letter in which the army ventriloquized the people's concern about the general's health. This letter showed both emotion and appreciation toward Velasco, the older "brother" who had led "the paths of liberation of the poor." It also highlighted a trope that had been very important for the revolution: the close connection and unity between the people and the armed forces, because the army had finally sided with the poor and excluded. The letter also highlighted how General Velasco was the embodiment of the Binomio Pueblo-Fuerza Armada, the collectivity of the Peruvian people and the army.

> Brother Velasco,
> We, the people, your cradle and your cause, stronger and more closely knit together than ever, come to you shouting your name, General of the Poor, along streets and plazas, to express our deepest solidarity and our support for the revolution that the armed forces began in 1968.
> We, who knew misery, hardships day after day . . . and exploitation by the bosses, have marched toward you because it is you who leads us through the paths of liberation and because you, General of the Poor, you are us.
> How could we not have come to demonstrate to you our love, our solidarity? You, who have put the sword to our service? It was because of you, General of the Humble, that we discovered that in each soldier of the nation lives one of our brothers, that their guns are ours, that their stubborn fight for a sovereign fatherland is our own battle, that the same Peruvian flag wraps us all. . . . That is why tonight we are all together with you. . . . We do trust you. . . . You trust us. General, feel our wounded hearts because you have been wounded. Feel our hearts as close to you as the first day because we the people, brother Velasco, never stopped being with you and we will never leave you.
> Everything is clear. Today, these people only want to greet you and tell you that millions of homes, brother Velasco, also take care of you, and they demand that you also take care of yourself because your life is ours, it is the life of the revolution that we soldiers and workers on duty, we take care of the country.
> Receive [General Velasco] the fatherland's gifts, with our flag and our roses. We also give you our Peruvian hearts.[58]

In a letter he wrote one month after his seizure and that was published in *Actualidad Militar*, Velasco used the familiar tone in which he had talked to Peruvians since his first days in power, and he commented on his commitment to the Peruvian Revolution. The physically diminished revolutionary warrior had to fight against his own bodily disease, and at the same time he had to ascertain that the army's revolutionary project needed to continue until the social justice that it pursued had been obtained.

Beloved Brothers and Sisters,
This is a message of gratitude and revolutionary reassurance. Difficult moments test a man and great causes. When they are authentic, however, they become stronger. For that reason, our revolution is stronger now.

Today, more than ever I feel that this revolution that both men and soldiers are undertaking in Peru is deeply rooted in my life. There is no room in me for sadness, because for a man, hard times are moments of affirmation and joy. For that reason, with optimism, we will keep on fighting the challenges that the future brings.

From the place where I am now, which is a moment of fight, I send a hug to each of you and I renew my faith in this revolution; it will not be stopped until we obtain authentic freedom for Peru and justice for its people.[59]

However, the revolution that was so "deeply rooted in his life" began to crumble when Velasco's health deteriorated more and more after 1973, and when various factions within the army decided to take control of the Revolutionary Government of the Armed Forces, bringing the end to the revolution in 1975.

In 1969, in his speech to commemorate the first anniversary of the revolution, General Velasco stated that among the officers who had led the coup there were no "predestined or irreplaceable" men and that they all belonged to a team that was leading the revolutionary process that Peru so badly needed. By 1975, however, the central role that Velasco had played in the revolution eventually went against him. He had been the image of the revolution, he *was* the revolution. Although in 1968 the revolutionary process had been a collective enterprise, after seven years, Velasco remained its biggest promoter, defender, and embodiment. His physical frailty in 1975 no longer positioned him as the powerful political authority that he had been before. A profound rhetoric had shaped him as the father and the maker of the revolution, and though in the beginning this was acceptable and understandable for implementing the initial transformations that were taking place within Peru, by the mid-1970s the revolution could no longer just depend on the sole figure and charisma of Velasco.

In February 1975, the police went on strike and there were riots in Lima. The city was exposed to looting and pillage, and the army had to occupy the streets to pacify its people. In a way, the violation of Lima's physical integrity was a demonstration that Velasco, the older brother, the protector of the nation, the embodiment of the revolution, no longer had the capacity to protect Peru and Peruvians as he had offered to do so many times. Thus, physically diminished and becoming too close to some sectors of the Peruvian left, Velasco became extremely vulnerable to the army's internal struggles and to the factions within his institution that no longer embraced his vision of the revolution. On July 29, 1975, General Francisco Morales Bermúdez, the minister of war, overthrew him.

In the September 1975 issue of *Actualidad Militar*, the military stated that the change in the regime did not represent an end to the Peruvian Revolution, and that there would be institutional continuity in the reforms implemented during the First Phase, because "Men are replaceable, the Revolution no! Men pass by, but the Revolution stays![60] Morales Bermúdez, however, would gradually dismantle many of Velasco's more radical measures and he would look for a path to a democratic transition. With Morales Bermúdez, the revolution had come to an end.

General Morales Bermúdez's rise to power revealed the internal tensions existing within the revolution and the Peruvian army. Although one of the revolution's basic notions was that the army came from the people and that it worked for the people, the fact was that the army was still a very heterogeneous institution, and not all of its officers identified themselves with the more radical components of the revolution's rhetoric. Velasco was well aware of the differences among army officers. As he stated in the interview he gave to César Hildebrandt in 1977, some months before he died, "Revolutionary intentions and conservative prejudices were intermingled among the military and within each military man's mind because the army was still an institution made up of different social classes, [and] they brought with them their virtues, limitations, prejudices, and resentments. This happened not only among the soldiers but also among the high-ranking officers . . . the challenge that they faced was between being loyal to their own origins or submitting to the comfortable present."[61]

For many high-ranking officers and for the more conservative sectors within the army, the tension between their origins and their comfortable present was stirred by anxieties about the revolution's deviations, and by Velasco's closeness with more radical left-wing sectors. Indeed, by the mid-1970s, the very concept of revolution had turned problematic for the army.

Conclusion

When democracy returned to Peru in the 1980s, the army no longer embraced its revolutionary ideals. If in the late 1960s and early 1970s being a revolutionary officer, a paternal figure who might talk to his children about Peru's need for social and economic transformations, was acceptable, in the 1980s that discourse had become dangerous. The word "revolution" had acquired threatening meanings and became associated with a group of people, the Shining Path, and with a specific region in Peru, the highlands. Paradoxically, the Shining Path guerrillas came from the sectors that Velasco and the armed forces' revolution had tried to elevate: the indigenous, the poor, and the excluded. During the years of the Peruvian internal armed conflict, the initial union between peasants and the Shining Path guerrillas created a new Binomio Pueblo–Fuerza Armada, a new entity that connected the people and an army that did not belong to the Peruvian state but to an insurgency, the Shining Path's. This new collectivity also attempted to radically transform Peru's social, political, and economic structures, and during the first years of the conflict (1980–1984), the Shining Path enjoyed more legitimacy in the countryside.

During the years of the internal armed conflict, Velasco's official memory faded even more. There were no public holidays promoted by the state to commemorate the revolution. October 9, the Day of National Dignity, was no longer a national holiday, and the new democratic regime rescued the memory of Miguel Grau, the Knight of the Seas, as a less polarizing historical figure to commemorate in October. The Peruvian state's official silence about Velasco was reproduced within the Peruvian army; he became the uncomfortable memory that senior officers did not want to remember and that only some younger, radical officers, such as the *etnocaceristas*, secretly admired.

The army silenced Velasco not only because he ended up being on the losing side when a more conservative military faction overthrew him in 1975 but also because the general threatened one of the institution's core ideals during the twentieth century: the primacy of a collective identity over an individual one. In its memory box, the army promoted devotion to great men and compelling heroic figures only as long as they were actors from the past, and they could provide officers with masculine and honorable referents for the military's contemporary present. The box was filled with images of military political figures from the present only in times of dictatorships dominated by strong figures such as Luis Miguel Sánchez Cerro (1931–1933) and Manuel A. Odría (1948–1956). Once the military figure's political power waned, his memory was sent to the bottom of the army's box, and he practically disappeared from the army's official record. Velasco's persona, however, turned highly problematic even for the bottom of the army's memory box because of the reforms that his regime promoted and, especially, because of the revolution's radical rhetoric regarding indigenous people and their incorporation into the Peruvian imagined community.

By omitting Velasco's leading role in the experience of 1968, as well as the impact that his reforms provoked in Peruvian society, especially in the Andean countryside, the army revealed the challenges it faces in critically examining its past and making sense of its own historical trajectory. Furthermore, by silencing Velasco's relevance in Peru's contemporary history, the army has positioned the general almost at the same level as the men who committed criminal acts within the army, such as General Nicolás de Bari Hermoza Ríos, one of the main supporters of Alberto Fujimori's regime, and whose picture was removed from every military premise, or the officers guilty of atrocities during the counterinsurgent war of the 1980s and 1990s.

Notes

1. Juan Velasco Alvarado, "Discurso en el CIMP [Círculo de Investigación Militar del Perú; Military Investigation Circle of Peru]," December 22, 1971, in *Solidaridad y continuidad* (Lima: Oficina Nacional de Información, Empresa Editora del Diario Oficial El Peruano, 1971), 31. Unless otherwise noted, all translations to English are mine.

2. See   http://www.ejercito.mil.pe/index.php/acerca-del-ejercito/introduc cion/historia-del-ejercito. (Author's note: When I wrote the chapter in 2013, these links gave an overview of the Peruvian army's history, which traced its evolution from pre-Columbian warfare to the army's contemporary role in the present. They made a marginal reference to General Velasco. The links, however, are no longer available because the army has restructured its official website. As of 2016, the army provides only a historical overview of its main divisions and no longer makes reference to the army's pre-Columbian past.) The Peruvian military sent peacekeeping missions to the Middle East after the Arab-Israeli War of 1973. The Batallón Perú was in Sinai (Egypt) and Kuneitra (Syria) from November 6, 1973, until July 19, 1975. See http://batallonperu .blogspot.com/.

3. http://www.ejercito.mil.pe/index.php/acercadelejercito/introduccion/ex comandantesgeneralesep/product/view/1/7. (Author's note: This link was avail-

able in 2013, but the army has since changed its website. For further clarification, see note 2 above.)

4. Steve J. Stern, *Remembering Pinochet's Chile: On the Eve of London 1998* (Durham, NC: Duke University Press, 2006), xxviii.

5. For a further analysis of the Peruvian heroes in the first decades of the twentieth century, see Carlota Casalino's PhD dissertation, "Los héroes patrios y la construcción del Estado-nación en el Perú (siglos XIX y XX)" (Lima: UNMSM, 2008).

6. The *etnocaceristas* were a group of nationalist army officers who openly expressed their admiration for General Velasco and vindicated Peru's pre-Columbian past. The organization was created at the end of the 1980s. The Peruvian president as of this writing, Ollanta Humala, and his brother Antauro Humala led an armed insurrection in Locumba (Tacna) in 2000 against President Fujimori's regime. The revolt provoked the sympathies of thousands of Peruvian military veterans (*licenciados*) who later became the Humala brothers' main constituency.

7. Daniel M. Masterson, *Militarism and Politics in Latin America: Peru from Sánchez Cerro to Sendero Luminoso* (Westport, CT: Greenwood, 1991).

8. Juan Martín Sánchez, *La revolución peruana: Ideología y práctica política de un gobierno militar, 1968–1975* (Seville: CSIC, Universidad de Sevilla, Diputación de Sevilla, 2002).

9. Cecilia Méndez G., "Las paradojas del autoritarismo: Ejército, campesinado y etnicidad en el Perú, siglos XIX al XX," *Íconos: Revista de Ciencias Sociales* (Quito: FLACSO) 26 (September 2006): 17–34; and "La guerra que no cesa: Guerras civiles, imaginario nacional y formación del Estado en el Perú," in *L'Atlantique révolutionnaire*, ed. Clément Thibaud et al. (Bécherel: Editions Les Perséides, 2013).

10. Víctor Villanueva, *Cien años del ejército peruano: Frustraciones y cambios* (Lima: Juan Mejía Baca, 1972); *¿Nueva mentalidad militar en el Perú?* (Lima: Juan Mejía Baca, 1969); and *El CAEM y la revolución de la fuerza armada* (Lima: Instituto de Estudios Peruanos, 1972).

11. Dirk Kruijt, *Revolution by Decree: Peru, 1968–1975* (West Lafayette, IN: Purdue University Press, 2003 [1994]).

12. Frederick M. Nunn, *The Time of the Generals: Latin American Professional Militarism in World Perspective* (Lincoln: University of Nebraska Press, 1992); Alain Rouquié, *The Military and the State in Latin America* (Berkeley: University of California Press, 1987).

13. Masterson, *Militarism and Politics*.

14. Villanueva, *Cien años del ejército peruano*, 139.

15. *Ley Orgánica del Ejército*, July 14, 1950.

16. Eduardo Toche Medrano, *Guerra y democracia: Los militares peruanos y la construcción nacional* (Lima: Clacso/Desco, 2008); Villanueva, *El CAEM y la revolución de la fuerza armada*.

17. "Decreto Supremo No. 1-GM," in *Reglamentación de los Decretos Supremos que Declaran Patronos del Ejército y de las Armas* (Lima: Ministerio de Guerra, Perú, 1951), 2.

18. Villanueva, *Cien años del ejército peruano*, 139.

19. Ibid.

20. Ocaña made the monument to pay homage to the heroes of the war against Ecuador in 1941.

21. Colonel Bolognesi said that he would fight in Arica (1879) until he "fired the last round."

22. Ministerio de Guerra, *Historia de la Escuela Militar del Perú* (Lima: Ministerio de Guerra, 1962), 130.

23. Ibid., 128.

24. "Editorial," *Actualidad Militar,* November 30, 1963, 2.

25. Ministerio de Guerra, *Historia de la Escuela Militar del Perú,* 141.

26. Michael S. Kimmel, "Masculinity as Homophobia: Fear, Shame, and Silence in the Construction of Gender Identity," in *Theorizing Masculinities,* ed. H. Brod and M. Kaufman (Thousand Oaks, CA: Sage, 1994).

27. Toche Medrano, *Guerra y democracia.*

28. *Ley Orgánica del Ejército,* 1950.

29. Kruijt, *Revolution by Decree.*

30. Mario Vargas Llosa, *The Time of the Hero* (New York: Grove Press, 1975 [1966]).

31. Diana Taylor has explored how military coups were a display of manliness and power among the Latin American militaries, and how they situated military males over other males in the region in *Disappearing Acts: Spectacles of Gender and Nationalism in Argentina's "Dirty War"* (Durham, NC: Duke University Press, 1997).

32. Brian Loveman and Thomas M. Davies Jr., eds., *The Politics of Antipolitics: The Military in Latin America* (Wilmington, DE: Scholarly Resources, 1997).

33. Ministerio de Guerra, *Historia de la Escuela Militar del Perú,* 23.

34. Velasco Alvarado, "Discurso en el CIMP," 31.

35. Juan Velasco Alvarado, "Discurso del Presidente de la República en el Día del Ejército," in *La política del Gobierno Revolucionario: Discursos pronunciados por el General de División Dn. Juan Velasco Alvarado, Presidente del Perú* (Lima: Oficina Nacional de Información, 1972), 10:109.

36. Juan Velasco Alvarado, "Mensaje a la Nación en el primer aniversario de la Revolución," in *Velasco, la voz de la revolución: Discursos del presidente de la República, General de División Juan Velasco Alvarado, 1968–1970* (Lima: PEISA, 1970), 36.

37. Juan Velasco Alvarado, "Discurso del Presidente de la República en la clausura del año académico del Centro de Instrucción Militar del Perú," in *La política del Gobierno Revolucionario: Discursos pronunciados por el General de División Dn. Juan Velasco Alvarado, presidente del Perú* (Lima: Oficina Nacional de Información, 1970), 5:125.

38. César Hildebrandt, "Entrevista con Juan Velasco Alvarado," *Caretas,* February 3, 1977.

39. Velasco Alvarado, "Discurso del Presidente de la República en el Día del Ejército," 5:109.

40. Juan Velasco Alvarado, "Discurso del presidente del Perú pronunciado ante la concentración cívica en la Plaza Grau de la Ciudad de Piura," in *Velasco, la voz de la revolución: Discursos del presidente de la República, General de División Juan Velasco Alvarado, 1968–1970* (Lima: PEISA, 1970), 119.

41. Teresa La Rosa Goyburu de Deacon, composer, "Himno de la Revolución," 1969, http://www.eurvi.com/himno-de-la-revolucion-juan-velasco-alva rado-hq_1842c69b7.html.

42. Velasco Alvarado, "Discurso del presidente del Perú pronunciado ante la concentración cívica en la Plaza Grau de la Ciudad de Piura," 119.

43. Ibid., 113.

44. See several issues of *Actualidad Militar* and *La Gaceta del Recluta* from the 1950s to the early 1970s.

45. Juan Velasco Alvarado, "Discurso del presidente del Perú pronunciado ante la concentración cívica en la Plaza de Armas del Distrito de Castilla, en Piura," in *Velasco, la voz de la revolución: Discursos del presidente de la República, General de División Juan Velasco Alvarado, 1968–1970* (Lima: PEISA, 1970), 123.

46. Velasco Alvarado, "Discurso del presidente de la República en el Día del Ejército," 10:109.

47. Velasco Alvarado, "Discurso del presidente del Perú pronunciado ante la concentración cívica en la Plaza Grau de la Ciudad de Piura," 119.

48. Juan Velasco Alvarado, "Mensaje a la nación del presidente del Perú, en el primer aniversario del Día de la Dignidad Nacional, dirigido desde la Ciudad de Talara," in *Velasco, la voz de la revolución: Discursos del presidente de la República, General de División Juan Velasco Alvarado, 1968–1970* (Lima: PEISA, 1970), 124.

49. Ibid., 119 and 127.

50. Juan Velasco Alvarado, "Mensaje a la nación con motivo de la toma de La Brea y Pariñas, 9 de octubre de 1968," in *Velasco, la voz de la revolución: Discursos del presidente de la República, General de División Juan Velasco Alvarado, 1968–1970* (Lima: PEISA, 1970), 5–7.

51. Juan Velasco Alvarado, "Discurso del presidente del Perú pronunciado en el almuerzo ofrecido por Petroperú Talara," in *La política del Gobierno Revolucionario: Discursos pronunciados por el general Juan Velasco, presidente del Perú* (Lima: Oficina Nacional de Información, Empresa Editora El Peruano, 1970), 4:96.

52. Ibid., 96.

53. Decreto Ley No. 17066, October 9, 1968.

54. Goyburu de Deacon, composer, "Himno de la Revolución," 1969.

55. Roxana Llerena Vera, "Entrevista a mi padre, un personaje revolucionario," *Actualidad Militar* 11, no. 182 (December 1972): 31.

56. Ibid.

57. Carmen McEvoy, "'Bella Lima ya tiemblas llorosa del triunfante chileno en poder': Una aproximación a los elementos de género en el discurso nacionalista chileno," in *El hechizo de las imágenes*, comp. Narda Henríquez (Lima: Pontificia Universidad Católica del Perú, 2000), 200.

58. "Mensaje del pueblo peruano al jefe de la revolución," *Actualidad Militar* 12, no. 185 (March 1973): 3.

59. "El mensaje del Presidente Velasco," *Actualidad Militar* 12, no. 185 (March 1973): 2.

60. Miguel Castillo Durand, "Pasarán los hombres, ¡la Revolución no!," *Actualidad Militar* 14, no. 213 (September 1975): 5.

61. César Hildebrandt, "Entrevista con Juan Velasco Alvarado," *Caretas*, February 3, 1977.

CHAPTER 8

Velasco and the Military:
The Politics of Decline, 1973–1975

GEORGE PHILIP

The period from 1973 to 1975 in Peru saw the rapid decline of the Velasco Alvarado regime. When Velasco fell ill in February 1973, the regime was still energetically pursuing its program of reforms and the
economy was still growing at full tilt. By late 1975, although the worst
was still to come, the whole experiment with military radicalism looked
to be failing. But it was not just the government of Velasco himself that
was ailing; it was the entire project with which he had become associated. By the time Velasco was overthrown in August 1975, it was evident that the experiment with left-of-center military government was
facing major problems. As soon as he became president, Francisco Morales Bermúdez embarked on a much more conservative course of action. While Morales was a far less radical political figure than Velasco
or some other radical generals, it was also evident that he had little
choice but to look for a different strategy. How do we explain the rapid-
ity and completeness of this reversal?

The Economy

Adverse economic developments played a significant part in the rapid
turnaround. The 1973–1975 period saw a fall in the living standards of
the majority of Peruvians and a broader decline in general economic optimism. Certainly there was an element of bad luck involved here. The
semifailure of the Selva oil play, the fact that Peru was still an oil im-
porter in 1973 and would be one for some years to come, the generally
depressed state of commodity prices (other than oil) due to the global

recession of 1974–1975, and the specific crisis in the fishmeal industry all combined to cause problems. These were made worse by high levels of government borrowing, largely in foreign currency, and a marked fall in private investment. Without tax reform, which the regime did not seriously attempt, there was a tendency to overborrow.[1] As a result, Peru's foreign debt was on a dangerously increasing trend as early as 1973.

Long-term factors mattered as well. Rosemary Thorp and Geoffrey Bertram argue that a long-term malaise was developing in Peru's export economy that was beyond the control of any government. The regime did make an effort to promote export growth, fomenting some major projects in copper and oil, but the export sector remained very dependent on commodities and vulnerable to adverse terms of trade. This was an increasing problem after the first oil shock of 1973–1974. The economy as a whole was also very reliant on the performance of a large number of newly created state enterprises, because many of the reforms of the Velasco regime had the effect of replacing foreign and domestic private capital with state enterprise. Despite the optimism of the time, this did not lead to better economic management—rather the reverse.

Additional problems with the domestic economy included the over-enthusiastic buildup of import substitution industrialization (ISI), which dates from the previous decade and left Peru with an inefficient and high-cost manufacturing sector. Policy direction was also a problem, as many government reforms ostensibly intended to combat poverty were either cynically designed to benefit the politically influential middle class or else poorly chosen. These included food subsidies and price controls and the underpricing of state-provided goods such as gasoline.[2]

Since global economic thinking has been revolutionized since 1975, it is hard to strip out all of the different factors that combined to produce Velasco's economic failure. Nevertheless, the failure itself was a fact. It is clear that the Peruvian economy was a source of weakness rather than strength during 1973–1975 and indeed for several years thereafter. The regime also ran deficits to an alarming degree and thereby set the scene for the later intrusion of the International Monetary fund (IMF) and Peru's loss of economic independence.

At least some of the reasons for these problems were political. The regime had promised too much in order to win support in its battles for power and subsequently suffered the political consequences of failing to deliver. As early as 1973, the British ambassador's annual report observed that "fearful of its popularity, the government is trying to shield the Peruvian consumer as much as possible from world economic realities."[3] In a small, commodity-dependent Latin American economy, this was a doomed enterprise.

While the relationship between popularity and economic performance is reasonably close in most countries in the world, Velasco's regime was probably more vulnerable to economic setback than most other governments in Latin America, and he failed to survive the 1975 downturn. By way of contrast, Chile's General Augusto Pinochet survived in power for sixteen years and presided over two very deep recessions. The Argentine military in the 1970s also for a time survived very high rates of inflation. One reason why Velasco's regime was more vulnerable to economic failure than the military dictatorships of the Southern Cone is that it was less repressive. Another factor is that, in ideological terms, Velasco was in a minority within the military. For both of these reasons, Velasco had to rely more on bread and circuses for his survival than most authoritarian regimes.

Peru: Some Historical Issues

The perception that the regime might pay a high political price if the economy performed poorly is congruent with evidence from Peru's twentieth-century history. Peruvian civil society has often been quite militant during hard times. Scholars have highlighted the violence of the Sánchez Cerro period in the 1930s, the militant early history of APRA at around the same time, and the bitter feuding between APRA and the army in the 1940s.[4] In later periods, there was the general strike of July 1977 and the murderous rebellion of Sendero Luminoso (Shining Path) in the 1980s. It is true that political institutions in Peru were weak, but this reflected mainly popular cynicism about democracy rather than political docility. The mind-set was nicely summed up by a sign on a building in a Lima suburb whose contents were reported in *Latin American Newsletters* on October 10, 1968: "This building is no longer used for political purposes. Please do not break the windows."[5]

We can regard the relationship between the economy and political stability as a kind of bargain. Public opinion tolerated dictatorship as long as the economy performed acceptably well. At first, the population was indeed quiescent even though it was not particularly supportive of the regime. After 1973, economic decline fed a loss of popular support and an accelerating tide of protests.

A similar assessment was made by the British ambassador in 1970 in his annual report for that year. It read as follows: "The regime is widely accepted; that does not mean it is popular. . . . I believe the Secretary General of the APRA controlled trade unions when he told me that if the government were to land in serious economic trouble, the attitude of the industrial workers would change at once."[6]

During 1973–1975, this judgment proved to be right. As noted, that period saw a considerable decline in living standards, and the effect on government popularity and social mobilization was as expected. It is likely that the generals anticipated such an outcome, since most outside observers clearly did. Economic setback had secondary consequences, too. The regime's efforts to mobilize public support via organizations such as Sistema Nacional de Apoyo a la Movilización Social (SINAMOS; National System of Support for Social Mobilization) could never have succeeded due to inherent design faults, but a declining economy made its task well nigh impossible.

International Factors

International issues need discussion as well. At the beginning of the 1970s, a number of leftist governments ruled in South America. By 1974 there were significantly fewer. The death of Juan Perón in 1974 was not an event of great significance for Peru, but it played its part in accentuating a general rightward movement among military regimes in South America. A number of Peruvian officers were admirers of Perón.

Of altogether greater significance to Peru was the Chilean coup. Relationships between the two countries during the Allende period were not as close as might have been expected if one considers ideological factors alone. Rivalry between the two countries was considerable and long-lasting. But it took on an additional dimension after the Chilean coup because the Pinochet regime was openly hostile to Peru. Conflict intensified further when Peru undertook a major program of tank purchases from the USSR during the 1970s. Yet a further influence was the inexorable approach of 1979, which was the one hundredth anniversary of the outbreak of the War of the Pacific. Bolivia, which had been the principal loser in the wars of the nineteenth century, made it clear that it wanted the whole border issue renegotiated. The result was a major arms buildup that involved Peru.

This arms buildup, in hindsight, probably had more to do with the bargain basement prices at which the tanks were offered for sale to Peru than with the desire of any country to go to war. However, Pinochet was not the most impartial of observers, and he may have found it helpful to raise the Peruvian threat in order to try to reduce Chile's international isolation.[7] Pinochet did not necessarily want war with Peru, but a tense international climate had its advantages for both countries. This higher degree of tension was seen by much of the Peruvian military as portending outright conflict. In the long run, though, the main significance for Peru of its arms buildup was budgetary. It was another factor in the increase in the country's foreign debt. Soviet weapons came cheap but not free.

The Politics of Nationalism

A more nuanced conclusion is warranted with respect to the regime's economic nationalism. This was genuine enough, but it conflicted with Peru's creditworthiness. There can be no doubt that the International Petroleum Company (IPC) expropriation was popular and played a significant part in the Velasco regime's triumph over its adversaries.[8] The regime gained, too, from its confrontation with the United States over the 1962 Hickenlooper Amendment. The political gains in both cases outweighed any diminished access to foreign capital.

The regime's nationalism was not just opportunism. In its own way, the regime was quite ideological. For example, General Jorge Fernández Maldonado, then energy and mines minister, tried to use a conflict with Cerro de Pasco, an Andean mining town, in 1973 to re-create the nationalist coalition that Velasco had originally formed around the IPC issue. A battle over compensation was prepared in the Energy and Mines Ministry with the code name "Plan Túpac Amaru." However, the willingness of the radicals to use the issue for domestic political capital had declined since the days of IPC. A large part of the reason for this had to do with Velasco's own priorities. Peru was at the same time involved in negotiating a comprehensive settlement with the United States that covered a range of matters. Velasco wanted the negotiations to succeed (in the end, they did) because success would help Peru's creditworthiness. Velasco therefore wanted to avoid a renewed confrontation with the United States, so he steered a moderate course on negotiations with Cerro de Pasco over compensation. Fernández Maldonado was kept on a leash.

Ironically, the settlement that was reached in 1973 had an element of "winner's curse" as far as Peru was concerned. This is because better relations with the United States made it easier for the Velasco regime to borrow from abroad and thereby take on even higher levels of debt. The IPC compensation package was seen by the British ambassador as being "of immense value" to Peru.[9] However, what it mostly did was to allow Peru to continue its deficit financing policy for longer. This made the financial crisis, when it finally came, even more painful.

A general point can be made here. At a global level, the early 1970s was a period in which there was a major increase in international liquidity. Peru was able to borrow much more than it could in the 1960s, when a cessation of US aid seemed capable of bringing down the regime.[10] However, it was for the same reason difficult to know where the safe limits to borrowing lay, especially during 1971–1973, when commodity prices rose sharply and real interest rates were negative for a time. International borrowing looked deceptively easy until the day of reckoning.

The other high-profile nationalizations were of even less benefit to Peru. The effect of the takeover of Marcona and some minor foreign assets in 1975 was negative economically in light of Peru's by then very serious debt problems. The nationalization of the state-run fishing industry was an excellent example of how the politics of expropriation had become a liability.

Military-Political Issues

The final set of issues to do with the decline of the Velasco regime are personal and organizational, but we need to consider these from a political perspective. It is claimed here that the specific way in which the regime organized itself in 1969, as well as its general policy orientation, initially helped Velasco stay in power but made the regime more vulnerable in and after 1973. Velasco essentially ran a personalist authoritarianism. When he fell ill and the economy started to go wrong, the coherence of the government suffered. A personal style of governance masquerading as an institutional one could work for a time when Velasco was fit and well, but his illness stimulated conflict between factions. This internal conflict was the proximate cause of his downfall.

The claim that Velasco was running a personalistic authoritarianism requires further elaboration. It is true that his regime was not particularly repressive by the Latin American standards of the time, but it frequently adopted arbitrary measures in order to wrong-foot its opponents. The IPC takeover was a template of this political style, but there were many other examples.[11] Velasco led a regime lacking in gratitude and loyalty. Friends often suddenly became enemies. Cases of this included, but were not limited to, the 1968 coup itself, the confiscation of IPC, the destruction of the Prado business empire, the dramatic though ultimately unsuccessful seizure of Peru's northern haciendas, the expropriation of Cerro de Pasco, the conflict with *El Comercio*, and the press nationalization of 1974. The truth was that Velasco fought his way to the top by adopting confrontational tactics when he thought he could win with them. He chose his enemies with care. A similar characterization was visible in respect of policy, which, according to Cynthia McClintock, was characterized by "a certain Machiavellianism."[12] This is true and may be putting it mildly.

For this reason, Velasco's list of friends became shorter over time as his list of enemies became longer. APRA's leaders took advantage of Velasco's adversarial style of politics to move from a reluctant acquiescence to a more openly oppositional standpoint after around 1974. The teachers struck and so did the police.[13] Nor was it only civilians who joined the opposition. Relationships with the navy also deteriorated sharply in 1974 due to Velasco's high-handed treatment of disaffected admirals.

There can be no doubt that Velasco won most of his confrontations. In a way, then, his style worked for him, but each successive battle left the regime more isolated and added to its list of enemies.

The question is whether Velasco had any choice but to act as he did. Would a more favorable set of external conditions have permitted a less personalistic style? Some skepticism is in order here.[14] Most Latin American military regimes were at that time politically to the right of center. It was widely assumed in 1968 that the Velasco coup would be similarly right-wing. The dawning awareness that this might not be so came as a real shock, particularly after the land reform. Left-wing governance did not prove impossible, but Velasco was insecure and never really controlled events. It could be argued that Velasco needed to govern as he did or not at all.

As noted, Velasco's rise to power involved the political victory of a minority of nationalist officers over the rest. Even so, Velasco was almost certainly less popular than he had hoped to be. He would surely have preferred to govern with more support from the rest of the military, with greater personal popularity, and with a broader base within civil society. But he did not have this option. Instead, once in power, he had to rely on surprise and tactical advantage to substitute for a lack of reliable support. This led to arbitrary governance.

The Militarized Nature of the Regime's Organization and Psychology

We also need to consider the outlook and orientation of the military as a whole. The success of the 1968 coup marked the high point of the military's quest for autonomy.[15] This quest was substantially a creation of the Centro de Altos Estudios Militares (CAEM), Peru's Military Academy, and of officers based in the intelligence community who had, prior to the coup, elaborated their own critique of Peruvian society. CAEM had a significant influence on the Velasco government, even though the best-known radical generals were not CAEM graduates.[16] Without the confidence imparted by the Military Academy, Peru's military regimes would not have dared to take on the US government and the domestic oligarchy so aggressively. Nor would they have governed with so little civilian input and with such a predominant military style.

The deeply military nature of the Velasco regime can be seen in a number of other ways. One of them was comparative. Military rule in itself was certainly not uncommon in Latin America at that time, but most military regimes included civilians at high levels of government. This gave them contacts with civilian interest groups and even with some traditional politicians. Augusto Pinochet (Chile), Juan Carlos Onganía (Argentina), Jorge Rafael Videla (Argentina), and all of Brazil's various post-1964 rulers had civilians in prominent positions in the cabinet.

However, this was not true of Velasco, whose cabinets were all military. This contrast did not go unnoticed. One of the first things that Morales Bermúdez did after he removed Velasco from power was to put a prominent civilian in his cabinet.

The same highly militarized nature of Velasco's style of governance could be seen in other respects. The Velasco regime, for example, never held elections at any level. By way of contrast, Pinochet's model of individual despotism was covered by a veneer of plebiscitary backing,[17] and the Brazilian regime regularly held local elections. The Brazilian regime in fact tried hard to organize a political party around itself, though this policy ultimately failed. These military-sponsored elections were for the most part meaningless as exercises in contestation—as was the case in authoritarian Mexico, where elections were routinely held and routinely won by the Partido Revolucionario Institucional (PRI). Never-theless, they were potentially an effective means of putting a check on any kind of cult of personality. In Argentina, the determination of some officers to block any form of Peronism without Perón emerging from within the military led to pronounced presidential weakness and may have gone too far in the other direction for the good of the regime.

Another factor that was distinctive about the Velasco regime was that there was no formal limit to the length of his term of office. In princi-ple, as commander in chief of the junta, he had no retirement date and no fixed term. This contrasted with arrangements in Argentina, Brazil, and Uruguay, where heads of government were not intended to remain in power indefinitely.

It is true that there was an official position of prime minister, but this conferred prestige rather than power. However, it was also an addi-tional means by which the president could divide and rule the military institution. At the beginning, the office of prime minister was used as a balancing mechanism within the military. It enabled Velasco to offer some kind of institutional recognition to officers such as Ernesto Mon-tagne Sánchez and Luis Edgardo Mercado Jarrín, who were seen as be-ing more politically moderate than Velasco, without offering them real power. This enabled Velasco to look as if the basis of his government was broader than was actually the case.[18]

The absence of term limits blocked an important means of resolving conflicts within the regime. If in 1969 Velasco had been made to agree to having a fixed term of office, this would have ended in 1974 or early 1975. It seems likely that disaffected officers would have been willing to wait for a change in government rather than taking the risk of planning a coup. While we cannot be sure, it would seem likely that the worst of the political turmoil of 1975–1978 could have been avoided.

Personalist Politics

It seems clear that Velasco's method of governance was intended to per-mit a radical minority of officers to dominate the nonradical majority without seeming to do so. Not only was there a pronounced divide-and-rule aspect to the pattern of policy making, but the military organiza-tion was made to look professional and bureaucratic even when it was biased toward a relatively small number of left-of-center officers. The Comité de Asesoramiento de la Presidencia (COAP; Presidential Advisory Board), for example, was explicitly a presidential instrument in which rising senior officers could be tested before being entrusted with cabinet responsibilities. There were a number of cases in which COAP challenged or second-guessed those military officers who occupied conventional cabinet positions. Some of them led to the resignation of the cabinet minister concerned. This made it clear that ministers were not necessarily masters in their own house. What COAP did was to give a bureaucratic veneer to a left-wing-led political project.[19] The regime also exploited a bureaucratic aura so as to make the observance of procedures a legitimating factor behind military rule. For example, Velasco invoked a violation of procedure when he removed the navy minister from the cabinet in 1974, even though it was obvious to all concerned that the real motive for his removal was political. Ironically enough, Guillermo O'Donnell's famous term "bureaucratic authoritarianism" applies much better to Peru under Velasco than to some other South American countries where the term was more familiar.

In reality, the Velasco regime was always precariously balanced. Most of its military leaders were not radicals.[20] Velasco's project was actively supported by no more than a minority within the military, based on the intelligence services plus COAP and CAEM. This minority could punch above its weight, but it could not hope to dispose of its opponents, who often had to be reckoned with and not simply be outmuscled.

This precarious political situation limited governing possibilities. It meant that Velasco had to appear to lead a coalition rather than a despotism even though he actually needed to be despotic if he was to pursue his agenda. This rather mixed system of governance worked well enough for a time, but it meant that Velasco had to be "personalist." In his annual report for 1973, British ambassador Hugh T. Morgan commented on Velasco's illness, saying that this demonstrated "not only how much Velasco had all along been a strong man of the revolutionary government but also how much it needed one."[21]

Meanwhile, civilian politicians were down but not yet out. APRA may have been a political party in decline at least when Víctor Raúl Haya de la Torre was alive, but it was a national party with a long history and it had no motive for making life easier for Velasco. It was because the regime wanted to avoid ordinary party politics that it tried hard to strengthen its hand via organizations such as SINAMOS. Only the Communist Party remained supportive of Velasco, and this carried little weight. However, as has been documented elsewhere, unresolved tensions grew between the military's desire to maintain control and the unpopularity that was pretty much the inevitable result of governing a declining economy. Efforts to build political support by "participation" only made the regime look even more manipulative than it actually was.

The Downfall

These weaknesses made Velasco's personal fitness to rule a matter of decisive importance, and this is why his physical decline was central to the entire process. His style of politics worked well for a time, but it was as vulnerable in the long run as any other form of personalism. Nor did Velasco enjoy any degree of personal magnetism in the manner of Perón. Some halfhearted efforts were expended in trying to portray him as a popular hero—without much success—but in any case, he was more comfortable in the role of military bureaucrat than charismatic politician.

When he fell ill, military factionalism once again became key to the struggle for power. A major conflict with the navy occurred in 1974, serious police disaffection existed in 1975, and a form of right-wing personalism in the shape of La Misión arose at the end. By 1975, Velasco had lost the confidence of the military, including that of some of the radicals featured in the coup that overthrew him.[22]

The final decisive development was that the military radicals were deceived in the succession. According to General José Graham Ayllón, a group of them approached Morales Bermúdez and invited him to lead a coup. This would feature support from the remaining radicals, military support, and a broad continuity of outlook with the Velasco regime. Morales Bermúdez ostensibly agreed, but it soon became clear that Morales was accepting support from military conservatives as well as from the radicals. As president, one of his main governing principles lay in seeking a settlement with APRA. When this happened, the military radicals woke up to find themselves in bed with their erstwhile opponents.

Just as Velasco in 1968 seemed to have launched his coup from the right and then radicalized, so Morales promised continuity and actually moved to the right. There were understandable reasons for this but no turning back. When Fernández Maldonado was forced out of the cabinet in 1976, Peru no longer had a left-wing government. The Peruvian government joined Operación Condor, a campaign of political repression, in 1978.

Notes

1. Rosemary Thorp and Geoffrey Bertram, *Peru 1890–1977: Growth and Policy in an Open Economy* (New York: Macmillan, 1978). Unless otherwise noted, all translations to English are mine.

2. Dennis Gilbert, "The End of the Peruvian Revolution: A Class Analysis," *Studies in Comparative International Development* 15, no. 1 (Spring 1980): 15–38.

3. Foreign and Commonwealth Office, Annual Report for Peru 1973; Morgan to Douglas-Hume, Foreign and Commonwealth Office 7/2629 C5676 (London: National Archives), 12.

4. Steve Stein, *Populism in Peru: The Emergence of the Masses and the Politics of Social Control* (Madison: University of Wisconsin Press, 1980); Peter F. Klaren, *Modernization, Dislocation, and Aprismo: Origins of the Peruvian Aprista Party, 1870–1932* (Austin: University of Texas Press, 1973); Víctor Villanueva, *El Apra y el ejército peruano (1940–1950)* (Lima: Editorial Horizonte, 1977).

5. *Latin American Newsletters*, October 10, 1968.

6. Foreign and Commonwealth Office, Annual Report for Peru 1970; Morgan to Douglas-Hume, FCO7/1942/C475838, 3.

7. US Department of State, Memorandum of Conversation, "U.S.-Chilean Relations" (Kissinger-Pinochet), June 8, 1976.

8. George Philip, "Nationalism and the Rise of Peru's General Velasco," *Bulletin of Latin American Research* 32, no. 3 (2013): 279–293.

9. Foreign and Commonwealth Office, Annual Report for Peru 1973; Morgan to Douglas-Hume, FCO7/26295676, 2.

10. Richard N. Goodwin, "Letter from Peru," *New Yorker*, May 17, 1969, 41.

11. Philip, "Nationalism and the Rise of Peru's General Velasco." See also Richard J. Walter, *Peru and the United States, 1960–1975: How Their Ambassadors Managed Foreign Relations in a Turbulent Era* (University Park: Penn State University Press, 2010).

12. Cynthia McClintock, "Velasco, Officers, and Citizens: The Politics of Stealth," in *The Peruvian Experiment Reconsidered*, ed. Cynthia McClintock and Abraham F. Lowenthal (Princeton, NJ: Princeton University Press, 1983), 284.

13. On military relations with APRA, see Carol Graham, *Peru's APRA: Parties, Politics, and the Elusive Quest for Democracy* (Boulder, CO: Lynne Rienner, 1992).

14. See the discussion in Alfred C. Stepan, *The State and Society: Peru in Comparative Perspective* (Princeton, NJ: Princeton University Press, 1978), passim.

15. Víctor Villanueva, *El CAEM y la revolución de la Fuerza Armada* (Lima: Instituto de Estudios Peruanos, 1972).

16. Stepan, *The State and Society*.

17. "Sultanism" is Karen Remmer's word for this type of rule. See Karen L. Remmer, *Military Rule in Latin America* (London: Unwin Hyman, 1989).

18. Peter S. Cleaves and Martin Scurrah, *Agriculture, Bureaucracy and Military Government in Peru* (Ithaca, NY: Cornell University Press, 1980).

19. Peter S. Cleaves and Henry Pease García, "State Autonomy and Military Policy Making," in *The Peruvian Experiment Reconsidered*, ed. Cynthia Mc-

Clintock and Abraham F. Lowenthal (Princeton, NJ: Princeton University Press, 1983), 209–244.

20. Liisa North, "Ideological Orientations of Peru's Military Rulers," in *The Peruvian Experiment Reconsidered*, ed. Cynthia McClintock and Abraham F. Lowenthal (Princeton, NJ: Princeton University Press, 1983), 245–274.

21. Foreign and Commonwealth Office, Annual Report for Peru 1973; Morgan to Douglas–Hume, FCO7/26295676, 12.

22. Interview with General José Graham Ayllón in Lima in 1981.

PART III

DECENTERING THE REVOLUTION: REGIONAL APPROACHES TO VELASCO'S PERU

CHAPTER 9

Promoting the Revolution: SINAMOS in Three Different Regions of Peru

ANNA CANT

The Juan Velasco Alvarado government is often characterized as an example of "revolution from above."[1] The absence of formal checks on the power of the executive allowed the military government to implement reforms that were more radical and wide-ranging than any introduced under democratic rule.[2] Political participation was also subject to top-down control, via the Sistema Nacional de Apoyo a la Movilización Social (SINAMOS; National System of Support for Social Mobilization). Scholars such as Julio Cotler have been highly critical of the government's "corporatist" approach to popular politics.[3] However, this critique has tended to focus on the actions of central government, with little attention to the ways in which the "revolution" was communicated on the ground. This chapter examines the work of government promoters in the regions of Cuzco, Tacna, and Piura. Focusing on government efforts to promote the 1969 Agrarian Reform Law, I argue that the local context had a defining influence on the style of communication used and what the revolution came to represent in different areas of the country.

As the historian Susana Aldana has observed, "The region is a fundamental element in the vision and imaginary of any Peruvian. However, the construction of the nation-state model led to the creation of a totally homogenizing official discourse. Lima is the capital of the nation and, therefore, its best—and almost single—representative; the Peruvian state is reflected in the capital and is a reflection of it."[4] This is particularly true of the historiography on the Velasco government. Perhaps influenced by the government's own intensely nationalist rhetoric, analysts of the regime have tended to confine themselves to its national political strategy and decisions taken in Lima.[5] Although valuable local studies were produced in the 1970s and 1980s—particularly on the impact of the agrarian reform—these often emphasized the separateness of policy outcomes from the intentions of central government. For example, in her study of agricultural cooperatives, Cynthia McClintock comments that "decrees made in a Lima government office often were never seen nor heard elsewhere. Laws were regularly subverted by citizens. Riddled by power struggles among distinct bureaucratic and socioeconomic groups, the Velasco government was not as strong as its adherents or its critics suggested."[6] It is undoubtedly true that local conditions shaped policy implementation and produced unanticipated consequences. However, this emphasis on the particularities of the local context implies that the agrarian reform was experienced as a set of disparate local processes, detached from national politics. In fact, as Linda Seligmann shows, peasants often invoked state narratives in their petitions to the Agrarian Tribunal, directly engaging with the national government's rhetoric.[7] There remains a need for research that integrates national and local perspectives. Using detailed local research within a comparative framework, I hope to provide a multilayered account of political communication under the Velasco regime.

Perspectives on the Regions

The idea of the region is a social construct that has historically been defined in different ways and for different cultural and political purposes. Peru's current system of regional governments did not exist until 1990. Before that, there was a system of departments governed hierarchically from the center, with each department containing a number of provinces.[8] In Peru, the region has more often been seen in terms of social and cultural identities than politically defined territories, most commonly in the formulation of three distinct geographical areas: the coast, the *sierra* (Andean mountain range), and the *selva* (Amazonian jungle). While framed in terms of naturally occurring geographical features, such descriptions are shaped by cultural assumptions and reflect broader ideological positions. As Evelyne Mesclier has shown, changing representations of Peru's regions have also served to legitimize particular government policies.[9]

In June 1971, the Velasco government created SINAMOS, a government agency that was designed to "achieve the conscious and active participation of the national population in the tasks that economic and social development demand."[10] SINAMOS established a new formulation of the region that combined political and cultural characteristics. The so-called system was organized into eleven regions, one of which was designated for the *pueblos jóvenes* (shantytowns) across the country, that is, not confined to a particular geographical area. The remaining ten regions each comprised two or more departments. Within each SINAMOS region there were several zonal offices, each of which took responsibility for the activities carried out by local promoters in one or more provinces. The overall organizational structure of SINAMOS therefore comprised four tiers: the local level (teams of promoters), zonal offices (OZAMS; Oficinas Zonales de Apoyo a la Movilización Social; Zonal Offices of Support for Social Mobilization), regional offices (ORAMS; Oficinas Regionales de Apoyo a la Movilización Social; Regional Offices of Support for Social Mobilization), and the national office (ONAMS; Oficina Nacional de Apoyo a la Movilización Social; National Office of Support for Social Mobilization).

The system of SINAMOS regions created a parallel political geography to the existing departmental and provincial boundaries.[11] Its regional divisions were also distinct from Peru's five military regions and its twelve agrarian reform zones, creating a complex set of institutional relations. The logic behind the SINAMOS regions was to introduce a kind of centralization in miniature, simultaneously creating administrative efficiency and releasing resources to be used at the local level. As the members of staff in most regular contact with local populations, SINAMOS promoters were charged with defending the government's policies and stimulating a new kind of political participation, reflected in the following excerpt from a SINAMOS pamphlet:

> Participation should start with those closest to us, our neighborhood, for example. There, there are many things to do, many problems that are waiting to be resolved by us, without expecting that the solution will come "from above," from the government or whichever other institution . . . in an ascending manner and in accordance with our practice of organized participation, we arrive at [the ability to] present and resolve the problems, be they economic, political, social, or cultural, that affect the destiny of our country as a whole.[12]

Although in practice more hierarchical chains of command tended to dominate, the government's discourse on popular participation attracted many people who were already employed at the community level, such as teachers, to work in SINAMOS. In addition, the organization recruited young graduates in the fields of psychology, sociology, anthropology, and journalism via a rigorous selection process. According to a former SINAMOS employee who worked in the communications department of the Piura Regional Office, this consisted of various stages.[13] Following a written application, she was given a simulation exercise: to devise a plan for promoting a new law among Piura's rural population and present it to a selection panel. Having passed this stage, she was interviewed by a military official, who asked questions about her personality and her interest in social issues. Finally, she was interviewed by the director and subdirector of the regional office. "So everyone, according to the role they were applying for, went through that process. No one was recommended just like that. At least in my time. All of us who entered—there were a lot of us—we went through that process of selection and we passed."[14] According to this SINAMOS worker, an important element of the selection process was to establish whether the candidates had "*mística*"—a term that in this context meant a personal commitment to tackling Peru's social problems. This did not necessarily imply strict adherence to the government's ideas and approach; many of those recruited to the organization had previously participated in antigovernment protests, for example, in opposition to Velasco's proposed university reforms.

Given that SINAMOS sought a set of skills and experiences not usually found among military personnel (activism, public engagement, knowledge of social science models), its recruitment process was driven by a strong degree of pragmatism and admitted people with a variety of political affiliations. At times this openness created problems for the government, with political parties such as Vanguardia Revolucionaria (VR; Revolutionary Vanguard)—which saw SINAMOS as an instrument of dictatorship—deliberately infiltrating the organization.[15] Members and former members of the center-right party Alianza Popular Revolucionaria Americana (APRA; American Popular Revolutionary Alliance) also took up roles within SINAMOS. It seems that this issue was tackled through internal propaganda rather than any disciplinary action. In Tacna, for example, the regional SINAMOS office circulated a pamphlet in July 1975 entitled "Alert! APRA is infiltrating! What do you think?," with instructions for all the zonal offices to include a copy in their staff library.[16] Although the government rejected claims that SINAMOS was acting as the party of the government, its political role became increasingly prominent. A government pamphlet published in 1974 declared that the technical functions of SINAMOS promoters were complementary to their political role: "Legal and financial assistance, infrastructural support, training, dissemination, etc., are nothing more than different means through which the political position and aims of the Peruvian Revolution are expressed."[17]

However, the politically engaged new recruits represented a relatively small proportion of SINAMOS staff. The organization was formed from eight existing state institutions and retained large numbers of civil servants from the previous regime. This was a pragmatic move to avoid unpopular redundancies, but it created a series of problems for the government. Many staff were either insufficiently motivated to implement the government's reforms effectively or were actively engaged in sabotage. A former employee of the SINAMOS regional office in Piura commented: "Within SINAMOS there were completely discordant voices, without feeling, bureaucratic. I would say that they had their backs to the reality, chained to their desks. . . . Perhaps they were not confrontational but they delayed things, I would say that they delayed on purpose resolutions or projects that could have come out in one or two days."[18] SINAMOS also struggled to overcome tensions between its military and civilian personnel. The military's control of key positions within SINAMOS meant that military ideas about political organization tended to prevail over the more activist tendencies of civilian recruits.

The armed forces' perspective on the regions exerted a powerful influence, both at the highest levels of government among Velasco's advisers and in the implementation of policies on the ground, as military personnel took up positions within the national bureaucracy. Contemporary military magazines such as *Actualidad Militar* reflect common regional stereotypes. For example, the coast was portrayed as a modern area of industrial growth, the Amazon (*selva*) was seen as exotic and disconnected from the rest of the country, while the highland region (*sierra*) was considered an area of cultural and economic "backwardness." However, the military also had a long history of recruiting among Andean populations, and there was an acknowledged affinity between the military and the peasantry, which Cecilia Méndez has described as one of the great paradoxes of authoritarian rule in Peru.[19] Thus, despite attempts to draw a separation between the centralized, professional institution of the army and "isolated" rural populations, the army was composed of those very populations and influenced by the provincial backgrounds of its recruits.

General Juan Velasco's provincial background and personal trajectory is a case in point. Born in 1910 in Castilla, Piura, Velasco was one of eleven children. His father worked as a medical assistant, and he described his early childhood as a life of "dignified poverty, working as a shoeshine boy in Piura."[20] As president, Velasco frequently referred to his humble origins to distinguish himself from the so-called oligarchy, whom he labeled enemies of the Peruvian nation and the revolution. Many of the intellectuals who collaborated with the Velasco government also had a strong awareness of different regional cultures. Francisco Guerra García, who was the director of SINAMOS's regional offices, grew up in Cajamarca and moved to Lima to attend university. His career path was typical of many of the civilians who participated in the Velasco government: "Lima is a melting pot. Velasco was *piurano*. Leonidas Rodríguez, the chief of SINAMOS, was *cuzqueño*. Carlos Delgado, who was the most important political adviser, and also the most important SINAMOS politician, was *chiclayano*. And I could continue."[21] This firsthand knowledge of Peru's regions was a guiding influence within the Velasco government.

Regional Cultures

Having outlined the government's approach to political communication in the regions, I will now examine three regional case studies: Piura, Cuzco, and Tacna. Piura, in the far north of Peru, is a coastal region that includes 20 percent coastal land and 2.8 percent highlands, with the remainder taken up by plains and desert. Rainfall is concentrated in the highlands, with water on the plains coming from the Rivers Chira and Piura, which begin in the northern highlands and extend through two-thirds of the region's surface area.[22] Growth in the export trade of cotton and sugar in the mid-twentieth century led to the development of large agro-industrial complexes that used increasing levels of mechanization and were owned by economic associations rather than single families. Piura's valleys and plains were characterized by large cotton-producing estates belonging to powerful landowners such as the Romero Onrubia group, which owned a total of 103,991 hectares (1,040 sq. km), while the highlands were occupied by smaller haciendas and peasant communities that farmed small plots of unirrigated land and produced livestock.[23] With the implementation of the Agrarian Reform Law, the major agro-industrial complexes were expropriated and handed over to large cooperatives of the former workers, known as Cooperativas Agrarias de Producción (CAPs; Agricultural Production Cooperatives), while smaller haciendas were adjudicated either to CAPs or peasant communities with an established connection to the land. In addition to agriculture, the oil fields of La Brea y Pariñas formed a key part of the Piura economy. One of the government's first actions, on October 9, 1969, was the expropriation of these oil fields from the American-owned International Petroleum Company, an act that dramatically boosted support for the government within the region.

Cuzco, in the southern highlands, has a subtropical climate that is generally dry and temperate, with two defined seasons: the dry season from April to October and the rainy season from November to March.[24] The varied landscape made it possible to produce a wide range of agricultural products, from tea and coffee in the high forests to wheat and barley in the lower altitude valleys. In contrast to the agro-industrial plantations in Piura, Cuzco farming methods were more traditional and less intensive, since the high altitudes and steep inclines did not permit the use of heavy machinery. In the late 1960s, agricultural land continued to be highly concentrated in the hands of a small number of powerful hacendados and religious orders. While it is important not to underestimate the extent of capitalist penetration in the region, the great haciendas of Cuzco were more commonly seen by their owners as displays of social status and regional power, rather than the centers of capitalist accumulation that the latifundios of the north had become.[25] The agrarian reform adjudicated land to a small number of CAPs in Cuzco, but land was more commonly given to groups of campesinos and newly established Sociedades Agrícolas de Interés Social (SAIS; Agricultural Social Interest Societies). These were looser cooperative associations made up of former hacienda workers and neighboring peasant communities.

Tacna, on the southern coast, presents a further contrast in both geography and patterns of land tenure. It has a varied landscape, predominantly flat but with some mountainous areas to the west, with a mild desert climate and large amounts of sunshine year-round.[26] Lack of irrigation and topographical limitations meant that in 1961, just 1.16 percent of the total surface area of Tacna was cultivated, and by 1978 this had increased to only 1.49 percent.[27] At the time of the agrarian reform, Tacna had a large number of small landowners and few latifundios of the kind found in northern Peru. In 1961, some 73.76 percent of Tacna's cultivated lands were held in plots of less than 5 hectares (classed as "minifundios"), 21.89 percent were extensions of between 5 and 50 hectares, and just 4.35 percent were more than 50 hectares.[28] Tacna's chief agricultural products were alfalfa and other food crops rather than international exports such as coffee, sugar, or cotton. Alongside agricultural production, Tacna's economy centered on mining, industry, and fishing, while its proximity to the border with Chile made it an area of intense commercial activity.[29]

As well as representing different social and economic contexts, the three regions had different cultural characteristics that shaped the implementation and promotion of the agrarian reform. A key difference between Cuzco and both Piura and Tacna was the high number of Quechua speakers in the former. According to the 1972 census, some 88.9 percent of the population of Cuzco were bilingual or monolingual Quechua speakers.[30] In Piura, by contrast, less than 1 percent of the population over five years old within peasant communities—a sector of the population in which indigenous languages tend to be more dominant—spoke Quechua as a first language.[31] There were also variations in literacy levels, which determined the kinds of government propaganda that could be deployed. In Tacna, 15.7 percent of the population over fifteen years old was illiterate in 1972, while in Piura the figure was more than double at 33.5 percent, and in Cuzco it was 53.0 percent.[32]

Tacna, Piura, and Cuzco also have very different political histories. In Piura, the peasantry was weakly organized across the region, especially in comparison with the large landowners, who operated powerful agricultural associations. The majority of peasants worked as temporary laborers on the large haciendas, with a high degree of unemployment due to the declining fortunes of Piura's agriculture, placing them in an economically and politically precarious situation.[33] By contrast, Cuzco had a history of peasant unions (beginning in the 1950s) and popular mobilizations against exploitative landowners. Although conditions varied across the region, labor scarcity in the remote highlands gave peasants a stronger bargaining position, particularly on the coffee-producing estates of La Convención and Lares.[34] Peasant activism ranged from strikes against abusive landowners to "illegal" occupations of hacienda land by groups of campesinos who claimed historic ownership of the land. The activities of Cuzco's campesino unions reached a peak in the period from December 1963 until March 1964, when numerous haciendas were invaded simultaneously across the region.[35] This history of peasant mobilization was to shape how the agrarian reform was received in Cuzco.

In Tacna, the great political struggles of the twentieth century had emerged in connection with the conflict with Chile rather than localized land disputes and labor conditions. The fifty-year Chilean occupation of Tacna following the War of the Pacific (1879–1883) deeply affected the history and identity of the region, forging a political discourse that was both nationalistic and defiantly independent.[36] This history meant that *tacneños* were generally more sensitive to the government's nationalist rhetoric than to the ideas of social justice promoted by the agrarian reform. An editorial in *La Voz de Tacna* in October 1971 claimed that the agrarian structure brought by the Incas had been maintained in Tacna: "For that reason we have not experienced the excesses of *gamonalismo* nor have we been subjected to the domination of the latifundios. And because neither the exploitation nor the abuse of the powerful were known in Tacna, that is why [the people] learned to love and defend liberty with passion and rebelliousness."[37] The picture painted here is of a people who do not need liberating from the yoke of the landowners or government intervention to change oppressive power structures. Rather, it is suggested that *tacneños* identify with the Velasco government because of a commitment to liberty and equality rather than personal circumstances. While the editorialist perhaps overstates the absence of land conflicts in Tacna, his comments indicate the context in which propaganda surrounding the agrarian reform was received in the region. Although broadly welcomed by the Tacna press, the agrarian reform was regarded as something happening "elsewhere."

The agrarian reform was national in scope, but certain areas of the country were prioritized for the implementation of the new law. In particular, the government saw the large agro-industrial complexes of the north as a valuable asset. The political strength of the center-right APRA Party in the northern departments also made it imperative for the government to quickly assert its authority there.[38] Just days after the promulgation of Decree Law 17716, which brought the agrarian reform into effect, army tanks rolled into the major latifundios of Cartavio and Cayaltí, and government officials began taking inventory of all assets in a dramatic show of the government's revolutionary intent. Implementation of the reform occurred at a much slower pace in the southern highlands and was often propelled into action only by the grassroots organizing of the campesinos. For example, despite being a prime target for expropriation according to the Agrarian Reform Law, by 1971 no action had been taken against the Hacienda Huarán, situated near Urubamba in the Sacred Valley of the Incas. On the contrary, that year the minister of agriculture paid a personal visit to the hacienda, promising that only unirrigated lands would be affected by the reform. This situation began to change only when the hacienda workers decided to take collective action, forming a union and occupying the hacienda by force.[39]

Although Piura was one of the first departments to be declared a zone of agrarian reform, in October 1969, implementation was often subject to protracted adjudication processes.[40] Frustration at the pace of the reform led to various "tomas de tierras" (land occupations), which took the government by surprise and forced it to ratify actions already taken on the ground. For example, on February 21, 1972, two thousand members of the Comunidad Campesina de Catacaos entered the property of the Compañía Irrigadora S.A. to reclaim their communal lands, occupying 1,000 hectares in total. As one of the largest campesino communities in the country, the Comunidad Campesina de Catacaos not only succeeded in maintaining control of the land but also gained approval to form the first Unidades Comunales de Producción (Community Units of Production), a variation on the standard cooperative model.[41] Implementation of the reform also took a different path in Piura's highlands as compared with the southern and central regions of the country, since no associative enterprises were created.[42] Instead, lands were adjudicated to groups of campesinos, a factor that changed the nature of the work being carried out by government promoters. The role of SINAMOS employees here was to collaborate with and assist the groups of campesinos rather than establishing and overseeing cooperatives.

In Tacna, both the nature of the reform's implementation and its results were less dramatic than in either Piura or Cuzco. In January 1975, the Federación Agraria Revolucionaria de Tacna y Moquegua (FARTAMO; Revolutionary Agrarian Federation of Tacna and Moquegua) observed: "In the region of Tacna and Moquegua, obvious structural changes have not been noted with the application of the agrarian reform, given that there were no large haciendas; except in the case of Totora and the colonization of La Yarada, the majority of the properties are medium and small."[43] As this comment suggests, the dynamics of the reform in Tacna were different from those in both Piura and Cuzco in that the terms of the Agrarian Reform Law tended to be used for the resolution of disputes between relatively small landowners rather than to reclaim communal territories or overthrow capitalist landlords.[44]

Having outlined the key differences between Cuzco, Piura, and Tacna, I now examine the government's promotional activities in these regions. Initially, posters and pamphlets to promote the Agrarian Reform Law were produced by a small team of artists and intellectuals based in the capital and distributed across the country as required, for example, to accompany official visits or local land expropriation processes.[45] Propaganda interventions in the regions were sporadic and limited. In one instance, to drum up popular support for a presidential visit to Chiclayo, military helicopters delivered an airdrop of promotional leaflets.[46] Over time, it became apparent that a more sustained regional presence would be required to maintain popular enthusiasm for the government's reforms, prompting the creation of SINAMOS in June 1971, as discussed above.

In Cuzco, the regional director of SINAMOS, General Luis Uzátegui Arce, seems to have enjoyed considerable popular support. Upon vacating the position in 1973, some fifteen thousand people gathered in the main square to honor the work he had achieved, and he was publicly declared "a son of Cuzco." Local newspaper *El Sol* described how "the Plaza de Armas became the scene of the greatest homage that has been given to a man who was at the head of an institution."[47] As regional director, Uzátegui was an astute political operator who successfully co-opted well-known local political figures to work for SINAMOS. He told one such leader that his criminal record for political activities would not bar him from joining the organization, commenting, "You've been in prison here and here, you've been in Sepa, no? . . . That's not important, for you it's a prize, a merit."[48] By contrast, the military general in charge of the Piura Regional Office was somewhat intolerant of efforts by SINAMOS promoters to engage with the local population. A promoter stationed in Ayabaca described how, when reviewing a bulletin produced by SINAMOS staff in collaboration with local people, the regional director told the promoters to scrap a section on local people's knowledge of their own history and replace it with more information on the government's agricultural policies.[49]

Beyond differences of personnel and working style, variations in the regional context directly influenced both the propaganda methods used and popular perceptions of the revolution. The history of land struggles in Cuzco meant that the SINAMOS regional office there could draw on a wealth of experience of popular mobilization. In the case of the Hacienda Huarán, referred to above, General Uzátegui recruited Vladimiro Valer Delgado, a well-known local figure in student and campesino politics, to help establish a SINAMOS presence on the hacienda. Valer was particularly familiar with Huarán, having helped organize a trade union among the hacienda workers. The day after he agreed to work for SINAMOS, Valer was taken straight to Huarán to begin collaborating with the hacienda workers and preparing them for the expropriation and adjudication processes. Until that point, the agrarian reform authorities had been unable to begin implementing the reform in Huarán and the surrounding area due to the political power of the landowners and the failure of the national government to prioritize the highlands as an area of agrarian reform.[50]

Collaboration with local campesino leaders gave SINAMOS a strategic advantage, but it also affected local perceptions of the agrarian reform. The continuity of personnel among individuals who participated in Hugo Blanco's political campaigns and subsequently went to work for SINAMOS meant that, for many *cuzqueños*, the agrarian reform formed part of a larger narrative of peasant struggle rather than arriving out of the blue, which is how it was commonly understood in the northern provinces. For example, the daughter of a mule driver in Catacaos, Piura, who began working on one of the Romero haciendas from the age of three, described a total ignorance about the agrarian reform among the local campesino population prior to its implementation, recalling that "we didn't know if it was a good or a bad thing."[51] As waged hacienda workers with low levels of unionization, many *piuranos* lacked the political resources with which to launch the kinds of struggles seen in Cuzco. In drawing this contrast, I do not wish to suggest that there was no political activism among Piura's campesinos before the Velasco government. Campesino communities such as Catacaos have a rich political history, and by the mid-1960s its leadership demonstrated a clear engagement with national politics.[52] However, the local social and economic context constrained the possibilities for peasant activism, and the tactic of *tomas de tierras* was used at a much later stage in Piura than in Cuzco. While some areas of Cuzco were weakly politically organized and vice versa in Piura, it is important to highlight the ways in which "red Cuzco" differed from Piura, and how these political characteristics were shaped by local social and economic circumstances.

As well as employing local campesino organizers to promote the agrarian reform on its behalf, SINAMOS officers in Cuzco selected communication methods that incorporated Quechua and highland cultural traditions, seeking to create a lasting impression among *cuzqueños*. The high degree of Quechua monolingualism in rural Cuzco led the regional office to produce radio programs and short films in Quechua. Government promoters were drawn from local populations to ensure they were fluent in the local dialect of Quechua. Quechua was also used in the slogans printed on flyers and posters. For example, the word "*causachum*," meaning "rise up," was used frequently regarding the government's actions, as in the slogan "Causachum Inkari! Causachum Revolución! Causachum Perú!" Against a historical background in which the Quechua language had been treated with contempt by state authorities and seen as a mark of backwardness within the education system, the government's use of Quechua held great symbolic and political significance.[53] During official ceremonies to mark the transfer of lands from government control to campesino groups and cooperatives, government officials spoke primarily in Quechua. The ceremonies also featured traditional instruments such as the *quena* (a vertical flute) and the conch shell.

A common method used by SINAMOS to convey the principles of the agrarian reform was the traveling puppet show. This art form had the advantage of being highly mobile, accessible to an illiterate population, and adaptable to the local context. The teams of puppeteers employed by SINAMOS went to surprising lengths to reflect local traditions in their shows. For each community they visited, the puppeteers altered the puppets' costumes to replicate the traditional clothing of the *comuneros* (community members).[54] A short documentary film from the time, directed by Alberto Giudici, includes footage of one of these puppet shows. While dealing with broad issues of capitalist exploitation, the show featured characters that would have been particularly recognizable to a rural Cuzco audience: the oppressive landowner, the authoritarian priest, and the browbeaten *peón*. Moreover, the show was conducted entirely in Quechua. As the camera pans around to the audience, it is clear from their laughter and close attention to the story that the performance struck a chord.[55]

SINAMOS's use of Quechua, local costumes, and recognizable Cuzco characters created a seemingly strong connection between Cuzco's peasantry and the agrarian reform. It also promoted the idea that Velasco's revolution as a whole served to vindicate and celebrate Peruvian indigenous identity. This idea was supported at the national level through popular festivals such as Inkari, an annual event that brought together hundreds of performers following a series of local and regional competitions that featured the folklore, dance, music, and artistic traditions of each region. The commemorative pamphlet produced for the 1973 Inkari festival combined photographs of the participants with extracts from a colonial text that prohibited the "*indios*" from retaining cultural practices or artifacts that celebrated their Inca heritage. (The text was originally issued by the colonial authorities in response to the 1780 Túpac Amaru rebellion as part of their efforts to prevent further indigenous revolts.)

The accompanying images were presented as proof of the endurance of cultural traditions and the ultimate failure of cultural domination in Peru. The government presented its reforms as part of a popular effort to reclaim power, expressed through political and cultural means: "All that began to end on October 3, 1968. . . . And then, the people in uniform and without uniform recovered the lost control of our oil, our mines, our sugar, our seas. And then also, under the bright clarity of a revolution in process, the artisans continued engraving their *mates*, the ceramicists modeling the clay, the campesinos dancing their dances, and the minstrels expressing the deepest suffering of the people."[56]

The government sustained its image as an ally of the people and heir to Túpac Amaru's political legacy through repeated use of Túpac Amaru iconography.[57] An interview conducted by Thomas Turino with two musicians of rural mestizo background in Cuzco in 1988 suggests that the government's narrative was broadly accepted:

T.T.: And why was highland music of concern to Velasco?

E.V.: Because his political position was Túpac Amarist. And Túpac Amaru was the first precursor of independence, the first mestizo who went out in defense of the Indian, the campesino. Hence, because he [Velasco] identified with the campesinos, it was necessary for him to give value, not only to the campesino himself, but also to his culture.[58]

Inkari was a national festival, with participants traveling from all regions of the country, but its association with the history and legacy of Túpac Amaru had particular resonance in the Cuzco region, Túpac Amaru's birthplace.

Tacna's history as an occupied territory shaped the population's response to the arrival of SINAMOS in a different way. When SINAMOS was first established, the SINAMOS office in Tacna was a zonal office, under the supervision of the regional office in Arequipa. Fredy Gambetta, who worked for the *pueblos jóvenes* section of SINAMOS in Tacna, recalled that "the day of the creation of the XI Regional Office, caravans took to the streets to thank the government for 'granting us independence' from the *arequipeños*."[59] The announcement was greeted by the local press as official recognition of the region's importance. Beneath the headline "Much justice has been done to Tacna," General Juan Sánchez González, chief of the new SINAMOS regional office, was quoted as saying: "The decision of the Revolutionary Government has been to give hierarchy to our region, nominating Tacna as head of the region."[60] Tacna's border location and intense nationalism meant that greater attention was given to the arrival of state institutions per se rather than the "revolutionary" messages they carried.

Government representations of the agrarian reform varied across different regions of the country. In Piura, the government emphasized the idea that the revolution was bringing liberation from *latifundista* control, along with a variety of social benefits for hacienda workers. For example, a commemorative booklet entitled *Catacaos: 24 de junio de 1973 día histórico para el campesino piurano* was produced to mark the transfer of lands in several parts of Piura. The booklet included images of workers riding the finely bred horses that had previously belonged to the hacendado, asserting their control over the property of the latifundio.[61] A propaganda film produced by the Dirección de Promoción y Difusión de Reforma Agraria (DPDRA; Office of Promotion and Diffusion of Agrarian Reform), using footage from the northern agro-industrial complexes, featured interview extracts with the workers, who told how "they treated us like animals" and "I was afraid, even of the guard." Images of animals kept in confined quarters were contrasted with the postreform situation of animals in large pens and the workers participating in leisure activities such as dancing the *marinera*.[62] The central theme of this propaganda was the idea of release from the oppression of capitalist landowners rather than reclaiming lands lost or celebrating an Inca past, as was the case in Cuzco.

A different propaganda film, also produced by the DPDRA, combined highland rural scenes with the following voiceover:

> Four hundred years ago the Spanish invaded Peru. In the first one hundred years of the conquest, eight million indigenous people and the system of the Inca leader were almost completely destroyed. Agriculture also suffered the consequences of the invasion. . . . Inca agricultural technology was destroyed. The indigenous were stripped of their lands and used as slaves. . . . The land now belongs to the tiller but that is not sufficient. So that the change is true and complete the campesino has to participate. The campesino has to organize and present his ideas. The campesino has to act.[63]

Although this message formed part of the government's overarching revolutionary narrative, the imagery and use of panpipe music in this film situated it in a highland context. Whereas propaganda in the north emphasized the provision of new health and education services that would accompany the establishment of agricultural cooperatives, in the south, greater stress was placed on the agrarian reform as a historic moment in which the peasantry was called upon to make the reform a reality.

Whereas government communication efforts in Piura and Cuzco engaged with regional histories of social injustice and portrayed the agrarian reform as a continuation of local struggles, SINAMOS promoters working in Tacna had limited "cultural capital" to work with and faced indifference among the population. In January 1974, staff completed a questionnaire that asked them to list, in order of importance, the main problems they met with in carrying out their daily work. A number of promoters referred to the apathy or resistance they encountered among the target population. One response stated that "rejection from the base population . . . [and] lack of awareness about the current process among the population" were the key problems, while another listed "the population's rejection of the system [i.e., SINAMOS], excessive individualism, [and] influence of some power groups" as the main difficulties.[64]

The predominance of small- and medium-sized landholdings in Tacna created a particular political dynamic among agriculturalists in the region. Rather than CAPs and SAIS (although these existed), there was popular support for the formation of Asociaciones Agrarias de Conductores Directos (Agricultural Associations of Owner Occupiers). Perhaps in the absence of a peasant union movement as in Cuzco, or a growth in community activism as in Piura, peasant organizations in Tacna did not take on the combative political role of their equivalents elsewhere. A SINAMOS report on Tacna's agricultural cooperatives concluded that they were mainly financial in nature, and consciousness about cooperatives was "at an initial stage."[65]

However, there are signs that opportunities for greater political engagement between SINAMOS promoters and local populations were missed in Tacna as a result of the government's misplaced assumptions. For example, the notion that Tacna was a fundamentally mestizo region meant that there was little provision for communication using indigenous languages, and the importance of Quechua in particular was underestimated. Evaluating a training course for peasant community leaders, a report by the zonal SINAMOS office in neighboring Moquegua stated: "While it is true that those attending the course speak Spanish, a better understanding and integration between the *comunidades campesinas* and presenters would have been achieved using the language of the zone (Quechua)."[66] The failure of government promoters to engage with

Tacna's regional cultures ultimately shaped how the agrarian reform has been remembered in the region. Whereas in Cuzco and Piura the agrarian reform is remembered as a period of great political tumult, in Tacna it has left a relatively small impression on the region's history.

Problems at the Local Level

As well as devising communication strategies that would appeal to particular regional audiences, SINAMOS promoters had to navigate local power structures to reach their target audience. A 1974 report by the SINAMOS zonal office in Cuzco identified the power groups it believed were obstructing SINAMOS's work in the region. These included the judiciary, landowners, tradesmen, and the police (Guardia Civil), which "in these historic moments we are living . . . do not comply with the proposals and conquests of the revolution . . . often they act in collusion with the landowners."[67] The report also criticized the clergy for evading the agrarian reform by selling Church lands and using their position of authority to actively oppose the government: "During Mass they preach against the current government and the leaders, telling the parishioners that the current process is Communist and promotes atheism."[68]

During the formation of the SAIS in Oropesa, a highland district of the province of Quispicanchi in the department of Cuzco, there was open confrontation between government promoters and local landowners. As was mentioned above, the SAIS was an alternative model to the CAP, and was used particularly in rural areas to bring dispersed groups of peasants into a single cooperative organization, in contrast to the large northern plantations, where a CAP could be formed from a single agro-industrial complex. In the case of Oropesa, establishing the SAIS required promoters to reach campesinos across a wide geographical area and in places where local landowners still exerted strong social and political control. A report filed by the chief promoter at the Cuzco zonal office complained that Alcides Velasco, the son-in-law of a local landowner, had disrupted a meeting organized to inform the smallholders of Chingo Chico about the SAIS. According to the report, the meeting had been organized by a team of SINAMOS and Ministry of Agriculture representatives. As they waited for participants to arrive, Alcides Velasco "presented himself suddenly in a thuggish and presumptuous manner without any consideration, given that women and children were present, and without any cause hurled vulgar abuse against the Ministry of Agriculture representatives, SINAMOS, and the beneficiaries that had gathered." The account includes verbatim quotes of what Alcides Velasco is reported to have said, such as "Don't think that I'm an ignorant *indio* like you and that you can trick me" and "I'm going immediately to see General Guzmán Fajardo, so that they get rid of you and your little bosses."[69] The language used here is significant, for it shows the persistence of racist attitudes among the landowners and the belief that even under the new regime, a word with the right person would see the removal of the "little bosses" of SINAMOS.

A later report on the same SAIS observed that the lengthy adjudication process had allowed landowners to obstruct the formation of the SAIS, for example, by occupying the hacienda house—required for training and organization purposes—and asset-stripping the estate. In addition, a number of landowners had requested to retain a portion of their property as "unaffectable" land, in accordance with the Agrarian Reform Law.[70] This had a negative impact on local support for the SAIS: "Such is the case of Estanislao Gonzales of the property Huambutío L-2, to whom an unaffectable area was granted, and as a consequence of this fact the smallholders of the property identify more with this gentleman, defending him and not wanting to know anything about the Company [i.e., the SAIS]."[71]

Developing and maintaining local campesino support for the cooperatives and associations established by the government required a continuous presence in the area. It was common practice for SINAMOS promoters to live in one of Cuzco's remote villages and base themselves there among the population. Establishing such a presence was not easy, however, and several interviews have revealed that certain sectors of the Cuzco region remained untouched by SINAMOS because the landowners' power was too great. In the case of Maras, situated 40 kilometers north of Cuzco, the newly arrived SINAMOS promoter was forcibly evicted by the "notable" residents of the village: "They gathered here on the corner, the notable residents, and they said: 'What? Promoter for what? And Campesino Community—what for?' They began to say, 'We'll tell this young man to vacate his room, we'll give him forty-eight hours. To the contrary, something will happen to him.' By the following day he wasn't there, he had left that night."[72] As this example illustrates, the fact that the Agrarian Reform Law had been passed was no guarantee that it could be implemented on the ground. Indeed, government promoters' inability to penetrate certain areas of Cuzco meant that SINAMOS was often seen as a distant organization, confined to the departmental capital. In Piura, by contrast, SINAMOS quickly acquired a reputation for authority and an "octopus grip" on local politics. Edita Herrera, who worked on communications for SINAMOS in the Piura Regional Office, recalled how, after visiting a remote village close to Ayabaca (in the highlands of Piura), a woman from the village came to Piura to seek her out: "After a few months, she appeared in the Piura Regional Office, asking for Señorita SINAMOS. That is, the woman had no idea what an institution or an organization was. For her, I was Señorita SINAMOS and she wanted to talk to 'Papá SINAMOS,' so that he would receive her. Why? Because the mentality of the campesinos was that the master was the father, the '*taita.*'"[73] It would be easy to interpret such anecdotes as evidence of political naïveté among Piura's peasantry. In Peru in particular, there is a strong tendency to characterize campesinos as politically "innocent" and disengaged from state institutions.[74] In fact, the woman in the story demonstrated a clear understanding of the political dynamics in operation by seeking out the person who could make state-backed decisions about her personal situation. The fact that this perception was formulated in terms of a family rather than a state-institution structure does not diminish the political understanding shown by her actions. Moreover, the anecdote shows how quickly SINAMOS gained recognition as a major power broker in the Piura region, even in remote areas. While the government's neat vision of a statewide structure of political organization did not necessarily match up with how SINAMOS was perceived on the ground, the organization successfully penetrated existing political structures in the Piura region.

Nelson Peñaherrera, who was the provincial coordinator for the SINAMOS zonal office in Ayabaca, Piura, described how civil servants and other local authorities feared any negative reports about their work being made to the SINAMOS authorities, believing they would lose their jobs. Peñaherrera was required to send a political report on the province every three months:

The political report was above all about the reality of the zone, the behavior of the institutions. For that reason, since we had to inform about more or less how this or that institution was performing, what were its merits and shortcomings, therefore the majority of people who worked in those institutions viewed us with certain distance, no? "With you,

I'm watching you but I'm not coming closer, because you are a risk for what I am doing." So that's why they said that we were the government's gossipers (*chismosos*).[75]

SINAMOS promoters also met with opposition from the left-wing political parties, particularly MIR Cuarta Etapa (a faction of the Movimiento de Izquierda Revolucionaria) and Vanguardia Revolucionaria (VR). In fact, government promoters and political activists pursued somewhat similar strategies to try to mobilize the local population, resulting in a constant battle for control. A former VR activist in Piura remarked that the fight between the MIR, VR, and SINAMOS was "palmo a palmo" (inch by inch).[76]

In Tacna, SINAMOS promoters also encountered opposition, but more frequently from conservative organizations than from left-wing activists. A SINAMOS evaluation produced in January 1976 noted that organizations such as the government-sponsored Agrarian Leagues were being displaced by the Provincial Council, which promoted "speakers that spoke in the name of base organizations but who are known political activists of the parties who oppose the Process (APRA-UNO)."[77] Internal reports of the Tacna zonal office also complained that its staff was insufficiently politically motivated.[78] Whereas in Cuzco SINAMOS had recruited politically conscious promoters from the ranks of the region's peasant unions, in Tacna many SINAMOS staff came from the technical professions, resulting in a more technocratic style of operation.

Although SINAMOS was more heavily funded and larger than any previous state institution, the work of government promoters was limited in all three regions by financial constraints. In Ayabaca, for example, there were four SINAMOS employees to cover an area of 80,000 hectares (approximately 800 sq. km).[79] SINAMOS promoters were also restricted by the censorship that came from higher up the organization. Hugo Herrera, a former coordinator of the SINAMOS zonal office in Ayabaca, recalls how the leadership pulled the plug on a touring theatrical production called *Revolutionary* in response to pressure from the police. Although the play showed unjust arrests made by the police, ultimately the protagonists were liberated—which was presumably the play's central message. However, for the SINAMOS authorities, the need to control political debate trumped the desire of local promoters to stimulate popular engagement through theater and other art forms.

In 1973, Velasco suffered a pulmonary embolism that resulted in the loss of one of his legs. As his health declined so did the so-called revolutionary process. In August 1975, General Francisco Morales Bermúdez took power in an internal coup, marking the end of "phase one" of the military government and a shift toward more conservative policies. In retrospect, Hugo Herrera feels that it would have been better to be open with people that the revolution had ended rather than continue to raise expectations: "We abandoned them. So that produced a doubly negative impact on them . . . We continued talking to them about revolution because the leadership kept talking of revolution. But it had been making a revolution, and now it wasn't. That's what SINAMOS did."[80] Rather than the top-down, militaristic style of government that is often conjured in reference to the Velasco government, the personal testimony of SINAMOS promoters suggests that there was considerable political engagement at the local level, even if it was short-lived.

Conclusion

Charged with promoting popular participation and generating widespread support for government reforms, SINAMOS introduced innovative communication methods and established an organizational structure that reached remote areas of the country. Drawing on their military experience and different provincial backgrounds, Velasco and his closest advisers showed a greater awareness of regional diversity than previous governments. However, SINAMOS also fell prey to the constraints of any large bureaucratic institution, summarized here by Héctor Béjar, one of the key directors of SINAMOS:

> For every social promoter that worked at the base level in the rural areas or directly with the popular urban organizations, there were no fewer than five office workers who were not exactly occupied with providing logistical support, but rather worked on the same routine and bureaucratic labor as always. . . . The power of the bureaucracy, its behaviors and reflections, did not cease to have effects on the whole system: the promoters that were responsible for the most delicate and important tasks, those for which [SINAMOS] had been created, earned the lowest salaries and were the men who acted without real political support in a frequently hostile environment.[81]

Meeting with resistance from an inherited bureaucracy is a problem that emerges in many studies of revolution or regime change. The incoming party is forced to deal with the old regime by rejecting it altogether, through a series of local compromises or by attempting to co-opt its members into the new regime. The Velasco government opted for the latter strategy, hoping to indoctrinate the existing bureaucrats, while at the same time introducing a new generation of ideologically committed promoters who would engage local populations in the revolution. As this chapter has shown, this process generated a series of tensions—between existing bureaucrats and new recruits and between SINAMOS promoters and local power groups and political activists.

In this chapter, I have outlined how efforts to promote the revolution varied between the regions of Piura, Cuzco, and Tacna. The local context dictated the story that SINAMOS representatives chose to tell, from a popular celebration of economic progress and liberation from latifundio control in Piura, to the vindication of indigenous land rights in highland Cuzco, and "revolutionary" nationalism in Tacna. Promoters used local historical and cultural resources to link the agrarian reform to the broader historical trajectory of each region, with varying degrees of success. While SINAMOS developed a reputation for its "octopus grip" on power in rural Piura, its representatives were forced out of villages in Cuzco and met with indifference in Tacna. Thus, while the day-to-day events of the agrarian reform across the regions played a central role in forming public opinion, so, too, did the political discourse and communications strategies deployed by SINAMOS and other government agencies. SINAMOS engaged with local politics and "translated" its message into locally meaningful discourse, bringing mass politics to remote areas and making the "region" a central notion within Peruvian politics.

Notes

1. Dirk Kruijt, *Revolution by Decree: Peru 1968–1975* (Amsterdam: Thela Publishers, 1994). Unless otherwise noted, all translations are my own.

2. Following the military coup of October 3, 1968, the Peruvian National Congress was suspended. Under military rule, all legislation was passed by legal decree.

3. Julio Cotler, "The Mechanics of Internal Domination and Social Change in Peru," in *Peruvian Nationalism: A Corporatist Revolution*, ed. David Chaplin (New Brunswick, NJ: Transaction Books, 1976), 35–71.

4. Susana Aldana Rivera, "Pensando la región: Una reflexión en torno al cambio y a la diversidad, al todo y a las partes," *Revista Interdisciplinaria de Historia y Ciencias Sociales* 1, (2012): 27.

5. Abraham F. Lowenthal, ed., *The Peruvian Experiment: Continuity and Change Under Military Rule* (Princeton, NJ: Princeton University Press, 1975); Juan Martín Sánchez, *La revolución peruana: Ideología y práctica política de un gobierno militar, 1968–1975* (Sevilla: Consejo Superior de Investigaciones Científicas; Universidad de Sevilla; Diputación de Sevilla, 2002); María del Pilar Tello, *¿Golpe o revolución? Hablan los militares del 68*, 2nd ed., 2 vols. (Lima: SAGSA, 1983); Carlos Franco, coordinator, *El Perú de Velasco*, 3 vols. (Lima: Centro de Estudios para el Desarrollo y la Participación, 1983).

6. Cynthia McClintock, *Peasant Cooperatives and Political Change in Peru* (Princeton, NJ: Princeton University Press, 1981), 46–47.

7. Linda J. Seligmann, *Between Reform and Revolution: Political Struggles in the Peruvian Andes, 1969–1991* (Stanford, CA: Stanford University Press, 1995).

8. Carlos Contreras, "El centralismo peruano en su perspectiva histórica," Documento de Trabajo No. 127 (Lima: Instituto de Estudios Peruanos, 2002), 28.

9. See Evelyne Mesclier, "De la complementariedad a la voluntad de 'aplanar los Andes': Representaciones de la naturaleza y pensamiento económico y político en el Perú del siglo XX," *Bulletin de l'Institut français d'études andines* 30, no. 3 (2001): 541–562. Mesclier argues that the characterization of the southern highlands as an area of isolation, poverty, and "backwardness" was particularly pronounced during the 1990s, when the turn to neoliberalism made it convenient to see the social problems experienced in the sierra as somehow endemic and particular to that region.

10. Art. 1, Decreto Ley No. 18896, June 1971, http://peru.justia.com/federales/decretos-leyes/18896-jun-22-1971/gdoc/.

11. Provincial councils and departmental prefectures remained in place throughout the military government, albeit with frequent intervention from the national government.

12. SINAMOS, *Movilización Social: ¿De quién? ¿para qué?* (Lima: SINAMOS, ca. 1972).

13. Interview conducted in Lima, May 7, 2013. The interviewee asked to remain anonymous.

14. Ibid.

15. Interview with former VR activist Armando Zapata, Piura, April 16, 2013.

16. SINAMOS, "Memorandum 067-75-DDR," Archivo Regional de Tacna (Intermedio): Gobierno Regional de Tacna, Legajo 07-0027.

17. SINAMOS, *Los promotores y la participación popular*, serie III, no. 2 (Lima: SINAMOS, 1974).

18. Interview conducted in Lima, May 7, 2013. The interviewee asked to remain anonymous.

19. Cecilia Méndez G., "Las paradojas del autoritarismo: ejército, campesinado y etnicidad en el Perú, siglos XIX al XX," *Íconos: Revista de Ciencias Sociales*, no. 26 (2006): 18.

20. Daniel M. Masterson, *Militarism and Politics in Latin America: Peru from Sánchez Cerro to Sendero Luminoso* (Westport, CT: Greenwood, 1991), 228.

21. Interview with Francisco Guerra García, Lima, August 27, 2012.

22. Nicole Bernex de Falen and Bruno Revesz, *Atlas regional de Piura* (Lima: CIPCA-PUCP, 1988), 8.

23. Ibid., 44.

24. Markus Kottek et al., "World Map of the Köppen-Geiger Climate Classification Updated," *Meteorologische Zeitschrift* 15, no. 3 (June 2006): 259–263.

25. E. J. Hobsbawm, "A Case of Neo-Feudalism: La Convención, Peru," *Journal of Latin American Studies* 1, no. 1 (1969): 31–50.

26. Kottek et al., "World Map," 261.

27. Oscar Panty Neyra, *Tacna, economía y sociedad: Introducción al período reformista-desarrollista, 1970–1980* (Tacna: Ediciones Liberación, 1980), 26.

28. Ibid., 30.

29. Ibid.

30. Felícitas Mendoza Salazar, "Los programas en quechua en la radiodifusión peruana," thesis for the title of Professional Journalist (Lima: Pontificia Universidad Católica del Perú, 1974), 11.

31. SINAMOS, *Comunidades campesinas del Perú: Información censal población y vivienda 1972*, Vol. 2 (Lima: SINAMOS, 1977).

32. Instituto Nacional de Estadística e Informática, *El analfabetismo en el Perú* (Lima: INEI, 1995).

33. Elmer Arce Espinoza, *La reforma agraria en Piura: 1969–1977* (Lima: CEDEP, 1983).

34. Alfredo Encinas Martín, Ángel Pérez Casado, and Rafael Alonso Ordieres, *Historia de la Provincia de La Convención*, Vol. 2, *Historia social y religiosa del siglo XX* (Lima: Centro Cultural José Pio Aza, 2008).

35. Hugo Neira, *Cuzco: Tierra y muerte* (Lima: Editorial Herética, 2008), 12.

36. William E. Skuban, *Lines in the Sand: Nationalism and Identity on the Peruvian-Chilean Frontier* (Albuquerque: University of New Mexico Press, 2007).

37. *La Voz de Tacna*, October 1, 1971, 3.

38. Although not tackled in this chapter, political parties such as APRA and the left-wing Vanguardia Revolucionaria (VR) and Movimiento de Izquierda Revolucionaria (MIR) played a vital role in shaping public reaction to the Velasco government and organizing political opposition.

39. Deborah Poole, "Corriendo riesgos: Normas, ley y participación en el Estado neoliberal," *Anthropologica* 30, no. 30 (2012), 83–100.

40. Arce Espinoza, *La reforma agraria en Piura*, 72.

41. Diego García Sayán, *Tomas de tierras en el Perú* (Lima: DESCO, 1982).

42. Bernex de Falen and Revèsz, *Atlas regional de Piura*, 38.

43. "Plan de Actividades de la FARTAMO, 1975–76," Archivo Regional de Tacna (Intermedio), Gobierno Regional de Tacna, Legajo 07-001.

44. For example, small landowners petitioned the reform authorities to expropriate small parcels of land and adjudicate in their favor where it could be demonstrated that the present landowner was not directly engaged in farming the land. See D. L. 17716, Art. 17.

45. For details on the early propaganda efforts of the Velasco government, see Anna Cant, "'Land for Those Who Work It': A Visual Analysis of Agrarian Reform Posters in Velasco's Peru," *Journal of Latin American Studies* 44, no. 1 (2012): 1–37.

46. Interview with Pedro Morote, former director of communications at the Ministry of Agriculture, Lima, October 2, 2012.

47. *El Sol,* January 5, 1973.

48. Interview with former SINAMOS coordinator Vladimiro Valer Delgado, Cuzco, May 28, 2013. "El Sepa" was an infamous penal colony in the remote Amazonian jungle of Loreto. In the early 1960s, Valer was arrested for his political activities and sent there along with numerous other associates of the peasant leader Hugo Blanco.

49. Interview with former SINAMOS coordinator Hugo Herrera, Piura, April 9, 2013.

50. The Dirección General de Reforma Agraria y Asentamiento Rural (General Office of Agrarian Reform and Rural Settlement), part of the Ministry of Agriculture, held overall responsibility for implementing the agrarian reform, but a number of other agencies were involved, including SINAMOS and the Agrarian Tribunal.

51. Interview with Catacaos community member Chepa Mena, Piura, October 14, 2013.

52. For details, see Alejandro Diez, "Gobierno comunal: entre la propiedad y el control territorial. El caso de la Comunidad de Catacaos," in *SEPIA XIV Perú: El problema agrario en debate,* ed. Raúl Asencio, Fernando Eguren, and Manuel Ruiz (Lima: Sepia, 2012): 115–148; Jan Douwe van der Ploeg, *El futuro robado: Tierra, agua y lucha campesina* (Lima: IEP, Walir, 2006); and Bruno Revesz, "Catacaos: Una comunidad en la modernidad," *Debate Agrario,* no. 14 (June–September 1992): 75–105.

53. The anthropologist Penelope Harvey argues that among bilingual populations, use of Quechua and Spanish reflects conscious efforts to define power relations rather than a set of given language domains. Penelope M. Harvey, "Language and the Power of History: A Study of Bilinguals in Ocongate (Southern Peru)," PhD diss., Anthropology Department (London School of Economics, 1987). Although not extensive, the Velasco government's use of Quechua crossed the boundary that had historically been maintained between Spanish as the language of power and officialdom and Quechua as the language of home life in rural communities.

54. Interview with a former SINAMOS communications officer who asked to remain anonymous, Lima, May 7, 2013.

55. The film, entitled *Causachu,* can be viewed online at https://www.you tube.com/watch?v=IuXUd8SBHuM.

56. SINAMOS, "Hermanos! Una mañana del mes de noviembre de 1781, y luego de la transitoria derrota de Túpac Amaru, apareció en bandos públicos diseminados a lo largo del Cuzco la siguiente sentencia contra el pueblo: . . ." (Lima: SINAMOS, 1973), 2–3.

57. See the chapter by Charles F. Walker in this volume.

58. Thomas Turino, *Moving Away from Silence: Music of the Peruvian Altiplano and the Experience of Urban Migration* (Chicago: University of Chicago Press, 1993), 143; Turino's translation.

59. Fredy Gambetta, *Confesión de parte.* Personal testimony published online at: http://www.peruan-ita.org/personaggi/gambetta/confesion.htm.

60. *Correo,* May 17, 1972, 1.

61. Zona Agraria I (Piura), *Catacaos: 24 de junio de 1973 día histórico para el campesino piurano* (Piura: Primero Perú, 1973).

62. *Videoteca histórica de la televisión pionera en el Perú*, DVD 01, Reforma Agraria. Available at the Sala de Mediateca, Biblioteca Nacional del Perú (Avenida Abancay), Lima. The *marinera* is a Peruvian coastal dance, particularly associated with the north of the country.

63. Ibid.

64. Archivo Regional de Tacna (Intermedio), Gobierno Regional de Tacna, Legajo 07-0042.

65. SINAMOS ORAMS XI, "Análisis socio-económico de las cooperativas agrarias en Tacna y Moquegua." Internal report, ca. 1972.

66. SINAMOS, "Informe 01: Desarrollo de cursillo de capacitación para dirigentes de comunidades campesinas, 20.08.75," Archivo Regional de Tacna (Intermedio), Gobierno Regional de Tacna, Legajo 07-0001.

67. SINAMOS, "Diagnóstico socio-político evaluativo de la Liga Agraria 'General Ollanta' de la provincia de Urubamba," (ca. 1974).

68. Ibid. On the relationship between the Catholic Church and the Velasco government, see Jeffrey Klaiber, *La Iglesia en el Perú: Su historia social desde la independencia*, 3rd ed. (Lima: PUCP, 1996), especially chapter 9, 393–428.

69. SINAMOS, "Informe de los promotores Luis Urquizo y Guillermo Guzmán al Jefe de la UPO," Cuzco, January 23, 1974.

70. Articles 30–34 of D. L. 17716 set out a series of conditions under which an area of land could be declared exempt from the reform, or "unaffectable," provided it was farmed directly by the landowner. The size of this allowance could be extended if the landowner demonstrated compliance with certain financial and labor requirements, creating an important loophole for some landowners.

71. SINAMOS, "Informe del promotor Luis Urquizo al Jefe de la UPO," Cuzco, February 2, 1974.

72. Interview with Juan de Mata Segovia Sosaya, Maras, Cuzco, May 24, 2013.

73. Interview with former SINAMOS employee Edita Herrera, Lima, May 11, 2013.

74. Florencia Mallon argues that such assumptions have formed the basis of orthodox thinking on state formation and national politics in Peru. Florencia E. Mallon, *Peasant and Nation: The Making of Postcolonial Mexico and Peru* (Berkeley: University of California Press, 1995), 4.

75. Interview with former SINAMOS coordinator Nelson Peñaherrera, Sullana, April 11, 2013.

76. Interview with VR activist Armando Zapata, Piura, April 16, 2013.

77. SINAMOS, "Informe final: Evento de evaluación y programación correspondiente al IV trimestral de acciones," Archivo Regional de Tacna (Intermedio), Gobierno Regional de Tacna, Legajo 07–0003. APRA-UNO refers to the right-wing coalition formed between APRA and the Unión Nacional Odriísta between 1963 and 1968.

78. SINAMOS, "Evaluación situación socio-política zonal—Tacna (enero 1975)," Archivo Regional de Tacna (Intermedio), Gobierno Regional de Tacna, Legajo 07-0027.

79. Interview with former SINAMOS coordinator Hugo Herrera, Piura, April 9, 2013.

80. Ibid.

81. Héctor Béjar, *La revolución en la trampa* (Lima: Ediciones Socialismo y Participación, 1976), 107.

CHAPTER 10

Watering the Desert, Feeding the Revolution: Velasco's Influence on Water Law and Agriculture on Peru's North-Central Coast (Chavimochic)

MARK CAREY

Introduction

In December 2013, the Peruvian government awarded a contract to the Brazilian-Peruvian consortium Río Santa Chavimochic to complete the $715 million third and final stage of one of the country's largest agro-industrial irrigation projects, the Chavimochic project (Proyecto Especial Chavimochic, or PECH) in the northern department of La Libertad. The consortium agreed to cofinance the project by contributing approximately $374 million.[1] Awarding this contract helps implement some of the desert fantasies that have motivated Peruvian irrigators and export-oriented agriculturalists for decades, including the Velasco administration in the 1970s. While Chavimochic construction did not start until 1986, the Velasco era paved the way legally, politically, technically, and even culturally for this large-scale irrigation project that has, for many people over the last century, offered a solution to Peru's water, economic, labor, and development problems.

Despite its importance and prominence for Peru, Chavimochic has been the subject of relatively few critical studies and limited historical scholarship. This chapter provides a history of the Chavimochic project, asking in particular what role Velasco's military government played in its development and eventual implementation. It makes three points about the Velasco administration and the long-term development of Chavimochic. First, the Velasco era had direct impacts on the project not only because the Revolutionary Government of the Armed Forces (RGAF) conducted studies and supported north-coast irrigation, but also because of the post-1969 changes in land tenure, water law, and the role of the state in allocating land and managing water in La Libertad (and throughout Peru). Second, environmental forces (climate, hydrology, topography) shaped the history of Chavimochic, thereby demonstrating that any analysis of Velasco's government and its agrarian developments should recognize the role of dynamic environmental factors. In particular, drought and El Niño–generated floods shaped political support (or dismissal) of Chavimochic. Third, the project subsequently emerged in the 1980s partly due to perceived failures of the Velasco era, which helped contribute to the post-1980 shift toward export agriculture and nontraditional crops.

Overall, Velasco implemented a transformation to state-controlled infrastructure and a rise of technocrats and engineers that had emerged earlier in the twentieth century but became more solidified during (and remained after) the Velasco government. Changes under Velasco expanded the ever-increasing role of engineers, who have managed the Chavimochic project ever since. But while the Velasco administration did inspire important historical shifts, his 1969 Agrarian Reform Law and the 1969 Water Law were not necessarily the all-important turning points in agro-industrial developments in north-central Peru's coastal region over the last fifty years. It was Alan García's 1985–1990 APRA (Alianza Popular Revolucionaria Americana) government, after all, that implemented the Chavimochic project. And once project construction began in 1986, there was a clear and marked shift away from the principles and policies that Velasco had pursued. Moreover, the post-1993 liberalization of land, industry, trade, and agricultural businesses put Chavimochic on a path more radically distinct than anything Velasco had imagined in 1969. Thus, while Velasco technocrats played a key role in twentieth-century shifts toward engineering, state-controlled infrastructure, and technocratic consolidation in Lima, it is also important to decenter the RGAF from larger historical transformations, avoiding a tendency to identify Velasco's rule as the watershed moment.

Chavimochic Overview

Chavimochic is an immense irrigation project that relies on water from the Santa River, one of western Peru's most voluminous rivers, which flows along the Ancash–La Libertad border (see map 10.1). The irrigation project sends the Santa's water northward beyond Trujillo as the mother canal passes through the *Cha*o, *Virú*, *Mo*che, and *Chica*ma Valleys (hence the name: Chavimochic). The upcoming Stage III invest-

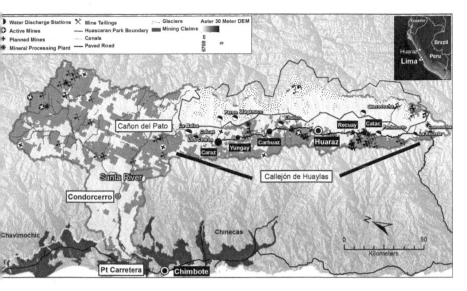

Map 10.1. Map of Santa River Watershed and Chavimochic Project (shaded section in lower left). Trujillo is near the coast, along the black line that represents the Pan-American Highway (Carretera Panamericana) in the lower-left corner. Map by Jeffrey Bury.

ment will fund construction of the massive 360-million-cubic-meter Palo Redondo reservoir, a 113-kilometer irrigation "mother canal" from the Moche Valley to the Chicama Valley north of Trujillo, and a 60-megawatt hydroelectric station, among other infrastructure and irrigation components in La Libertad. Stage I of the project was completed in 1994, and Stage II was mostly completed in the late 1990s, with some final minor aspects finished in 2011.

To date, Chavimochic has improved irrigation on approximately 28,000 hectares and opened agriculture on roughly 46,000 hectares of unproductive land that was previously sand and desert.[2] Since the 1980s, agriculture in La Libertad has increasingly shifted to export-oriented nontraditional crops such as asparagus, avocados, mangos, and *maracuyá* (passion fruit)—planted and managed by large agro-industrial companies supplied with water from the Chavimochic project. This shows a marked shift from the 1970s sugar cooperatives formed after President Juan Velasco Alvarado's military government (1968–1975). Accompanying this agro-industrial development have been a host of linked societal and environmental changes to land and water use, employment, livelihoods, economic conditions, urban expansion, and demography. A full

understanding of Chavimochic, and how and why it came to emerge—
as well as its long-term influence on labor, potable water supplies, hydroelectricity generation, and the colonization and creation of new fertile land for La Libertad and Peru—requires analysis of the Velasco
government and its legacies related to north-coast development.

Chavimochic Antecedents

Engineers first started fantasizing about using Santa River water to irrigate La Libertad as far north as the Chicama Valley in the 1910s—and
the dreams continued even since Stage I of Chavimochic was finished
in the early 1990s. Like much of Peru's coastal area, La Libertad is an
exceptionally dry desert with scant rainfall and intermittent floods associated with El Niño events and other extreme weather changes. Despite the desert conditions, irrigated agriculture has existed for millennia in these regions, implemented by such pre-Columbian groups as the
Moche and Chimú. With the rise of development-oriented engineers in
the late nineteenth century, interest in coastal irrigation grew markedly.
In 1912, the Peruvian engineers Eduardo Villarán Godoy and Manuel
Flores Romero proposed a canal from the Santa River to Trujillo. Plans
for what eventually became Chavimochic reemerged in 1936 when the
central government's Dirección de Aguas e Irrigación conducted studies for a 76-kilometer canal to irrigate 30,000 hectares of agricultural
lands in the Chao and Virú Valleys. More thorough studies were carried out in the early 1940s under the direction of the Ministerio de Fo-
mento by the US engineer Charles Sutton, who essentially envisioned
the project as it stands today, with a mother canal intake from the Santa
River above 400 meters above sea level, high enough to allow for construction of a hydroelectric station along the canal's route all the way
to the Chicama Valley. The most robust and detailed studies were then
conducted from 1957 to 1961 by the Peruvian Santa Corporation, which
managed the Cañón del Pato hydroelectric station on the Santa River
and promoted agricultural, irrigation, and industrial development using Santa River water in Chimbote and Ancash.[3] The company's work
clearly demonstrated the growing role of engineers in Peruvian development through the course of the twentieth century.

Yet, despite much government support for Chavimochic, it was not
until 1967 that the central government took definitive steps toward its
implementation. On July 21, Law No. 16667 officially named the Chavi-

mochic project as the entity to deliver Santa River water to the Chao, Virú, Moche, and Chicama Valleys. The law also established an executive council and directorate to oversee the project. Importantly, the law referred to it as "necessary and useful for the public," thereby suggesting its national and regional value to Peruvians.

The period from the 1910s to the 1960s also witnessed a trend that Velasco's government would partially break, or at least try to free the country from: the encouragement of foreign expertise, investment, and agro-industrial development. The 1961 Santa Corporation study, for example, actively sought out foreign investment for and involvement in Chavimochic.[4] The Velasco government did not completely reject foreign expertise, but it favored worker-owned cooperatives and small-scale farmers that came about after implementation of the 1969 Agrarian Reform Law. Up to the 1960s, "traditional" agroexport industries dominated the Peruvian coastal region, with cotton and sugarcane as the most important crops, covering 349,000 hectares, or 53 percent, of the coast's agricultural area and representing half of all Peruvian exports.[5] These trends would change with the Velasco administration and Chavimochic project.

Velasco and Chavimochic: Land

Even though the Velasco government did not construct—or even start constructing—the Chavimochic project, his administration paved the way for eventual implementation of the project after 1986 in two important ways: land and water. One of the most influential acts of the Velasco government was the Agrarian Reform Law of 1969, which led to one of the most comprehensive and far-reaching land reform programs in Latin American history.[6] Velasco's land reform immediately tackled the large sugar estates in La Libertad, especially in the Chicama Valley where Velasco expropriated the Cartavio and Casa Grande haciendas just two days after announcing the Agrarian Reform Law. Several reasons explain Velasco's decision to target estates in this region.[7] La Libertad had historically been a critical support base for APRA, which had been construed as key opposition to the military. Velasco officials thus hoped that by giving campesinos and farmworkers their own land they could undermine political opposition to his RGAF.[8] In addition, these sugar estates had not been part of the 1964 agrarian reform, so they remained as huge haciendas in 1969. Further, the Velasco administration targeted these haciendas because they were productive and unlikely to decline in production after expropriation, redistribution of land, and the formation of cooperatives. Consequently, a major transformation occurred after 1969 from the centuries-old power of the large estates and haciendas—combined with some poor, smallholder agriculture—to the post-1969 cooperatives, which excluded migrant workers and did not necessarily reduce the quantity of poor campesinos, since the cooperatives were formed primarily by those who were previously regularly employed estate workers.[9]

Two important aspects of agrarian reform in La Libertad affected the eventual implementation of the Chavimochic project fifteen years later. First, agrarian reform put the state in control of dividing land, and the military government sought explicitly to eliminate the haciendas that had dominated agrarian politics, landholdings, and water allocation for centuries. Second, after removal of hacienda control, it became possible for the government to later sell the land, thereby facilitating the arrival of private companies. These private companies did not arrive in force until Fujimori's neoliberal reforms in the 1990s, but that process may not have played out as it did if the Velasco government had not first wrested control of the land from its previous owners during the 1970s. In the 1970s, land in the intervalleys (the desert or unproductive lands between each of the Chao, Virú, Moche, and Chicama Valleys) was divided by the state. Then, after 1980, when the military government gave way to a civilian administration, a long period of dividing up the land resulted in average landholdings shrinking to 6 hectares per family by the end of the 1980s.[10] The land was increasingly sold after 1985—and even more after Fujimori's liberalization in 1993—through a process that promoted the intrusion of private companies oriented toward export agriculture because of the high amount of capital required to invest in the land. The price of land was not necessarily high, but the government required a US$2,000 investment per hectare, as well as $2,800 minimum equity per hectare. Agrarian reform in the 1970s had helped the process for Chavimochic because it fragmented landholdings in the old valleys when haciendas were expropriated and redistributed to each worker, rather than remaining in such large plots as previously.[11] In return for the investment in the land, each buyer was guaranteed by the state and Chavimochic to receive a minimum of 10,000 cubic meters of water per hectare per year, which they also had to pay for at the rate they used. There was also in the intervalleys a competitive process of selling lands through bidding, and by 2006 about 44,000 hectares had been allocated.[12] Another 5,100 hectares were sold directly, and

1,000 hectares were given as a concession to the agricultural community in San José.[13]

The post-1986 influx of private export-oriented companies selling nontraditional crops to Europe and the United States represents a complete shift from the objectives of Velasco's agrarian reform. Yet it was the elimination of haciendas and the change of land ownership that paved the way toward the liberalization of landholding and the agro-industry after Chavimochic was under way. There was a slow change of landholdings within the Chavimochic area, from the cooperatives of the early 1970s after the agrarian reform to the small- and medium-sized landholdings, which have in most cases surpassed the productivity and investments of the cooperatives.[14] A 1980s assessment report of the Chavimochic project suggested that the past era proved that land ownership should switch to private hands, as individual properties, or be in private company hands, rather than in the cooperatives that did not work and did not have enough capital to invest in boosting production. The Chavimochic path, then, was through the purchasing of lands to put into private and company ownership—with an extraordinary state subsidy to private companies in the form of irrigation infrastructure and the flow of water through desert lands.[15] Backlash to and reactions against the Velasco government's cooperatives were evidently still justifying the Chavimochic project in the late 1980s.

Velasco and Chavimochic: Water

When the Velasco government announced Decreto Ley 17752 at the same time as the Agrarian Reform Law in 1969, water became a public good under state control, to be managed for the good of society. In short, the law declared all water the property of the state. There was clearly intent for Velasco officials to radically change water law in Peru, as revealed by the planning that took place prior to the 1969 water law. In 1968, Velasco officials asked a group of advisers to produce a new Water Code to update and revise the one that had been in effect in Peru since 1902. Those drafting the new code concluded, however, that a code did not go far enough: "Public law," the water law architects argued, "due to its social and economic content, is dynamic and changing, not in keeping with the characteristics of a code, which is static, exclusive, and excluding."[16] The advisers apparently wanted to make the new water law both more flexible and more powerful.

This new 1969 Water Law established the central government's Autoridad de Agua as the final adjudicator in all water requests and conflicts, thereby strengthening state control over water.[17] Government organizations such as the Autoridad de Agua, the Administración Técnica del Distrito de Riego (ATDR), and the Plan de Cultivo y Riego (PCR) had authority over allocating water. They decided how much water certain crops required, using technical equations for how much water each crop deserved. The 1969 Water Law also established the state as the owner and manager of both water infrastructure and its maintenance. The Ministry of Agriculture held the authority and hired the personnel in charge of allocating and managing water for La Libertad. Previously, the haciendas had held almost complete control over their water. After 1969, the cooperatives and individual landholders were much weaker than haciendas in advocating for and securing their water rights, which empowered the central government technocrats even more. These engineers in Lima could decide how much water to supply at what time of year, what crops should be planted, and how irrigation operations should proceed. As Jeroen Vos summarizes, "The Velasco regime wanted complete control over water, and that is what they achieved."[18] At least they attempted to control it. The on-the-ground reality was that the state did not seize complete control, thus signifying that the transformation was as much discursive as it was material.

Under Velasco, engineers and technicians in Lima held the right to exclusively manage irrigation and water, replacing the previous arrangement in which commissions and the farmers themselves determined water use and irrigation practices. Even after 1979, when a restructuring of water management led to the supposed inclusion of irrigators and users, the central government still retained the fundamental role in water-allocation decisions, even if those decisions were contested or ignored in practice.[19] Cooperatives, communities, campesinos, haciendas, and small-scale farmers were all lumped into the irrigator Comisiones de Regantes and Juntas de Usuarios after 1979. But they were all considered "midsize proprietors" completely subordinate to the Ministry of Agriculture's ATDR.[20]

A technocratic change in water management and discourse also happened after Velasco came to power. Although engineers such as Sutton and those in the Santa Corporation had always described water in volumetric measures and in technical language focusing on cubic meters per second, those disparate engineering reports became law and practice after 1969, once the engineers in Velasco's Ministry of Agriculture sought near-complete control over Peru's irrigation water through the

ATDR and other governmental offices. Some locals lamented this shift in control of the region's land and water to a *limeño* professional class of engineers, as well as to foreigners—or at least to those with English and German language skills—who could work with the technical instruments and manuals published in those foreign languages.[21] The haciendas had lost control by the early 1970s, and the cooperatives that replaced them never were able to control water or dictate the language or terms of its management to the extent that the engineers and technocrats in Lima did through the Ministry of Agriculture subagencies such as the ATDR.[22]

In addition to water-allocation decisions, there was also a technical transition in irrigation canal maintenance, again replacing the actual water users and farmworkers, who had previously cleaned and maintained the infrastructure and technology, with engineers from Lima. Such a shift broke up community work and traditional social organization, replacing it with a technical apparatus overseen from Lima rather than from local communities.[23] Other scholars have noted how even just the discursive shift in language can erode local power, autonomy, and cultural relationships with water and rivers.[24] And in the Andes, ample evidence shows how irrigation is part of local customs and traditions, with water-allocation decisions embedded in a ritual that is as much spiritual and about community relations as it is about agricultural productivity.[25] The engineering language and power over water triggered a significant change after 1969. It also facilitated implementation of the Chavimochic project later because engineers and technocrats managing the project did not have to wrestle control of the water away from previously powerful hacienda owners in Ancash and the upper Santa River watershed. Instead, they had the authority and the discursive approach to justify the Chavimochic project in the face of early 1980s drought conditions and with support from García's post-1985 Aprista government.

Chavimochic eventually became an export-oriented agro-industrial irrigation enterprise favoring private companies, which obviously stood in sharp contrast to the populist-oriented agrarian reform and state-controlled economy favoring import substitution industrialization under the Velasco administration. Ideologically, the RGAF and the post-1985 direction of Chavimochic are oppositional. Yet, at the same time, Chavimochic has always been a state-managed project—first selling the land and then providing the hydrological infrastructure and negotiating power to bring Santa River water into La Libertad. Initially run by the Instituto Nacional de Desarrollo (INADE) from the early 1980s, and after 2003, by the La Libertad regional government, Chavimochic's irrigation, water treatment, and hydroelectricity components (among others) were run by the state. And this emphasis on the state gained significant momentum during the 1970s. Overall, through the twentieth century there was a transition from private to public control of water, with a shift from haciendas to the central government deciding on and managing water allocation in Peru after 1969 in particular.[26]

The technocratic thrust of the Velasco era was also carried into the Chavimochic project. This elite group of engineers, planners, and infrastructure specialists played an increasing role in Peru and gained rising prominence in state policies. Technocrats such as agronomists, for example, managed the production and policies for all the new cooperatives formed through land reform. And, ever since, Chavimochic has been managed and run by engineers. Chavimochic itself obviously has radically different values and ideals compared to the Velasco-driven cooperatives and water-allocation agendas. Yet it was the wresting of control over land and water away from haciendas that Velasco's government achieved after 1969 that later helped facilitate the rise of private, export-oriented companies and individuals operating in the Chavimochic lands after the 1980s, especially after the neoliberal reforms of the 1990s.

Regional Support for Chavimochic

Although Velasco's military government did not start actual work on the Chavimochic project, his Ministry of Agriculture did support its construction and conduct studies for its implementation, especially after 1973. In early February 1971, Velasco offered 1.5 billion soles to invest in seventeen small and midsized irrigation projects over the subsequent four years.[27] Expectations for this investment were that it would put 30,000 hectares of land under production, which would benefit five thousand families and bring in an estimated 460 million soles annually from this agricultural production. In the first year, however, none of the money supported projects in La Libertad (or Ancash), according to the newspaper article. Yet there was significant interest in moving Chavimochic forward in the early 1970s, with much hope that the project would help thirty thousand families just through Stage I, and that it would yield significant benefits for infrastructure, social services, the economy, the environment, and the expansion of Peru's productive capacity—the same suggested achievements of the project discussed when the 2013 contract was awarded to the Río Santa Chavimochic Consortium. The writer Juan Vicente Requejo summarized all these benefits in 1972 and hoped China could provide the necessary capital investment to complete Stage I, estimated at 3 billion soles. He complained that 100 million soles had been invested in studies to date, but that the project had still not gotten under way.[28] Moreover, he noted that the Mochica and Chimú societies had irrigated the area thousands of years ago, and that most agricultural lands and irrigation canals in the area were abandoned as a result of the Spanish Conquest. During the early 1970s, the RGAF did initiate work on the Chira-Piura project, as well the Majes project. The government conducted studies on Chavimochic, Chinecas, Jequetepeque-Zaña, Olmos, and Puyango-Tumbes.[29] There was clearly some support for large-scale irrigation projects on Peru's coast, but only two of those projects were under way a decade later. It seems the emphasis was more on technical improvements to existing irrigation infrastructure than to opening up new lands or developing original projects.

Nevertheless, some attention was paid to the Chavimochic project during the Velasco era. Local policy makers, residents, irrigators, and the newly established cooperatives all continued to recognize the critical importance of water for effective agriculture and agrarian reform in La Libertad during the early 1970s. Some claimed that agrarian reform meant that men and women in La Libertad could live "without anguish or fear" due to the redistribution of land, but many others recognized that water shortages relentlessly worked against productive and efficient agriculture in the desert region.[30] An article urging both large- and small-scale irrigation projects in the Chicama Valley pointed to the need not only to guarantee water supplies but also to match crops to the season and quantity of water available, adding livestock production when water supplies increased. The article lamented, but in an optimistic tone, that "there is much to be done in the Chicama Valley; there are lands to irrigate at low cost."[31] To irrigate these new lands, the newspaper concluded, it was necessary to control the flow of the Chicama River and to build a dam to make a reservoir in the upper watershed.

These were precisely the kinds of measures the Chavimochic project sought to achieve. Other pleas for such water-control infrastructure arose as well. In February 1970, for instance, the Trujillo newspaper *La Industria* argued that "better and more profitable crops are not a utopia. There is only one thing missing: abundant water. Reservoirs and power stations must be built; the flows of rivers must be managed."[32] The report pointed to progress on the Tinajones irrigation project in Lambayeque. But while Stage I of that project was finished, the authors suggested that the lack of other similar projects was holding back agricultural development on the north-central coast. A year later, the newspaper was still lamenting that the lack of progress on irrigation infrastructure meant that without more water, lands remained unproductive year after year.[33] And for some, this meant a significant loss not only of agricultural production but also of money and tax inputs for the national government and the people of Peru. Consequently, many argued that the lack of irrigation capacity in La Libertad had a profound national impact. At the Casa Grande Cooperative alone in 1971, the lost production of a million quintales of sugar cost an estimated 257 million soles in lost revenue. This translated into an annual loss of 28 million soles for the central government, which supposedly reduced government investment in the construction of schools and the expansion of hospitals.[34] Expanded irrigation through projects such as Chavimochic, in other words, could have far-reaching positive socioeconomic impacts on the region, people claimed at the time.

Newly formed cooperatives argued strongly in favor of the Chavimochic project, especially after 1973 when years of ample rainfall gave way to a drought. Representatives of the Casa Grande Cooperative in the Chicama Valley, for example, wrote in 1973 that "The consolidation of the agrarian reform process can be achieved only when a steady supply of water is assured. . . . Reports and technical information should be made available immediately to carry out the plans to divert Santa River water toward the Chao, Virú, Moche, and Chicama Valleys. The socioeconomic benefits have already been clearly demonstrated, and they are incalculable for the region and the country."[35] The cooperatives remained supportive of Chavimochic even after the 1970s. According to one report, government officials noted that agricultural cooperatives were going to help fund the construction of Chavimochic in order to reduce government costs and ensure that the project moved forward. Cooperatives, the report continued, also supplied labor and equipment, especially the large ones such as Casa Grande, Cartavio, and Laredo.[36] Cooperatives had another impact on Chavimochic through the language of community building and cooperation. These ideas were still emphasized after the Velasco era, when some argued that the "agrarian politics" of Velasco's government and its values that emphasized protecting and respecting the people as well as focusing on the "spirit of cooperation and fraternity" and not on "hatred or sterile clashes" were still critically important for coastal irrigation projects.[37]

More complaints than these were broadcast in newspapers and reports about the lack of water for irrigation and agriculture in the early 1970s—and these complaints had existed for decades until Chavimochic began bringing Santa River water into La Libertad. These problems fall into various categories: irregular water flow in the rivers, lack of potable water for the residents and industries of Trujillo, and an unstable and insufficient supply of electricity for people and industries in La Libertad. *La Industria* carried news articles complaining about these issues every few weeks during the 1970s. The electricity went out, the water dried up for several days, potable water vanished from Trujillo homes, a flood washed away people and crops, a drought wreaked havoc because there were no reservoirs—these were the kinds of reports appearing in newspapers regularly throughout the Velasco period.

Velasco and the Politics of Drought

Obstacles to irrigation and farming proliferated, but floods and drought were consistent, albeit irregular, setbacks. El Niño years often brought floods that destroyed irrigation canals.[38] But there were, on the other hand, also frequent periods of drought and lack of water.[39] This led to repeated efforts to tap groundwater reserves as a way to make up for seasonal and decadal deficiencies of water. In one case in the Moche Valley in 1980, a plan passed to use subterranean water to help irrigate 1,600 hectares of land. As the Moche farmer Guillermo Caffo Rosales explained about the need for the project, "Water is the key to development for the entire country."[40] The Chavimochic canal helped regularize water flow as soon as it was constructed. This was important in the Virú Valley, among others, because it was particularly variable in the dry season.[41] With Chavimochic, the water flow was both regularized and augmented markedly. While scholarship to date has focused on the politics and agrarian economy (especially land reform) under Velasco's government, it is also important to recognize the role of drought, floods, and other environmental factors that shaped the history of Velasco's government and the evolution of the Chavimochic project.

Drought—or the opposite of drought, *huaycos* (flash floods)—played a role in the historical development of Chavimochic. The region has historically been plagued by droughts and El Niño–related floods going back millennia. These factors had shaped the region for fifteen hundred years, since the Moche society and before.[42] Over the last several decades, droughts have also played a role in justifying the Chavimochic project. For example, the mid-1960s drought that hit north-central Peru was brutal for farmers. By 1968, the agronomist Alfredo Santa María Calderón estimated the drought had caused 1 billion soles of damage in Trujillo Province alone. Santa María Calderón saw the Chavimochic project as offering salvation from such socioeconomic suffering.[43]

But the lack of drought and periods of consistent water supply also affected agrarian and irrigation politics, such as during the Velasco administration. Although there had been a significant drought in the mid-1960s, which may have partly motivated passage of the 1967 law that officially established Chavimochic, by 1969 the drought had ended, and the early 1970s was a period of ample water supplies in the various La Libertad rivers.[44] Combined with this period of relatively high international sugar prices, the cooperatives formed through agrarian reform and the sufficient water supply may have made the Chavimochic irrigation project less important for the military government. What's more, the devastating 1970 earthquake that killed an estimated seventy thousand Peruvians in Ancash and La Libertad destroyed the north-coast economy. Subsequent years were devoted to the recovery and rebuilding of infrastructure rather than to investment in new projects. Though not a climatic event, the earthquake demonstrates how other environmental forces shaped the trajectory of the Velasco years.

In 1973, drought returned and the Velasco government's interest in Chavimochic surged. Officials transferred administration of Chavimochic planning to the Ministry of Agriculture, and many local cooperatives offered to take an active role by supplying labor for its construction. In part because of this unskilled labor supply, engineers and cooperative leadership proposed changing the Santa River intake from the planned point at 412 meters above sea level to 295 meters, believing that this lower intake would make canal construction much simpler, quicker, and thus cheaper.[45] Although money for Chavimochic studies was generally included in annual central government budgets, no progress was made on actual construction under Velasco's government, and the estimated US$300 million (or more depending on the route and components such as hydroelectric stations or not) was never allocated.

In the early 1980s, however, the Peruvian government jump-started Chavimochic, once again because of severe drought. In 1980, the government announced a new law (Decree Law 22945) that identified Chavimochic as a "preferred national interest." The decree allocated 78 billion soles (US$300 million) to Chavimochic over the next twelve years, with the hope that the project could expand the agricultural frontier by adding 81,000 hectares of new land for agro-industrial development. Further, the law stipulated that interest rates and borrowing privileges would be "the most favorable" for Chavimochic and La Libertad.[46] The government was responding in 1980 to the years of drought that had inflicted suffering, crop loss, and economic hardship on the region. José Ramos Arnao lamented in 1979 in Lima's *La Prensa* that "drought and *huaycos* once again lash the region of Ancash affected profoundly by the May 1970 earthquake."[47] A major "agrarian campaign," he concluded, was necessary in the region to hold off the onslaught of nature during the previous several years. The president of the Organismo de Desarrollo de La Libertad (ORDELIB), the engineer César González Vásquez, also noted the powerful impact of the drought on the region. He explained to *La Industria* that "the three consecutive years of drought that lashed this region" represented definitive proof of the need to speed up the implementation of the Chavimochic project.[48] González Vásquez noted the important support for Chavimochic from both the Ministry of Economy and Finance and the Regional Directorate of Agriculture and Food. This joint support for the project, combined with the ongoing impact of the drought, helped justify increased government expenditures for the project in 1980. And while the government decreed funds for Chavimochic, emergency funds were simultaneously flowing into La Libertad, for example, to help drought victims with relief and recovery.[49] Yet, just as the funds were allocated, the national government changed and the project did not actually move forward in 1980 as planned and as decreed in Law 22945.

Drought and politics continued to intersect through the 1980s. By 1982, engineers settled on the high route for the mother canal intake on the Santa River at 412 meters instead of 295 meters. The project would thus include not only vast irrigation canals but also hydroelectric generation and potable water for the city of Trujillo. But just as the 1981 drought had sparked regional and national interest in Chavimochic construction, the end of that drought and the onset of the major 1982–1983 El Niño event hushed voices in favor of the project. The public outcry and political maneuvering of the early 1980s vanished, and project development stalled until 1985, when President Alan García repaid his APRA support base in La Libertad by allocating hundreds of millions of dollars between 1986 and 1989 to actually start Chavimochic construction.[50]

From the 1960s to the 1980s, climatic conditions played a major role in stimulating political support (or lack thereof) for the project—just as climate change concerns in the last decade have helped fuel the implementation of Chavimochic's Stage III. James Kus explains the waning support for Chavimochic that occurred when the 1982 El Niño event started: "Once again, the end of an episode of drought reduced interest in this project. . . . For more than seventy years there have been proposals to build the Chavimochic project in northern coastal Peru. Most efforts to build this intervalley canal system have come during extended droughts; return of normal water volumes in the region's rivers has usually ended interest in the Chavimochic project."[51] Overall, it seems that drought did play a role in the push to construct Chavimochic, though it must also be contextualized within the politics of the country, since environmental forces alone were not enough to push the project through.

As a result, one cannot simply consider the political aspirations and agendas of Velasco's administration (or other governments) as a driver of his agrarian reform and water law policies. These must be contextualized within, among other things, the fluctuating yet always active environmental forces at play in Peru, such as climate and water dynamics in the geographical context of a desert that led to fluctuating periods of drought followed by ample water. Kus, writing before any Chavimochic canals actually diverted any Santa River water into La Libertad, argued more broadly that Chavimochic could be seen as a success historically even though it had not been implemented. That's because it allowed government officials to rally behind it and produce technical studies that proved that "something is being done to solve the problem of drought in the region." In this way, I suggest, there was a politics of drought that involved repeated claims of government support for Chavimochic, which were always embedded in the specific political, economic, and technical contexts that increasingly, during and after Velasco, emphasized a techno-hydraulic approach to water. Such discourse in periods of drought offered hope—hope that Chavimochic could resolve problems such as the farmworkers and cooperatives wanting irrigation, the Trujillo inhabitants needing drinking water, the industries requiring hydroelectricity, and the landless campesinos hoping for new land or jobs. It also suggested that the government was making progress and moving forward on their dreams—but without actually investing hundreds of millions in the actual Chavimochic project. The mobilization of this environmental narrative—the politics of drought—was an important way in which the state and its technocratic engineers interacted with society, and not only during the Velasco government.

Chavimochic Construction

Several issues in the early 1980s led to the implementation of the Chavimochic project. The first was a major shift in orientation and scale of Peruvian coastal agriculture toward a more international, export-oriented agriculture.[52] The change occurred because of the growing demand in Europe and North America for crops that could be produced in Peru, Chile, and elsewhere in the Southern Hemisphere during the northern winter. In addition to the international demand, Peru also had cheap and abundant labor. Further, the early 1980s was characterized by state support and investment through the Corporación Financiera de Desarrollo (COFIDE) and the Banco Agrario del Perú (BAP), as well as by the intrusion of private companies and new or updated technologies. These changes were particularly prominent in Ica and La Libertad.

Part of the motivation to construct Chavimochic in the 1980s was the backlash against perceived failures in Velasco-era cooperatives and the ensuing unproductive agriculture of the late 1970s. One commentator in La Libertad argued in favor of the Chavimochic project in early 1985 by saying that the internal focus of agriculture since the 1970s reduced demand and thus decreased production and profits, as well as taxes. This writer believed a more export-oriented agro-industrial focus would help resolve these problems that had plagued the region for fifteen years. Specifically, he suggested more "industrial investment" in the production of tomatoes, asparagus, tubers (potato, yucca, sweet potato), and alfalfa.[53] José Benites Vargas, candidate to the Chamber of Deputies for the Acción Popular Party, also explained in March 1985 that the irrigation projects were essential for the region. As *La Industria* summarized on March 15, "The principal base for creating new sources of wealth and work in La Libertad is the increase in agricultural production, which requires technical inputs, a guaranteed supply of water, available low-interest credit to farmers, and cheaper inputs, which will all stimulate sustainable agro-industrial development in La Libertad."[54] The goals of the Chavimochic project did in fact diverge markedly from those of the agrarian reform of 1969 because they sought to expand production and productivity, generate more jobs, increase available credit, and enhance exports.[55] Agricultural productivity had clearly been important to Velasco. But in the 1980s, the emphasis was on commercialization, new technologies, international crop exportation, and providing loans—as well as ensuring a stable water supply for irrigation.

The most important immediate factor in the implementation of Chavimochic was party politics and the Aprista government of Alan García, who became president in 1985. After more than a half century of fantasizing and fussing about Chavimochic's ability to tap the Santa River, it took the APRA Party, with a stalwart base in Trujillo, to invest in the project. In fact, García did not even wait to be sworn into office before he started expressing his solid support for Chavimochic.[56] This was in many ways part of a long trend of using Chavimochic as a rallying point in local and national elections, especially for APRA with its historical support base in Trujillo and La Libertad.[57] As the local resident Julio Isla Cabanillas put it, "We applaud how Aprismo is loyal to its support base. We also believe that compatriots in the entire region, and not just Trujillo, will benefit from it."[58]

Chavimochic has significantly changed La Libertad. For one, Chavimochic claims to have generated more than sixty thousand jobs in the region.[59] Such opportunity for employment has also caused considerable immigration into Trujillo and La Libertad. Trujillo, for example, has grown from 355,000 inhabitants in 1981 to approximately 800,000 today, indicating roughly a doubling of the urban population since the Chavimochic project began.[60] There has also been a transformation of land ownership from the haciendas before 1969, to the cooperatives after Velasco's agrarian reform, to today, when eleven companies have come to control approximately 86 percent of the newly cultivated land in the intervalley areas. Between 1994 and 2006, these companies accumulated nearly 44,000 hectares of intervalley areas previously uncultivated until the arrival of Chavimochic irrigation canals. The Peruvian company Camposol, which is the world's largest producer of avocados and one of the world's leading asparagus growers, acquired more than 10,000 hectares (23 percent) of these new lands by 2006, while other companies such as Compañía Minera San Simón (6,185 hectares), El Rocío (4,901 hectares), Empresa Agroindustrial Laredo (3,790 hectares), and Rego Corporation (3,778 hectares) acquired an additional 34 percent of the new intervalley desert lands to come under cultivation within the Chavimochic project.[61]

During the past several decades, Chavimochic has become one of Peru's largest and most lucrative agro-industrial projects. According to the Ministry of Economy and Finance, the Chavimochic project will generate US$1.5 billion annually for Peru once Stage III is completed, which represents 30 percent of La Libertad's gross domestic product (GDP).[62] Peru has also become one of the world's leading exporters of asparagus and avocados, with cultivation in Chavimochic (and Ica) accounting for a significant portion of the country's production.[63] In short, the Chavimochic project has helped La Libertad blossom into one of the leading agro-industrial regions of the country. In addition to providing the crucial ingredient (water) for this billion-dollar agro-industrial economy, Chavimochic also supplies drinking water to the vast majority of Trujillo's 800,000 residents, as well as hydroelectric energy to people and industries. But it all hinges on the Santa River, whose water flow is increasingly variable and declining, given global climate change and the shrinking of the Cordillera Blanca glaciers that are a key source of the Santa's flow, especially during the tropical dry season.[64]

Conclusion

Analysis of Chavimochic antecedents and implementation illuminates several important trends both for the Velasco years and for longer-term implications up to the present. First, for all the professional engineering and scientific studies conducted by Peruvians and foreigners over more than half a century, there was little accounting for any short- or long-term fluctuations in the Santa River water supply. All the studies assumed that Chavimochic could extract a regular minimum amount of water at a rate of 45 m³/sec (cubic meters per second). In the last decade, however, dry season flow rates in the Santa River have fallen to 30 m³/sec or lower, and today Chavimochic officials express tremendous worry about declining water supplies in the glacier-fed Santa River.[65] But now hundreds of thousands of people depend on the project and this Santa River water, making them extremely vulnerable to climate change and glacier shrinkage that affect the river's water flow. Further, before the 1980s, there was little understanding or even acknowledgment among these coastal experts of the source of the Santa River, which is born in the Cordillera Blanca and is significantly glacier fed. These glaciers, as highland experts were realizing by the 1940s, can shrink and reduce long-term water supplies, especially in the dry season when most Santa River water flow is glacier fed.[66] Evidently, Peru's coast-sierra divide blinded professional engineers, too. There was—and still is to some degree—a static view of the upper watershed, assuming that people, farmers, industries, and mines would not remove more Santa River water over time to restrict water flow at the point where Chavimochic wanted to remove the water at the intake. Engineers seemed to assume that future water supplies would remain constant for people and agro-industries in La Libertad. What's more, a consistent mantra among the engineers persisted—and persists today—that any water flowing into the ocean was "wasted." As Figallo and Vattuone explain, "Their objective could be summarized in the following phrase: not even a drop to the sea."[67]

From a more social-hydrological perspective, there was little concern by the Santa Corporation or other engineers about taking water from the Santa River and the people of Ancash. As the 1960s Santa Corporation study clearly shows, they proposed to extract an additional 24 percent of the dry season Santa River water for the Chavimochic project. They assumed that they had the right to take the water from Ancash. Such thinking, however, has yielded a never-ending source of conflict, in particular because the *bocatoma* (intake) for Ancash's Chinecas irrigation project is below the Chavimochic *bocatoma*. In 1985, as plans for Chavimochic solidified, Ancash–La Libertad (Chinecas-Chavimochic) tensions heightened, and Trujillo's leading newspaper, *La Industria*, carried almost weekly articles about *ancashino* worries and frustrations with Chavimochic. Today, as Santa River water declines, tensions continue and struggles for water will likely only increase in the future, as they have already in the upper Santa watershed.[68] Thus, while Chavimochic has yielded tremendous profits and income for Peru, it has also heightened the vulnerability of nearly a million people who depend on one water source (the glacier-fed Santa River), and it may generate future water conflicts that are only just now heating up among various social groups throughout the watershed.

Velasco's military government did not build the Chavimochic project, but it did shape its evolution. Agrarian reform and the 1969 Water Law ended the grip of haciendas on both land and water, empowering the state, which was subsequently able to divide and sell lands within the Chavimochic project and to keep control of the water flowing through the canal. The engineers, agronomists, and other technocrats managing Chavimochic since its early days had also gained prominence and power during the Velasco era, and this real and discursive transformation thus had important long-term consequences. The drought politics of the twentieth century, including from the late 1960s to the early 1980s, also played a critical role in Chavimochic's history and demonstrate how states can mobilize environmental narratives to retain authority and discursively claim state action (through engineering studies but not actual projects) in the name of societal benefits, thereby quelling political discontent. Support for irrigation projects like Chavimochic surged when droughts hit, and interest waned when water was sufficient. Such environmental factors are crucial to remember in the history of agrarian reform, agricultural politics, and Velasco's military government. In short, Chavimochic emerged through a variety of political, socioeconomic, cultural, technological, and environmental variables that interacted in both time and space.

Notes

This chapter is based on work supported by the National Science Foundation Grants #1253779 and 1010132. Special thanks to Kelsey Ward and Nicolas Montoya for research assistance, as well as to Adam French, Carlos Aguirre, Paulo Drinot, and participants of the 2013 Velasco workshop at University College London for valuable comments on the manuscript.

1. Proyecto Especial Chavimochic, "Consorcio Río Santa Chavimochic gana buena pro III etapa de Chavimochic," *Boletín del Proyecto Especial Chavimochic* 12, no. 120 (December 2013): 1. For preliminary contract discussions, see http://www.chavimochic.gob.pe/portal/ftp/informacion/boletines/2012/b _agosto_2013.pdf. Unless otherwise noted, all translations are my own.
2. Chavimochic, *Chavimochic en cifras 2000–2010* (Trujillo: Gobierno Regional La Libertad/Proyecto Especial Chavimochic, 2012), 6. Also, Huber Vergara Díaz, Gerente General de Chavimochic, "Desarrollo y logros, Proyecto Especial Chavimochic," presentation in Trujillo, June 2011.
3. For the studies and antecedents, see INADE, "Proyecto de irrigación de Chavimochic," *Revista de Obras Públicas* 146, no. 3387 (1999): 76–79; James S. Kus, "Chavimochic: A Peruvian Irrigation Project," *Yearbook, Conference of Latin Americanist Geographers* 13 (1987): 19–24; Humberto M. Landeras Rodríguez, *Así se hizo Chavimochic: Historia del megaproyecto liberteño de alcance internacional* (Trujillo: Impresiones Peruanas, 2004); Alfredo del Carpio Zavala, *Proyecto de la irrigación de Chao, Virú, Moche y Chicama*, 2 vols. (Lima: Corporación Peruana del Santa, 1961).
4. Carpio Zavala, *Proyecto de la irrigación de Chao, Virú, Moche y Chicama*.
5. Marcel Valcárcel, "Agroexportación no tradicional, sistema esparraguero, agricultura de contrata y ONG," *Debate Agrario* 34 (2002): 31.
6. Enrique Mayer, *Ugly Stories of the Peruvian Agrarian Reform* (Durham, NC: Duke University Press, 2009); Cristóbal Kay, "The Agrarian Reform in Peru: An Assessment," in *Agrarian Reform in Contemporary Developing Countries*, ed. Ajit Kumar Ghose (New York: Routledge, 2011 [1983]), 185–239.
7. James S. Kus, "The Sugar Cane Industry of the Chicama Valley, Peru," *Revista Geográfica* 109 (1989): 57–71.

8. George Philip notes, on the other hand, that leading to the 1968 coup, Velasco was "already tending to see APRA as pointless rather than threatening" (285); see George Philip, "Nationalism and the Rise of Peru's General Velasco," *Bulletin of Latin American Research* 32, no. 3 (July 2013): 279–293.

9. Ismael Muñoz Portugal, "Grupos de regantes y acción colectiva en la distribución del agua en el valle de Virú," *Debates en Sociología* 34 (2009): 87–104.

10. Ibid., 89.

11. Anaïs Marshall, "El proyecto especial Chavimochic: Contratos agrarios establecidos entre agro exportadores y pequeños agricultores en los valles de Virú y Chao," in *Perú: Seminario Permanente de Investigación Agraria (SEPIA) XII*, ed. G. Damonte, B. Fulcrand, and R. Gómez (Tarapoto, Peru: SEPIA, 2008), 553–584.

12. Zulema Burneo, *The Process of Land Concentration in Peru* (Rome: The International Land Coalition, 2011), 14, online at http://www.landcoalition.org /sites/default/files/documents/resources/PERU_ENG_web_21.06.11%202.pdf.

13. "Cambiando los desiertos en tierras agrícolas—Peru," *Grid: Revista de la Red IPTRID* 24 (2006): 6–8.

14. Julio Ernesto Gianella, "Proyecto de desarrollo rural integrado de los valles de Chao y Virú: Planeamiento Físico Rural. Informe Preliminar," ed. Ministerio de Agricultura/PRONADRET (Trujillo: Archivo del Proyecto Especial Chavimochic, 1989).

15. Ibid., 4–6.

16. Quoted from Dale B. Furnish, "The Hierarchy of Peruvian Laws: Context for Law and Development," *The American Journal of Comparative Law* 19, no. 1 (Winter 1971): 91–92.

17. Laureano del Castillo, "Lo bueno, lo malo y lo feo de la legislación de aguas," *Debate Agrario* 18 (1994): 1–20.

18. Jeroen Vos, *Pirámides de agua: Construcción e impacto de imperios de riego en la costa norte del Perú* (Lima: Instituto de Estudios Peruanos [IEP]/Water Law and Indigenous Rights [WALIR], 2006), 75.

19. María Teresa Oré, "From Agrarian Reform to Privatisation of Land and Water: The Case of the Peruvian Coast," in *Searching for Equity: Conceptions of Justice and Equity in Peasant Irrigation*, ed. Rutgerd Boelens and Gloria Dávila (Assen, the Netherlands: Van Gorcum, 1998), 268–278.

20. María Teresa Oré, *Agua: Bien común y usos privados. Riego, estado y conflictos en la Archirana del Inca* (Lima: Pontificia Universidad Católica del Perú/Soluciones Prácticas ITDG/Wageningen University/Water Law and Indigenous Rights, 2005), 151.

21. Jorge Zavaleta Alegre, "¿Quienes conducen la reforma agraria?," *La Industria* (Trujillo), February 22, 1970, Suplemento Dominical.

22. Vos, *Pirámides de agua*.

23. Oré, "From Agrarian Reform to Privatisation of Land and Water."

24. Linda Nash, "The Changing Experience of Nature: Historical Encounters with a Northwest River," *The Journal of American History* 86, no. 4 (2000): 1600–1629.

25. See, for example, Paul H. Gelles, *Water and Power in Highland Peru: The Cultural Politics of Irrigation and Development* (New Brunswick, NJ: Rut-

gers University Press, 2000); Paul B. Trawick, *The Struggle for Water in Peru: Comedy and Tragedy in the Andean Commons* (Stanford, CA: Stanford University Press, 2003).

26. Ricardo Apaclla et al., "Las políticas de riego en el Perú," in *Gestión del agua y crisis institucional: Un análisis multidisciplinario del riego en el Perú*, ed. Grupo Permanente de Estudio sobre Riego (Lima: Tecnología Intermedia (ITDG)/Servicio Holandés de Cooperación Técnia (SNV), 1993), 59–78.

27. "1,500 millones invertirán en pequeñas irrigaciones," *La Industria* (Trujillo), February 2, 1971, 1.

28. Juan Vicente Requejo, "Chao-Virú-Moche-Chicama," *La Nueva Crónica* (Lima), September 12, 1972.

29. Flavio Figallo and María E. Vattuone, "Tecnología: El lado oscuro de la reforma agraria," *Debate Agrario* 7 (1989): 103–125.

30. "La revolución agraria," *La Industria* (Trujillo), February 22, 1970.

31. "Plan de regadío económico en el valle de Chicama," *La Industria* (Trujillo), January 11, 1970, Suplemento Dominical.

32. "El Perú necesita agua y especialistas en irrigación de Tinajones: Es el comienzo," *La Industria* (Trujillo), February 15, 1970, Suplemento Dominical.

33. "Aceleran trabajos de irrigación: Angasmarca," *La Industria* (Trujillo), January 15, 1971, 9.

34. "Regantes del Valle Chicama se reunen para tratar sobre el reparto de agua," *La Industria* (Trujillo), March 8, 1971, 7.

35. Cooperativa Agraria de Producción Casa Grande No. 32, *Informe de actualización del proyecto de desarrollo agrícola de los valles Chao-Virú-Moche-Chicama (Chavimochic)* (Trujillo: La Cooperativa, 1973), 7.

36. "Alan García aseguró que hará Chavimochic," *La Industria* (Trujillo), May 25, 1985, 1.

37. Hernán Miranda Cueto, "Chavimochic, algo más que una irrigación," *La Industria* (Trujillo), March 24, 1985.

38. Víctor Arcila Cáceres, "Una irrigación económica," *La Industria* (Trujillo), December 5, 1985.

39. Humberto Landeras Rodríguez, "Sequía en el norte y el Proyecto Chavimochic," *La Industria* (Trujillo), December 20, 1985.

40. For example, "Aguas subterráneas utilizarán para riegos en Distrito Moche," *La Industria* (Trujillo), March 6, 1980.

41. Muñoz Portugal, "Grupos de regantes y acción colectiva," 87–104.

42. Izumi Shimada et al., "Cultural Impacts of Severe Droughts in the Prehistoric Andes: Application of a 1,500-Year Ice Core Precipitation Record," *World Archaeology* 22, no. 3 (1991): 247–270.

43. Alfredo Santa María Calderón, *La sequía del siglo: Gran argumento de justificación económica para el proyecto irrigación de Chao, Virú, Moche y Chicama* (Trujillo: Unpublished manuscript in Sala de Investigaciones, Biblioteca Nacional del Perú, 1968), 1.

44. Kus, "Chavimochic: A Peruvian Irrigation Project," 19–24.

45. Ibid.

46. "Dan crédito por 78 mil millones a Chavimochic," *La Industria* (Trujillo), March 22, 1980; "Urge participación para materializar Chavimochic," *La*

Industria (Trujillo), March 18, 1980; "En menos de 60 días se inicia Chavimochic," *La Industria* (Trujillo), March 16, 1980.

47. José Ramos Arnao, "Pasión y esperanzas del campesino de Ancash," *La Prensa* (Lima), April 7, 1979.

48. "Satisfacción en ORDELIB por proyecto Chavimochic," *La Industria* (Trujillo), March 17, 1980.

49. "A víctimas de sequía darán préstamos," *La Industria* (Trujillo), March 22, 1980.

50. Landeras Rodríguez, *Así se hizo Chavimochic*.

51. Kus, "Chavimochic: A Peruvian Irrigation Project," 23.

52. Valcárcel, "Agroexportación no tradicional," 29–44.

53. Carlos Neyra Medina, "¿Por qué Chavimochic?," *La Industria* (Trujillo), March 13, 1985.

54. "Irrigaciones son la base para aumentar producción," *La Industria* (Trujillo), March 15, 1985, 3.

55. Dirección Ejecutiva del Proyecto Especial de Rehabilitación de Tierras, *Proyecto Planrehati III. Sub-proyecto: Rehabilitación y mejoramiento de riego valles Virú y Chicama (Paiján). Estudio de factibilidad, Volumen I, Informe Principal* (Lima: Ministerio de Agricultura/Ministerio de la Presidencia, 1986), 11.

56. "Alan García aseguró que hará Chavimochic," *La Industria* (Trujillo), May 25, 1985, 1; "Alan García pondrá en marcha CHAVIMOCHIC," *La Industria* (Trujillo), December 18, 1985, 1.

57. Kus, "Chavimochic: A Peruvian Irrigation Project," 23.

58. "Aplauden anuncio por Chavimochic," *La Industria* (Trujillo), December 20, 1985.

59. Chavimochic, *Chavimochic en cifras 2000–2010*, 20.

60. Instituto Nacional de Desarrollo (INADE), *Informe: Proyecto Especial Río Santa—Chavimochic* (Lima: INADE, File P10 I46R, No. 6612 in Autoridad Nacional de Agua, 1985), 4; Instituto Nacional de Estadística e Informática (INEI), *Censos Nacionales 2007: XI de población y VI de vivienda. Perfil sociodemográfico del Departamento de La Libertad* (Trujillo: INEI, 2007).

61. Burneo, *The Process of Land Concentration in Peru*, 14; Barbara Lynch, "River of Contention: Scarcity Discourse and Water Competition in Highland Peru," *Georgia Journal of International and Comparative Law* 42, no. 1 (2013): 90.

62. "Proyecto Chavimochic aportará US$1.500 millones anuales al PBI nacional," *El Comercio* (Lima), July 15, 2013, http://elcomercio.pe/economia/1604227/noticia-proyecto-chavimochic-aportara-us1500-millones-anuales-al-pbi-nacional.

63. Tatsuya Shimizu, "Expansion of Asparagus Production and Exports in Peru," *Institute of Developing Economies (IDE) Discussion Paper No. 73* (2006); Valcárcel, "Agroexportación no tradicional."

64. Michel Baraer et al., "Glacier Recession and Water Resources in Peru's Cordillera Blanca," *Journal of Glaciology* 58, no. 207 (2012): 134–150; Jeffrey Bury et al., "New Geographies of Water and Climate Change in Peru: Coupled Natural and Social Transformations in the Santa River Watershed," *Annals of the Association of American Geographers* 103, no. 2 (2013): 363–374; Mark Carey et al., "Toward Hydro-Social Modeling: Merging Human Variables and the So-

cial Sciences with Climate-Glacier Runoff Models (Santa River, Peru)," *Journal of Hydrology* 518, Part A (2014): 60–70.

65. Personal communications with at least a dozen Chavimochic officials and engineers, La Libertad, July 2013.

66. J. A. Broggi, "La desglaciación andina y sus consecuencias," *Actas de la Academia Nacional de Ciencias Exactas, Físicas y Naturales de Lima* 6, no. 6 (1943): 12–26.

67. Figallo and Vattuone, "Tecnología: El lado oscuro de la reforma agraria," 117.

68. Mark Carey, Adam French, and Elliott O'Brien, "Unintended Effects of Technology on Climate Change Adaptation: An Historical Analysis of Water Conflicts below Andean Glaciers," *Journal of Historical Geography* 38, no. 2 (2012): 181–191; Barbara Deutsch Lynch, "Vulnerabilities, Competition, and Rights in a Context of Climate Change toward Equitable Water Governance in Peru's Rio Santa Valley," *Global Environmental Change* 22, no. 2 (2012): 364–373.

CHAPTER 11

Chimbotazo: The Peruvian Revolution and Labor in Chimbote, 1968–1973

NATHAN CLARKE

On May 24, 1973, thousands of residents in the northern port of Chimbote, Peru, went on strike. Frustrated with the Revolutionary Government of the Armed Forces' (RGAF's) attempts to control the labor movement, members of three dozen union and popular organizations took to the street, demanding that the state stop interfering in the fishermen's syndicate and that the union leadership step down from the posts it had held since 1968.[1] Various agencies of the state's repressive forces met the strikers on the streets, matching the protesters' rocks and sticks with tear gas and bullets. At the end of the day, one protester had died, another lay in critical condition in a hospital, and the citizenry's relationship with the military government had fractured. This strike, now known as the Chimbotazo, became a crucial moment not only in Chimbote but also for the RGAF.

This event represents perhaps the largest protest of the labor movement against the Velasco government's many dictates.[2] The unionized workers of Chimbote—many of whom had become state employees during the course of the revolution, including the fishermen just seventeen days before the strike—demonstrated their discomfort with the penetration of state power in their institutions through the government's co-optation of local union leadership and the creation of two state-controlled labor organizations: the Revolutionary Labor Movement (Movimiento Laboral Revolucionario; MLR) and the Central Organization of Workers of the Peruvian Revolution (Central de Trabajadores de la Revolución Peruana; CTRP), a national labor confederation. While not necessarily opposed to the RGAF's project to create a more progressive and participative Peru, the strikers did not want to forego their union autonomy to achieve the regime's goals.

This chapter focuses on the state's intervention in the labor movement in Chimbote, one of the nation's most unionized cities. During the postwar era, Chimbote grew from an insignificant fishing village to become the world's largest fishing port and home to the nation's first steel mill. Likewise, the industrial workers belonged to two of the nation's most important and most active unions, the Chimbote Fishermen's Union (Sindicato de Pescadores de Chimbote y Anexos; SPCHA) and the Steel Plant Workers Union (Sindicato de Trabajadores de la Planta Siderúrgica; STPS), both with membership in the several thousands.[3] The events of May 1973 changed both Chimbote and the RGAF. The Chimbotazo reveals the state's anxiety over the autonomy of the masses and over Chimbote itself, perhaps the nation's strategically most important city aside from Lima. This event also demonstrates civil society's inclination to push back against the state, even though the state proved willing to use violence in return. Scholars generally considered Velasco's regime to have avoided the use of violence, especially when compared to contemporary military regimes throughout South America.[4] The Chimbote experience, however, shows the state willingly used violence to co-opt and coerce civil society. Finally, the Chimbotazo altered the image and relationship between the military regime and the people of Chimbote (and all of Peru), as the regime's bullets shattered its image of a humanist, participatory regime it had cultivated since assuming power.

Chimbote emerged after World War II as Peru's fastest-growing city, based around the development of steel and fishing industries. The state selected Chimbote as the site to build the nation's first steel mill, beginning production in 1958. By 1970, the plant had around four thousand workers. Dedicated almost exclusively to the production of fishmeal, a high-protein additive for hog and poultry feed, fishing propelled Peru's economy from 1955 to 1972, eventually overtaking copper as the nation's leading export.[5] Major fishing centers emerged along the Peruvian coast, from Ilo in the far south to Chancay in the north, but none as large as Chimbote, home to 35 percent of the industry's boats and factories. Entrepreneurs from Peru and abroad turned the peaceful and fecund Ferrol Bay into the world's largest fishing complex: Chimbote's fishermen landed more fish than any other port in the world from 1965 to 1972. In total, over five thousand people worked in one of the industry's thirty-odd factories and on more than four hundred boats.

The fishmeal industry grew with little restraint during the 1960s: the anchoveta (*Engraulis ringens*), fishmeal's prime material that accounted for over 95 percent of the national catch, abounded off the coast, a seemingly inexhaustible resource. Banks readily extended high-interest, short-term credit to interested entrepreneurs, while politicians and bureaucrats showed little interest in slowing or regulating the industry. This laissez-faire atmosphere saw entrepreneurs build over one hundred plants along the coast and put over fifteen hundred boats of increasing size into the water, leading to constantly increasing catch levels. Every year between 1965 and 1971, the Peruvian catch surpassed its ecological limits; in 1970, fishermen officially landed 12.3 million metric tons (MMT) of anchoveta, nearly 50 percent more than the state's oceanographic institute, the Peruvian Institute of the Sea (Instituto del Mar del Perú; IMARPE), had recommended.[6] By 1972, the Peruvian fishing industry had stretched the ecological limits of the anchoveta to its breaking point.

The fishing industry brought the northern port of Chimbote to international prominence and national concern. Under the influence of fishing and steel, Chimbote developed into a classic boomtown: a place where tens of thousands of men and women from all parts of Peru came to earn a fortune exploiting the *oro gris*, or gray gold, as many knew the anchoveta. It also suffered greatly as a result of the boom: Chimbote became an externality of industry. Its terrestrial, aquatic, and atmospheric environments received an incessant onslaught of pollution from the factories and boats. Chimbote became the pride (its residents proudly proclaiming they held the title of *primer puerto pesquero del mundo*, or leading fishing port in the world) and embarrassment (an uncontrollable tragic city personified by pollution, prostitution, and poverty) of the Peruvian fishing boom.[7]

President Fernando Belaúnde Terry (1963–1968) paid little attention to the fate of the fishing industry, but the sector composed an important part of the revolutionary government's plans. In 1970, the military government created the Ministry of Fisheries (Ministerio de Pesquería; MIPE), separating the fishing bureaucracy from the Ministry of Agriculture. The creation of MIPE spoke to the significance the sector had attained for the Peruvian state and economy; it also represented an important symbolic achievement for the fishing community. During the first years of the military government, fishing's role increased in the nation's plans: not only had fishmeal become a leading export, but MIPE asserted control over international sales of fishmeal and attempted to promote the domestic consumption of fish.[8] The military emphasized the potential Peru's vast and abundant aquatic resources had for solving the nation's nutritional deficiencies: they set into motion plans to open refrigerated fish warehouses throughout the nation and centers of artisanal fishing dedicated to the promotion of fish for direct human consumption:[9] the generals would fish for food, not for feed.[10]

The ever-present and energetic role of the state in the fishing sector between 1968 and 1973 could not correct the deficiencies of the industry during the years before its coup, as productive capacity continued to outstrip the biological sustainability of the anchoveta. Peruvian producers managed to extract over 33 MMT of fish between 1969 and 1971, well above the cumulative 27 MMT limit set by IMARPE.[11] Again, regardless of its newfound potency, the state could neither protect the anchoveta from overfishing nor convince fishmeal industrialists to limit or redirect their efforts. As fishmeal exports brought in significant capital to the national coffers, limiting fishing did not align with the state's interests either.

Meanwhile, the union movement had begun to develop and strengthen a close relationship with the military government. According to the secretary general of the national Peruvian Fishermen's Federation (Federación de Pescadores del Perú; FPP), which represented dozens of fishing unions and over twenty thousand members, fishermen used this relationship—not too close, not too far—to win a series of benefits for their workers, like vacation pay, worker's compensation, and accident insurance, which the entrepreneurs had resisted affording them previously.[12]

After fifteen years of intense and abundant fishing, catch levels fell dramatically in 1972, as the warming of the coast waters by the El Niño Southern Oscillation alienated the anchoveta from the shore, sending them to cooler temperatures to the south and in the ocean deep, beneath the fishermen's nets.[13] By April 1972, boats began returning empty as anchoveta captures dropped from 12.3 MMT in 1970 to 4.4 MMT in 1972 and 1.5 MMT in 1973.[14] The effects of this decline during 1972–1973 devastated the industry, especially in Chimbote, where people had still not completely recovered from the 1970 earthquake.[15]

With the industry facing mounting debts and few prospects of recovery, the military government undertook one of its boldest moves: the wholesale expropriation of the entire fishmeal industry. On May 7, 1973, fisheries minister General Javier Tantaleán Vanini announced two radical measures: Decree Law (DL) 19999, creating the new national fishing company Pesca Perú, and DL 20000, expropriating the entire anchoveta fishing industry. Through this law, the federal government seized control of the fishmeal industry's assets—boats, factories, stored fishmeal—and its substantial debt, setting both the rationale for the expropriation (that the anchoveta, a natural resource that belongs to the Peruvian people, had disappeared, and that the industry's debt and role in the national economy demanded action) and the conditions for the repayment of seized capital goods. With the stroke of a pen, the Peruvian government became the owner of the world's largest fishing company, a unified enterprise with over twenty-seven thousand employees, fifteen hundred boats, and over one hundred factories, with the ability to confront the structural deficiencies of the industry's boom.

Pesca Perú embodies the struggles of the revolutionary government. The mismanagement of the fishmeal industry since its inception forced the regime's hand. Faced with the bankruptcy of one of the nation's largest income earners, the government opted to take over the industry, warts and all, much like it had the nation four and a half years before. The RGAF thought only it could save the fishing industry. But, as with the country, the military found they could not solve the industry's problems: the disappearance of the anchoveta limited its ability to pay Pesca Perú's enormous inherited debt.[16] For the workers of the fishmeal industry, the intervention altered their relationship with the state and the industry.

Chimbote's industrialization spurred the growth of the union movement in the city. SPCHA, formed in 1945, demanded that all fishermen join the union in order to work on one of the boats, a closed shop. The steel mill formed its first union in 1956, two years before the plant officially opened. Practically all the formal sectors of the economy had unions, from bank employees to construction workers and taxi drivers. The high level of union activity and solidarity in the 1950s and 1960s came to define the city.[17] Until 1965, members of the Alianza Popular Revolucionaria Americana (APRA; American Popular Revolutionary Alliance) Party dominated the city's unions. APRA members held sway in most of the city's major unions and in the Syndical Union of the Province of Santa (Unión Sindical de la Provincia de Santa; USPS), the provincial labor confederation, which coordinated union activity among the different sectors. APRA formed, without a doubt, the major force for labor in Chimbote.[18]

The omnipresence of APRA did not sit well with everyone in Chimbote's unions. During the late 1950s and 1960s, the national APRA leadership moved further to the right in search of political recognition following the Convivencia.[19] Many union members, especially those coming from the growing left-wing and Communist parties, began perceiving APRA union leaders as subservient to management. In the fishing industry, for example, APRA congressmen and senators formed a key part of the "Fishing Caucus," which helped the industry's interests pass through the belabored Belaúnde legislature.[20] Locally, Chimbote's union leaders faced accusations of not fighting intensely enough at the negotiating table and of being on the industry's payroll.[21] According to Nigel Haworth, labor—and in this sense APRA-led labor—before 1968 "lacked the institutional, ideological, and numerical strengths necessary" to challenge capital at the bargaining table.[22] As a result, by the mid-1960s, the questioning of their loyalty and ability to represent the rank-and-file's true interests reached its tipping point.

The absolute predominance of APRA in SPCHA's leadership lasted for close to two decades. The Aprista leadership, called a "mafia" by its critics, became known for quelling worker debate and dissent, while adhering to the APRA national leadership's increasingly probusiness positions. According to the sociologist Beatriz Gil:

> The predominance of the APRA Party among fishermen lasted throughout the emergence of the anchoveta industry. A system of union control—the "mafia"—assured the protection of the interests of fishing capitalists over the possible movements of worker reward. The "mafia," which originally consisted of a repression and "gangsterism" in favor of industry mixed with Aprista bullying to the point where . . . from 1960 to 1965 one can speak of one single mafia consisting of Apristas, criminals, and industrialists.[23]

According to one fisherman I interviewed, the conservative nature of APRA control defined the unionism of the 1960s.[24] Another fisherman argued that "APRA has always been a prejudicial element in Chimbote. [The fishmeal magnate Luis] Banchero Rossi used APRA, and APRA supported Banchero, who always sought to pay his workers as little as possible.[25] In short, two positions dominated Chimbote unionism before the mid-1960s: pro-APRA and anti-APRA.[26]

Two key struggles from 1965 and 1966 demonstrate the breakdown of APRA's control over the fishing union in Chimbote. Throughout these two crucial years, fishermen all along the Peruvian coast held two major labor actions. The first, spearheaded by the newly created FPP, sought to create a pension system for fishermen, which it successfully did with the creation of the Fishers' Benefits and Social Security Fund (Caja de Beneficios y Seguridad Social del Pescador; CBSSP). The second sought to increase the per-ton share fishermen received from S/.80 to S/.115. In both labor actions, the APRA-controlled Chimbote union, the nation's largest and most influential local, refused to cooperate with the national-level strike. In the former, the Chimbote union signed the agreement last, stalling the monumental achievement of the FPP and all fishermen; in the latter, Chimbote's secretary general, Hugo Beltrán, agreed to a raise from S/.80 per ton to S/.92. This proved problematic on two levels. First, it severely undercut the stated goal of S/.115; second, he made this agreement without consulting the rank-and-file or the national strike leadership. Many fishermen had felt betrayed by the union leadership on several occasions, but to members of the nation's burgeoning left-wing political scene, Beltrán's actions demanded response.

With the triumph of the Russian, Chinese, and Cuban Revolutions, the influence of Communist and left-wing parties within the Peruvian labor movement had grown substantially. In Chimbote, the first of these groups to assert itself, the Dionisio Horna Vásquez Clasista Group (Agrupación Clasista Dionisio Horna Vásquez; ACDHV),[27] espoused an independent version of unionism, called *clasismo. Clasismo*, according to Catherine Conaghan, "identified class struggle as the strategy through which industrial workers and popular classes could secure their long-denied rights and reclaim their dignity in Peruvian society. That struggle, *la lucha*, was manifested in persistent mobilization. Protests, demonstrations, marches, work actions, and strikes were the currency of clasismo."[28] *Clasistas* perceived any collaboration negatively, and autonomy from the state was the goal of the union's actions. The importance of *clasismo* resided in the autonomy of workers and political independence from traditional parties (like APRA) and the state.[29] The ACDHV, composed of many supporters of APRA Rebelde,[30] and the pro-Chinese faction of the Communist Party[31] opposed the "mafia's" subservience to the needs of the industrial elite and the omnipotence of APRA over the union movement in Chimbote. The ACDHV, under the leadership of the veteran fisherman Máximo Gonzales Castillo, led a coup against the Aprista leadership, ousting Beltrán from the head of the union and setting up a Transitional Leadership Junta (Junta Directiva Transitoria; JDT).[32] The JDT named a young fisherman with less than two years' experience in the sector, Franco Baca Bazán, as the assistant secretary for social assistance. He would dominate the fishing union until 1975.

Nineteen-year-old Franco Baca Bazán had arrived in Chimbote on New Year's Day 1964, fleeing the police in his hometown Chiclayo. A member of the (pro-Chinese) Communist Youth, Baca, by the time he stepped foot in Chimbote, had a long history of leftist activism, including a short jail term as a political prisoner during the military junta of 1962–1963.[33] He quickly caught on with a fishing crew, whose members he knew through his leftist contacts, to avoid capture by the police, and began his rapid ascent in the union. Within six months of becoming a fisherman, he had been named the union delegate for his boat and the director of debates during union meetings. With the emergence of the ACDHV, Baca sparked the end of the era of APRA dominance of the union movement.

The transition to *clasista* control signified a reorientation of the goals and actions of SPCHA. The *clasista* leadership took a different stance toward the industrialists and the environmental impact of fishing than the Aprista-led factions had. The collaborationist attitudes of APRA had disappeared, and union leadership began to challenge industry instead of accepting its mandates. For example, in its 1967 *Memoria*, the union railed against increasing foreign ownership in the fishmeal industry:

> As the interests of the foreign capitalists are not the same as those of Peruvian capitalists, our development does not concern them: they are interested in fishing and only fishing. They are not concerned if the ichthyological richness could one day expire, because they can just pick up stakes, leaving our fishermen and our country mired in unemployment and misery. We as fishermen must realize that this approach is completely harmful for us, as both workers and citizens of this country.[34]

The new leadership's focus on the ecological effects of the extensive fishing marked a significant change in union rhetoric. Before the *clasista* leadership, the APRA-led union did not consider the impact that the intensive fishing had on the coastal ecology; instead, it focused on economic issues. By the time the *clasistas* took control of the union, the industrial structure established by the decades of Aprista control and corruption had become too well entrenched to change drastically. The status quo remained in place until the military government seized the industry in 1973.

In 1967, Franco Baca led a diverse slate of fishermen from both the *clasista* and traditional party ranks (Acción Popular and APRA) to victory in the union election.[35] His term should have finished at the end of 1968, but the RGAF's coup overthrew democracy in SPCHA as well. Baca immediately identified with goals and aspirations of the RGAF, recounting that the Velasco government made an impression on him by undertaking impactful policies, like the expropriation of the International Petroleum Company—one of the left's rallying cries—and the agrarian reform. It shocked him to see military officers showing landowners to the street and not trampling on the rights of the peasantry, as had long been the history in Peru.[36] Baca quickly made contact with the regime: within two weeks of assuming power, the minister of the interior, General Armando Artola, called Baca to his office in Lima to convince him to support the RGAF. The relationship between Baca and the RGAF grew closer, particularly as the state's role in the fishing industry and popular movements increased. From our interview, it seemed apparent that Baca became the RGAF's go-to guy in Chimbote, its source for any information about the city or its people: "Tantaleán, Velasco . . . they would call me, they used my opinion."[37] The closeness of this relationship between the leader of the country's largest union and the military government did not become clear to the residents of Chimbote until the events of May 1973.[38]

Over the following four years, Baca ran the union without holding elections or meetings. He produced several notable achievements, including opening the Fisherman's Hospital (Policlínico del Pescador), which provided free medical care for fishermen and their families, and building a new union hall on the city's main thoroughfare, Avenida Pardo. Four stories tall, the union hall had three floors of offices, classrooms, and libraries; the ground floor could accommodate meetings of several thousand fishermen (or social events). Baca used his growing connections within the military government to acquire the funds to build the union hall, calling on President Velasco directly to help him secure the support of the CBSSP to use the fishermen's own money to finance construction.[39] Given the achievements of his time as union head, many fishermen saw (and still see) Franco Baca as a true leader of the working class, a "bastion" who "did not seek personal fortune, unlike others."[40] Not everyone supported this sentiment, however, especially as the crisis of 1972–1973 progressed. Independent *clasista* forces began to mobilize to oust Baca and his cohort from the posts they had held for four years; they did not know they would have to face down the national government as well as Baca and his supporters to do so.

The corporatist project of the RGAF included an attempt to control civil society. The most notable incidence of this "top-down" revolutionary approach, the National System of Support for Social Mobilization (Sistema Nacional de Apoyo a la Movilización Social; SINAMOS), served as the regime's propaganda arm and provided its presence in the countryside (aiding the peasantry with their new cooperatives) and in the coast's innumerable shantytowns.[41] As its rule continued, the military government perceived the labor movement as another of the cogs it needed to co-opt. The nation's existing labor confederations and unions did not welcome military rule as the government had expected. By 1970, Peru had three main union confederations. The oldest, the Aprista-dominated Peruvian Workers' Confederation (Confederación de Trabajadores del Perú; CTP) had controlled labor until the mid-1960s, but still remained powerful. The Moscow-line Communists controlled the General Workers' Confederation of Peru (Confederación General de Trabajadores del Perú; CGTP); originally created by the prominent intellectual José Carlos Mariátegui in the 1920s, the CGTP rekindled in the late 1960s after a period of dormancy. The third group was the National Central Workers' Organization (Central Nacional de Trabajadores; CNT), a tiny confederation controlled in large part by the Catholic Church and the Christian Democratic Party.[42] The RGAF had expected labor and the left to support its reforms, yet this did not come to fruition. Initially, it did receive the support of the Moscow-line Communist Party, but the APRA and Beijing-line Communists resisted.[43] The government realized it needed to assert greater control over the labor movement in order to lead its revolution forward; in 1972, it created the institutions to bring labor under its power.

Two main government organizations would attempt to control workers. First, in May 1972, it created the MLR during a meeting of 160 fishermen held outside Lima.[44] The head of SINAMOS, General Leonidas Rodríguez Figueroa, spoke at the conference, giving the MLR his institution's backing, exhorting the fishermen to carry the revolution not only to the west (in this case, the ocean) but also to the north, east, and south.[45] The MLR has a difficult history to trace, as its former members do not place much importance on the group: Franco Baca called it "embryonic." Its opponents described the MLR as "mafiosos" and "gangsters" (as the *clasistas* had called the Apristas). Contemporary analysts described it as "proto-Fascistic" and "ultrarightist" and under the direct control of fisheries minister General Javier Tantaleán Vanini, though they do not justify those assertions.[46] The MLR ultimately became the Velasco government's "shock force," which it used to combat the *clasista* "workers' guard" (*guardia obrera*);[47] Franco Baca claimed the MLR "was something small, inflated surely by those kids who had been paid to fight this terrible enemy group. Now, maybe there were some scuffles [*trompeaderas*] and a few swollen eyes, but it's bullshit [*cojudeces*]; there weren't any deaths or anything like that."[48] The MLR attempted to infiltrate unions across the country; in Chimbote it had a solid foothold in SPCHA and had made inroads into STPS, though without success.[49] This shock force made its presence felt in Chimbote during May 1973.

The second institution created by the RGAF to control the labor movement was CTRP. Created in November 1972, according to its foundational "Declaration of Principles," the CTRP sought to carry the revolutionary changes forward, to support and sustain the revolutionary government, and to eschew politicking and sectarianism that had defined the union movement to this point. The document concluded by stating that "we have faith in the Peruvian Revolution." The new CTRP leadership included prominent leaders from the phone company, construction workers, and fishermen's unions, like the adjunct general coordinator, Franco Baca Bazán.[50] The FPP played an important role in the operation of the CTRP; a high-ranking FPP leader, Daniel Bossio da Silva, became the CTRP's second president. Indeed, the FPP became the most important cog in the RGAF's union structure, including both the MLR and the CTRP.[51] The CTRP grew quickly, doubling its presence within the labor movement in its first year of existence.[52]

After rallying fishermen disaffected with Aprista control during the mid-1960s to the side of *clasismo*, Franco Baca repeated the sins of his forefathers and allied with the bosses, in this case, the military government.[53] The close collaboration with the regime's MLR and official labor confederation contradicted the *clasista* conviction of constant struggle and opposition to all forms of authority. As the ecological crisis of 1972–1973 continued, fishermen began to resent the lack of transparency in SPCHA, evidenced by the absence of both union assemblies and elections. Baca came under increasing criticism from his fellow union members for not supporting the interests of the fishermen, many of whom had been out of work for several months. According to the anonymous *clasista* union members who authored *Chimbote: Una experiencia revolucionaria de masas*, Baca and SPCHA did not defend its members: "Facing this situation, neither the leaders of the [SPCHA] nor the leaders of the [FPP] truly assumed the role their positions demanded in order to solve the economic and social problems the fishermen faced."[54] Instead, they quieted demands and supported the regime, thus pushing the weight of the crisis—which the authors blamed on the unrestrained capitalist exploitation of the 1960s and early 1970s—onto the shoulders of the fishing proletariat.[55] The deal struck by the FPP with the CBSSP and the Banco Asociado in October 1972 to alleviate the workers' economic plight epitomizes their discontent. The parties agreed to a loan of S/.4,000, less than three weeks' wages and definitely not enough money to make up for not having fished in several months.[56] The *clasistas* believed their leadership needed to take a more combative course.

In Chimbote, attendance at union meetings dropped as alienated workers stopped participating in union activities.[57] The *clasista* forces began fervently criticizing Baca near the end of 1972, arguing in the press that he did not attempt to solve, even temporarily, the "sad reality" in which the fishermen lived. The *clasistas* avoided rankling the official power structure—which fully supported Baca—by not attacking the government itself. Rather, their critiques focused on the state's union apparatus (such as the MLR and the CTRP). They also made sure not to frame themselves as a political party—as the RGAF rejected political parties—instead, the *clasistas* remained in the middle of the road so as not to be labeled either ultraleftist or revanchist.[58] Rather than oppose the entire revolutionary process, the fishermen instead insisted that the union leadership engage in class struggle (*posición de lucha*). In many senses, Baca's collaboration with the regime exposed him and his rule to many of the same critiques that he and his compatriots had leveled against the Apristas in the 1960s: *clasistas* routinely called him a mafioso or gangster. With his affiliation with the MLR, they added a new epithet: *matón*.[59]

In early 1973, the *clasista* forces reacted to the confluence of calamity they faced: a prolonged ecological crisis, the creation of the CTRP and the growth of the government's role in subordinating union autonomy, and a recalcitrant union leader who ignored their demands. After a series of marches and protests in April 1973, fishermen elected a Transitional Directive Junta (JDT) for SPCHA as a direct challenge to Franco Baca. *Clasista* fishermen, including Máximo Gonzales Castillo, whom Baca had sent to serve on the CBSSP in the late 1960s, revived the ACDHV, which had entered a period of dormancy and, much like it had done to the Apristas seven years earlier, sought to oust Baca.[60] The *clasistas* elected the JDT under the leadership of Hugo Callán Castillo and established a committee to look into the union's financial situation, as they questioned the Baca regime's accounting practices. Throughout April 1973, one of the hardest months of the crisis, the JDT amassed the support of over one thousand fishermen and formed an election committee. On April 21, they even managed to seize control of the SPCHA headquarters, where they hunkered down.[61]

Seizing the union headquarters, while definitely a show of force from the *clasistas*, proved a somewhat presumptuous action, especially given the ability of Franco Baca and the MLR to utilize the state's security and repressive forces to its advantage. It also became one of the *clasistas'* biggest mistakes, according to *clasistas* themselves, as they ultimately did not have enough personnel or ability to hold the union hall. On May 1, the International Day of the Worker, several dozen Baca supporters, including a busload of fifty MLR members from Lima and other ports, violently took back the union hall from the twenty-five *clasistas* standing guard there.[62] According to one interviewee present at the union hall, at noon, the "mafiosos" showed up with several types of armaments—wrenches, chains, and even guns—and beat him and his fellow protestors, kicking them out of the union hall. Once on the street, he met with the police, who almost arrested him. At least four of the JDT members did get arrested,[63] but none of the MLR members—the paid aggressors, including the Callao MLR leader, Rolando Riega—did.[64] My interviewee remarked that he did not know until then the amount of power that Franco Baca had accrued with the government; he and the other members realized at that point that they had to fight not just Baca and his supporters but the state's repressive forces, like the police and army, as well.[65]

Both union factions scheduled rallies for May 7. The JDT called its meeting for the morning, rallying at their headquarters in the old union hall located along the seafront *malecón*. When the fishermen arrived, however, they found representatives of the state's security apparatus, including the Civil Guard (Guardia Civil; GC), Republican Guard of Peru (Guardia Republicana del Perú; GRP), and Peruvian Investigative Police (Policía de Investigaciones del Perú; PIP) waiting for them. From 8:30 a.m. to 11:30 a.m., as fishermen waited to enter the old union hall, the police arrested the JDT leadership. At the same time, Minister of Fisheries Tantaleán prepared to announce the expropriation of the fishing industry. It remains unclear why the police detained the JDT leadership or who ordered their detention, but the *clasistas* writing about the events of May 1973 point to the possibility that the orders came from Lima, a convincing prospect given the important announcement that came later in the day (and the time of their release).

At the union hall, Baca Bazán waited until 5 p.m., shortly after Tantaleán announced the expropriation, to begin an extraordinary general assembly.[66] This meeting, according to contemporary accounts, devolved into a declaration of war between the *clasistas* and the MLR.[67]

After a series of *¡vivas!* of support for the revolution, for Velasco and Tantaleán, and for May 7, the "Day of Dignity for the Fisherman,"[68] Franco Baca and his directorate, according to the bulletin produced by SPCHA, received a vote of confidence. Finally, the crowd saluted the MLR for recovering the union hall.[69] A *clasista* pamphlet describing the meeting claimed the police and members of the state security surrounded the union hall, and the mention of the MLR started boisterous whistling (*rechifla*) from the union members present.[70] The Lima newspaper *El Comercio* reported that in the scuffle that ensued, three people were injured, including one gravely.[71]

The government continued its assault on workers, including holding a press conference on May 9 to show off the thirty-eight Molotov cocktails and other propaganda it had found at the old union hall, evidence that the local state officials (the GC, GRP, PIP, and Marines [Capitanía de Puerto]) claimed proved the *clasistas'* intentions to start a terrorist campaign against the interests of fishermen and the revolution.[72] *Clasistas* argued that the police or the MLR had planted the bombs, an old police trick.[73]

The aggression initiated against the *clasistas* on May 1 and compounded on May 7 outraged the labor movement in Chimbote and throughout the country, sparking a notable outpouring of solidarity. Over the following three weeks, the JDT and *clasista* forces worked with other local unions and allies—most notably the large and powerful STPS as well as student groups and teachers unions—to challenge the state's increasing presence in the labor movement.

The early May offensive against the *clasistas* started a "pamphlet war" in which supporters from both sides of the struggle began issuing communiqués and newspapers expressed their outrage at either the MLR or the JDT. Pro-government forces, like the MLR committee at the steel plant and the SPCHA leadership, still under the official control of Baca, argued that the *clasistas* and protesters had engaged in "counterrevolution": by attacking SPCHA and its leader Franco Baca, they had essentially attacked the government and the revolution. Likewise, the MLR pamphlets challenged the right of outside unions, like the STPS or Department of Ancash Workers Federation (Federación Sindical Departamental de Trabajadores de Ancash; FESIDETA), the successor to the USPS, to intervene in SPCHA's internal affairs, questioning how it would feel if SPCHA attempted to intervene in the STPS's next union election.[74] Through SINAMOS, the state also led a campaign against the *clasista* cause in the local press.[75]

Several themes emerge from reading the pro-*clasista* pamphlets. The main issue for the *clasistas* was the RGAF's incursion into the labor movement. The state, as a signatory to various International Labor Organization treaties, had agreed to the principle of labor autonomy, but the creation of the MLR and the CTRP directly violated those treaties, as had the use of state power to arrest JDT members. Likewise, these documents share a profound rejection of Baca and his cohort, calling them sellouts and mafioso thugs. They called for the ouster of the subprefect, the state's top direct political appointee in Chimbote, and the demotion of two bureaucrats from the Labor Ministry.[76] Finally, the documents called for a general strike to start on May 24.

Interestingly, both sides cast the same aspersion on the other: *¡Aprista!*. By this time, the APRA Party's reputation had soured to the point where neither side wanted to have any association with it. Both sides accused one another of being dominated by the Apristas. On the one hand, the pro-government forces claimed "FESIDETA belongs to the Aprista CTP, and APRA receives 'Yankee dollars,' which it uses to promote imperialism and challenge the revolution,"[77] and on the other, according to *clasistas*, both the FPP, under its leader Alberto Gil Peñaranda, an Aprista during his youth, and the minister of fisheries himself, General Tantaleán, had APRA ties.[78] Likewise, interviewees alternatively told me that the APRA basically transitioned into the MLR,[79] and that the government formed the MLR to combat the APRA's shock troops.[80]

The rift in the fishing union reached its apex on May 24, a day now known as the "Chimbotazo." In a city where the labor movement had played a dominant role in the postwar era, this perhaps represents the most significant union action on a single day in its history. The events of May 24 altered the nature of the relationship of many of Chimbote's residents with the revolutionary government. The *clasista* authors of *Chimbote: Una experiencia revolucionaria de masas* called the Chimbotazo "the most impressive and largest march that Chimbote had ever seen."[81]

Outraged at the actions of the government and its violations of union autonomy, the regional labor confederation, FESIDETA, called for a general strike and organized its member institutions to stop all work in Chimbote.[82] The strikers had four main demands, all reflecting the discomforts that labor felt regarding the role of the state in union business: remove political authorities from union affairs; reject the CTRP and the MLR; guarantee new elections in SPCHA, monitored by FESIDETA; and, replace the subprefect (the state's highest ranking official in Chimbote) because he had collaborated with Franco Baca.[83] These political demands united workers and their allies from all levels of Chimbote society and demonstrated the growth of class solidarity across the city over the previous months. *Clasista* teachers, steelworkers, construction workers, and students joined the march through the streets of downtown Chimbote. The fishermen peacefully marched from the edge of the downtown core to the SPCHA hall where the steelworkers and others joined them. The police met the protesters in front of the SPCHA union hall, dispersing the crowd with tear gas and by shooting at it. According to one of the protesters, the police had prepared for violence. The morning and afternoon turned bloody.

The strikers split into several groups. One group continued protesting in the city center, meeting near the FESIDETA and STPS offices, located within five blocks of one another. The police, who had come to shoot, opened fire on the crowd several times. In total, they shot seven unarmed people, killing two. The first victim, CGTP national secretary of press and propaganda and former head of STPS, steelworker Cristóbal Espinola Minchola, thirty-nine, was shot in the back trying to flee police bullets.[84] The police took Espinola first to the local Hospital del Obrero and later by helicopter to a Lima hospital, where he perished on June 13.[85] The second victim, Humberto Miranda Estrada, fourteen, was the child of a steelworker. Even with blood running in the street, the many protesters continued facing down the military and police, barricading themselves behind brick walls.

By 2:15 in the afternoon, smoke from tear gas covered the city streets. The workers refused to cede their position, fighting the state's bombs and guns with rocks and bricks. The strikers retreated to the steelworkers' hall, where they held an emergency assembly; incensed by the presence of Miranda's (unidentified) corpse, the assembly put forth several (overtly political) demands: release of political prisoners, removal of local political authorities, and getting the Guardia Republicana out of the steel plant. They also called for justice for Espinola's shooting and Miranda's murder. They promised to continue with an indefinite strike until that time.

Incensed by the violence, part of the crowd turned its attention toward the most notorious example of the RGAF's presence in Chimbote, SINAMOS. Protesters sacked, or attempted to sack, three SINAMOS offices, angered by its (*antipopular y antiobrero*) actions that went against the people and workers. Turned back at the first office, located downtown, the protesters left. At the second office, located to the south in the

Miraflores Alto shantytown, demonstrators broke down the brick wall and entered the offices with the intention of setting fire to the installation. Their jerry cans of gasoline turned out to be nonflammable oil, and they had to flee police bullets into the neighboring countryside (*chacra*). Finally at 9 p.m. or 10 p.m., they set upon the SINAMOS office in the El Progreso shantytown, a populous neighborhood located east of the downtown core. The protesters burned the offices and its installations, including several archives.[86] The attacks on SINAMOS symbolize the growing discontent with the overbearing presence of the revolutionary state in Chimbote; the SINAMOS office in El Progreso had been working to help shantytown dwellers and informal landholders acquire permanent and legal property titles, one of the key desires of the people of Chimbote.[87] Regardless of its intentions, the protesters perceived SINAMOS as one of the most obvious (and civilian) examples of the government presence.

The following day, the strike continued but with less worker support and diminishing unity. The focus of the workers' actions turned toward the steel plant, where during the course of the strike on the 24th, the lamination plant suffered damages costing (according to the state) over S/.50,000,000. The government accused the strikers of damaging the plant, and therefore sabotaging Peru's (revolutionary) economic development; no one on the *clasista* side claimed responsibility for the damages, arguing that the state deliberately damaged the plant to defeat the strike.[88] On May 29, the government promulgated DL 20043, declaring SIDERPERU to be in reorganization.[89] The police stepped in and seized control of the steel plant and the steelworkers' union hall, arresting a dozen labor leaders and firing forty-eight steelworkers.[90] The steelworkers continued their strike into June, yet the atmosphere of solidarity of May dwindled. By mid-June, many unions had stopped supporting the STPS, and some steelworkers had even begun to cross picket lines. By June 19, fishermen had begun to work again.[91]

The violence of May 24 had mixed results for the labor movement. The government defeated the *clasistas* in 1973, as both steelworkers and fishermen went back to work. Neither the MLR nor the CGTP disappeared.[92] Franco Baca did eventually step down from the secretary general position of the union, but not because of the pressure from his colleagues. He played an instrumental role in the election of a new, pro-RGAF slate of union leaders, led by Manuel Zúñiga Franco,[93] and took a position as float supervisor and adviser in Pesca Perú. *Clasista* demands quieted but did not disappear. In short, the fishermen remained split;

this fracture reemerged in 1976, when the fishermen fought after the state began the process of privatizing Pesca Perú, which included offering the expropriated boats to worker cooperatives. In 1976, fishermen led a seventy-day strike to defend Pesca Perú and protect the labor stability their new employer provided them. As in 1973, their efforts to protect their jobs and their rights ended futilely.[94]

The events of April and May 1973 hold a greater significance than just some internal squabbles among local fishermen. Chimbote's workers led the nation's rejection of the RGAF's attempt to co-opt the labor movement, receiving support from workers throughout the country. The Chimbotazo demonstrates the anxiety the state had over the development of Chimbote and the growing discontent of the masses with the overbearance of the RGAF. The Chimbotazo also marks a crucial moment for both Chimbote and the military government: no longer could Chimbotanos consider the RGAF as a benevolent force. The events of 1973 took the veneer off the government. It demonstrated it would willingly use violence to impose order, which it had not done previously. The events of May 1973 in Chimbote changed the Peruvian Revolution.

Notes

1. I use the gendered term "fishermen" instead of the neutral term "fishers," since no women worked on fishing boats in Peru. Indeed, bringing women on board was considered bad luck, though some captains reportedly dressed up their wives or girlfriends like men and snuck them aboard. Interview TRM003, May 10, 2005. The author conducted all interviews in Chimbote, unless otherwise noted. With few exceptions, interviewees were given codes to protect their anonymity; interviewees without codes agreed to have their real names used. Unless otherwise noted, all translations from Spanish are mine.

2. In-depth studies of the labor movement during the military regime are surprisingly scarce, given the importance of organized labor to the regime and the spike in unionization during the first phase. Several scholars mention the rise of the Central de Trabajadores de la Revolución Peruana (CTRP) and Movimiento Laboral Revolucionario (MLR), yet no monograph-length study of the RGAF's labor policies exists to date. Notably, the sociologist Denis Sulmont covered the period briefly in his analysis of the history of the Peruvian labor movement, and Jorge Parodi Solari and Carmen Rosa Balbi analyzed the rise of the *clasista* labor movement in Lima factories. See Denis Sulmont, *El movimiento obrero peruano, 1890–1980: Reseña histórica*, 2nd ed. (Lima: Tarea, 1980); Jorge Parodi, *To Be a Worker: Identity and Politics in Peru*, trans. James Alstrum (Chapel Hill: University of North Carolina Press, 2000); and Carmen Rosa Balbi, *Identidad clasista en el sindicalismo: Su impacto en las fábricas* (Lima: Centro de Estudios y Promoción del Desarrollo, 1989). See also Alan Angell,

Peruvian Labour and the Military Government since 1968. University of London Working Papers Series, 3 (London: University of London, Institute of Latin American Studies, 1980). The most sustained discussion of the CTRP can be found in Evelyne Huber Stephens, "The Peruvian Military Government, Labor Mobilization, and the Political Strength of the Left," *Latin American Research Review* 18, no. 2 (1983): 57–93.

3. SIDERPERÚ, nationally owned until 1996 and in private hands since, has two unions, one for the blue-collar workforce (*trabajadores* or *obreros*) and the other for the white-collar workforce (*empleados*). The union split in the 1960s and has been an effective method of controlling the workforce, as management often plays both sides off each other.

4. The regime also made this claim. The head of the state's social movement organization, SINAMOS, stated in 1972 that the Peruvian Revolution is peaceful and will not be imposed at the end of a stick. Leonidas Rodríguez Figueroa, cited in "Preludios navideños," *Oiga* 502, December 22, 1972, 13–16.

5. Fishmeal remains an underappreciated component of the national economy. It is difficult to find references to the fishmeal industry in some of the more prominent textbooks and economic monographs published in the last few years. For example, see John Sheahan, *Searching for a Better Society: The Peruvian Economy from 1950* (College Park: Pennsylvania State University Press, 1999); Peter F. Klaren, *Peru: Society and Nationhood in the Andes* (New York: Oxford University Press, 1999). For an important exception, see Rosemary Thorp and Geoffrey Bertram, *Peru, 1890–1977: Growth and Policy in an Open Economy* (New York: Columbia University Press, 1978). Fishmeal is now used in feeds for aquaculture.

6. This official figure does not consider the important role played by *pesca negra*, the unreported and illegal catch that often composed 30 percent of the total catch. Therefore, it is quite possible that in 1970, Peruvians took over 15 MMT out of the ecosystem, a devastating total for the existence and reproduction of the biomass.

7. In an infamous 1968 newspaper article, a Limeña reporter described Chimbote unfavorably, drawing attention to the massive shantytowns surrounding the city and the high number of bars and brothels. See María Tellería Solari, "Chimbote: Ciudad trágica," *Expreso*, July 4, 1968. On Chimbote, see Juan Carlos Sueiro, *El olor del dinero: La contaminación por la industria de harina de pescado en Chimbote* (Lima: Instituto para el Desarrollo de la Pesca y la Minería, 1994); and Nathan Clarke, "Traces on the Peruvian Shore: The Environmental History of the Fishmeal Boom in Chimbote, Peru, 1940–1980" (PhD diss., University of Illinois at Urbana-Champaign, 2009). Many people referred to, and still do, Chimbote as the *primer puerto.*

8. *Aprueban ley orgánica de la Empresa Pública de Servicios Pesqueros,* 1970, http://www.leyes.congreso.gob.pe/Documentos/Leyes/18252.pdf; *Decreto Ley 18212, Norman régimen del comercio de la harina y aceite de pescado,* 1970, http://www.leyes.congreso.gob.pe/Documentos/Leyes/18212.pdf; *Decreto Ley 18253, Ley orgánica de la Empresa Pública de Comercialización de Harina y Aceite de Pescado que se produzca en el país,* 1970, http://www.leyes.congreso.gob.pe/Documentos/Leyes/18253.pdf.

9. One of my interview subjects claimed that upon assuming power, General Francisco Morales Bermúdez ordered these refrigerated warehouses closed, as promoting the consumption of fish clashed with his family's interests in the poultry industry. Interview with Franco Baca Bazán, Lima, September 11, 2014. Direct human consumption refers to the consumption of fish in a fresh, canned, or frozen state. Indirect human consumption refers to the consumption of fish through another form; in this case, humans consumed fishmeal indirectly through chicken and pig meat.

10. "Pesquería: Una marcha sin descanso," *Oiga* 478, June 9, 1972, 24–26 and 53, details the military government's programs for incentivizing the consumption of fish in the highlands.

11. If we consider *pesca negra* as well, the total catch might have surpassed 40 MMT.

12. Interview with Alberto Gil Peñaranda, September 23, 2014. Speaking over forty years after the fact, Gil, who held the post of secretary general from 1967 to 1975, did not want to portray his federation's relationship with the government as being too close; the FPP, according to many sources, had a much closer relationship than Gil now admits to.

13. On the 1972–1973 El Niño event, see César N. Caviedes, "El Niño 1972: Its Climatic, Ecological, Human, and Economic Implications," *Geographical Review* 65, no. 4 (1975): 493–509. The collapse of the Peruvian anchoveta fishery in 1972–1973 remains a controversial topic. Scholars like Michael Glantz pointed to several factors that combined to cause the collapse: the size of the fleet and productive capacity of the factories; the dependence of the industry's twenty-seven thousand workers, both white and blue collar, as well as those working in secondary enterprises (net companies, food providers); the state's increasing reliance on the taxes and foreign exchange garnered from exports; and the never-ending search for profits. See Michael H. Glantz, *Currents of Change: Impacts of El Niño and La Niña on Climate and Society*, 2nd ed. (Cambridge: Cambridge University Press, 2001); and Michael H. Glantz and J. Dana Thompson, eds., *Resource Management and Environmental Uncertainty: Lessons from Coastal Upwelling Fisheries*, Advances in Environmental Science and Technology series (New York: John Wiley and Sons, 1981). Since 2004, oceanographers have begun to argue that the anchoveta did not collapse in 1972; rather, they suggest that a multidecadal shift emerged that saw the anchoveta replaced by the pilchard (*Sardinops sagax*). See Jürgen Alheit and Miguel Ñiquen, "Regime Shifts in the Humboldt Current Ecosystem," *Progress in Oceanography* 60, nos. 2–4 (2004): 201–222, among others.

14. Figures from Pier M. Fontanot, "The Peruvian Fishmeal and the United States Soybean Meal in the Feed Protein Crisis" (master's thesis, Southern Illinois University, 1974). The anchoveta catch continued its decline throughout the 1970s, bottoming out at 720 thousand MT in 1980, a 94 percent drop.

15. On May 31, 1970, a massive earthquake shook the department of Ancash, including Chimbote. In total, seventy thousand people died—around five hundred people in Chimbote—and a half million lost their homes. The state undertook an ambitious reconstruction program, which sought to create Chimbote as a decentralized industrial power. On the earthquake, see Teobaldo

Arroyo Icochea, *Y . . . no nos fuimos!* (Chimbote: Editorial é Imprenta Chimbote E.I.R.L., 1990); Barbara Bode, *No Bells to Toll: Destruction and Creation in the Andes* (New York: Scribner, 1989); and Anthony Oliver-Smith, *The Martyred City: Death and Rebirth in the Andes* (Albuquerque: University of New Mexico Press, 1986). On the reconstruction program in Chimbote, see Nathan Clarke, "Revolutionizing the Tragic City: Rebuilding Chimbote, Peru, after the 1970 Earthquake," *Journal of Urban History* 41, no. 1 (2015): 93–115.

16. On the problems with Pesca Perú's inherited debt, see Carlos Malpica Silva Santisteban, *Anchovetas y tiburones* (Lima: Editora Runamarka, 1976).

17. For example, "Los sindicatos de Chimbote tuvieron un año muy activo en 1958," *Centinela* (Chimbote), January 1, 1959, 10, lists twenty unions in Chimbote.

18. It held similar levels of power in municipal government, as most mayors and council members also belonged to APRA.

19. The Convivencia refers to how APRA, shut out from formal politics in the 1950s and having failed to obtain the presidency in the 1962 election, abandoned its foundational left-of-center policies and joined with its former persecutors—first with President Manuel Prado y Ugarteche (1956–1962) and later with the followers of General Manuel Odría (1948–1956) and his right-wing Unión Nacional Odriísta—in order to access political power and eventually control parliamentary debate and complicate Belaúnde Terry's legislative agenda. For many Apristas, uniting with Odría proved problematic, given the former dictator's persecution of party members from 1948 to 1956. Disaffected Apristas split from the party and formed APRA Rebelde, joining with guerrilla movements to promote change through alternative means. See Carol Graham, "Peru's APRA Party in Power: Impossible Revolution, Relinquished Reform," *Journal of Interamerican Studies and World Affairs* 32, no. 3 (Autumn 1990): 75–115; and Osmar Gonzales, "La izquierda peruana: Una estructura ausente," in *Apogeo y crisis de la izquierda peruana: Hablan sus protagonistas,* ed. Alberto Adrianzén (Lima: IDEA Internacional; Universidad Antonio Ruiz de Montoya, 2011), 15–44.

20. Alberto Gil Peñaranda recounted meeting APRA founder Víctor Raúl Haya de la Torre and other top-level APRA figures in (presumably) 1967 or 1968. Gil complained to Haya de la Torre about some of the problems facing fishermen; Haya de la Torre instructed his assistants to call "Lucho," referring to the fishmeal magnate Luis Banchero Rossi, to solve the issue. Interview with Alberto Gil Peñaranda, September 18, 2014. On the fishing caucus (*célula pesquera*), see "El caso Ramírez del Villar, Banchero y la caja del pescador," *Oiga 194*, October 7, 1966, 9–11; and "Obsequio ministerial: Nueve millones para Banchero," *Oiga 201*, November 25, 1966, 4, 7. Also see interview with Alberto Gil Peñaranda, September 23, 2014.

21. Interview with Franco Baca Bazán, Lima, September 11, 2014.

22. Nigel Haworth, "Political Transition and the Peruvian Labor Movement, 1968–1975," in *Labor Autonomy and the State in Latin America,* ed. Edward C. Epstein (Boston: Unwin Hyman, 1989), 198.

23. Beatriz Gil, *El aprismo y el movimiento sindical chimbotano,* Centro de Investigaciones Sociales, Económicas, Políticas y Antropológicas 7 (Lima: Ponti-

ficia Universidad Católica del Perú, Departamento de Ciencias Sociales, Area de Sociología, 1974), 3. The epithets "mafia" and "gangster" were employed throughout the era under study to refer to someone who was perceived to have sold out his/her class.

24. Interview LIH001, April 7, 2005.

25. Interview PEH002, April 25, 2005.

26. Gil, *El aprismo y el movimiento sindical chimbotano*, 1.

27. Dionisio Horna Vásquez was a fisherman who died saving a coworker who had fallen into a boat's holding tank. The ACDHV took this name in remembrance of his sacrifice. Gil Farías Mogollón, *Así nacimos: Orígenes del sindicalismo en la pesca* (Lima: Instituto para el Desarrollo de la Pesca y la Minería, 1983), 71.

28. Catherine M. Conaghan, "Introduction to the English Edition," in Parodi, *To Be a Worker*, xiii.

29. Balbi, *Identidad clasista en el sindicalismo*, 13–14.

30. Gil, *El aprismo y el movimiento sindical chimbotano*, 5.

31. Interview PEH1410, September 29, 2014.

32. "Cayó la directiva que presidió Beltrán: Los pescadores nombran junta transitoria," *El Faro* (Chimbote), March 20, 1966.

33. The biographical information in this paragraph comes from my interview with Franco Baca Bazán, Lima, September 11, 2014.

34. *Memoria del Sindicato de Pescadores de Chimbote y Anexos*, 1967, cited in *Chimbote: Una experiencia revolucionaria de masas* (Chimbote, Peru: N.p., 1974), 9.

35. Interview PEH1409, September 16, 2014.

36. Interview with Franco Baca Bazán, Lima, September 11, 2014. Baca remarked that he had witnessed a massacre of peasants by police on an hacienda as a fifteen-year-old that made a major impression on his ideological development.

37. Interview with Franco Baca Bazán, Lima, September 11, 2014.

38. Interview PEH1410, September 29, 2014.

39. Numerous interviewees mentioned the solid construction of the union hall, as it was one of the few buildings to survive the devastating 1970 earthquake. For example, Interview PEH1402, August 28, 2014.

40. Interview PEH1003 and PEH1004, July 14, 2010.

41. In Chimbote, SINAMOS played a major role in organizing the shantytowns after the 1970 earthquake. See Clarke, "Revolutionizing the Tragic City."

42. Stephens, "The Peruvian Military Government," 65–66. A Patria Roja (Beijing-line Communism) pamphlet from May 1973 described the CNT as being an appendage of the present government and the CTP as reactionary. See "¡Hacia la unidad clasista del proletariado y las masas populares!," May 1, 1973, located in CENDOPES (Centro de Documentación, Investigación y Desarrollo Pesquero; hereafter CENDOPES), folder Los Sucesos de Mayo 1973 I.

43. Interview PEH1005, July 25, 2010. See as well "El sindicalismo debe ser revolucionario," *Oiga* 498, October 27, 1972, 12–14.

44. On May 1, 1972, the FPP published its yearly International Workers' Day salute. In it, they argued that the reason Peru had yet to achieve a "just and socially dignified society" was the lack of unity among the working class, given

the tripartite division in the union movement. The unbreakable and indestructible unity of the working class would be the determining factor in the success of the revolution. Federación de Pescadores Peruanos, "Primero de mayo: A los trabajadores peruanos," published in *Expreso*, May 1, 1972. This document clearly lays the foundation for the creation of the MLR and later the CTRP.

45. "En cita de pescadores nace el Movimiento Laboral Revolucionario: Jefe de Sinamos: Le damos nuestro respaldo," *Expreso*, May 23, 1972, 3.

46. Denis Sulmont, for example, calls the MLR "ultra-right." Sulmont knew Chimbote intimately during the period under study, as he had done his doctoral work in the port in the 1960s and has become one of the leading experts on the labor movement in Peru. See Sulmont, *El movimiento obrero peruano, 1890–1980*, 103–104; Liisa North, "Ideological Orientations of Peru's Military Rulers," in *The Peruvian Experiment Reconsidered*, ed. Cynthia McClintock and Abraham F. Lowenthal (Princeton, NJ: Princeton University Press, 1983), 252; and Philip Mauceri, *State under Siege: Development and Policy Making in Peru* (Boulder, CO: Westview, 1996), 21. General Tantaleán denied these claims in his autobiography: Javier Tantaleán Vanini, *Yo respondo* (Lima: Talleres de Manturano-Gonzales, 1978), 177–182. Tantaleán headed a faction of generals called "The Mission," which was also accused of using gangsterish and "McCarthy-like" tactics, including the creation of corporate institutions to control civil society. See Cynthia McClintock, *Peasant Cooperatives and Political Change in Peru* (Princeton, NJ: Princeton University Press, 1981), 51–55. The MLR formed a key part of this "Mission's" project.

47. The *guardias obreras*, according to former FPP president Alberto Gil Peñaranda, were present in all the factories, a concept the Communist-influenced *clasistas* adopted from factories in the Eastern Bloc. Interview with Alberto Gil Peñaranda, September 3, 2014.

48. Interview with Franco Baca Bazán, Lima, September 11, 2014.

49. Steelworker Union leaders with whom I spoke minimized the importance of the MLR within their union. Apparently the plant's executives—high military officials in the 1970s—would attend the MLR meetings. Interview SDH1401, August 14, 2014. In May 1973, during the lead-up to the May 24 strike, the MLR group from within SIDERPERÚ published a pamphlet denouncing the planned strike. See "SIDERPERÚ: Comando del Movimiento Laboral Revolucionario (M.L.R.) de los trabajadores de SIDERPERÚ," undated document located in CENDOPES, folder Los Sucesos de Mayo 1973 I. The MLR was active in other unions at the time, such as in the Marcona iron mines of the Ica region, but the miners rejected them there.

50. Central de Trabajadores de la Revolución Peruana, I Convención Nacional, 11 y 12 noviembre 1972, "Declaración de Principios," published in *Expreso*, November 19, 1972, 19.

51. Mauceri, *State under Siege*, 21.

52. "CTRP: Sindicalismo de nuevo estilo," *Oiga* 556, December 21, 1973, 39–40. Evelyne Huber Stephens notes that the recognition of new unions spiked during the Velasco regime, which could account for the growth of support for the CTRP. Only twenty workers were needed to form a union in a particular plant. Stephens, "The Peruvian Military Government," 61, table 1.

53. Farías Mogollón, *Así nacimos*, 125. During our interview, it also seemed like he grew close to the industrialists as well, intimating a close relationship with Luis Banchero Rossi. Baca talked about accompanying Banchero to Portugal to help him sell fishmeal and would, apparently, routinely provide Peru's richest man with advice. Interview with Franco Baca Bazán, Lima, September 11, 2014.

54. *Chimbote: Una experiencia revolucionaria de masas*, 7.

55. Ibid., 11–12.

56. *Revista de la Cámara de Comercio de Chimbote* 2, no. 15 (October 1972): 15; "Con 400 millones mensuales: Gobierno prestará dinero a pescadores mientras dure veda," *Expreso*, September 15, 1972; "Dan préstamos a pescadores por larga veda," *Prensa*, November 4, 1972.

57. *Chimbote: Una experiencia revolucionaria de masas*, 17–19.

58. Ibid., 13–14.

59. *Matón*, or murderer. During our interview, Baca casually mentioned four times that he carried a revolver during the 1960s and 1970s, including stating that he was not "afraid of anyone. He had a dog that bites and barks but doesn't eat." Interview with Franco Baca Bazán, Lima, September 11, 2014.

60. Interview PEH1410, September 29, 2014.

61. *Chimbote: Una experiencia revolucionaria de masas*, 15–18; Farías Mogollón, *Así nacimos*; Interview PEH1410, September 29, 2014. Franco Baca, when asked about the seizure of the union hall by the *clasistas*, did not seem to think it was a big deal at the time, stating it was their union hall, too. Interview with Franco Baca Bazán, Lima, September 11, 2014.

62. *Chimbote: Una experiencia revolucionaria de masas*; Farías Mogollón, *Así nacimos*, 116; Gil, *El aprismo y el movimiento sindical chimbotano*, 29; "Comunicado del Sindicato de Pescadores de Chimbote y Anexos Junta Directiva Transitoria," May 3, 1973, located in CENDOPES, folder Los Sucesos de Mayo 1973 I.

63. It's unclear how many JDT members were arrested. My interviewee said he did not get arrested, yet his name is included on one of the lists of those leaders who were taken in. Likewise, some of the existing documents located in CENDOPES, folder Los Sucesos de Mayo 1973 I, state that four JDT members were arrested, and others say nine. This confirms how hectic the events of early May 1973 truly were.

64. This point was made by the Agrupación Clasista de Pescadores Dionisio Horna Vásquez in their *Boletín Informativo Proletariado*, no. 11, on May 4, 1973, document located in CENDOPES, folder Los Sucesos de Mayo 1973 I. Rolando Riega is the brother-in-law to the notable guerrilla warrior Hugo Blanco and was one of the primary forces within the MLR. Interview with Alberto Gil Peñaranda, September 23, 2014.

65. Interview PEH1410, September 29, 2014.

66. Baca surely knew about the expropriation plans, given his close relationship with Tantaleán, and that the discussion before the meeting pointed toward a major revolutionary act about to take place. Furthermore, Baca told me that the generals had had their eye on the expropriation since the first meeting he

had with Interior Minister Artola in October of 1968. Interview with Franco Baca Bazán, Lima, September 11, 2014.

67. *Chimbote: Una experiencia revolucionaria de masas*, 25. The authors of *Chimbote: Una experiencia revolucionaria de masas* reported that Baca resigned at the meeting, yet in SPCHA's document, Baca received the support of fishermen. In our interview, Baca intimated that he had been asked to step down from all union activities by the RGAF, as he was going to be named as the replacement for Enrique León Velarde as director of the Interior Government, one of the highest civilian positions in the military government. Baca ultimately did not assume the position for unclear reasons, including Velasco's failing health and the end of the first phase of the revolution. Interview with Franco Baca Bazán, Lima, September 11, 2014.

68. An allusion to October 9, 1968, the Day of National Dignity on which Velasco had announced the expropriation of the International Petroleum Company's operations, ostensibly the spark for the coup six days before.

69. SPCHA, "Comunicado #2," May 8, 1973.

70. El Comité de Defensa de los Pescadores, "Boletín No 1," undated documented located in CENDOPES, folder Los Sucesos de Mayo 1973 I.

71. "Se produjeron incidentes entre pescadores: Chimbote," *El Comercio*, May 8, 1973.

72. *El Faro*, October 5, 1973.

73. Interview PEH1410, September 29, 2014, and Sindicato de Trabajadores en Construcción Civil de Chimbote, "Comunicado de Prensa," undated document located in CENDOPES, folder Los Sucesos de Mayo 1973 I.

74. See, for example, "SIDERPERÚ: Comando del Movimiento Laboral Revolucionario (M.L.R.) de los trabajadores de SIDERPERÚ," undated document located in CENDOPES, folder Los Sucesos de Mayo 1973 I; Movimiento Laboral Revolucionario M.L.R., "Comunicado," undated document located in CENDOPES, folder Los Sucesos de Mayo 1973 I; an untitled SINAMOS pamphlet, undated document located in CENDOPES, folder Los Sucesos de Mayo 1973 I; and Motoristas Revolucionarios de Embarcaciones Pesqueras de Chimbote, "Comunicado 1," May 20, 1973, document located in CENDOPES, folder Los Sucesos de Mayo 1973 I.

75. For example, see "Los ultra'izquierda [*sic*] y derecha intentaron sabotear tranquilidad de los pescadores: dijo Franco Baca n [*sic*] reunión de prensa en Sind. Pescadores," *Últimas Noticias*, May 10, 1973, 1. Also see *Chimbote: Una experiencia revolucionaria de masas*, 24.

76. The SPCHA JDT issued several communiqués, as did the ACDHV and other local *clasista* unions, the various factions of the Peruvian Communist Parties, and other unions' social movements. These documents are located in CENDOPES, folder Los Sucesos de Mayo 1973 I.

77. Movimiento Laboral Revolucionario M.L.R., "Comunicado," undated document located in CENDOPES, folder Los Sucesos de Mayo 1973 I.

78. In our four interviews, Gil claims he de-affiliated from APRA in the 1960s and during his tenure as FPP secretary general attempted to take a nonpartisan line. One recurring theme from the interviews is his repudiation of

Communism, as he considers his ouster from the FPP in 1975 to have been at the instigation of Communists within the federation. Interviewee PEH1410 claimed that Gil maintained those APRA ties. Likewise, Javier Tantaleán Vanini's son, the historian Javier Tantaleán Arbulú, held a number of high-ranking posts in the APRA Party and in Alan García's first government (1985–1990). Interview PEH1410, September 29, 2014.

79. Interview SDH1001, July 2, 2010.

80. Interview with Franco Baca Bazán, Lima, September 11, 2014.

81. *Chimbote: Una experiencia revolucionaria de masas*, 36.

82. On the role of regional labor federations, see Angell, *Peruvian Labour and the Military Government since 1968*. FESIDETA replaced the USPS, but it was essentially the same entity, with its area of coverage expanded from the provincial (like a county) to a departmental (equivalent to a state) level.

83. *Chimbote: Una experiencia revolucionaria de masas*, 32; Gil, *El aprismo y el movimiento sindical chimbotano*, 29.

84. Interview PEH1410, September 29, 2014. This interviewee had been near Espinola shortly before the shots were fired and managed to escape the bullets by ducking into a nearby restaurant. Espinola did not have as much luck. He received bullet wounds in his right semithorax, liver, kidney, and vertebra. "Un muerto en incidentes producidos en Chimbote: Subprefectura del Santa emitió Comunicado Oficial," *La Prensa*, May 25, 1973.

85. "Continuaron ayer los disturbios en la ciudad de Chimbote: Dirigente herido de Sider-Perú fue traído a Lima," *El Comercio*, May 26, 1973; "Falleció dirigente sindical herido durante paro: Chimbote. Las tres balas destrozaron su organismo," *La Industria*, June 14, 1973.

86. Interview PEH1410, September 29, 2014; "Seis detenidos por estar complicados en destrucción de oficina de Sinamos: Pasaron a la Cárcel Pública de Chimbote," *La Industria*, June 23, 1973.

87. SINAMOS had begun a massive program to attempt to get Chimbote's shantytowns under control in the wake of the 1970 earthquake. See Clarke, "Revolutionizing the Tragic City."

88. See "Editorial: Sabotaje al Perú," *El Comercio*, June 3, 1973; "Todo indica que es sabotaje lo ocurrido en siderúrgica: Afirmó Cáceres Graziani en conferencia" and "Más de 90 millones de soles deja de vender SIDERPERÚ: Empleados de Oficina de Lima, Laboraron," both in *La Industria*, June 1, 1973.

89. See *DL 20043: Se declara en reorganización a la empresa SIDERPERÚ*, 1973, http://www.leyes.congreso.gob.pe/Documentos/Leyes/20043.pdf.

90. Interview SDH1402, August 23, 2014. Most of the fired steelworkers were important union leaders. Several of the steelworkers sued SIDERPERÚ to get their jobs back, which they achieved fifteen years later.

91. "Acuerda continuar la huelga Sindicato Unico de Siderperú," and "Maltratan a empleados que se oponen a huelga," both in *La Industria*, June 4, 1973; "No habrá clases, taxis ni mercados en Chimbote," *La Industria*, June 5, 1973; "Importante sindicato de Ancash levantó la huelga," *Expreso*, June 9, 1973; and "Pescadores laboran siguiendo normas de Pescaperú: Chimbote," *Expreso*, June 17, 1973.

92. The MLR died with the end of the first phase of the revolution in 1975. The CTRP continues to exist but has little influence.

93. According to one source, Manuel Zúñiga Franco and Franco Baca were cousins. Interview PEH1410, September 29, 2014.

94. The lessons of May 1973 have not disappeared. Among labor leaders in Chimbote, the massacre of Minchola and Miranda, as well as the general use of violence, remain a part of the landscape of struggle, even in the present. In May 24, 2005, I attended an event remembering the events of thirty-two years before held in the same SPCHA union hall. Likewise, Espinola's portrait still hangs in the office of the STPS secretary of defense.

CHAPTER 12

Generals, Hotels, and Hippies: Velasco-Era Tourism Development and Conflict in Cuzco

MARK RICE

When Peru's minister of industry and commerce arrived in Cuzco on October 18, 1974, he found a warm welcome printed in the local newspaper. "Cuzco Progresses through Tourism" proclaimed *El Comercio* in an endorsement of the efforts by Peru's military government to transform the region into a global destination.[1] The slogan also reflected a new phase for tourism in Cuzco. Promoted since the 1920s as a strategy to bolster local pride and serve as a supplemental source of profit, under the government of Juan Velasco Alvarado, tourism transformed into a potential source of regional development. In the wake of agrarian revolts and the collapse of the area's traditional agricultural economy, regional and national leaders searched for strategies to restore economic and political stability to Cuzco. Numerous scholarly studies have analyzed the course and legacy of these efforts, especially related to agrarian reform.[2] Often overlooked, however, is the fact that tourism also emerged as a potential solution to reform Cuzco's economy and society during this era.

No institution symbolized the hopes to employ tourism as a force for social change in Cuzco better than COPESCO (Plan Turístico y Cultural Perú-UNESCO; Peru-UNESCO Tourist and Cultural Plan), a joint operation between Peru and UNESCO. Promoting cultural tourism as development, COPESCO sought to unite the goals of historical preservation, economic development, and social inclusion. COPESCO, along with the overall tourism policies pursued by the Velasco government, draws attention to several still understudied aspects of the era, especially in regard to the regime's investment in nontraditional economic sectors and its effects on regional development. However, the narrative of tourism development in Cuzco also reflects historical narratives of the Velasco era. Unfortunately, like many other initiatives of the military government, tourism plans promoted as paths to social cohesion ultimately provoked conflicts between differing visions regarding the character and direction of development in Cuzco. The policies pursued by the Velasco government to develop tourism proved prophetic, both for envisioning the potential of cultural tourism in Cuzco and for the conflicts these plans would ultimately produce.

Efforts to use state resources to promote tourism in Cuzco predated the military government. In 1964, President Fernando Belaúnde Terry approved the creation of the Corporación de Turismo del Perú (COTURPERU; Peruvian Tourism Corporation) to manage tourism funding and planning.[3] COTURPERU emerged as a response to the dramatic increase in international travel to Peru following the introduction of regular commercial jet service to Lima in 1960 and, by 1968, to Cuzco.[4] These advances, along with the inauguration of new airport facilities in Lima and Cuzco, made leisure travel to Peru's interior convenient and quick.[5] Peru's annual international tourist arrivals increased dramatically from 62,000 to 108,000 between 1963 and 1967.[6] Cuzco emerged as one of the primary benefactors of state investment in tourism. One early planning report noted that "if Peru has a single attraction known throughout the world—it is Machu Picchu."[7] COTURPERU allocated more than 5 million soles for various restoration and infrastructure projects in the region in its 1965 budget.[8] The efforts bore fruit, and between 1960 and 1970, annual tourist arrivals to Cuzco doubled from 26,026 to 52,834. Equally important, the coveted international market composed a large part of the tourism increase in Cuzco, which went from 40 percent to 63.6 percent of the overall tourist demographic (chart 12.1).[9] The Peruvian media joined Cuzqueños in embracing the concept of fashioning the country into a destination for the cultured international traveler. The November 1963 edition of *Caretas* magazine sponsored a photo shoot of "Nordic Vicuñas" at Machu Picchu. The photos of European models, wearing modern fashions posing among the stones of Machu Picchu, reinforced the image of tourism as a force of modernization and progress for Cuzco.[10] These images, as well as those of passenger jets flying over Machu Picchu, emerged as a point of regional pride and the promise of modernization for Cuzco well into the 1970s.[11]

However, behind the glossy images of modern travel, multiple problems still afflicted Peru's tourism development. Beginning in 1958 with

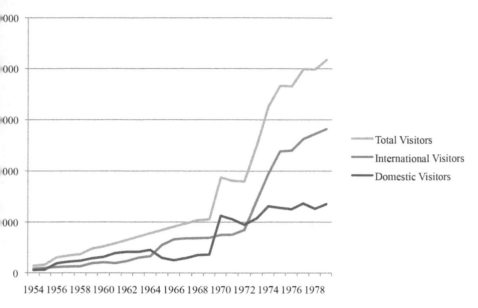

Chart 12.1. Total Annual Tourist Arrivals to Cuzco, 1954–1979. COPESCO, *Plan de desarrollo II etapa* (1980), 14, Archivo COPESCO del Cusco.

the La Convención agrarian movement, land seizures, strikes, and protests had rocked Cuzco.[12] By February of 1964, at least thirty-five people had died in confrontations with the police over land seizures, and in March, Belaúnde declared a state of siege in Cuzco.[13] In 1965, foco guerrilla groups,[14] the Movimiento de Izquierda Revolucionaria (MIR; Movement of the Revolutionary Left) and the Ejército de Liberación Nacional (ELN; National Liberation Army), engaged the military in a failed uprising in Mesa Pelada.[15] The ongoing social chaos did not go unnoticed by visitors. One *Boston Globe* columnist, visiting Machu Picchu in 1960, characterized highland Peru as a mix of "beauty, squalor, and angry voices."[16] Economic unrest and budgetary woes in the latter years of Belaúnde's government spread to affect directly the tourism sector through a series of strikes, worker actions, and reduced spending on tourism projects.[17]

After the coup, the Velasco government continued state investment in tourism and, in December of 1969, inaugurated the Dirección General del Turismo (DGTUR; General Office of Tourism) within the Ministry of Industry and Commerce to act as the key coordinating office for tourist development.[18] More importantly for Cuzco, the military government pushed forward the creation of COPESCO—an institution that pledged to integrate the goals of tourism, social development, and preservation. Since 1966, UNESCO had studied the possibility of aiding cultural tourism in Peru and announced the Plan Turístico y Cultural Perú-UNESCO in the final months of the Belaúnde government.[19] The new military government continued COPESCO and, in April of 1969, organized an executive committee headed by the minister of industry and commerce to assume and direct administrative control of the institution, aided with advisers partially funded by UNESCO and the United Nations Development Programme. Although the Ministry of Industry and Commerce and DGTUR would fund many tourism projects, most proposals originated as COPESCO plans.[20] The military government proved adept at securing international financing for COPESCO, and by 1972, the institution's total spending had reached US$70,752,000, 60 percent of which was provided by a loan from the Inter-American Development Bank (IDB) and 40 percent by the Peruvian state.[21]

Overseeing 84,735 square kilometers extending from Lake Titicaca in Puno Department to La Convención in Cuzco, COPESCO promoted tourism as a central tool in the military's efforts to fundamentally change the economic and social structures of Peru's southern Andes.[22] COPESCO's mission won approval from the generals administering the revolutionary government. For Velasco and his allies, the uprising in La Convención and the experience of fighting the MIR and ELN in 1965 had served as formative moments in their political evolution, highlighting the stark underdevelopment of Cuzco and the potential danger of ignoring the region's social and economic conditions.[23] A 1972 COPESCO planning report best summarized the new mission of tourist development, stating: "In the Cusco-Puno zone, tourism is the sector that can channel investment for its own development and simultaneously provide an infrastructure base for the social-economic development of the zone."[24] Tourism, like the agrarian reform, would become a motor for development and social change in Cuzco.

It appears that COPESCO planners recognized that agrarian reform alone would not resolve the problems of a general lack of arable land and overpopulation that affected highland Peru's rural economy.[25] COPESCO planning documents noted that even with the agrarian reform, 56 percent of Cuzco's economically active rural population lacked access to employment opportunities in 1969.[26] To combat the region's underdevelopment, planners envisioned an immediate injection of state spending in "fixed social capital" through the construction of roads, hotels, and tourism infrastructure. Such spending would encourage private investment in a service economy in the region.[27] COPESCO predicted that the combined public and private investment would quickly begin a "chain reaction of auto-generated profits and spending that will extend to all economic sectors." As a result, "tourism activity, not needing skilled labor, will become a generator of profits to absorb the workforce in a rapid, easy, and cheap process."[28] In the eyes of COPESCO, tourism would provide a crucial role in absorbing rural labor into a modern service economy.

COPESCO also dedicated extensive funds toward preservation. Restoring historical sites served to foment cultural tourism while simultaneously appealing to the military's nationalism. Working with the United Nations Development Programme, COPESCO helped create Project PER-39 as an extensive program to document and catalog archaeological sites.[29] Between 1973 and 1975, COPESCO worked in coordination with the PER-39 project to coordinate the restoration of twenty-seven different historical sites in and around Cuzco, produced catalogs of archaeological sites in Cuzco, and funded artisan workshops to repair artifacts in Cuzco.[30] The PER-39 project included funding for photography and inspection of stonework in Machu Picchu in 1974.[31] In September 1974, the IDB awarded the Peruvian government a loan of US$5,478,000 for historical preservation projects. With this start-up funding secured, the government formed a special unit to oversee a comprehensive maintenance and preservation program for Machu Picchu between 1975 and 1981.[32]

The dual goals of preservation and economic development received a warm reception in Cuzco, where the regionally focused mission of COPESCO promised to reform a tourism economy that had begun to be dominated by non-Cuzqueño commercial interests. As early as 1967, *El Comercio del Cusco* criticized the increasing stratification of tourism development in the region. "Tourism promotion for Cusco should be guided to give this city some positive benefit," noted the editorial. The paper concluded that the new tourism economy threatened to "place us in the role of the 'willing stooge' (*tonto útil*) in favor of outside companies and people."[33] Cuzqueños welcomed the state spending of the COPESCO project as an alternative to private, Lima-based capital interests. Emphasizing the importance of Cuzco's tourism development, Velasco personally arrived in the city on September 27, 1971, to formally approve a Cuzco–Machu Picchu highway project.[34] *El Comercio*

La majestuosidad de Machupijchu y la grandiosidad del Cusco, siguen atrayendo a millares de turistas de todo el mundo. Diariamente llegan de todas partes del mundo a admirar a es ta Capital Arqueológica de América. Que 1974 sea de realizaciones para que tengamos mejores vías de comunicación y siga creciendo el turismo receptivo. (Grabado de Emiliano Franco).

Figure 12.1. Even at the height of the Velasco populist period, tourism in Cuzco remained imagined as elite, jet-set, and white. *El Comercio del Cusco*, January 1, 1974, 1.

del Cusco applauded Velasco's visit and the state's recent investment and claimed: "They constitute a true rise in tourism promotion that Cusco needs and longs for."[35]

However, if COPESCO aimed to broaden the social impact of tourism in Cuzco, the character of the international travelers it sought to attract remained unchanged. COPESCO plans endorsed earlier recommendations that argued for continued state investment toward creating upscale hotels to market to elite international tourists—primarily originating from the United States.[36] The Velasco government did use tourism to support its leftist rhetoric. By 1972, dignitaries from the People's Republic of China and the Soviet Union visited Cuzco.[37] However, the government maintained friendly relations with international tourism interests by signing lucrative hotel contracts with Holiday Inn, Marriott, and Braniff Airways. With the exception of a dispute over AeroPerú's landing rights, tourism served as a source of positive commercial and diplomatic cooperation.[38] Even at the height of the military government's populist and revolutionary message in 1974, the imagery of tourism remained associated with cultured, modern travelers from the global north (fig. 12.1).[39]

However, in order to attract lucrative international travelers, Cuzco needed massive investment in its hotel capacity. COPESCO planners estimated that by 1975, Cuzco could face a deficit of over five thousand hotel beds.[40] COPESCO put forward an ambitious proposal to construct three new two-hundred-bed hotels for Cuzco; one at Machu Picchu and two in Cuzco City to serve international visitors.[41] The Machu Picchu hotel received priority, and by February 1972, the national government had completed formal estimates on construction costs and locations for the new hotel.[42] All proposals under consideration featured modernist designs and several floors of rooms. Most proposals also placed the new hotel adjacent to the archaeological complex, often dug into the hillside (fig. 12.2).[43]

So convinced were they of the benefits of tourism development that

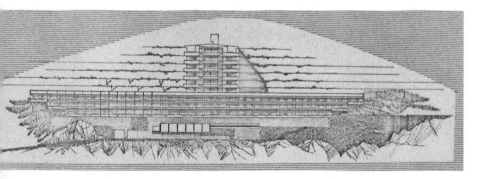

Figure 12.2. Elevation of proposed hotel. Note construction into terraces of the mountain. *COPESCO: Estudio de factibilidad del hotel Machu Picchu,* vol. 1, Biblioteca del Ministerio de Cultura.

the military and COPESCO planners never predicted that proposals to construct a large hotel adjacent to Machu Picchu would cause an outcry. Employing Machu Picchu as a nationalist symbol, the military did not foresee the possible negative reaction produced by granting elite travelers prime access to the site. More importantly, the Velasco government created and empowered new bureaucratic institutions that proved ideally suited to provide state resources *against* the hotel project. In March of 1971, the government created the Instituto Nacional de Cultura (INC; National Culture Institute) to centralize national cultural policy and historical preservation.[44] Following new policy, COPESCO sent the hotel plans to the INC for review. In October 1971, the INC responded with a conditional "favorable opinion," but cautioned that the National Archaeological Council (now under the control of the INC) needed to provide final approval for the hotel.[45] More ominously, the report warned that the hotel project could potentially conflict with several national preservation laws.[46]

Opposition to the project emerged at a forum held on June 12, 1972, by the Ministry of Industry and Commerce. Five panel members, all representing tourism interests, expressed approval of the project. However, the remaining fourteen members argued against the hotel. The architect Santiago Agurto declared the project a "cultural injury." A forestry engineer, Benjamín Almanza, noted that a new hotel would threaten the biodiversity surrounding Machu Picchu. The scholar Luis E. Valcárcel also spoke against the project, and the artist Fernando de Szyszlo warned that "it would be insensitive to only consider the tourist-commercial element" embodied by the hotel project. Others in attendance argued that the hotel project ran contrary to the aims of the Velasco government's revolutionary and nationalistic rhetoric. The architect Roberto Wakeham noted that constructing a hotel largely for wealthy foreign travelers did not conform to the current revolutionary goals of the military government. Leopoldo Chiappo also argued that the plan of hotel construction needed to be reviewed "from the point of view of a revolutionary society that one wants to establish in the country."[47] As a response, the national government sent an INC team to Machu Picchu in early June to assess the hotel site,[48] but this action was too late to prevent international pressure against the hotel project. Scholars meeting in Mexico City for a conference in August, including John Murra and María Rostworowski, both eminent ethnohistorians of Peru, signed a petition protesting the hotel project.[49] By August of 1972, even

US dailies printed news articles regarding the uproar over the proposed hotel.[50]

In Cuzco, opposition to the hotel smacked of Lima-centric machinations against regional development. "Sabotage of an already-approved project?" questioned *El Comercio del Cusco* on June 12, 1972, following the first delays of the hotel in preparation for the INC review.[51] However, if preservationists appealed to the military's sense of national pride, Cuzco backers sought to remind leaders of the social benefits of tourism development. The August 5, 1972, editorial of Cuzco's *El Comercio* petitioned the government to proceed with hotel construction, citing the "mindfulness that the people support said project."[52] Another editorial from August 22 argued that "the stubborn persistence of hidden but powerful economic forces encysted in Lima" were the true sources of opposition to the Machu Picchu hotel in the view of *El Comercio del Cusco*.[53] For Cuzqueños, COPESCO and the Machu Picchu hotel represented the region's best chance for independent economic development, and the military had to ignore well-financed investors in Lima who wanted to scuttle the project.

Hotel promoters received another defeat in September of 1972 when the Education Ministry recommended a protected zone of 1,400 hectares surrounding Machu Picchu, prohibiting construction at the preferred site.[54] *El Comercio del Cusco*'s editorial board reacted to rumors of the relocation as another threat from Lima-based economic interests, arguing that "enemies of Cusco do not relent."[55] Tensions mounted until the provincial mayor of Cuzco called an open town meeting on October 10 to demand construction of the Machu Picchu hotel on the current lodge site or an alternate location selected by COPESCO. Denouncing the INC head, Martha Hildebrandt, a linguist, the meeting participants threatened a general strike if their demands were not answered within fifteen days. Reporting on the meeting, *El Comercio del Cusco* proudly noted that "it had the virtue of certifying the unity of Cusqueños when they see the goals of progress in danger for those who have a right to their land (*tiene derecho a su tierra*)."[56] Although the calls for a general strike failed to materialize, two days later, Cuzco's leaders sent a formal petition to Lima to press the hotel project with Velasco directly.[57]

As Cuzqueños rallied to protect what they viewed as their economic independence, in Lima INC director Hildebrandt criticized the mobilizations in Cuzco as a short-sighted pursuit of local development over the long-term needs of preservation. Interviewed by Lima's *El Correo* on October 17, Hildebrandt retorted: "It's incredible but odd that we, not the Cuzqueños, are the ones concerned with Cuzco."[58] The remarks of Hildebrandt did little to diminish Cuzqueños' suspicions of Lima's centralism and paternalism. In fact, Cuzco's mayor demanded that Hildebrandt travel to Cuzco, mocking her as one of "these *señores* that, at the eleventh hour, become *cusqueñistas* and look down from their balcony trying to devise tactics for the solutions that afflict Cusco."[59] *El Comercio del Cusco* criticized Hildebrandt and the INC as pawns used by monopolistic tourism interests in Lima that "will not have this valuable prey to suckle on," once the state-owned Machu Picchu hotel was completed.[60] Cuzco's regional leadership continued to view the hotel project as a vital link in Cuzco's revolutionary and populist development. To bolster this view, in early October labor unions representing the region's brewers, bank workers, hotel employees, drivers, industrial workers, and even employees of the Coca-Cola bottling plant formally petitioned the national government to back the hotel in the name of workers' rights.[61]

In response, Hildebrandt also appealed to the nationalist rhetoric of the revolutionary government in her recommendations against the hotel project. In her October 1972 official report to the council of ministers, Hildebrandt noted: "Monuments of our old culture represent cash capital (*capital contante y sonante*). *It is necessary to put the ruins to work*, it is true, but not in a hurried search for the ephemeral dollar, but in the employ of affirming our national identity." The report went on to detail that "Peru has many ruins, large ruins, magnificent ruins. But among all of them, only Machu Picchu has reached the dimension of a symbol. Machu Picchu is Peru, just like Túpac Amaru." Hildebrandt backed the preservationists arguing for the need to preserve Machu Picchu's natural environment. Hildebrandt ended the report noting, "Conservation of cultural patrimony and tourism development has led to the creation of seemingly equitable but false expression: *cultural tourism*"[62] The conclusion appeared to refute one of the central goals promoted by COPESCO: the compatibility of development with preservation in Cuzco.

On October 31, 1972, the Ministry of Industry and Commerce and the Ministry of Education agreed on a compromise that promised to continue the locally supported construction on the hotel while addressing the INC concerns regarding conservation of the area surrounding Machu Picchu. Issuing Decree Law 19597, the government declared that the new hotel for Machu Picchu was an "urgent necessity," but that the project would not take place in a new, "protected zone" marked by the Ministry of Education and the INC that surrounded the immediate environs of the ruin.[63] A new commission composed of COPESCO, INC, and government representatives arrived at the site in November and recommended the lower zone of the Hacienda Mandor, located along the Urubamba River at the base of the ruin, as the best alternative option for the hotel.[64] By February of 1973, the minister of industry and commerce still predicted "four or five weeks" until authorities finalized the exact location for the new hotel. As usual, *El Comercio del Cusco* blamed "large economic interests sealed off in Lima" for delays with the hotel.[65] However, press reports from Lima suggest that Cuzco's suspicions were overblown. For example, Lima's *El Comercio* editorial line continued to support efforts to construct the Machu Picchu hotel.[66]

By February 1973, Velasco's deteriorating health, growing opposition to the regime's controversial labor laws, and worsening economic outlooks emerged as the most serious threats to the COPESCO mission.[67] Despite optimistic announcements, work on nearly all large tourism projects, including the hotel and highway to Machu Picchu, failed to progress through 1973.[68] With the hotel project virtually suspended, local interests lobbied the government to at least complete the highway to Machu Picchu. "Open the doors of Cusco's own house to all nonprivileged Peruvians," pleaded *El Comercio del Cusco* in an October 11, 1973, editorial.[69] If appeal to the government's populist rhetoric failed, the local press exploited the military's nationalist tone. Relations reached a nadir in November of 1973 when locals attacked and burned the Cuzco headquarters of SINAMOS.[70] Efforts continued on paper to build a modern hotel near Machu Picchu. The government continued to pledge its plans for a modern Machu Picchu hotel as late as 1976.[71] However, as the military's revolution turned to the right under the leadership of General Morales Bermúdez, tourism spending by the state declined dramatically. By 1976, austerity measures forced even a modest restoration of the 1933 Machu Picchu lodge to be scaled back.[72]

Even the military's vaunted agrarian reform brought different government institutions into conflict over its role in relation to preservation and tourism at Machu Picchu. Officials in the cultural preservation bureaucracy raised objections over the effect of increased land use surrounding Machu Picchu following the 1969 agrarian reform. Concerns grew after September 1971, when the owner of the adjacent Hacienda Mandor burned undergrowth to clear a zone for sheep grazing, causing a fire to grow out of control and threaten Machu Picchu. Two weeks later, another set blaze ascended Huayna Picchu and "entered the ruins, burning the plaza of the sacred rock and the eastern slope of the Intihuatana hill." After this incident, the head of the Cuzco Archaeology Council, Manuel Chávez Ballón, concluded that "this should serve as a motive to resolve for once and for all the need for Machu Picchu to be considered as a national park."[73] Like Chávez Ballón, the INC opposed the social goals of agrarian reform, citing its danger to preservation at Machu Picchu. In a 1975 report, the INC presented the results of the agrarian reform and distribution of lands as a direct threat to Machu Picchu. The INC predicted a "total acquisition of lands into a cooperative, social company, or whatever it may be called," a "future avalanche of people," and "indiscriminate exploitation of forests." The report recommended that the INC leadership work to acquire as much surrounding land as possible to prevent it from being redistributed to campesinos.[74]

Conflict over land redistribution, preservation, and tourism emerged from beyond the INC. The government faced difficulty justifying the reservation of prime tracts to serve foreign elite tourists while continuing its rhetoric of populist land reform. In October of 1973, campesinos invaded the territory reserved in the San Sebastián neighborhood for one of Cuzco's proposed tourism hotels. Despite the government's rhetoric, the "*toma*" (occupation) of the hotel property provoked a rapid police response to dislodge the campesinos.[75] In other instances, campesinos themselves rejected the goals of the agrarian reform in favor of tourism profits. Campesinos residing near major tourist attractions showed little interest in forming agricultural cooperatives. Although not part of a cooperative, by the mid-1970s residents in the village of Aguas Calientes at the base of Machu Picchu negotiated with private developers to sell land for future hotel construction.[76]

As the original goals of social development and historical preservation became sources of conflict, the military's plans faced another unpredicted threat when the arrival of new countercultural travelers caused locals to question the "modernization" promised through tourism. COPESCO documents estimated that the average traveler to Peru in 1971 would be "a business man or professional between thirty-five and forty, with a high degree of education and cultural level. It is almost guaranteed this man will travel with his family."[77] As a result, Peruvians were slightly surprised when *El Comercio de Lima* reported a new wave of "travelers with long hair, worn-out blue jeans, or dressed in colorful clothing" in July 1972. *El Comercio de Lima* noted that hippie arrivals to Peru were indeed a global phenomenon. "Our country's embassy in France is literally assaulted with requests for information or for visas from young students who want to 'share in the life of the Quechua Indian,'" remarked the article. The report concluded with the observation: "In the age of Aquarius, Machu Picchu is one of the most sacred places of the world."[78]

For many countercultural travelers of the late 1960s and early 1970s, Peru and the Andes did indeed serve as icons for the mystic. One US backpacker who arrived in Cuzco with her husband in the 1970s recalled how visiting Peru was an opportunity for "going back to Earth."[79] Transnational economic and cultural links also helped reintroduce the Andes into the counterculture's subconscious. In 1970, Simon and Garfunkel released their Grammy-winning album *Bridge over Troubled Water*, featuring a renewed version of the Cuzqueño composer Daniel Alomía Robles's "El cóndor pasa." Recorded using Andean instruments, Simon and Garfunkel's "El Condor Pasa (If I Could)" increased global awareness of Cuzco's folkloric music.[80] Peruvians themselves helped recast the image of Peru and Cuzco as antidotes to the modern world. When a young German filmmaker named Werner Herzog arrived in Peru in 1971 to film a television special and ran low on funds, a future hotel owner hoping to generate global interest in Peru stepped in to provide financing for the project. The final version of Herzog's film, *Aguirre, the Wrath of God*, quickly developed a following in art houses across Europe and the United States.[81] By the mid-1970s, the government-owned AeroPerú promoted Machu Picchu as an antimodern, mysterious destination emblematic of Peru, "the most mysterious country on earth."[82] For countercultural travelers, regional political changes, particularly the Mexican state's crackdown on hippies following 1968, most likely played an important role in elevating Peru as an appealing destination.[83] Although the military government was suspicious of youth counterculture, Peru's leftist political stance and general lack of state violence made it an attractive destination in an era when Latin America was experiencing the rise of numerous authoritarian regimes.[84]

Locals did recognize the potential benefits of serving backpacking and independent travelers. By 1973, *El Comercio del Cusco*, in cooperation with local tourism promoters, began to publish an English-language "Tourist Supplement" that offered content geared especially toward travelers touring without an agency or guide.[85] However, for many, hippie tourism brought more imagined threats than profits. According to Cuzco's Archaeology Council chief, Chávez Ballón, the new international visitors to Machu Picchu "do not want to pay for anything and create problems by wanting to violate policies."[86] The increase in backpacking tourism taxed the limited staff at Machu Picchu. Chávez Ballón complained that "tourists leave fruit peels, cans, paper, food scraps, plastics, etc." Even worse, "many times, unable to find a bathroom, they do their 'business' (*necesidades*) inside the ruins." When not leaving refuse, Chávez Ballón complained, such visitors wanted to scale walls, damaging the ruins and causing personal injury. Problems of supervising backpackers increased in archaeological sites adjacent to Machu Picchu, where the Archaeology Council staff had less vigilance. In these sites, "the backpackers sunbathe naked or attempt to explore difficult zones," reported Chávez Ballón.[87] The lack of lodging facilities for backpackers also placed strains on Machu Picchu. Chávez Ballón estimated that, on any given night, twenty backpackers slept in unregulated tents surrounding the ruin.[88]

In Cuzco, the arrival of hippie travelers with beards, long hair, and wearing indigenous clothing proved especially shocking to locals. As early as 1969, *El Comercio del Cusco* warned local parents to look out for "the appearance of Cusqueño hippies that constitute grotesque caricatures of their overseas peers."[89] One can imagine the shock of many of *El Comercio del Cusco*'s readers when they saw the June 1, 1971, headline announcing that hippies had turned Machu Picchu into a "nudist paradise."[90] In the wake of such news, a report appeared in *El Comercio del Cusco* warning: "'Hippismo,' born in the West and in North America, equal to *rocanrolerismo* and other forms of juvenile misconduct, has extended through America, threatening to destroy the most vital elements of the nation."[91] By the end of 1973, the local press expressed concern that Cuzco had become a center of hippie life. "Cusco is converting into an operations center of international 'hippismo,'" complained *El Comercio del Cusco*.[92] In fact, the local press reported that Cuzco's Plaza de Armas had been transformed into a makeshift "Hippie Market" where backpackers sold their own artisan goods and travel material to the chagrin of local merchants.[93] Relations between locals and hippies reached a low point in June of 1974 during a student civic campaign to pick up litter in Cuzco named "Operation Cleaning." Participants began hanging makeshift signs in Cuzco's Plaza de Armas stating: "Cusco: Clean of Hippies," much to the applause and approval of locals.[94]

Figure 12.3. *El Comercio del Cusco* documents the "hippie threat" brought by tourism, September 5, 1972.

Local media quickly associated rumors of increased drug use with the arrival of hippies in Cuzco. In early September 1972, police arrested two hippies—one Peruvian and one Uruguayan—on charges of marijuana possession. *El Comercio del Cusco* published photos of the Uruguayan suspect and reminded readers of the "grave danger" drugs posed to the community (fig. 12.3).[95] Local concerns over the relationship between hippie backpackers and drug consumption increased in June 1973 when authorities discovered marijuana cultivations in backpacking lodges near Machu Picchu.[96] Later that month, police arrested another suspect on charges of possession of marijuana inside Machu Picchu.[97] Drugs proved to be just one of the moral dangers of hippie tourism, according to many observers. In April 1973, Lima's *La Prensa* newspaper reported that backpacking shelters around Machu Picchu "were converted into 'refuges' for groups of hippies that stayed there weeks and had all kinds of orgies."[98] It appeared that the search for cultured tourists had missed its mark.

Conclusion

How do we assess the legacy of tourism development in Peru under Velasco, and, more importantly, what can it tell us about larger questions regarding the revolutionary military government? As Abraham Lowenthal has noted, although the military government did not achieve many of its goals, the broad reach of its programs makes it difficult to judge the regime a failure.[99] By this standard, tourism policy was quite successful. COPESCO oversaw US$93 million in investments in Cuzco and Puno, and tourist arrivals increased steadily throughout the 1970s—an achievement not matched in other economic sectors during the military government (see chart 12.1).[100] In addition, COPESCO completed important infrastructure projects, including 322 new kilometers of paved highways and electrification projects that benefited residents living in rural towns along tourist routes.[101]

Even so, many observers concluded that COPESCO and the tourism policy was a failure. First, the contradictory goals of cultural tourism—modern projects to endorse preservation, developing elite hotels to redistribute wealth, and its highly technocratic nature—resulted in a policy endorsed to create social and political unity in Cuzco becoming a point of conflict. Julio Cotler notes: "Contrary to its hopes, however, the GRFA [RGAF] became tangled up in the hostile actions its policies unleashed."[102] It appears that tourism policy in Cuzco suffered the same fate, and the military saw its own bureaucratic institutions and rhetoric employed in increasingly bitter fights regarding regionalism, preservation, and land redistribution. Even the unpredicted arrival of hippie travelers caused many to question the social cost of tourism policy. Second, tourism plans, like many of the military's economic policies, ultimately failed to redistribute wealth.[103] COPESCO's strategy to absorb Cuzco's underemployed rural workforce in tourism proved overly optimistic and ambiguous.[104] Even at the height of COPESCO's hiring in 1974, the local press reported thousands of laborers unsuccessfully seeking employment with the institution.[105] COPESCO's plans to use tourism spending as a trickle-down or multiplying factor also largely failed. By 1981, jobs and investment provided by tourism employed only 3 percent of the Cuzco regional workforce.[106]

The failure to redistribute wealth points to the final problematic legacy of tourism development in Cuzco under the military. Tourism policy failed to resolve Cuzco's economic and political dependence. Historians of Cuzco have noted the paradoxical effect of the Velasquista government's reforms that, instead of empowering locals, contributed to increased regional dependence on the state.[107] Unfortunately, the highly technocratic and centralized nature of tourism development under the military continued this pattern. Although COPESCO did create jobs, most positions ultimately provided little training or savings for workers to actually reinvest as small entrepreneurs in the tourism economy. Materials, plans, and investments for COPESCO projects originated from outside Cuzco.[108] Finally, by focusing on attracting elite international travelers to Cuzco, COPESCO ensured that tourism development would require capital investment and technical skill beyond the ability of local actors. After 1972, domestic travel to Cuzco leveled, while the elite-oriented international tourism dominated by Lima and international capital increased (see chart 12.1). An IDB report assessing COPESCO warned that its policies led to the creation of a "dual economy" of separate agrarian and tourism interests.[109] The opening of Cuzco's Libertador Marriott in 1976 signaled the lost opportunity for public-sector and locally controlled tourism development envisioned by the military government and COPESCO. In 1975, an INC report alerted the government that its strategies had led to "consolidation of groups of power, in sectors dedicated to commerce, industry, and tourism."[110] The INC concluded: "This reflects a clear loss of initiative on the local level, as well as the entrepreneurial sector, leadership, and social conditions."[111] It appeared that the seeds of inequality endemic to Cuzco's present-day tourism economy were planted during the era of revolutionary military nationalism.

Notes

1. See advertisement in *El Comercio del Cusco* (hereafter *ECC*), October 18, 1974, 3, archived at Biblioteca Municipal del Cusco (hereafter BMC). Unless otherwise noted, all translations to English are my own.

2. Agrarian unrest and reform has been investigated by José María Caballero, *Economía agraria de la sierra peruana antes de la reforma agraria de 1969* (Lima: Instituto de Estudios Peruanos, 1981); Eduardo Fioravanti, *Latifundio y sindicalismo agrario en el Perú: El caso de los valles de La Convención y Lares (1958–1964)*, 2nd ed. (Lima: Instituto de Estudios Peruanos, 1976); David Guillet, *Agrarian Reform and Peasant Economy in Southern Peru* (Columbia: University of Missouri Press, 1979); Howard Handelman, *Struggle in the Andes: Peasant Political Mobilization in Peru* (Austin: University of Texas Press, 1975); Enrique Mayer, *Ugly Stores of the Peruvian Agrarian Reform* (Durham, NC: Duke University Press, 2009); Hugo Neira, *Los Andes: Tierra o muerte* (Santiago de Chile: Editorial Zyx, 1965). For studies on the Velasco military government,

see Cynthia McClintock and Abraham F. Lowenthal, eds., *The Peruvian Experiment Reconsidered* (Princeton, NC: Princeton University Press, 1983); George D. E. Philip, *The Rise and Fall of the Peruvian Military Radicals, 1968–1976* (London: Athlone, 1978); Richard J. Walter, *Peru and the United States, 1960–1975: How Their Ambassadors Managed Foreign Relations in a Turbulent Era* (University Park: Pennsylvania State University Press, 2010).

3. Archivo General de la Nación del Perú (hereafter AGNP), Lima, Fondo de Hacienda, H-6, Legajo 2396, Cámara de Comercio de Lima, *Boletín Semanal*, no. 726, March 16, 1964. The state hotel chain was also placed under the supervision of COTURPERU.

4. Faucett Advertisement, *Caretas*, no. 372, May 7–20, 1968, n.p.; see advertisement in *ECC*, June 7, 1968, 5, BMC.

5. Lima's Jorge Chávez International Airport opened in 1960, with its terminal facilities completed in 1965. Cuzco's new Alejandro Velasco Astete International Airport opened in 1965 in the Quispiquilla zone, to the east of the original airfield opened in the 1930s. See "Hilbck y los aeropuertos," *Caretas*, no. 208, November 10–24, 1960, 39; "Aeropuerto del Cuzco en Quispiquilla," *ECC*, March 6, 1964, 2, BMC.

6. Archivo del Ministerio de Comercio Exterior y Turismo (hereafter Archivo MINCETUR), Dirección General del Turismo (hereafter DGTUR), Serie Documental Estudio de Estrategia Turística (hereafter EET), VII–XIII, Caja 4, Jorge Merino Silva, *COPESCO, Estudio general del trabajo (Parte I): El turismo en Sud América con especial énfasis en el Perú* (June, 1971), Gráfico No. IV, n.p.

7. "Turismo, una industria de gran porvenir en el Perú," *Boletín de la COTURPERU*, no. 15, December 1965, 28, Biblioteca Nacional del Perú (hereafter BNP).

8. "Presupuesto de COTURPERU para 1965," *Boletín de la COTURPERU*, no. 5, January 1965, 4–6, BNP; "El Valle Sagrado de los Incas," *Boletín de la COTURPERU*, no. 5, January 1965, 18–22, BNP; "5 millones: Pavimentación carretera 'Valle Sagrado,'" *ECC*, December 30, 1964, 1, BMC.

9. 08.01.01–04-1, folder "Zona monumental—Informes en General, Cusco—año 1970–1990," "Bases para una política de conservación y desarrollo del Centro Histórico del Cusco," 9–10, Archivo Instituto Nacional de Cultura (hereafter Archivo INC).

10. César Villanueva (photographer), "Vicuñas nórdicas invaden Machu-Picchu," *Caretas*, no. 278, November 8–21, 1963, 44–47.

11. See illustration in *ECC*, June 2, 1970, 3, BMC.

12. Handelman, *Struggle in the Andes*, 81–83, 101; Niera, *Los Andes*, 95–99; Fioravanti, *Latifundio y sindicalismo agrario*; José Tamayo Herrera, *Historia regional del Cuzco republicano: Un libro de síntesis, 1808–1980* (Lima: Tarea, 2010), 191–213.

13. Handelman, *Struggle in the Andes*, 113–115.

14. "Foco" is a type of guerrilla combat popularized by Che Guevara that uses dedicated cells to radicalize the surrounding área.

15. Peter F. Klarén, *Peru: Society and Nationhood in the Andes* (Oxford: Oxford University Press, 2000), 329–336.

16. Otto Zausmer, "Filthy Gutter Where Gold Once Flowed," *Boston Globe*, June 1, 1960, 32.

17. See "Un paro como justa protesta," *ECC*, June 2, 1965, 1; "Huelga hotel en suspenso," *ECC*, November 17, 1965, 1; "COTURPERU no dá 500 mil, consejo dejará de operar," *ECC*, June 1, 1967, 1—all archived at BMC.

18. Biblioteca del Congreso del Perú, Decreto Ley 17525, March 21, 1969. COTURPERU was replaced with the Empresa Nacional del Turismo (ENTURPERU; National Tourism Company), a smaller institution tasked with managing the state hotels; DGTUR was formally created with Decreto Ley 18059, December 19, 1969.

19. DGTUR, EET VII–XII, Caja 4, Jean Marie Sertillange, *COPESCO: Estudio general de turismo (Parte IV), Necesidades y requerimientos en infraestructura de transportes en la zona Cusco-Puno*, September 1971, 1–4, Archivo MINCETUR.

20. DGTUR, EET VII–XII, Caja 4, Sertillange, *COPESCO: Estudio general del turismo (Parte IV)*, 3–4, Archivo MINCETUR.

21. DGTUR, EET VII–XII, Caja 4, *Plan COPESCO, Estudio económico financiero*, Archivo MINCETUR.

22. Ibid., 39, Archivo MINCETUR.

23. Philip, *Rise and Fall of the Peruvian Military Radicals*, 78; Liisa L. North, "Ideological Orientations of Peru's Military Rulers," in McClintock and Lowenthal, *The Peruvian Experiment Reconsidered*, 250, 256.

24. DGTUR, EET, VII–XII, Caja 4, *Plan COPESCO, Estudio económico financiero*, 305, Archivo MINCETUR.

25. Caballero, *Economía agraria de la sierra peruana*, 109.

26. DGTUR, EET I-VII, Caja 3, José Ignacio Estévez, *COPESCO: Estudio general del turismo (Parte III), Análisis y proyecciones del turismo en el eje Cuzco-Puno*, June 1971, 50–52, Archivo MINCETUR; Unidad Orgánica: Dirección Nacional del Turismo, Serie Documental, Estudio de Estrategia Turística COPESCO I–VII, Caja 3, Archivo MINCETUR.

27. DGTUR, EET I-VII, Caja 3, *Plan COPESCO, Un caso de desarrollo regional en función del turismo*, 1972, 3, Archivo MINCETUR.

28. Ibid., 4, Archivo MINCETUR.

29. DGTUR, EET VII–XII, Caja 4, *Plan COPESCO, Estudio económico financiero* (Lima: January 1972), anexo "PER-39," Archivo MINCETUR.

30. José de Mesa, "Prólogo," in *Cusco: La traza urbana de la ciudad inca* (Cuzco: Proyecto Per-39, UNESCO, INC), 1980, 13–17, Biblioteca, Centro Bartolomé de Las Casas (hereafter CBC).

31. The PER-39 project was led by Alfred Valencia Zegarra, Arminda Gibaja Oviedo, and José González Corrales under the supervision of the Mexican anthropologist José Luis Lorenzo. See Alfredo Valencia Zegarra, "Historia y evaluación de las investigaciones arqueológicas en el santuario histórico de Machu Picchu," in *Seminario-taller internacional arqueología del santuario histórico nacional y sitio patrimonio mundial de Machu Picchu: Estado de la cuestión y propuestas para un plan maestro* (Cuzco: N.p., 1993), 100, CBC.

32. Unidad Especial Ejecutadora, INC-Cusco, *Informe Final, obra de restauración: Conjunto arqueológico de Machupicchu, 1975–1981*, vol. 1 (Cuzco: N.p.,

1983), section 5.00, Biblioteca Ministerio de Cultura del Cusco (hereafter BMCC).

33. "¿A quiénes beneficia el turismo en el Cuzco?," *ECC*, June 20, 1967, 2, BMC.

34. "¡Autopista a Machupijchu es un hecho!," *ECC*, September 27, 1971, 1, BMC.

35. "Cinco trascendentes decretos," *ECC*, September 28, 1971, 2, BMC.

36. DGTUR, EET VII–XII, Caja 4, Silva, *COPESCO, Estudio general del trabajo (Parte I): El turismo en Sud América con especial énfasis en el Perú*, 41, 64–65, Archivo MINCETUR. Although some COPESCO scenarios recommended that the national government focus on attracting more tourists from South America, the North American market remained a development goal in all tourism plans.

37. "Productos cusqueños irán a China Popular," *ECC*, August 5, 1972, 1; "Soviéticos muy felices de conocer Machupijchu," *ECC*, June 13, 1972, 1—both archived at BMC.

38. ENTURPERU's hotel contracts are discussed in Charles T. Goodsell, *American Corporations and Peruvian Politics* (Cambridge, MA: Harvard University Press, 1974), 162; the landing rights dispute is reviewed in Walter, *Peru and the United States*, 303–304. Walter argues that relations between the Velasco government and the United States were generally friendly, especially after Allende's 1970 election in Chile made the Peruvian military government appear relatively moderate.

39. See front page of *ECC*, Jan. 1, 1974, 1, BMC.

40. DGTUR, EET, Caja 3, José Ignacio Estévez, *COPESCO: Estudio general del turismo (Parte III), Análisis y proyecciones del turismo en el eje Cuzco-Puno*, June 1971, 184, Archivo MINCETUR.

41. DGTUR, EET VII–XII, Caja 4, *Plan COPESCO, Estudio económico financiero*, 185–197, Archivo MINCETUR.

42. "Nuevo hotel Machupijchu costará s/. 240 millones," *ECC*, Feb. 4, 1972, 1, BMC.

43. *Estudio de factibilidad hotel Machu-Picchu*, vol. 2 (Lima: N.p., 1973), gráfico III, 1–32, Biblioteca del Ministerio de Cultura del Perú, Lima (hereafter BMCP).

44. Decreto Ley 18799, March 9, 1971, Biblioteca del Congreso del Perú. The INC replaced earlier efforts by the Prado and Belaúnde governments to consolidate cultural coordination in Peru under an institution named Casa de Cultura. Created by Decreto Supremo 48 on August 24, 1962, the Casa de Cultura acted as the national coordinating agency for cultural affairs, museums, and preservation. The institution suffered from budgetary and bureaucratic instability and was dissolved on March 9, 1972, to cede control to the INC.

45. PRO 25.002, "Aspectos legales y de procedimiento en la conservación y defensa de Machu Picchu," October 24, 1972, 1–2, Biblioteca de la Pontificia Universidad Católica del Perú, Colección Gobierno de las Fuerzas Armadas (hereafter CGRFA).

46. Ibid., 2–3, CGRFA. The report cited concerns regarding the 1929 "Tello

Law" protecting archaeological sites, the 1933 Athens Charter, the 1964 Venice Charter, and the 1967 Norms of Quito—all professional agreements emphasizing the importance of landscapes and environments surrounding historical sites.

47. "Del hotel en Machu Picchu," *El Comercio de Lima*, Dominical, June 18, 1972, BNP.

48. PRO 25.002, "Aspectos legales y de procedimiento en la conservación y defensa de Machu Picchu," October 24, 1972, 5–6, CGRFA.

49. "Americanistas dicen: No al hotel de Machupijchu," *ECC*, August 17, 1972, 1, BMC.

50. David F. Belnap, "'Lost City' Hotel," *Los Angeles Times*, August 6, 1972, F8.

51. "Comisión ejecutiva dirá dónde se ubica hotel en Machupijchu," *ECC*, June 12, 1972, 1, BMC.

52. "Hotel en Machupicchu: ¿Esperanza que se aleja? No," *ECC*, August 5, 1972, 12, BMC.

53. "Hotel en Machupicchu, tema que quema en Lima," *ECC*, August 22, 1972, 2, BMC.

54. "Señalan 1,400 hectáres de zona intangible: Machu Picchu," *ECL*, September 23, 1972, 1, BNP.

55. "Enemigos del Cusco, no cejan," *ECC*, September 6, 1972, 2, BMC.

56. "Piden respetarse ubicación de concurso para construir hotel del Machupijchu," *ECC*, October 11, 1972, 1, BMC.

57. "Cusco pidió audiencia a Velasco para exigir hotel en Machupijchu," *ECC*, October 12, 1972, 1, BMC.

58. "Directora del Instituto Nacional de Cultura: 'Ahora . . . hay que defender Machu Picchu de los cuzqueños,'" *El Correo*, October 17, 1972, 6, BNP.

59. "Directora de cultura debe venir para ver situación del turismo," *ECC*, October 18, 1972, 1, BMC.

60. "Otra vez el centralismo limeño vuelve sus garras contra Cusco," *ECC*, October 18, 1972, 2, BMC.

61. "Trabajadores con el Cusco," *ECC*, October 26, 1972, 1, BMC.

62. PRO 25.002, Martha Hildebrandt, Directora General del INC, "La política de conservación del patrimonio monumental y el caso de Machu Picchu," October 24, 1972, CGRFA; emphases in original.

63. Decreto Ley 19597, October 31, 1972, Biblioteca del Congreso del Perú.

64. COPESCO, *Estudio de factibilidad Hotel Machu Picchu*, vol. 2, 7–18, BMCP.

65. "Grave denuncia," *ECC*, June 1, 1973, 2, BMC.

66. "El hotel de Machu Picchu y el problema de su ubicación," ECL, September 25, 1973, 2, BNP.

67. Philip, *Rise and Fall of the Peruvian Military Radicals*, 131–136.

68. "Con más de mil millones harán obras infraestructura turística," *ECC*, September 13, 1973, 1; "Cientos de visitantes no conocen a Machupijchu a falta de carretera," *ECC*, October 5, 1973, 1—both archived at BMC.

69. "Machupicchu: Sueño irrealizable para gran mayoría de cusqueños," *ECC*, October 11, 1973, 2, BMC.

70. Tamayo, *Historia regional del Cuzco republicano*, 227.

71. "A costo mil mlls. se construye Hotel Machupijchu; 20 niveles," *ECC*, October 8, 1976, 1, BMC.

72. "Recortan partida para hotel de Machupijchu," *ECC*, September 11, 1976, 1, BMC.

73. Manuel Chávez Ballón, *Informe Machupijchu*, 12–13, CBC.

74. Ministerio de Cultura, 08.13.04–03-6, "Informe—Delimitación de áreas arqueológicas en los fundos de Q'ente y St. Rita de Q'ente," December 18, 1975, Archivo INC.

75. "Invaden el predio destinado a hotel," *ECC*, October 24, 1973, 1, BMC.

76. Interview with José Koechlin, December 3, 2011.

77. DGTUR, EET VIII–XIII, Caja 4, Silva, *COPESCO, Estudio general del trabajo (Parte I): El turismo en Sud América con especial énfasis en el Perú*, June 1971, 115, Archivo MINCETUR.

78. Luis Delboy, "Machu Picchu: La otra tierra prometida," ECL, Dominical, July 16, 1972, n.p., BNP.

79. Wendy Weeks, interviewed by Mark Rice, October 26, 2011.

80. "Top Grammies Won by Simon-Garfunkel," *New York Times* (hereafter *NYT*), March 17, 1971, 34.

81. Koechlin, interview by Rice, December 2, 2012; for an account of filming *Aguirre*, see Paul Cronin, ed., *Herzog on Herzog* (London: Faber and Faber, 2002), 76–94.

82. Display ad 1239, *NYT*, April 13, 1975, 252.

83. Eric Zolov, *Refried Elvis: The Rise of the Mexican Counterculture* (Berkeley: University of California Press, 1999), 141–146.

84. The Velasco state was no friend to youth counterculture as evidenced in the actions it took against Lima's budding rock 'n' roll culture as documented by Eric Zolov, "Peru's Overlooked Place in the History of Latin American Rock," *NPR Online*, April 21, 2011, http://www.npr.org/blogs/alt latino/2011/04/21/135042157/perus-overlooked-place-in-the-history-of-latin -american-rock.

85. "Tourist Supplement," no. 3, in *ECC*, September 5, 1973, BMC.

86. Chávez Ballón, *Informe Machupijchu*, 15, CBC.

87. Ibid., 5.

88. Ibid., 9.

89. "Los hippies y el crimen," *ECC*, December 5, 1969, 2, BMC.

90. "Paradiso de nudistas Machupicchu: Hippis," *ECC*, June 1, 1971, 1, BMC.

91. Ernesto Valdivia Pezo, "Influencia negativa en la juventud," *ECC*, June 22, 1971, 2, BMC.

92. "El Cusco se está convertiendo . . . ," *ECC*, December 31, 1973, 1, BMC.

93. "'Mercado Hippie' Plaza de Armas," *ECC*, June 21, 1974, 1, BMC.

94. "'Cusco: Limpio de Hippies' protest in streets and plazas," *ECC*, June 20, 1974, 4, BMC.

95. "Hallan marihuana en poder de hippie," *ECC*, September 5, 1972, 1, BMC.

96. "En Machupijchu descubren plantaciones de marihuana," *ECC*, June 5, 1973, 5, BMC.

97. "A un 'hippie' loretano la GC. capturó volando," *ECC*, June 24, 1973, 23, BMC.

98. Germán Alatrista, "Instalarán centros de información en las atalayas de Machu Picchu," *La Prensa*, April 18, 1973, 26, BNP.

99. Abraham F. Lowenthal, "The Peruvian Experiment Reconsidered," in McClintock and Lowenthal, *The Peruvian Experiment Reconsidered*, 419.

100. Arthur D. Little Co., *Estudio de orientación estratégica para inversiones en turismo en la región inka: Informe final—Abril de 1996* (1996), 6, CBC.

101. Oficina de Evaluación de Operaciones, Oficina del Contralor, *Una revisión interina del impacto económico y social del Plan COPESCO*, December 1981, 3–9, CBC.

102. Julio Cotler, "Democracy and National Integration in Peru," in McClintock and Lowenthal, *The Peruvian Experiment Reconsidered*, 28.

103. Rosemary Thorp and Geoffrey Bertram, *Peru, 1890–1977: Growth and Policy in an Open Economy* (London: Macmillan, 1978), 305–307.

104. Gerardo Lovón Zavala, "Dinámica interna de la sierra," in *Estrategias para el desarrollo de la Sierra*, ed. Alvaro Ortiz (Cuzco: Universidad Nacional Agraria La Molina and Centro de Estudios Rurales Andinos Bartolomé de Las Casas, 1986), 151–171.

105. "Mucha desocupación hay en el Cusco," *ECC*, October 22, 1974, 1, BMC.

106. Gerardo Lovón Zavala, *Mito y realidad del turismo en el Cusco* (Cuzco: Centro Bartolomé de Las Casas, 1982), 9–21.

107. Tamayo, *Historia regional del Cuzco republicano*, 220; José Luis Rénique, *Los sueños de la sierra* (Lima: CEPES, 1991), 266.

108. Lovón Zavala, *Mito y realidad del turismo*, 9–21.

109. Oficina de Evaluación de Operaciones, Oficina del Contralor, *Una revisión interina*, 19, CBC.

110. 08.01.01-04-1, folder "Zona monumental—Informes en General, Cusco—año 1970–1990," "Bases para una política de conservación y desarrollo del Centro Histórico del Cusco," 11–13, Archivo INC.

111. 08.01.01-04-1, folder "Zona monumental—Informes en General, Cusco—ano 1970–1990," "Bases para una política de conservación y desarrollo del Centro Histórico del Cusco," 23–28, Archivo INC.

CHAPTER 13

From Repression to Revolution: Velasquismo in Amazonia, 1968–1975

STEFANO VARESE

A Personal Prologue

The guiding theme of these reflections is related to my intellectual and activist itinerary spanning twenty years of my life in Peru and Mexico. In this opportunity I would like to focus on the relation between the postoligarchic nation-state of Peru and the ethnically diverse peoples and ethnicities that constitute the national community, especially in Amazonia.

I fell in love with Amazonia when, at age seventeen, I traveled to the upper Huallaga River with my father and during seven days we went downriver on a raft of balsa wood guided by two local *balseros*. We were going to visit an old friend of my father, a socialist intellectual who had decided to spend the rest of his life in Puerto Tocache, a small village with no electricity or communication by road with the rest of Peru. It was at the end of the 1950s. By 1967, I had completed my doctoral dissertation in anthropology with a study of the Campa-Asháninka of the Gran Pajonal, published in 1968 as *La sal de los cerros: Una aproximación al mundo campa*.[1]

In October 1968, the Revolutionary Government of the Armed Forces (RGAF), under the leadership of General Juan Velasco Alvarado, put in motion a series of radical social reforms aimed at transforming the indigenous and peasant regions of Peru from a semifeudal system of land tenure and exploited labor into modern forms of self-managed cooperative and communal rural enterprises. I had the privilege, or the bad taste, according to others, of working for the revolutionary government of Juan Velasco Alvarado since the beginning of 1969 until the beginning of 1975, charged with organizing and promoting the "agrarian" and territorial legislation regarding the indigenous peoples of Amazonia. As head of the Division of Native Communities of the Jungle (jefe de la División de Comunidades Nativas de la Selva), I was incorporated into the Ministry of Agriculture and the General Office of Agrarian Reform and Rural Settlement (Dirección General de Reforma Agraria y Asentamiento Rural; DGRAyAR). A few years later, I was transferred, with the Program of Indigenous Peoples of Amazonia, to a branch of the Sistema Nacional de Apoyo a la Movilización Social (SINAMOS; National System of Support for Social Mobilization) and a supporting project of the UN-ILO (International Labour Organization; Oficina Internacional del Trabajo de Naciones Unidas; UN-OIT) directed by the Brazilian anthropologist Darcy Ribeiro. In 1974, the RGAF enacted Decree Law 20653, Ley de Comunidades Nativas,[2] a substantial piece of revolutionary legislation that was the result of five years of research; social and ethnic mobilization of Amazonian people through congresses and workshops; and consultations with indigenous communities, their emerging organizations, and the few experts on Amazonian anthropology that were available in Peru and Latin America at that time.

Peruvian Amazonia: Terra Nullius

I had joined the Velasco revolution thanks to an "invitation" from the sociologist Carlos Delgado delivered to me personally by Mario Vásquez, an anthropologist involved in the revolution. Delgado and Vásquez were playing an important role in the ideological and institutional construction of SINAMOS and the agrarian reform institute. Both had earned degrees from Cornell University (Delgado an MA and Vásquez a PhD), both were former members of the APRA Party, and both were pragmatic idealists. Mario Vásquez was a Quechua speaker, a member of an indigenous community of the Ancash region, and together with Carlos Delgado went to Cornell University to study with Allan Holmberg, the director of the Vicos Project of applied anthropology. During the late 1950s and 1960s, Peru had developed a substantial school of Andean archaeology and anthropology, housed mainly at the Universidad Nacional de San Marcos and partially at the Universidad Católica. In Peru, starting with founding scholars such as Julio C. Tello, a Quechua speaker from the central Andes, and the Cuzqueño Luis E. Valcárcel, the scholarly emphasis had always been on Andean studies. Amazonia had been left out of national academic interest and was reserved mostly for a few foreign scholars and educated travelers.[3]

Vásquez and Delgado challenged me with the formidable task of extending into the Amazon area the land reform process initiated by the military revolution in the coastal and highland regions, starting by defining the needs of the "tribal indigenous people" of the rain forest and developing a legal framework for protecting their territorial rights and guaranteeing their language, cultural, and political rights—all of which, Vásquez reminded me, had to be done swiftly and with scarce financial and technical resources. Most importantly, these studies and the policy planning had to take place against the backdrop of long-held cultural and racial prejudices against the indigenous peoples of Amazonia, biases that were shared by the majority of criollo and mestizo Peruvians, the politically threatened oligarchy, the state bureaucracy, and even some of the progressive military officers who were running a government intended to bring social and cultural democracy to all Peruvians.[4]

In the early months of 1969, I founded the Division of Native Communities of the Jungle as a branch of the Ministry of Agriculture, the DGRAyAR, and SINAMOS. I chose the names "Native" and "Community" with the ethnopolitical intention of debunking the old colonial lexicon used at that time in Peru to address the Amazonian indigenous peoples and all things related to the Amazonia: *"tribus indias," "chunchos," "salvajes," "selvícolas," "charapas,"* nomads without agriculture, hunter-gatherers living unorganized in the middle of the forest, and so forth. The official terminology used by the RGAF to refer to the indigenous peoples of the Amazonian region, even before the enactment of Decree Law 20653, became "Natives" and "Native Communities." The agrarian reform of 1969 had already substituted the terms *"indios"* and *"indígenas"* for those of *"campesinos"* and *"comunidades campesinas" (peasants* and *peasant communities,* respectively). These changes of terminology were an essential part of the social and historical reconfiguration of the national Peruvian community as a whole and the self-perception and representation of the Peruvian peoples. None of these decisions were taken lightly by the urban criollos and mestizos, especially the elites and the middle class, who were losing ground on their historical monopoly on Peru's national identity.

Precedents and Context

The enormity of the undertaking I was charged with by the revolutionary government was augmented by my own awareness that my expertise was really limited to the Asháninka people of the Gran Pajonal, the

Yánesha of the Selva Central, and some other indigenous communities that I had visited briefly along the Ucayali, Marañón, Santiago, and Amazon Rivers. I suppose that at my then twenty-eight years of age I was enough of a risk taker and an idealist to underestimate the consequences of my limited anthropological knowledge. In any event, housed in an ugly and dilapidated office in the old Ministry of Labor building, and staffed with a few former anthropology students of mine, a "constitutional" lawyer, an agronomist, and a Peruvian sociologist of Chinese descent whose cousin had been in the Che Guevara guerrilla movement in Bolivia, the Division of Native Communities started its mission by producing a social assessment of the indigenous peoples of Peru's Amazonia. With no reliable demographic data or information about territorial occupation, land tenure, or forest management, the survey task soon became an overwhelming challenge. Peru's academia and government administrations had no tradition whatsoever of social studies or even censuses of the region.[5] The Amazon area—encompassing more than half the national territory of the country—had never been seriously taken into consideration by the ruling elites or by academia.

The ethnic survey that we were initiating had to rely on missionary sources: archives of Catholic orders such as the Franciscans, Dominicans, and Jesuits, or Protestant and Evangelical sects; documentation prepared by groups such as the Summer Institute of Linguistics/ Wycliffe Bible Translators, the New Tribes Mission, and various other evangelical missions, all of which became our most important—albeit contested—sources of information. The desolate landscape the state administration inherited after more than one hundred and fifty years of systematic neglect of the peoples and lands of Amazonia began to burden us. What were the key problems of the Amazon indigenous communities? What were their claims? What were their demands? Were there any forms of indigenously generated political programs, agendas, and platforms? Who and where were the indigenous leaders, the representatives of dozens of ethnic groups and literally thousands of local communities?

During the final months of 1969 and part of 1970, the small team of social scientists of the Division of Native Communities carried out a pilot study of the Aguaruna (Awajún) communities of the Alto Marañón River. Through this study we were able to show the subordinate position of the Aguaruna (today, Awajún) and Huambiza (today, Wampi) peoples within the regional market economy and political system, as well as the dramatic loss of indigenous territorial possessions and control of resources at the hands of the state-planned military colonization, which, since the administration of Fernando Belaúnde Terry (1963–1968), had encouraged the occupation of indigenous territories and land by civilians and demobilized army personnel from the coast and the Andean highlands. By 1971, the division had issued a broader assessment of the indigenous peoples of Peruvian Amazonia. The study was labeled "Confidential Document" and stowed away in the bureaucratic maze of the Ministry of Agriculture. I was able to rescue the document in its entirety when I was appointed principal investigator at the UN-ILO/SINAMOS Centro de Estudios de Participación Popular and used it as a basis for the numerical experimentation and modeling that was coordinated and directed by Óscar Varsavsky and Darcy Ribeiro.[6]

Gloomy Diagnosis, Optimistic Outlook

Our diagnosis of Peruvian Amazonia and its indigenous peoples/Native Communities was confirming that five centuries of systematic political oppression, economic exploitation, and ethnic-racial discrimination had had a profound impact on the ability of some of the indigenous peoples to recover a sense of autonomy and political and cultural sovereignty, as well as the social energy needed to assert their collective rights in the new revolutionary legal system. I myself was misled by my field experience with the Asháninka people into thinking that their proud resistance and cyclical return to higher levels of autonomy in their relations with colonial and modern Peru were common historical traits to be expected in other indigenous peoples of Amazonia. We soon discovered that a historical and cultural fracture existed between the indigenous peoples of pre-Andean Amazonia (Selva Alta or Ceja de Selva) and the indigenous peoples of the Amazonia lowlands (Selva Baja). Of the almost seventy ethnic nationalities of Peruvian Amazonia, the most successful in resisting the ravages of colonialism and the expansive wild capitalism were the pre-Andean native peoples: the Asháninka, the Yánesha, the Nomatsiguenga, the Quechua of San Martín, the Machiguenga, the Yine (Piro), and the Aguaruna. We could only speculate that the geographical difficulties of colonizing these inhospitable terrains of the upper jungle during the colonial centuries and the early years of the republic allowed these communities to maintain a higher degree of independence in relative isolation. Even the massacres and genocidal wars of the rubber era, at the end of the nineteenth century, may have been somehow less intense in parts of these marginal indigenous areas. The relative demographic stability of these Native Communities confirmed these hypotheses: the Asháninka, for example, are one of the largest groups of the whole Amazonian basin. They numbered an estimated 40,000 people in the 1970s, and today they number around 70,000, in spite of the massive tragic losses of lives at the hands of Shining Path, the Movimiento Revolucionario Túpac Amaru (MRTA; Túpac Amaru Revolutionary Movement), and the army and police in the decade of the 1980s.

All of these pre-Andean Amazonian indigenous communities were also showing a remarkable ability to adapt to the challenges brought about by the expansion of the capitalist frontier and the penetration of the extractivist agroforestry and cattle ranches. The Campa-Asháninka of the Upper Perené River, who were "given" to the British Corporation, together with thousands of hectares of tropical rain forest, by the Peruvian government as payment for the British sale of arms to Peru during the War of the Pacific in 1879, had organized themselves by the early twentieth century into a rural labor union demanding fair labor treatment and better salaries. The rest of Amazonia—the lowlands, the hinterlands, the interfluvial Tierras Altas, and the inundated Igapós that had become regions of refuge for the Indian survivors of centuries of killings, persecutions, *correrías*, slavery, and unashamed capitalist exploitation—presented a very different image. There, the communities that had maintained some relations with the mestizo *ribereño* peoples and the regional state representatives were disguising their Indian identity in a strategy of survival that they had adopted since the times of colonial missionaries. I myself was deceived by this hidden "indigeneity" when, in the early 1960s, I spent three months in what I thought was a mestizo village of the Lower Ucayali River, Flor de Punga, but that years later turned out to be a village of Kukama/Cocamilla, founded in the eighteenth century by Guaraní Indians who were navigating the Amazon basin from their original location, probably in southeastern Brazil or Paraguay. These mestizo *ribereños* became Nativos and Indians again when years later the Law of Native Communities gave them the opportunity to claim collective possession of their lands as indigenous inhabitants.

In light of these findings and the long relationship that I had with the Native peoples of the upper jungle (Montaña/Selva Alta), I was biased in favor of starting the division's program of social mobilization and participatory consultation with the communities of the central and northern jungle: the Campa-Asháninka, the Yánesha, the Nomatsiguenga, the Aguaruna (Awajún), and the Huambiza (Wampi). Soon I realized, however, that more important than mobilizing the Native Communities was to address the more difficult task of sensitizing the revolutionary cadres and the bureaucrats about the Native Peoples of Amazonia and the complexity of the environmental/ecological issues of the Amazon tropical rain forest.

Indian Knowledge Meets Modern Obscurantism

In the late 1960s and early 1970s, the anthropological and ecological information about Peruvian Amazonia was abysmal. My own doctoral dissertation bibliography, compiled in 1967, registered only a couple of texts that could be considered of anthropological and environmental interest. The remaining sources were ethnohistorical documents; missionaries' apologies and official reports; and a few writings of travelers, mostly foreigners. Some of the key studies of Peruvian Amazonia, such as those by Michael Harner, John Bodley, William Denevan, and Gerald Weiss, were written and published in the early, mid-, and late 1970s.[7] This desolate academic landscape and the general ignorance among Peruvians regarding Amazonia constituted a colossal obstacle for achieving even a minimal consensus among the policy makers of the Peruvian Revolution on what to do in Amazonia and how to carry forward a radical program of social justice, cultural and political equity, and ethnic diversity. Among the few informed urban intellectuals and technocrats, the dominant mode of thinking about the Amazonian region and the tropical rain forest was highly influenced by the analyses of Betty Meggers and her pessimistic vision of Amazonia as an environment too harsh and hostile to humans to allow for the development of complex forms of communities and sophisticated political and economic organizations. Amazonia and its people were destined to remain at a primary level of social and economic organization, oppressed by an unforgiving environment and reduced to a life of subsistence and mere survival.[8]

Betty Meggers's studies did, however, show that the Amazonian Indians had developed to the maximum of their potential all the technologies and techniques that had allowed them to implement an economy of subsistence sufficient for a stable reproduction of the community. The slash-and-burn horticulture and the polyculture combined with fishing, hunting, and gathering was productive enough to guarantee the reproduction and survival of the community. This much was clear even to the skeptical urban observers. If there were still Indians in Amazonia, it was because of their adaptation to a hostile and complex environment and their ability to innovate, modify, and adapt their productive technologies to the social and environmental transformations brought in by external colonists.

During centuries and millennia, the occupation and use of the Amazonian landscape by indigenous peoples had produced thousands of well-adapted and dynamic communities that could manage the diverse and complex ecosystems of the tropical rain forest and establish a network of communication and trade that facilitated the exchange of valuable items such as salt; stone axes; curare (*Strichnos toxifera*) poison for hunting; some basic technologies of production, consumption, and transportation; and, most importantly, a great number of cultivars and semidomesticated plants that came from different Amazonian ecosystems and niches of domestication.

What was not really clear at that time to all of us researchers of Amazonia was the fundamental anthropogenic characteristic of the whole Amazonian tropical forest. Starting in the 1990s, geographers, anthropologists, ecologists, and bioarchaeologists began to rediscover the hidden history of Amazonia. This was a history of at least ten thousand years of intensive agriculture, agroforestry, fruit tree cultivation, raised fields surrounded by water and navigable channels, and dense populations living in large towns connected by roads with other towns and villages—all of these evidence that the whole greater Amazonian region had been an area of multiple and complex civilizations. The "fantasies" of the sixteenth-century Spanish explorer Francisco de Orellana and his chronicler Fray Gaspar de Carbajal about hundreds of heavily populated towns along the Napo River and the Amazonas, so close to each other that they could be considered one long city, turned out to be true. Over millennia, the indigenous peoples built Amazonia as a vast anthropogenic cultivated forest that hosted and supported millions of people and thousands of different communities.[9]

What we thought at the time was the highest achievement of the Amazonian Indians, the slash-and-burn rotating polyculture, turned out to be a consequence of the Iberian invasion and colonialism that brought and disseminated metal axes and machetes, allowing for a faster landuse rotation, increased deforestation, and the adoption of short-cycle cultigens rather than fruit tree plantations that demanded long-term planning and more stable residency. The dramatic population decline of the first few decades of European occupation due to exogenous diseases, mistreatment, starvation, and lack of production caused the migration of the surviving Amazonian Natives to seek refuge in the interfluvial zones—Tierras Altas—and in Upper Amazonia—Montaña. These are more isolated and protected areas, but at the same time they are less productive in terms of soil quality and access to gaming and fishing. In Peru's 1970s social and cultural environment of fervent evangelical modernists, it was difficult to present and illustrate the state of Amazonian Indians as another case of postcolonial adaptation rather than the normal slow evolutionary stage achieved by "primitive savages."

Revolutionary Inventiveness

I had invited to the Division of Native Communities a few former students of mine to work with me on the proposed legislation (Law of Native Communities) and on the operational definitions that would accompany the law and its implementation. One of these collaborators, Alberto Chirif, quickly became the most informed and knowledgeable Peruvian anthropologist specialized in Amazonia, and he is still today the prime researcher and activist of Peru's Amazonian indigenous peoples. In the Division of Native Communities; in the SINAMOS/UN-ILO Centro; and during field visits that included participation in Native Communities' assemblies, observations, conversations with Native members of emerging local organizations, and the administration and analysis of a few surveys, we began the construction of possible models of communal land tenure and territorial control and management. One of the first issues we had to clarify for the ideologues and policy makers of the coastal and Andean agrarian reform was the fundamental differences that existed between Andean indigenous peasant communities—usually congregated around a stable endogamous village—and the residential and kinship system of most of the Amazonian Natives, which usually follow a pattern of social segmentation and dispersed exogamic-neolocal residency. Faced with the need to simplify and generalize the definition of the Native Amazonian social unit beyond the family (nuclear or extended), we literally invented the term "Comunidad Nativa," and we assigned a quantitative and qualitative value to it. The Division of Native Communities began to survey regional samples—Selva Central and Marañón River to begin with—designating groups of indigenous families and lineages as Comunidades Nativas with a specific geographical position in the region, and defined boundaries and native names for people and places, if possible in the local indigenous language. In a sense, I can say that in the division we were deconstructing the colonial understanding of Amazonian Indians and attempting to restore for the Peruvian people the image of the real social, cultural, and ecological entities that were still called tribes of *chunchos* by most Peruvians.

The anthropologist Shane Greene has recently traced back to the Velasco era the contemporary emergence of an Andean social movement that is reindigenizing itself, abandoning the decades-old social self-representation as peasants: "Up until this recent [2008–2010] multicultural turn most community organizing was characterized by a distinct lack of alliance between Andeans, mostly self-representing as peasants, and Amazonians, mostly self-representing as indigenous. One is forced to reflect on the fact that the Velasco period was a critical moment. The state took a major step toward consolidating the peasantization of indigenous Andeans and a major step toward explicitly indigenizing Amazonians via the Native Communities Law."[10]

Legitimizing the Native Community and Fostering Territoriality

By the time I had moved from the Division of Native Communities to the Centro de Estudios de Participación Popular within SINAMOS,[11] the idea of Native Community as the initial social unit to be used for analysis and administrative actions for the Amazonian indigenous people was consolidated and accepted in the official revolutionary language. At this point, through a tight cooperation with the staff of Alberto Chirif, who had become the head of the Division of Native Communities, we began to review critically the "land and resources" tenure system and introduce the concept of territory for the whole ethnic group (ethnolinguistic communities/nationalities comprising dozens or hundreds of dispersed local communities). The task was to debunk the modern urban definition of an Andean community as a compacted localized social unit living in a village located in a contiguous and continuous larger area of communally managed land, which had been applied to Amazonian Indians. We had to make the argument that Amazonian indigenous peoples do not think of land as family-managed arable plots that can be occupied generation after generation by the legitimate members of the community. The Amazonian Indians conceive the temporary place where they have their houses and cultivated plot (the *cha-cra*) as part of a larger place/space that they claim together with all the other lineages of the ethnic group in an orderly way and regulated by unwritten customary laws that are based on a complex cosmological rationality that many years later I came to define as *cosmocentric*, in opposition to the *anthropocentric* rationality of Mediterranean-European origin.[12] I take the opportunity here to summarize the main arguments that I made to expound my hypothesis about *cosmocentrism*, reminding the readers that in the early 1970s, when I was working for the Velasco revolution, I was just beginning to conceptualize these ideas based on my empirical ethnographical knowledge and my reading of indigenous peoples' history.[13]

Cosmocentrism and Spiritual Ecology

We must keep in mind that during more than five hundred years, millions of indigenous peoples of the Americas have struggled to maintain or regain their independence in the social and economic spheres, their political self-determination, and fundamentally their ethnic sovereignty, understood and practiced as an exercise of authority and dominion over their autonomous intellectual, spiritual, and cultural life. Forms of combined active and hidden resistance have been collectively and individually practiced in the realm of intangible culture, in the secrecy and clandestinity of their inner personae, where language, culture, and consciousness intersect in the daily task of reading the universe and living and acting in it. As we well know, under colonial occupation this immense indigenous labor of interpreting, stewarding, and nurturing the world could not always be accomplished. While imperial and colonial intentions were aimed at controlling the totality of the subjugated peoples—their spirit, reason, bodies, and labor—the larger, more systematic and continuing effort has been directed toward the expropriation of land and resources, as well as of the associated indigenous systematic knowledge and technologies. And this is why even a superficial revisionist look at the history of indigenous peoples' resistance to imperialism reveals the centrality of both the territorial issue and the "environmental" question since the very beginning of Indians' opposition to Europeans and Euro-Americans.

In the specific case of Amazonia, the indigenous peoples' epistemological and axiological approach to the relationship between individual and society and between these and "nature" is based on what a Lakota scholar, Elisabeth Cook-Lynn, has called the "language of place": a language embedded in the locality, that is, the concrete space where culture is grounded and reproduced in a familiar landscape where the naming of things, space, objects, plants, animals, living peoples and the dead, the underworld and the celestial infinity evokes the total cosmic web as an awesome and mysterious social and divine construction.[14] This is why I believe that a paradigmatic shift that accentuates "topos" rather than "logos" is needed to understand the Amazonian indigenous peoples. Their cultural language is constructed around a number of principles and a cultural logic or topology that privileges diversity and heterogeneity over homogeneity, eclecticism over dogma, and multiplicity over bipolarity. As I deepened my understanding of Amazonian Natives together with my colleagues in the division and the Centro, I became aware of the powerful symbolic meaning of the Indian chakra, the always-present polyculture that represents, reproduces, and mimics the necessary biodiversity of the tropical rain forest and is a constant reminder to the members of the community that what they do daily is to reproduce at a smaller scale the cosmogonic/foundational act of the deities, whichever they may be. The chakra becomes a metaphor for the relational reality of the indigenous world where every biological and physical entity is part of a larger cosmic network of relations, a system of kin, a net of relatives.

These conceptions hold that concentrating, nourishing, and developing diversity in the reduced space of human agricultural and agroforestry intervention, as well as in the larger space of the economic activity of the entire group, is the most appropriate way of dealing with land, water, animals, trees, plants, the conservation of resources, and in general the preservation of the environment and the nurturing of nature. Another important characteristic of Amazonian civilizations (plural) is that some of their historical expressions took the complementary route of "foraging the forest" while minimizing the horticultural intervention. Foraging—or what traditional anthropologists used to call "hunting and gathering"—is always present among Amazonian Natives and can be seen as a permanent, thousand-year-old anthropogenic transformation and regeneration of the forest. Foraging, as we have now learned from the Huaorani of Ecuador, implies a transgenerational refined knowledge of the forest: palms, fruit trees, hunting grounds, burial sites, sites of old cultivars of yuca (*Manihot esculenta*), and places of longhouses (*malocas*) are visited in seasonal cycles year after year.[15] So that jungle, which to modern Western eyes appears to be a chaotic mix of thousands of plants and insects, becomes a "cultivated" and nurtured environment that is constantly "humanized" by one of the members of the cosmic net of relatives: the humans.

Clearly, Amazonian Natives' agricultural biodiversity and environmental management are millennial practices and sciences that resulted from early intentional and planned domestication of plants such as yuca, corn, beans, squash, *ají*, sweet potato, peanuts, coca, tomato, avocado, tobacco, and thousands of other cultigens and semidomesticated plants. What needs to be pointed out is that the extreme variety of indigenous cultigens and semidomesticated plants is matched by an equally diverse and multiple use of the environment and a systematic cultural preoccupation with maintaining and increasing the diversity of the biosphere. Polyculture and the intentional maintenance of biodiversity are historical realities but also metaphors of the indigenous peoples' cultural gravitation toward diversity rather than homogeneity, eclecticism rather than dogma.

Polyculture, the nurturing of biodiversity, and the multiple uses of the environment seem to constitute the crucial conception of what has been called by James Scott and others the "moral economy" of indigenous peoples.[16] This axial cultural notion, which operates along the "principle of diversity," accompanies and shapes the whole cosmology of innumerable Amazonian indigenous societies that place at the *center* of the universe not the man (the anthropocentric, patriarchal, dominant character of both the sacred and secular history of Euro-America), but rather diversity itself, expressed in the multiplicity of deities/sacred beings with their polymorphic characteristics and at times contradictory functions. I can mention the case of the Asháninka people as an example of this type of ontology. The Asháninka maintain that the cosmogonic creator is incarnated in the cultural heroes Pachacamaite (Giver of Goods), Oriátziri (Sun), and Katziri (Moon), who delivered the first cultivated plants and allow year after year the regeneration of the forest—but only if nurtured and treated respectfully.[17]

Amazonian indigenous people, in contrast to Euro-Americans and their anthropocentrism, seem to have constructed over millennia *cosmocentric* and polycentric cosmologies based on the logic of diversity and the logic of reciprocity. A diverse cosmos in which no center is privileged, no singularity is hegemonic, a world that is constantly enriched by the interaction of each of its elements, even those that are antithetical, requires a moral code (a customary code of behavior) based on the logic of reciprocity. Whatever is taken has to be returned in similar and comparable "value." Whatever I receive (goods, gifts, services, resources) I will have to reciprocate at some point with similar and comparable value. What I take from Earth has to be returned, and what I give to Earth or to the gods or my human counterparts will be given back to me. Many decades ago, the sociologist of religion G. Van der Leeuw synthesized this civilizational logic with the Latin formula "Do ut possis dare" (I give so that you may be able to give).[18]

Social Economy, Modernity, and the Peruvian Revolution in Native Amazonia

At this point it may be clear that during the years of the Peruvian Revolution it was unrealistic to raise the political and administrative debate regarding the Amazonian indigenous communities to these types of specialized anthropological arguments. The cadres of Velasco's revolutionary government were mostly "traditional" sociologists, economists, Andeanist anthropologists, and agronomists who were not particularly trained to deal with the Amazonian tropical rain-forest or indigenous communities.

Our challenge was to bring the discussion to the need for state-guaranteed territorial titles for groups of Native Communities of the same ethnolinguistic family. These territories had to be continuous, ideally ethnically homogeneous, respectful of historical occupation by the same group, and identifiable by indigenous toponymy. In cases where there was a presence of nonindigenous Peruvians or foreign occupants—either small farmers (colonos) or larger agricultural, cattle, and forestry firms—the state would expropriate these lands, pay compensation for the "improvements," compare these costs to unpaid retroactive taxes (as was done in the agrarian reform law), and offer relocation to the small farmers and liquidation or new concession contracts to the larger enterprises. We included in the law the possibility that the Native Community could decide in its general assembly if they wanted to continue to "host" Peruvian colonists within their new territorial boundaries. In the law proposal, we were careful to separate the issue of the "social economy" (subsistence economy) of the community from the emerging cases of "market economy" activities being adopted by some of the communities, especially those that were close to roads or other means of communication. We wanted to establish the principle that guaranteeing "traditional" territorial occupation and the free choice of continuing to practice indigenous social economy would not be interpreted by the state and its government as a license to marginalize Native Communities from the market and the state services provided to the rest of Peruvian citizens (communication and transportation, energy, education, political rights, fair marketing practices, and access to loans). We also included in the law a mechanism for community self-administration of justice according to customary law (excluding criminal charges), and we provided the administrative mechanisms for each Native Community to open their "office" of Civil Registration (Registro Civil) that would record births, deaths, and civil unions. A special note was made to allow the Native commoners to register themselves with their own Indian names, breaking the colonial, missionary, and republican practice of giving Spanish names to every Amazonian Native they would come in contact with. One extremely important measure included in the law was the establishment of legal mechanisms to allow the communities to associate themselves in federations of the same ethnicity and then to associate those federations into multiethnic confederations.

What Was Achieved?

By the time the Law of Native Communities (Decree Law 20653) was approved and began to be implemented from 1974–1975 (during the administration of General Velasco) until 2006 (the administration of Alejandro Toledo), 1,212 Native Communities were titled for a total of 10,105,505 hectares. The highest percentile of titles occurred during a period of barely two years of the Velasco revolutionary regime (1974–1975).[19] The process of defining the territorial claims and issuing the titles to Native Communities during this thirty-one-year period (1975–2006) was mostly done by Peru's civil society, NGOs, grassroots organizations (*organizaciones de base*), and Amazonian indigenous organizations, with a reduced number of actions also taken by the various pro–free market administrations of Francisco Morales Bermúdez, Fernando Belaúnde Terry, Alan García, Alberto Fujimori, Valentín Paniagua, and Alejandro Toledo. Most of these limited state actions were the result of popular mobilization and pressures by indigenous organizations, activists, and NGOs.

According to Alberto Chirif and Pedro García Hierro, what appears to be the most important result of more than thirty years of Amazonian

Native Communities' struggle to regain territorial sovereignty is their amazing ability to organize ethnopolitical civil institutions and establish a dynamic platform of social demands to present to the various government administrations. It is now impossible in contemporary Peru to disregard the active presence of the Amazonian Indians/Native Communities and their local, regional, national, and even international organizations, which put forward clear proposals; advance their own social and cultural projects of political and ethnic autonomy; and demand environmental, social, and political justice as well as cultural democracy.[20]

A few political analysts of the RGAF led by Juan Velasco Alvarado have often asked rhetorically if those of us who were involved in different capacities in the process could or would have done anything different. I can only speculate from my own very limited perspective that such a question should be addressed not to us, active participants in the movement, but rather to those Peruvian citizens of the whole political and ideological spectrum, from the oligarchic extreme right to the Maoist extreme left. We should ask if their condescending abstention, critical sidelining, or socialist perfectionism have contributed in any tangible way to the betterment of the peoples of Peru, that is, to a higher level of social justice, a more culturally democratic system, and the improvement of the lives of millions of Andean and Amazonian indigenous peoples.[21]

"El Chino Velasco" would probably be comforted and relieved to know that at least one of his utopian dreams has flourished in the midst of Amazonia.

Notes

1. The first edition was published in Lima by Universidad Peruana de Ciencias y Tecnologías in 1968. Subsequent editions appeared in 1976 (Lima: INIDE), in 2002 in English (Norman: University of Oklahoma Press), in 2006 (Lima: Fondo Editorial del Congreso del Perú), in 2011 (La Habana: Fondo Editorial Casa de las Américas), and in 2015 in French (Paris: L'Harmattan). Unless otherwise noted, all translations to English are my own.

2. Decreto Ley 20653, "Ley de Comunidades Nativas y de Promoción Agropecuaria de las Regiones de Selva y Ceja de Selva."

3. See Stefano Varese, Guillermo Delgado, and Rodolfo L. Meyer, "Indigenous Anthropologies beyond Barbados," in *A Companion to Latin American Anthropology*, ed. Deborah Poole (Malden, MA: Blackwell, 2008), 375–398. For this section, I rely on my book *Witness to Sovereignty: Essays on the Indian Movement in Latin America* (Copenhagen: International Group for Indigenous Affairs-IWGIA, 2006).

4. Varese, *Witness to Sovereignty*, 61–63.

5. In fact, I was officially charged with providing an estimate of the indigenous population in Amazonia to the National Census Office and to the National Institute of Planning (Instituto Nacional de Planificación; INP).

6. See Óscar Varsavsky, Ignacy Sachs, and Carlos de Senna Figueiredo, *Planificación y participación* (Lima: Ediciones del Centro de Estudios de Participación Popular, 1974).

7. Michael J. Harner, *The Jívaro: People of the Sacred Waterfalls* (Garden City, NY: Anchor Books, 1972); John Bodley, "Campa Socio-Economic Adaptation" (PhD diss., University of Oregon, 1970); William Denevan, "Campa Subsistence in the Gran Pajonal, Eastern Peru," *Geographical Review* 61, no. 4 (1971): 496–518; Gerald Weiss, "The Cosmology of the Campa Indians of Eastern Peru" (PhD diss., University of Michigan, 1969).

8. Betty J. Meggers, *Amazonia: Man and Culture in a Counterfeit Paradise.* (Chicago: Aldine, 1971). In 1958, Betty Meggers had published "Ambiente y cultura en la cuenca del Amazonas: Revisión de la teoría del determinismo ambiental," in *Estudios sobre ecología humana*, Estudios Monográficos No. 3 (Washington, DC: Unión Panamericana).

9. For an outstanding summary of the reconceptualization of the long history of Amazonia, see Charles C. Mann, *1491: New Revelations of the Americas Before Columbus* (New York: Knopf, 2005).

10. Shane Greene, *Customizing Indigeneity: Paths to a Visionary Politics in Peru* (Stanford, CA: Stanford University Press, 2009), 140.

11. The Centro de Estudios de Participación Popular (Centro; Center for the Study of Popular Participation) was created in 1971 as a joint program of the revolutionary government, represented by SINAMOS, and the United Nations Development Program (UNDP), represented by the International Labor Office-ILO. A short description of the Centro can be found in my book *Las minorías étnicas y la comunidad nacional* (Lima: Ediciones del Centro de Estudios de Participación Popular, 1974). Other texts of interest on this aspect of the Velasco revolution can be found in Roberto Magni, *Autogestione e sottosviluppo: Il caso del Perú* (Rome: Coines Edizioni, 1975); and Rubén Ramos, *Velasco: El pensamiento vivo de la revolución* (Maracaibo, Venezuela: Imprenta Internacional, 2009 [1975]).

12. I have developed this conceptual tool of "cosmocentrism" in a few papers and articles, most of them published in Spanish during the last fifteen years. A summary version of this idea in English can be found in Stefano Varese, "The Territorial Roots of Latin American Indigenous Peoples' Movement for Sovereignty," *HAGAR: International Social Science Review* 2, no. 2 (2001), 201–217. See also my book *Witness to Sovereignty.*

13. See especially the 4th and 5th editions of my book *La sal de los cerros.* In these two editions, I added a few more texts written since the first edition, in which I developed the ideas of "indigenous territorialities" and their link to "indigenous epistemologies and cosmologies."

14. Elisabeth Cook-Lynn, "American Indian Studies: An Overview," *Wicazo Sa Review, A Journal of Native American Studies* (Fall 1999): 14–24.

15. See the excellent study by Laura M. Rival, *Trekking through History: The Huaorani of Amazonian Ecuador* (New York: Columbia University Press, 2002).

336 Stefano Varese

16. James C. Scott, *The Moral Economy of the Peasant: Rebellion and Subsistence in Southeast Asia* (New Haven, CT: Yale University Press, 1976).

17. Stefano Varese and Moisés Gamarra, "Deux versions cosmogoniques campa: Esquisse analytique," *Annales, Économies, Sociétés, Civilisations* 31, no. 3 (May–June 1976): 469–480.

18. G. Van der Leeuw, *La religion dans son essence et ses manifestations: Phénoménologie de la religion* (Paris: Payot, 1955).

19. For accurate quantitative information and excellent critical social analysis of the relation between land/territory and Native Communities, see Alberto Chirif and Pedro García Hierro, *Marcando territorio: Progresos y limitaciones de la titulación de territorios indígenas en la Amazonía* (Copenhagen: IWGIA, 2007).

20. For a detailed analysis of the aftermath of the Law of Native Communities during the forty years following its promulgation, see Alberto Chirif, "Prólogo: A casi 40 años de *La sal de los cerros*," in Varese, *La sal de los cerros*. Chirif points out that after 1975, few institutional consolidations took place in the state apparatus with regard to the Amazonian indigenous peoples. In fact, the continuation, expansion, and consolidation of the mandates of the Ley de las Comunidades Nativas were carried forward mostly by indigenous peoples' organizations, such as AIDESEP (Asociación Interétnica de Desarrollo de la Selva Peruana), and NGOs supporting Amazonian communities.

21. For readers unfamiliar with Peru's political landscape in the 1970s, I should clarify that until the "First Act of War" of Shining Path (the splinter of the Communist Party of Peru—Bandera Roja) in May 1980, the left was fragmented into a great number of relatively small groups claiming doctrinal adherence to sometimes obscure ideological principles that would cause the separation of the group from the rest of the others—especially from the pro-Soviet Communist Party of Peru (PCP) that had critically supported Juan Velasco Alvarado's revolution. The center and the right of the political spectrum were dominated by the APRA Party and various other incarnations of populism and liberalism. All of the leftist groups (with the exception of the Communist Party of Peru) and the populist and liberal parties had opposed the RGAF of Juan Velasco Alvarado, arguing either that it was not the "true socialist revolution" or that it was too much of a socialist takeover by a pro-Soviet and pro-Castro military dictatorship. For some intellectuals and academics, abstention from actively participating in the opposition (risking deportation and exile) or eagerly joining the revolution became their ways of choosing freedom of opinion.

Notes on the Contributors

Carlos Aguirre is a professor of history at the University of Oregon. He obtained his MA at the Universidad Católica del Perú and his PhD at the University of Minnesota. He is the author of five books: *Agentes de su propia libertad: Los esclavos de Lima y la desintegración de la esclavitud, 1821–1854* (Lima: Pontificia Universidad Católica del Perú, 1993), *Breve historia de la esclavitud en el Perú: Una herida que no deja de sangrar* (Lima: Fondo Editorial del Congreso del Perú, 2005), *The Criminals of Lima and Their Worlds: The Prison Experience (1850–1935)* (Durham, NC: Duke University Press, 2005), *Denle duro que no siente: Poder y transgresión en el Perú republicano* (Lima: Fondo Editorial del Pedagógico San Marcos, 2008), and *La ciudad y los perros: Biografía de una novela* (Lima: Pontificia Universidad Católica del Peru, 2015). He is also coeditor of seven books on banditry, crime, prisons, intellectuals, and popular culture. He was a MacArthur Fellow at the University of Minnesota (1990–1996) and a John Simon Guggenheim Fellow (1999–2000). He is currently working on a book project on intellectuals and military nationalism in Peru.

Anna Cant completed a PhD in history at Cambridge University in 2015. Her dissertation, supervised by Gabriela Ramos, examines the cultural and political impact of the radical agrarian reform introduced by the Velasco government in 1969. Her research uses a regional comparative approach to reveal how the government's "revolutionary" project was implemented on the ground, drawing on oral history interviews as well as various Peruvian archives. Before beginning the PhD, she studied for an MPhil in Latin American Studies at the Centre of Latin American Studies, Cambridge University. Anna is interested in many aspects of twentieth-century Latin American history, especially developments in mass communication, the history of land reform, and debates on citizenship. She is currently engaged in a postdoctoral research project funded by the Leverhulme Trust on the impact of radio education in rural Colombia during the 1960s and 1970s.

Mark Carey is an associate professor of history in the Robert D. Clark Honors College at the University of Oregon, where he teaches environmental history, history of science, and Latin American history. His book *In the Shadow of Melting Glaciers: Climate Change and Andean Society* (New York: Oxford University Press, 2010) won the American Historical Association's Conference on Latin American History (CLAH) 2011 Elinor Melville Prize for the best book on Latin American environmental history. He also won the Leopold-Hidy Prize for the best article published in the journal *Environmental History* during 2007. He has held major grants and fellowships from the National Science Foundation, Social Science Research Council, American Meteorological Society, Fulbright, Inter-American Foundation, and many others. He is a contributing author to the 2014 United Nations Intergovernmental Panel on Climate Change (IPCC) report, and his current research is funded by a five-year National Science Foundation CAREER grant.

Nathan Clarke is an associate professor of history at Minnesota State University Moorhead, where he teaches classes in Latin American, African, and environmental history. His paper on the revolutionary government's development program in Chimbote following the 1970 earthquake appeared in the *Journal of Urban History* in 2015. He presently is working on a book-length manuscript on the environmental history of Chimbote's boom and bust in the postwar period, using oral and archival sources. He has presented his research at conferences in Mexico, the United States, Canada, and the United Kingdom. He is a graduate of McGill University (BA in Latin American Studies, 1997), the University of California–San Diego (MA in Latin American Studies, 2001), and the University of Illinois (PhD in Latin American History, 2009).

Paulo Drinot is a senior lecturer in Latin American history at the Institute of the Americas, University College London, and coeditor of the *Journal of Latin American Studies*. He holds an undergraduate degree in economic history from the London School of Economics and Political

Science, an MPhil in Latin American Studies from the University of Oxford, and a DPhil in modern history from Oxford. He is the author of *The Allure of Labor: Workers, Race, and the Making of the Peruvian State* (Durham, NC: Duke University Press, 2011), editor of *Che's Travels: The Making of a Revolutionary in 1950s Latin America* (Durham, NC: Duke University Press, 2010), and *Peru in Theory* (New York: Palgrave, 2014), coeditor (with Leo Garofalo) of *Más allá de la dominación y la resistencia: Estudios de historia peruana, siglos XVI–XX* (Lima: Instituto de Estudios Peruanos, 2005), and coeditor (with Alan Knight) of *The Great Depression in Latin America* (Durham, NC: Duke University Press, 2014).

Jaymie Patricia Heilman is an associate professor of Latin American and Caribbean history at the University of Alberta in Edmonton, Canada. She did her graduate work at the University of Wisconsin-Madison, completing her PhD in 2006. Her book *Before the Shining Path: Politics in Rural Ayacucho, 1895–1980* (Stanford, CA: Stanford University Press, 2010) uses oral history interviews and archival research to examine rural indigenous political projects in the century preceding Peru's 1980–2000 civil war. She has published several articles on Peruvian history, including works on indigenous political mobilization, the populist APRA Party, and peasant anti-Communism, in journals such as *The Journal of Latin American Studies*, *The Americas*, *A Contracorriente*, and *The Latin American Research Review*. She has just published a testimonial biography titled *Now Peru Is Mine: The Life and Times of a Campesino Activist* with coauthor Manuel Llamojha Mitma, an indigenous political activist who led the Peruvian Peasant Confederation in the 1960s and 1970s. This biography was supported by a grant from Canada's Social Sciences and Humanities Research Council. Her next project explores popular participation in the Peruvian cocaine trade during the 1970s and 1980s.

Lourdes Hurtado is an assistant professor of history at Franklin College (Indiana). She has a PhD and a master's degree in Latin American history from the University of Notre Dame (Indiana) and a bachelor's in anthropology from the Universidad Nacional Mayor de San Marcos (Lima, Peru). Her research focuses on the history of the interactions between the military and civilian society in Peru, memory, and the history of the Cold War in South America. Her most recent academic interests are related to the intersections between memory and local identity in the province of Canta (Lima, Peru).

Adrián Lerner is a student in the history PhD program and a member of the first cohort of the Interdisciplinary Graduate Concentration in the Humanities at Yale University. His dissertation project at Yale focuses on the environmental aspects of the history of urban growth in Amazonia in Brazil and Peru during the twentieth century. Before moving to the United States, he obtained undergraduate degrees in history from the Universidad Católica, where he also taught, and worked as a researcher at the Instituto de Estudios Peruanos in Lima, Peru. He is the author (with Marcos Cueto) of *Indiferencias, tensiones y hechizos: Medio siglo de relaciones diplomáticas entre Perú y Brasil, 1889–1945* (Lima: IEP, 2012); author of "Esterilizaciones masivas y esfera pública en el Perú, 1994–1998," in *"Nosotros también somos peruanos": La marginación en el Perú, siglos XVI a XXI*, ed. Claudia Rosas Lauro (Lima: Pontificia Universidad Católica del Perú, 2011); and coeditor (with Marcos Cueto) of *Desarrollo, desigualdades y conflictos sociales: Una perspectiva desde los países andinos* (Lima: IEP, 2011).

George Philip studied politics and economics at Oxford University, where he started his university career in 1969. He was awarded his first degree from Oriel College in 1972, and went on to do postgraduate research at Nuffield College during 1972–1975 with an extended stay in Peru. Since 1972, his main academic interests have revolved around Latin America, although he has occasionally ventured further afield. He was awarded his doctorate in 1975 for a thesis titled "Policymaking in the Peruvian Oil Industry with Special Reference to the Period October 1968 to September 1973," which focused to a significant degree on the Velasco regime. He moved to London in 1975, where he finished his book *The Rise and Fall of the Peruvian Military Radicals 1968–1976*, published by Athlone in 1978. He has worked in London ever since, moving to the London School of Economics and Political Science (LSE) as a lecturer in 1976, being granted tenure at LSE in 1981, becoming a reader in 1985 and full professor in 2001, and serving as head of the Department of Government during 2004–2007. He has written extensively on Latin American politics, including books on the military, the oil industry, and a jointly authored book on the rise of the left. He has continued to follow events in Peru.

Patricia Oliart is a senior lecturer in Latin American Studies at Newcastle University. She is the author of *Políticas educativas y la cultura del sistema escolar en el Perú* (Lima: Instituto de Estudios Peruanos, 2011) and coauthor with Gonzalo Portocarrero Maisch of *El Perú desde la escuela* (Lima: Instituto de Apoyo Agrario, 1989). Her numerous publications about education in Peru consider the school system as a realm for cultural and social analysis. Using ethnography as her main approach, she studies the contradictory nature of education as an area where social transformation and reproduction of social relations are always in tension. From 1996 to 2002, she was part of the research team on education at the Institute of Peruvian Studies, where she led fieldwork research on rural schools. She holds a BA in social sciences (Pontificia Universidad Católica del Perú), an MA in Latin American Studies (University of Texas at Austin), and a PhD in human geography (Newcastle University).

Mark Rice is an assistant professor of history at CUNY-Baruch College. He has published his research most recently in the *Journal of Latin American Studies* and has presented at academic events in North America, Latin America, and Europe. Over the course of his graduate studies, he has earned fellowships from various institutions, including the Tinker Foundation and the Social Sciences Research Council.

Stefano Varese, an Italian-Peruvian anthropologist, is a professor emeritus at the University of California, Davis, and currently director of the Indigenous Research Center of the Americas at UC Davis. He began his research on Peruvian Amazonia with the publication of his dissertation *La sal de los cerros* (*Salt of the Mountain*), which has five editions and one English translation. In 1975, Varese accepted an invitation from Guillermo Bonfil, director of Mexico's National Institute of Anthropology and History, and joined a team of researchers in the state of Oaxaca, continuing his ethnohistorical and cultural interests in the indigenous peoples of southeastern Mexico. In the 1980s, Varese was appointed director of the Research Center of Popular and Indigenous Cultures in the state of Oaxaca. Beginning in the 1990s, Varese moved to California, where he taught at UC Berkeley, Stanford University, and UC Davis. His books include *Las minorías étnicas y la comunidad nacional* (Lima: Ediciones del Centro de Estudios de Participación Popular, 1974); *Proyectos étnicos y proyectos nacionales* (Mexico City: Fondo de Cultura Económica, 1983); *Indígenas y educación en México* (Mexico City: GEFE, 1983); *Pueblos indios, soberanía y globalismo* (Quito: Ediciones Abya-Yala, 1996); coeditor with Sylvia Escárcega of *La ruta mixteca: El impacto etnopolítico de la migración transnacional de los pueblos indígenas de México* (Mexico

City: UNAM, 2004); *Witness to Sovereignty: Essays on the Indian Move-ment in Latin America* (Copenhagen: IWGIA, 2006); coeditor with Fré-dérique Apffel-Marglin and Róger Rumrril of *Selva Vida: De la destruc-ción de la Amazonia al paradigma de la regeneración* (Copenhagen: Grupo Internacional de Trabajo sobre Asuntos Indígenas, 2013).

Charles Walker is a professor of history and director of the Hemi-spheric Institute on the Americas at the University of California, Davis. He studied Latin American Studies at UC Berkeley (BA) and Stanford University (MA) and has a PhD in history from the University of Chi-cago. He has been associated with the Centro Bartolomé de Las Casas in Cuzco since 1988 and has taught at the Universidad Nacional San Anto-nio Abad del Cuzco. His books include *Smoldering Ashes: Cuzco and the Creation of Republican Peru, 1780–1840* (Durham, NC: Duke University Press, 1999)/*De Túpac Amaru a Gamarra: Cuzco y la formación del Perú re-publicano* (Cuzco: CBC, 1999); *Shaky Colonialism: The 1746 Earthquake-Tsunami in Lima, Peru, and Its Long Aftermath* (Durham, NC: Duke University Press, 2008)/*Colonialismo en ruinas: Lima frente al terremoto y tsunami de 1746* (Lima: Institut français d'études andines, 2015); and *The Tupac Amaru Rebellion* (Cambridge, MA: Harvard University Press, 2014). He has also coedited several volumes in Peru, including a compila-tion of his essays, *Diálogos con el Perú*, and, with Carlos Aguirre and Wil-lie Hiatt, has edited and translated Alberto Flores Galindo's *Buscando un Inca/In Search of an Inca* (Cambridge: Cambridge University Press, 2010). He has held fellowships from the NEH, University of California Presi-dent's Fellowship in the Humanities, American Council of Learned So-cieties, SSRC, the American Philosophical Society, the Tinker Founda-tion, and the MacArthur Foundation.

Index

Italicized page numbers indicate figures.